Nonviolent Social Movements

NONVIOLENT SOCIAL MOVEMENTS

A GEOGRAPHICAL PERSPECTIVE

Edited by

Stephen Zunes,
Lester R. Kurtz,
and Sarah Beth Asher

© 1999 by Blackwell Publishing Ltd
except for editorial material and organization © 1999 by Stephen Zunes, Lester R. Kurtz, and Sarah Beth Asher

BLACKWELL PUBLISHING
350 Main Street, Malden, MA 02148-5020, USA
9600 Garsington Road, Oxford OX4 2DQ, UK
550 Swanston Street, Carlton, Victoria 3053, Australia

First published 1999 by Blackwell Publishing Ltd
Reprinted 2000, 2003, 2004 (twice)

6   2007

Library of Congress Cataloging-in-Publication Data

Nonviolent social movements: a geographical perspective / edited by Stephen Zunes, Lester R. Kurtz, and Sarah Beth Asher.
    p. cm.
  Includes bibliographical references and index
  ISBN 978-1-57718-075-3 (hardcover: alk. paper) — ISBN 978-1-57718-076-0 (pbk: alk. paper)
    1. Nonviolence. 2. Passive resistance. 3. Social movements. I. Zunes, Stephen.
  II. Kurtz, Lester R. III. Asher, Sarah Beth.
  HM278.N695   1999
  303.6'1—dc21   99-17510
                                                              CIP

A catalogue record for this title is available from the British Library.

Set in 10 on 11pt Sabon
by Kolam Information Services Pvt.
Printed and bound in Singapore
by Fabulous Printers Pte Ltd

The publisher's policy is to use permanent paper from mills that operate a sustainable forestry policy, and which has been manufactured from pulp processed using acid-free and elementary chlorine-free practices. Furthermore, the publisher ensures that the text paper and cover board used have met acceptable environmental accreditation standards.

For further information on
Blackwell Publishing, visit our website:
http://www.blackwellpublishing.com

Stephen Zunes To Albert McQueen, a teacher, scholar, mentor and friend, who believed I could succeed

Lester R. Kurtz To Elise and Kenneth Boulding, who helped clear the path

Sarah Beth Asher To Richard, who has taught me that those who may look to be an enemy can, in fact, be a best friend

Contents

Sources and Acknowledgments

The authors and publishers gratefully acknowledge the following for permission to reproduce copyright material:

Matthew Lyons, "The Grassroots Movement in Germany, 1972–85" was excerpted from his book *The "Grassroots" Network: Radical Nonviolence in the Federal Republic of Germany, 1972–1985* (Ithaca, NY: Cornell University Press, 1988).

Pamela McAllister, "You Can't Kill the Spirit: Women and Nonviolent Action" was excerpted from her book *You Can't Kill the Spirit* (Philadelphia: New Society Publishers, 1988), the first of the Barbara Deming memorial series of stories of women and nonviolent action.

Stephen Zunes, "The Role of Nonviolence in the Downfall of Apartheid" originally appeared in the *Journal of Modern Africa Studies*, vol. 37, no. 1 (January, 1999).

Ronald Pagnucco, "Advocating Nonviolent Direct Action in Latin America: The Antecedents and Emergence of SERPAJ" originally appeared in Bronislaw Misztal and Ansun Shupe, *Religion and Politics in Comparative Perspective* (Praeger, 1992).

The postcards used in Chapters 8 were created by Thai artist Naphas Assawachaicharn and are reproduced courtesy of her organization Sarn Fan (Weaving the Dreams).

The Publishers apologize for any errors or omissions in the above list and would be grateful to be notified of any corrections that should be incorporated in the next edition or reprint of this book.

This volume was the inspiration of Sarah Beth Asher and Lester Kurtz, who originally planned to combine case histories with interviews of major actors in nonviolent movements. I was brought into the project later as principal editor as time constraints and other obstacles were delaying publication.

When it became apparent that our collected material, if published, would be a tome of more than 1,000 pages, I took upon myself the unenviable task of dropping the interviews (which we hope to resurrect in a subsequent book), eliminated about half of the remaining chapters and added a couple of new ones for geographic balance. This is the final product which resulted.

We are particularly appreciative of talented and extremely patient people at Blackwell Publishers: Susan Rabinowitz, the commissioning editor at the US office; editorial controller Simon Eckley; and Helen Rappaport, the desk editor. We are also grateful to Paul Joseph, Souad Dajani and Robert Irwin, who gave us important insights and critiques through earlier drafts. But first and foremost, we are grateful to the men and women who really made this book possible: those on the front lines in nonviolent struggles around the world.

Stephen Zunes

Notes on Editors and Contributors

Editors

Sarah Beth Asher is a Physician Assistant in general surgery practice in Austin, Texas. She has a Master's Degree in Public Health from the University of Texas Health Science Center and Master's Degree in Physician Assistance Practices from FUHS/the Chicago Medical School. Her work both in the US and abroad, particularly with women and women's health issues has led to a keen interest in the efficacy of nonviolent movements in the fight for equal rights. She has done research on international public health issues and has written about violence for *Clinician Review*. She currently resides with her daughters, Poeta and Patience, in Austin, Texas.

Lester Kurtz is Professor of Sociology and Asian Studies at the University of Texas at Austin and Past Chair of the Peace Studies Association and the Peace and War section of the American Sociological Association. He has written books and articles on peace and conflict, social change and the sociology of religion including *The Web of Violence* (edited with Jennifer Turpin, University of Illinois Press), *Gods in the Global Village* (Pine Forge), *The Nuclear Cage* (Prentice-Hall), "Third World Peace Perspectives" (edited with Shu-Ju Ada Cheng, a special issue of *Peace Review*) and *The Politics of Heresy* (University of California Press). He is Editor-in-Chief of a four-volume *Encyclopedia of Violence, Peace and Conflict* (Academic Press) and is currently writing a book on *Fighting with Gandhi: The Paradox of India's Nonviolence*. Kurtz has been a visiting professor at the University of Chicago, Northwestern University, Tunghai University, and Delhi University, and has lectured in Asia, Europe, Africa, and North America.

Stephen Zunes is an associate professor of Politics and Chair of the Peace and Justice Studies Program at the University of San Francisco and serves as Chair of the nonviolence commission of the International Peace Research Association. He received his PhD from Cornell University, has taught and lectured widely, holding faculty positions at Ithaca College, the University of Puget Sound, and Whitman College. He served as founding director of the Institute for a New Middle East Policy and as a research fellow at the Institute for Policy Studies and the Institute for Global Security Studies. His articles have appeared in *Middle East Policy, Current History, Arab Studies Quarterly, The Progressive, Z, In These Times*, the *Christian Science Monitor* and other publications. He serves as editor of the *International Journal of Nonviolence* and as an associate editor of *Peace Review*. He is currently completing a book on the conflict in Western Sahara to be published by Syracuse University Press. He lives in a cohousing community in Santa Cruz, California with his wife, Nanlouise Wolfe, and their children Shanti, Kalila, and Tobin.

Contributors

Michael Beer is director of Nonviolence International and has done extensive nonviolence training throughout Southeast Asia.

The late **Kenneth Boulding** was an eminent economist, Quaker, and prominent founder of the peace studies movement.

Charles Chatfield is H. O. Hirt Professor of History at Wittenberg University and is widely published in the areas of peace history and social movements.

Joshua Cooper is a human rights activist and doctoral candidate in Political Science at the University of Hawaii.

Souad Dajani is a sociologist and an independent scholar living in Boston.

Matthew Lyons is a freelance writer living in Albuquerque, New Mexico whose research on German nonviolent movements was the basis of his senior honors thesis at Cornell University.

Pam McAllister is a writer and speaker based in Brooklyn, New York, and author of *Reweaving the Web of Life: Feminism and Nonviolence* (New Society Publishers).

Chaiwat Satha-Anand teaches political science at Thammasat University in Bangkok and is the founder and director of the Peace Information Center, Foundation for Democracy and Development Studies in Thailand.

Lee Smithey is a graduate student in sociology at the University of Texas at Austin.

Daniel Zirker is dean of the College of Arts and Sciences and Professor of Political Science at Montana State University-Billings and specializes in democratization and civil–military relations in Latin America and Africa.

Introduction

Nonviolent action campaigns have been a part of political life for millennia, challenging abuses by authorities, spearheading social reforms and protesting militarism and discrimination. In recent years, however, there has been an increase in movements that have not only led to significant political and social reforms, but have toppled governments from power and forced governments to change the very nature of the regime itself. In the twentieth century, nonviolence became more of a deliberate tool for social change, moving from being largely an *ad hoc* strategy growing naturally out of religious or ethical principles to a reflective, and in many ways institutionalized, method of struggle.

Indeed, the past 20 years has witnessed a remarkable upsurge in nonviolent insurrections against authoritarian regimes. Many of the individual revolts have received major media attention and certain political consequences of these largely pro-democracy movements have certainly been examined. However, there has been little recognition of the significance of the increasing utilization of nonviolent methods in situations where guerrilla warfare was once seen to be the only path to liberation and the extent to which nonviolent struggle has emerged as a central cultural movement throughout the globe. Despite its widespread diffusion as a conscious movement around the world in recent decades, and its central role in tectonic shifts in geopolitics of the late twentieth century, we still understand little about nonviolence as a technique for social change. "Nonviolence" is not even a category in the mainstream academic lexicon.

This volume is intended as a step toward a more systematic, comparative study of nonviolent social movements and the efficacy of unarmed struggle. Although nonviolence is as ancient as violent struggle, nonviolent strategies have not been developed or analyzed with the same energy and resources as military and other violent means, and its widespread deliberate use is a relatively new phenomenon in human history. We have no large nonviolent academies that parallel our military academies or widespread units of peace brigades stationed to intervene nonviolently in crisis situations.

Primarily nonviolent "people power" movements have overthrown authoritarian regimes in nearly two dozen countries over the past two decades, have
forced substantial reforms in some, and seriously challenged still others.
These nonviolent insurrections are distinguished from armed struggles in
that they are movements of organized popular resistance to government
authority which – either consciously or by necessity – eschew the use of
weapons of modern warfare.[1] They also distinguish themselves from more
conventional political movements in that their tactics are primarily outside
the normal political process, such as electioneering and lobbying. Tactics may
include strikes, boycotts, mass demonstrations, the popular contestation of
public space, tax refusal, destruction of symbols of government authority
(such as official identification cards), refusal to obey official orders (such as
curfew restrictions), and the creation of alternative institutions for political
legitimacy and social organization. Its power is based in noncooperation.

Until the twentieth century, nonviolent actions had been primarily matters of individual initiative or at most small-scale collaboration, although
cultivated by aspects of religious and ethical cultures.[2] Now, both the
problems that nonviolent movements seek to address are increasingly global issues and the nonviolent philosophies and strategies used are borrowed
from movements around the world. As theories and strategies of resistance
are disseminated through the media, transnational organizations, and the
published works of Mohandas Gandhi, Martin Luther King, Gene Sharp
and others, participants in social movements are sharing their wisdom with
one another to challenge a system of social control that is increasingly
global in nature. Even the social problems that do not have global structures are being repeated in a similar fashion in local communities and
grassroots activists are drawing upon the experience and successes of social
movements everywhere.

The focus in this volume is primarily on the political questions of nonviolent change rather than on exclusively ethical concerns, which deserve
their own separate treatment. We also concentrate primarily on nonviolent
insurrections, not on civilian-based defense or various forms of nonviolent
intervention from the outside, which similarly deserves more extensive
study. In our study of these unarmed insurrections, we hope to contribute
to the growing understanding of nonviolent action, of its nature, its possibilities and limitations, and the conditions of its success and failure. We
have not tried to be comprehensive but to present an instructive sample of
case studies and offer some scholarly analysis.

The Diffusion of Nonviolent Movements

The roots of contemporary nonviolent theory and practice are in ancient
teachings of most of the world's religious traditions. In the Eastern religions, the teachings of such central figures as Lao Tzu (sixth century BCE),

founder of Taoism, and Mo Tzu (ca. 479–391 BCE) contended that violence goes against the very grain of the universe. Similarly, the Buddha (ca. 563–483 BCE) taught that the first precept of his eightfold path was not to kill, and the ancient Hindu teachings of the Vedas stressed the importance of *ahimsa*, that is, nonharmfulness or nonviolence.

The earliest recorded instance of nonviolent resistance of which we are aware is in ancient Egypt about 3,000 years ago (ca. 1300 BCE). According to the Hebrew scriptures, Hebrew midwives hid slave babies in defiance of the Pharaoh's decree that they should be killed. This nonviolent strain in ancient Judaism – admittedly a minor motif – became prominent in the teachings of Jesus, who himself engaged in frequent struggle with the political and religious authorities of his day, but avoided harming individuals, failed to mount the armed rebellion some of his followers anticipated, and emphasized love for one's enemies.

Mohandas Gandhi (1869–1948) drew heavily on those historic nonviolent elements of traditions from both East and West, as well as their manifestations in more recent thought such as Henry David Thoreau's writings about civil disobedience, Leo Tolstoy's radical Christian pacifism, the peace churches (such as the Quakers and Mennonites), and others. Gandhi not only taught the religious virtues of nonviolence, but actualized the principles in his political struggles, first in a South African campaign against the injustice towards the Indian community in that country, and then with his colleagues in the Indian movement in order to gain independence from the British colonial empire. While his nonviolence was grounded in his deep religious faith, Gandhi was also a sophisticated political strategist who greatly advanced nonviolence as a successful method of political struggle even by those who did not share his entire moral framework.[3]

The Indian success story was watched with considerable attention by people in a number of other contexts of oppression, from African Americans' struggle with racism in the United States, to people suffering under European colonialism in Africa and elsewhere. Indeed, recent years have witnessed a dramatic growth in nonviolent resistance movements in the Third World, an issue that we will examine in particular detail in the concluding chapter of the book.

An Outline of the Book's Structure

The chapters that follow provide an overview of nonviolent social movements around the world. While we recognize the unfortunate preponderance of North American male writers, we nevertheless hope that the wide geographical range covered offers a somewhat representative scope of the power of nonviolent action.

We begin with an introductory unit consisting of two overviews, one by an economist, the late Kenneth Boulding, who takes a broad historical approach, and the second is by Pam McAllister, who offers an important perspective on the often overlooked role of women in nonviolent movements around the world.

Our geographic tour begins with the Middle East, in part because it is not a region of the world that most people normally associate with the idea of nonviolent movements, and which includes an overview of recent nonviolent movements, particularly in the Palestinian independence struggle against Israeli occupation.

We then move on to Europe, where some of the more well-known of the recent nonviolent movements of recent years took place, in the democratic revolutions of 1989 that played a pivotal role in the disintegration of the Soviet bloc and the cessation of the Cold War, 200 years after the violent French Revolution shook the foundations of geopolitics in its time as well. Both the struggles against Communist regimes in Eastern Europe, as well as nonviolent action campaigns in the democratic Federal Republic of Germany, are examined.

From Europe we turn our attention to the motherland of modern non-violence, Asia, where Gandhi provided the impetus for much of the kind of nonviolent direct action that we are examining here, where one of the better-known nonviolent insurrections occurred in the People Power movement of the Philippines. We also take a look at nonviolent movements in Burma and Thailand.

In Africa we focus on a detailed study of nonviolence in the anti-apartheid movement in South Africa as well as the struggle of the Ogoni people of Nigeria for political and environmental rights.

Latin America has also seen its share of violent struggle and violent oppression by military regimes determined to immediately suppress any dissent, yet here too the depth and impact of nonviolent struggle on the continent has been impressive. We focus on the nonviolent organizing of Servicio Paz y Justicia (SERPAJ) and other church-related institutions which provided the organizational infrastructure for significant nonviolent movements in several areas, especially Brazil.

We conclude with an overview of the history of nonviolent action in the United States.

In each section we provide a brief overview of some significant aspects of nonviolence in the region in order to orient the reader and to hopefully inspire more detailed examinations of these movements and others that we do not examine in detail. In our final chapter we offer some tentative conclusions about the nature of nonviolent social movements and what we might expect from them in the future.

We would like to be more comprehensive, but that would take many volumes. This survey, like a whirlwind world tour, is intended to provide a tantalizing introduction prompting further travel and research. A more complete exploration and evaluation of these profound movements would require an army of scholars and a research budget the size of the US Army

Research Bureau.[4] We do not expect that to happen in the near future, but we do hope that this preliminary analysis will show the promise of this sort of investigation and inspire students and scholars to undertake the kind of in-depth and comparative studies that we need to understand how non-violent social movements might help us transform human social organization in the coming centuries.

Notes

1 Studies such as James Scott's *Weapons of the Weak: Everyday Forms of Brazilian Resistance* (New Haven: Yale University Press, 1985) on the Malaysian peasantry have documented a long-standing and widespread tradition of passive resistance to authority. This tends to be quiet and individualistic, however, and would thereby not constitute a nonviolent insurrection.
2 There have been episodes of mass resistance going back even into ancient history, however, such as the plebeian withdrawal from ancient Rome.
3 See Sharp, *Gandhi as a Political Strategist* (Boston: Porter Sargent, 1978).
4 The Army Research Bureau's annual research budget exceeds the total social science research budget of all US government agencies combined, including the National Science Foundation, the National Institutes of Health, and the US Institute of Peace.

PART I

Perspectives on Nonviolent Movements

1

Nonviolence and Power in the Twentieth Century

Kenneth E. Boulding

The twentieth century has seen almost unprecedented change in the total system of Planet Earth. The world human population has increased at least threefold. There has been an enormous increase in human knowledge and the discovery of human artifacts. In cosmology we have expanded into virtually the ends of the universe in space and time. In biology we have come to understand the genetic basis of life and the real meaning of heredity. We are still a long way from knowing exactly how the genotype produces the phenotype: a fertilized bird's egg, a chicken; a fertilized human egg, Einstein. We have developed aerial warfare and the nuclear weapon; we have increasingly become a single world economically – the volume of international trade increased six times between 1950 and 1980 – and we have established the United Nations, however small and weak it may be. We have a world communication system; a fair proportion of the human race can now talk to anybody anywhere in the world almost immediately. We have mapped Venus and Mars and sent our artificial eyes to the edge of the solar system. We have almost gotten rid of empires. There has been a real spread of democratic institutions around the world, though the process is very incomplete.

We have seen two world wars, the rise and collapse of both fascism and communism. We had a grave world depression from 1929 to 1933, and in spite of the enormous growth in population, the per capita gross world product – whatever that is – has almost certainly increased, though with a widening disparity between the rich temperate zones and the poor tropics.

A really striking phenomenon in the twentieth century – not enough noticed by historians! – has been the rise of organized nonviolence as an instrument of social and political change. Something like this has happened many times in human history, but in the twentieth century it became conscious thanks due largely to Gandhi, who was certainly the philosopher if not the Newton of nonviolence, and who played a dominant role in liberating India from British rule and liberating Britain from the burden of empire. We could argue indeed that the power of nonviolence in the world has increased almost throughout the twentieth century to produce a great change in race relations in the United States inspired by Martin Luther King, who was a disciple of Gandhi; the expulsion of Ferdinand Marcos from the Philippines; and the extraordinary economic expansion of Japan under the military domination of the United States.

Finally, the almost entirely nonviolent transformation of the Soviet Union and the Eastern European communist countries, with the exception of Romania, certainly indicates a crumbling of the power of organized threat in the face of the withdrawal of legitimacy from existing rulers by very large numbers of ordinary people. We still have, of course, close to 200 independent national states, all but one (Costa Rica) committed to national defense by an organized military. Each year, however, something new is happening in the world that never happened before, particularly in regard to the general structure of power. There has been a decline in "power over" or dominance, which is largely though not entirely the power of threat, and the rise of "power to do" or "empowerment," which is the ability not only to get what we want, but to change what we want, when we find that what we want is not really worth having. The rise in feminism and the shift from male domination of women into mutual partnerships between the sexes is another remarkable aspect of the twentieth century.

In order to understand what is going on, we need to examine both the conscious and the unconscious processes of the great complex, overall system of Planet Earth. The conscious processes are those which are guided in some degree by decision. Decision involves a choice between the different conscious images of the future. The extent and the magnitude of these images reflects the power of the decision-maker to change the world through some kind of action. A prisoner in a jail has little power over his own behavior, and very little power over others. The president of the United States, by contrast, has the power to declare war, and to order the military force of which he is the commander-in-chief to risk their lives, to kill larger numbers of other people, and to destroy property. He may not have the power to be re-elected except through the control which he may have over his public image.

Power is clearly a very complex phenomenon. I distinguish "three faces" of power,[1] though these categories are by no means unambiguous or complete: The first of these is threat power, which involves the threatener saying to the threatened, "You do something I want or I'll do something you don't want." The power of the law rests on rather specific threats, which can have a considerable effect on human behavior. Thus, the law says, "Put a coin in the parking meter or else you will be fined." Or "Calculate and pay your income tax obligation according to the rules or you will get into serious trouble." Military threats are apt to be much more vague: "You do something unspecifiedly nasty to me and I will do something unspecifiedly nasty to you!" Their weakness in influencing behavior has something to do with the indeterminacy and uncertainty of the threat, as the 1991 Gulf War showed very clearly. The dynamics of the threat system depend very much on the response of the threatened. One response is submission, as when I pay my income tax. Another is defiance: "I am going to drive over the speed limit" or "I won't pay my income taxes." Then, of course, what happens depends on the response of the original threatener. If the threat was in the first place a bluff, as it often is, there may be no response, or, of course, the threatener may try to carry out the threat.

Another response is flight, which depends on the principle that the power of the threatener is a diminishing function of the distance between the threatener and the threatened. This has been very important in human history and probably accounts for the spread of the human race all around the world. A fourth possibility is counterthreat: "If you do something nasty to me, I'll do something nasty to you," which may lead to deterrence, that is abstention on the part of the original threatener from carrying out the threat. It may lead to a breakdown, for instance, in war, if each tries to carry out the threat on the other. A last possibility, important in the theory of nonviolence, might be called "disarming behavior," which seeks to turn the threatener into a friend, drawn into a larger community which includes the threatened. This is very important in the theory of nonviolence.

A second form of power is economic power, most simply defined as what the rich have more of than the poor. This sometimes emerges out of the successful use of threat power, as in the conquest of land. On the whole, however, economic power comes out of the skills of production and exchange and the distribution of economic power is very largely the result of a long history of different human experiences in learning and in luck. In matters of pure exchange, economists believe, either participant has a veto. The seller can refuse to sell and the buyer can refuse to buy. This means that exchange will not take place unless both parties feel at the time that they will both benefit from it. There can be exceptions to this, especially in the case of superior threat power on the part of one of the parties, as in the labor market.

The third, and I argue the most important, source of power is what I have called "integrative power." This is the power of legitimacy, persuasion, loyalty, community, and so on. In a very real sense power is a gift to the powerful by those over whom the power may be exercised, who recognize the power as legitimate. Threat power and economic power would be hard to exercise if they were not supported by integrative power, that is if they were not regarded as legitimate. King George III had the illusion that he had the power to tax the American colonists, who then proceeded to withdraw legitimacy not only from the tax but from the monarch himself. The sources of integrative power are very complex and rather obscure. Why the French in Quebec submitted to an alien monarch, whereas the English speakers further south did not is an interesting question. The ability to persuade is clearly important. History has something to do with it. Old legitimacies have a certain tendency to persist. Pay offs have something to do with it. We tend to regard as legitimate those structures from which we feel we can benefit. On the other hand, there is the phenomenon that I have called the "sacrifice trap," where if we make sacrifices for something it is hard later to admit that they were in vain, and this in turn may enhance the legitimacy of the imposer of the sacrifice. We see this in the case of the military. Sometimes, however, the sacrifice is perceived as too great and the response is revulsion or an overturn of legitimacy.

Any actual exercise of power tends to involve all three "faces," but they are able to co-exist in very different proportions. Threat power is certainly dominant in the military, but unless it has a certain base in economic power, of course, the means of destruction and threat cannot be produced. Unless a military organization has "morale," and if it ceases to believe in the legitimacy of its officers and generals and admirals, no amount of internal threat on ordinary soldiers or sailors can be effective. The greater the internal threat, the more likely there is to be a revolt and rebellion. This happened sometimes with the French army in the First World War, when ordinary soldiers simply refused to obey orders they knew were designed for their sacrifice. The economic power of property is supported by the threat power of the law, yet where ownership of property becomes illegitimate, as it did, for instance, in Russia in 1917, no amount of threat power can preserve it. In democratic elections, while economic power may be used to some extent to buy votes and even a certain amount of threat power in terms of possible loss of jobs and so on, the overwhelming source of power is legitimacy. Threat does not make people vote for you, and people may be suspicious of wealthy candidates.

It is often the unconscious processes of history that govern the way in which power in any of its forms comes to be exercised. We are too much accustomed to thinking of history as consisting of the decisions of the powerful and the effects of these decisions. All history books tend to be written in terms of military victories, and of leaders such as Genghis Khan or Napoleon, and so on. This leads to a neglect of the unconscious processes that come out of the underlying dynamics of human learning and interaction. It could be argued indeed that conscious decision processes in history, which make for empires, wars, revolutions, and so on, can often be seen as interruptions in the underlying unconscious processes of the accumulation of human knowledge – inventions and technology, the rise of religions and ideologies, changes in culture and ethics – all of which come out of the small decisions of large numbers of ordinary people, rather than not out of the big decisions of the powerful. I believe very profoundly that a real world does exist, in spite of some possible evidence to the contrary, and that if our image of that world does *not* correspond to the reality, we are more likely to change it than if it does; that is, that injustice is not permanent, however long it may persist, and that there is a very real power of truth, which will eventually prevail. The Inquisition in the Catholic Church, the KGB in the Soviet Union, the mentality of Nazi ideology have all faded with time.

Economic development itself is a learning process, spread over very large numbers of people, and an attempt to impose development from above often slows it down. Japan is a good example. While it is true that the leaders of the Meiji Restoration around 1870 removed previous obstacles to development imposed by authority, the actual development that resulted was due to the newly acquired skills of very large numbers of people. The rise of the Japanese military interrupted this development, to a small extent during the Korean and Chinese conquests of the 1930s, and to a disastrous extent in the Second World War. Nevertheless, the defeat of Japan in the war removed the obstacles to development which the military had been imposing. One might even consider the war as an interlude in the economic development of Japan, for where Japan is today, or where it was even by the late 1960s, is just about where it would have been if its development had proceeded at the pre-war pace and there had been no conflict.

The Soviet Union is an even more interesting example of an imposed development, because it was imposed by a tyranny which, under Stalin, surpassed even the Spanish Inquisition, then gradually lost legitimacy, until the whole structure collapsed almost overnight, with virtually no violence. The empires of the European powers are another case in point. The historical evidence suggests that the empires of the British, the French, and the Dutch slowed the internal economic development of the imperial powers in the nineteenth century. The countries in Europe that became prosperous in the second half of the nineteenth century were not those that pursued the acquisition of an empire, but countries such as Sweden and Denmark, that concentrated on their own domestic economies. Germany is another striking example. It was the cultural center of Europe in the eighteenth century, producing talents such as Bach, Beethoven, Kant, and Hegel. Its economic development from the mid-nineteenth century onwards, again, like Japan, was largely achieved outside of government. Then, when the military took over after Bismarck, and even more so under Hitler, (even though Hitler did achieve full employment), the economic results were catastrophic. And like Japan, after its military defeat in 1945, postwar economic development proceeded in Germany at an accelerated pace until it again about caught up to where it would have been if there had been no world wars.

The Ottoman Empire is another good example of the economic failure of military success. Its conquest of Byzantium in 1453 was followed by a long period of economic and cultural decline, lasting almost 500 years, whereas disorganized and relatively powerless Europe literally went off, eventually, into exploring outer space. Spain is another example. Its huge empire crippled it both economically and culturally, and it made practically no contribution to modern science until the twentieth century. Indeed the modern world as we know it came out of the politically disorganized and rather powerless triangle of territory located between northern Italy, Britain, and Sweden, and while the development of the modern world helped to create European domination over the rest of the world, domination alone did not create it. In fact, it grew out of a learning process which involved very large numbers of fairly ordinary people, on the whole separate from the political system. The rise of modern science represents the establishment of a subculture that denied the use of threat as a means of persuasion and power. The agricultural and industrial revolutions likewise were the product of people who were not themselves politically powerful and many actually dissociated themselves from the political system.

Societal evolution, like biological evolution, can be influenced by political power but it is not guided by it. Human power, indeed, distorts the ecosystem in favor of human values, as when a farmer adapts his land to grow wheat instead of prairie grass. Government in many ways is rather like social agriculture, discouraging weeds such as crime and encouraging the growth of organizations and social behavior which are supportive of fundamental human values. Farmers, of course, can destroy the soil on which they work; governments have often destroyed the social soil which supports them. The ecosystem is the most fundamental system. It may be distorted by human power, but still remains an ecosystem, still guided to a large extent by Adam Smith's famous "invisible hand." The wild woods have no "government," although on an increasingly crowded earth they may only exist because government prevents their destruction by private individuals. Government and the exercise of human power may still have to be used to manipulate ecosystems towards the achievement of higher human objectives. The "invisible hand" can sometimes turn into an "invisible fist." The intrusion of a parasite may destroy a forest. The ecosystem of commodities (in other words the economy itself) can go into retrograde motion, such as those which produced the Great Depression of 1929–33. Using a visible hand, or even occasionally using a visible fist, may be defensible.

Where, then, does nonviolence fit into the larger picture? Almost unconscious nonviolence in the form, for instance, of disarming behavior, has been very important in human history. Indeed, I would argue that most human development has been nonviolent. At least 90 to 95 percent of human activity is nonviolent – or what I have called "unviolent" – in terms of growing crops, making things, exchanging things, raising children (there is a little violence in this), and so on. Organized nonviolence, however, is very largely a twentieth-century development, beginning with Gandhi, who was perhaps the first nonviolent philosopher and theorist, stressing the power of truth and the capacity of undeserved suffering to produce shame in the perpetrators of it. I remember Gandhi making his famous visit to Lancashire when I was young. In spite of the fact that his boycott of imported English textiles in India was affecting the Lancashire economy adversely, he made a great impression on the people. I remember a popular song which went something like this: "We don't like the black shirts, / we don't like the brown shirts, / we don't like the red shirts, / but here's to Gandhi with no shirt at all."

Popular songs, indeed, are a very interesting indicator of what is happening to integrative structures. The fact that the First World War produced rousing war songs, while the Second World War produced practically none, and the Vietnam War produced mostly anti-war songs, with the possible exception of country music, certainly indicates that a profound change has been taking place in the legitimacy of war. Even the Gulf War, while it produced a lot of popular enthusiasm, did not, I think, produce anything in the way of war songs.

A feature of nonviolence in the twentieth century, for which we owe a great deal to Gandhi, is the movement of what might be called "informal and unorganized nonviolence" into "formal and organized nonviolence" as a political tool. Besides the three faces of power mentioned above, a case can be made for introducing a fourth face, which is organizational power. This involves the development of organizations, ranging from churches to governments and corporations, which have members and usually some sort of hierarchy. It is hard indeed to have a large organization that does not have some sort of hierarchy. Organizations, like any other structure, beyond a certain point exhibit diminishing returns in relation to size, which is why small is often not only beautiful but has survival value. The cockroach survived the extinction of the dinosaurs and may even survive our extinction.

Certain changes in organizational structure, however, tend to increase the size at which the economies begin to malfunction. I have argued,[2] for instance, that the tremendous rise in the size of organizations of all kinds since about 1870, especially corporations and governments, has a lot to do with the invention of the telephone, which enabled upper members of a hierarchy to communicate with a great many more lower members than had previously had been the case. Nowadays it is hard to imagine how either General Motors or the United States government managed to run, in the days when the main means of communication were young boys running around with slips of paper, or letters that took weeks to arrive! The development of computers and email may further extend the point at which diminishing returns in relation size to begin, though this is not wholly clear.

As we move into organizational structures, both the social and the biological ecosystems tend to shift in the direction of hierarchy and "bosses," and the various forms of human power may become more important. The rise of nonviolence in the twentieth century, however, is an indication of the fact that even with the increase in conglomerate organizations the power mix is beginning to include much more integrative power and much less threat power, with economic power perhaps lying somewhere in between. I have sometimes argued that if we are looking for any single element in the social system on which everything else depends – something which we should probably not do – the best candidate would be integrative power in the shape of legitimacy, for without legitimacy neither threat power nor economic power is very effective. People don't get rich by bullying, but by complex interactions with the market and other people. Even when threat is used for bullying, it tends to weaken because of the erosion of legitimacy. Even the Gulf War may have increased the hostility towards the United States all around the world. Military defeat, as we saw earlier, often results in more cultural and economic development on the part of the defeated than on the part of the victors.

The prospects for organized nonviolence in the twenty-first century, therefore, look rather good. The problem here is that organizations for nonviolence tend to be temporary, put together for a particular occasion or to fulfill a particular objective, and if that objective is fulfilled, the organization tends to disintegrate. Gandhi's own organization is a good example. His "victory" over the British and the establishment of an independent India led to the virtual dismemberment of the Gandhian movement and to an appalling civil war between Muslims and Hindus resulting in millions of casualties. It produced also an India which actually rejected Gandhian principles and became what might almost be called a "Victorian European nation," with a large military force and a constant threat of war with Pakistan and China. I was in India during the war with China and witnessed a huge military procession in Delhi, with regiments of women in saris doing the goosestep and a most moving display showing the dove of peace defending her young!

The continuing power of the military may very well be the result of its embodiment in permanent organizations even in peacetime – armies, navies, and air forces – which have a very distinctive culture of their own, and which train the people in them to believe in the legitimacy of war in almost any form, a belief which can easily be expanded when there is a war. The peacetime military organizations also can have very profound effects on civilian government. There are many examples of the military taking over civilian government in a coup, though these military governments do seem to be a little unstable and there is a noticeable tendency after a while for a civilian government to return. Perhaps this is because the military is not really very good at government, but only specialized in threat, whereas government involves the careful exercise of integrative and economic power. The military may be skilled at having integrative power over their own soldiers, but that does not necessarily give them integrative power over the general public. Indeed, it is a fundamental principle of democracy that military power must be subordinate to civilian power. Beyond a certain point, if the military dominates the civilian power, this is the end of democracy, though ironically enough it was Hitler's integrative power over the German people, that is, his rhetoric, that produced the remilitarization of Germany and the Second World War. Here again, military defeat often delegitimates military power and permits the restoration of civilian power, which is much more successful in stimulating cultural and economic development.

A very interesting question for the twenty-first century, therefore, is whether organized nonviolence can develop into a permanent organization for training and developing specialists in the art. There are small signs of this in institutions like peace brigades and the development of what is almost like a new profession – conflict management, mediation, and so on – but so far this is very small-scale. Some European governments, especially, have become interested in what is sometimes called "defensive defense," that is, internal means of dealing with external threat and even occupation, without creating a threat to the threatener. This may lead to the organization of "disarming behavior" and training for nonviolent responses to violence before violence occurs.

It is not impossible, therefore, that the twenty-first century may see a real blossoming of the organization of nonviolence, though this may face some of the difficulties that the military have in maintaining their legitimacy and morale when there is no war. In the military this has developed into practice maneuvers, marching exercises, and so on, which can keep the members of the military from being bored during peacetime. Whether we can do this for organizations of nonviolence is an interesting question which only the future can answer. Nevertheless, it is not unreasonable to have real hope for more sophisticated and organized structures of nonviolence in the twenty-first century and we may eventually view the twentieth century as the seeding ground for their development.

Notes

1 K. E. Boulding, *Three Faces of Power* (Newbury Park, Calif.: Sage Publications, 1989).

2 K. E. Boulding, *The Organizational Revolution: A Study in the Ethics of Economic Organization* (New York: Harper & Brothers, 1953; reissued: Westport, Conn.: Greenwood Press, 1984).

2
You Can't Kill the Spirit: Women and Nonviolent Action[1]

Pam McAllister

What has drawn me most strongly to nonviolence is its capacity for encompassing a complexity necessarily denied by violent strategies. By complexity I mean the sort faced by feminists who rage against the system of male supremacy but, at the same time, love their fathers, sons, husbands, brothers, and male friends. I mean the complexity which requires us to name an underpaid working man who beats his wife both as someone who is oppressed and as an oppressor. Violent tactics and strategies rely on polarization and dualistic thinking and require us to divide ourselves into the good and the bad, assume neat, rigid little categories easily answered from the barrel of a gun. Nonviolence allows for the complexity inherent in our struggles and requires a reasonable acceptance of diversity and an appreciation for our common ground.

Barbara Deming wrote convincingly of the "complicated truth" in her 1977 essay, "Remembering Who We Are."

> how can one any longer make neat distinctions between oppressors and oppressed? Won't it often happen that we would have to name the very same person both an oppressed person and an oppressor? Yes, it will very often happen. Life is precisely that complicated. And to pretend that it isn't that complicated doesn't help. We need rescue from neat distinctions that are illusions...

> if the complicated truth is that many of the oppressed are also oppressors, and many of the oppressors are also oppressed – nonviolent confrontation is the only form of confrontation that allows us to respond realistically to such complexity. In this kind of struggle we address ourselves always both to that which we refuse to accept from others and to that which we can respect in them, have in common with them – however much or little that may be.[2]

Barbara wrote about the two hands of nonviolence. She wrote that nonviolence gives us two hands upon the oppressor – "one hand taking from him what is not his due, the other slowly calming him as we do this."

In another essay she wrote, "We can put more pressure on the antagonist for whom we show human concern. We put upon him two pressures – the pressure of our defiance of him and the pressure of our respect for his life – and it happens that in combination these two pressures are uniquely effective."[3]

This visual metaphor is particularly helpful in describing the basic attitude underlying the nonviolent sensibility. With one hand we say to an oppressor, "Stop what you are doing. I refuse to honor the role you are choosing to play. I refuse to obey you. I refuse to cooperate with your demands. I refuse to build the walls and the bombs. I refuse to pay for the guns. With this hand I will even interfere with the wrong you are doing. I want to disrupt the easy pattern of your life." But then the advocate of nonviolence raises the other hand. It is raised outstretched – maybe with love and sympathy, but maybe not – but always outstretched with the message that "No, you are not the other; and no, I am not the other. No one is the other." With this hand we say, " I won't let go of you or cast you out of the human race. I have faith that you can make a better choice than you are making now, and I'll be here when you're ready. Like it or not, we are a part of one another." The peculiar strength of nonviolence comes precisely from the dual nature of its approach – the two hands.

The women at the Seneca Peace Encampment in New York State used the two hands of nonviolence in the summer of 1983. Barbara was with the peace camp women the day they went on a women's history walk past the homes of Harriet Tubman and Elizabeth Cady Stanton and past the site of the first Women's Rights Convention. But during their walk, the women were met by a fierce and frenzied mob in Waterloo. People jabbed the pointed tips of their little American flags like tiny spears at the peace camp women and screamed, "Commie dykes, go back to Russia!" and "All you girls need is a little rape." Barbara saw then the two hands of nonviolence used at the most crucial moment when the women were blocked from proceeding and danger was imminent:

> I saw that a number of women had sat down, then formed a circle together...I can remember the reassurance I felt at once, at the sight of those quietly seated figures. Without words they made the statement it was essential that we make. The statement that we posed no threat – had no intention of trying to thrust our way through the mob. But the statement that we had no intention of retreating, either. We knew our Constitutional rights. We had a right to walk here. The two-fold message that gives nonviolent struggle its leverage: We won't be bullied; but you needn't fear us. You needn't fear us; but we won't be bullied.[4]

My response to my world requires such complexity as is embraced by nonviolent strategies. As I have learned and continue to learn more about nonviolence, I have realized that, despite first impressions, nonviolence not only allows but requires me to act from the full range of my feelings and reactions. It is about speaking the whole complicated truth, responding to the fullness of the struggle, and it requires my most bitter words, my most hearty laughter, my deepest compassion, my sharpest wit.

Tactical Nonviolence

The above discussion of the spirit and sensibility of a nonviolent philosophy of resistance may seem lofty, especially in contrast to its practical applications. In fact, most of the people who participate in nonviolent action are not in the least concerned with the underlying philosophy, nor would they know to call their actions nonviolent. Most would be surprised to learn that they are quite adept at using tactical nonviolence or that they have done so every time they have gone on strike, signed a petition, participated in a boycott, stood silently in a candlelight vigil, or joined a demonstration. While bombs bursting in air are given prominence in anthems, headlines, and national budgets, and the impulse for revenge is celebrated in folktale and box office hits, nonviolent tactics have been used more often and more successfully than violent tactics ever have. The majority of people who've successfully relied on tactical nonviolence have simply understood it to be a direct, commonsense way to protest, intervene, in or refuse to cooperate with circumstances they deem unjust.

Nonviolent action is often used by those who would be equally willing to use violent tactics in some circumstances. People who have no qualms about taking up the gun to defend flag or family are the same people who vote to go on strike at their workplace (the classic nonviolent tactic), and who can be found on picket lines every day (another nonviolent tactic). Furthermore, tactical nonviolence is the backbone of most national liberation struggles, struggles popularly called "violent revolutions." These revolutions do rely on fighters who are able and willing to use violent tactics and lethal weapons. But they also rely on countless acts of nonviolent resistance by workers, students, women, elders, and children who use a full range of tactics including strikes, physical obstruction, sanctuary, hunger strikes, petitions, slowdowns in factories, mass protest demonstrations, acts of economic noncooperation such as boycotts and tax resistance, civil disobedience, and the development of underground presses and/or secret organizations. In these struggles, even teaching people to read is sometimes a revolutionary act of civil disobedience taken at great risk. Nonviolent actions have especially made sense to unarmed or insufficiently armed people whose adversaries are not only equipped with a range of weapons and military apparatus but are rigorously trained, ready, and willing to use violence.

Nonviolent actions were used long before the word nonviolence was first used in print in 1923 by Clarence Marsh Case in *Nonviolent Coercion: A Study in Methods of Social Pressure*. For centuries people sought ways to live without causing injury to others and experimented with ways to fight injustice without employing violence, but they had no name with which they could identify or give shape to this commitment as an intentional philosophy. Historians studying nonviolence will find it possible only to identify the occasions when a specific nonviolent action was used, but must leave to conjecture any attempt to identify a nonviolent philosophy or strategy.

Theorist Gene Sharp identifies three basic tactical categories of nonviolent action. The first is nonviolent protest and persuasion. With these actions we name what we think is wrong, point our fingers at it and try to help others understand. This category would include such tactics as petitioning, picketing, demonstrating, and lobbying. The second category is nonviolent noncooperation. With these actions we deliberately fold our hands and turn our backs, refusing to participate in the wrong we have named. This category would include such tactics as boycotts, strikes, and tax resistance. The third category is nonviolent intervention. With these actions we face the wrong we have named, the wrong we have refused to aid, and we step into the way, interfere, block. This category would include such tactics as physical obstruction, blockades, civil disobedience, and sit-ins.

Subversive Activity: Women Resisting Disappearance

A few years ago I received a call from a university professor who said he was teaching a class on the history of nonviolence – you know, all about the contributions of Thoreau, Tolstoy, A. J. Muste, Gandhi, Martin Luther King – but he felt he should include something about women. Trouble was, he just didn't have any substantial information about women and nonviolence, and he wondered if I could help. "Had women ever contributed anything toward the history of nonviolence?" he asked.

Men like Thoreau, Tolstoy, Muste, Gandhi and King usually get the credit for the development of active nonviolence, but women – around the world and from the beginning of history have consistently experimented with ways to resist oppression and challenge injustice without endorsing violence. In fact, most of what we commonly call "women's history" is actually the history of women's role in the development of nonviolent action.

Feminist historian Dale Spender has written that the most subversive and powerful activities women can engage in are those activities which celebrate our lives and help us resist disappearance. Mary "Mother" Jones, the great labor organizer, knew this. It is said that every speech she gave was a history lesson: she wanted working women and men to know that their courageous acts were not isolated, that they were part of a tradition of struggle. I too want to tell stories which will empower us, lift us out of our isolation, sustain us in times of personal despair, heal our brokenness. I want to tell stories that will stimulate our imaginations, incite us to action.

At his request, I taught the professor's class. I told stories for over two hours to students whose only knowledge of Susan B. Anthony was that she appeared on an odd-sized coin. That day I limited myself to stories of how women in North America (primarily in the United States) have used non-violent action in their struggles for social justice. The students were spell-bound, abandoning their frantic note-taking after the first half hour to simply listen.

I told about the Lysistrata action taken in 1600 by the women of the Iroquois nation. They threatened to boycott love-making and childbearing until the men conceded some of their power in decisions about war and peace.

I told about Anne Hutchinson and Mary Dyer and the nonviolent tactics they used in the fight for religious freedom in the Massachusetts Bay Colony. I told about the women fighting against slavery: Lucretia Mott, Sarah and Angelina Grimke, Prudence Crandall, Harriet Tubman, Mary Shadd Cary, the women who worked on the Underground Railroad.

I told about the fight for women's suffrage and the nonviolent actions of Susan B. Anthony, Sojourner Truth, Alice Paul, and the suffragists.

I told stories from the civil rights movement, stories about Fannie Lou Hamer and Rosa Parks.

I told about women's anti-lynching campaigns, about Ida B. Wells, and women's labor movements. I told of women's long history of fighting for peace: stories about Jane Addams, Jeanette Rankin, Dorothy Day, Barbara Deming, the women at the peace camps.

I illustrated how, in all of these campaigns, women found creative ways to struggle collectively and nonviolently. The stories opened the door for us to talk, not only about women's history, but about nonviolent action – what it is, how it works, why it's used. In the discussion that followed my storytelling, the students, professor, and I seemed to feel ourselves empow-ered by the rich history of women activists who had created an ongoing global laboratory in which nonviolence theory is continually tested and transformed.

That experience also opened my eyes to the difficulty we have in finding these stories, this history. I was startled that such a learned professor had been at a loss in his search for examples of women's participation in the development and use of nonviolence – especially since his area of expertise was the history of nonviolence.

As I began hunting for more stories I soon discovered why he had had such a hard time. Women's stories have been buried. In 1705, English feminist Mary Astell observed, "Since the Men being the Historians, they seldom condescend to record the great and good Actions of Women." Oh Mary, how true.

Texts on nonviolence make little if any mention of women's use of nonviolent action. The classic text on nonviolent action is Gene Sharp's *The Politics of Nonviolent Action, Part Two: The Methods of Nonviolent*

Action.[5] Sharp lists 198 specific nonviolent tactics with several documented examples to illustrate each one. But in this fascinating volume, so popular with students of nonviolence, women are underrepresented to a shocking degree. For example, of the nine instances he cites of the use of mass petitions, Sharp includes none by women, though petitioning is a tactic critical to women's history. Of the ten stories he tells of revenue refusal, he cites no examples of women's use of tax resistance. Of the ten examples of protest meetings, he cites none by women. This is not to say that he leaves out women entirely. He has included a number of examples of women's use of nonviolent action, but they are unnecessarily scarce, made conspicuous by their rarity.

Nor is Sharp the only researcher and theorist of nonviolence to largely disregard women's contributions. *Blessed Are the Peacemakers: The Voices of Peace – From Isaiah to Bob Dylan* edited by Allen and Linda Kirschner and published in 1971, includes passages by such diverse thinkers and doers as Buddha, Pope John XXIII, Thoreau, Linus Pauling, Pete Seeger, and Daniel Berrigan, but Joan Baez is the only woman deemed fit to be included in what would appear to be the otherwise all-male club. Of the 535 pages which constitute the important volume *Nonviolence in America: A Documentary History*, edited by Staughton Lynd in 1966, only 46 pages are given to words by women. *The Quiet Battle: Writings on the Theory and Practice of Non- Violent Resistance* edited by Mulford Q. Sibley, features case studies in nonviolent resistance from modern-day United States as well as from India, colonial Pennsylvania, ancient Rome, South Africa, Hungary and Norway. However, out of twenty-seven essays only one is by a woman.

In the preface to his 1970 political science text *Twentieth Century Pacifism*, Dr. Peter Brock thanks his wife (who remains nameless) "for typing the greater part of the manuscript of this book" but lists only six references to women in the index of his 274-page book. Of these six women, only three were accorded a full sentence each in the text itself. No wonder the professor who called me for help wondered if women had ever contributed to the history of nonviolence. They have, but you wouldn't know it from many of the books we use.

I found the same problem in other areas of published research and soon learned that if I wanted to know about women's actions, I had to look for resources specifically about women. If I wanted to know about a strike by women workers in Japan, or South Africa, or Peru, books about the labor struggles in these countries rarely helped. Instead, I had to seek books specifically about women in Japan, South Africa and Peru. I repeatedly found that books which claimed to offer general information were often actually accounts specifically of men's thoughts and actions. I shouldn't have been surprised. After all, throughout most of my formal education, the "history" I studied had been filtered through the voices and point of view of North American white males. Their history was labeled "world" history though it left out most of what had happened to the non-kings, not to mention whole continents like Africa, Australia, and most of Asia and South America. These places, when they were mentioned, served as props for European explorers, men like Columbus who "discovered" a new world, albeit a world inhabited by people who had settled on the land centuries before, people with long traditions, laws, religions, cultural inheritances, history. But it was new to the European white males and so it became "the new world," a world theirs for the finding, its history theirs for the telling. The stories I heard were told in the conqueror's tongue with the conqueror's emphasis.

All history books are biased, they tell a story from a point of view. While white, male European history is often passed off as world history, what little "history of nonviolence" seeps into the lessons is similarly distorted and still reflects the white male European bias. The danger is that the bias is so often unacknowledged, the point of view mislabeled "universal" or "objective."

I am not particularly more interested in women's nonviolent actions than men's, but I am dismayed that so many wonderful stories have systematically been denied us and deemed less vital, less important than other stories simply because they are about actions taken by people who are not male. The denial and suppression of these stories is no accident given that we live on a planet which is overwhelmingly patriarchal. And if mere oversight accounts for their exclusion from history, it is an oversight which both reflects and reinforces patriarchal ideology. I believe this is why Dale Spender suggested that telling our stories as women and thus resisting disappearance is a subversive activity.

The Gestures of Courage are Repeated

Stories of resistance have been taken from us, the books burned, the songs stifled or forbidden, the troubadours sent wandering in the wilderness where no one will hear the stories they have to tell. Some stories have been told but the storyteller failed to hold our interest: we didn't pay attention. And now, the one who would destroy freedom of speech grins amiably on our television sets.

What can we do? There is talk that soon some people among us will be rounded up, given numbers, sent away. What can we do? This has happened before. Often. What have others done in times like these? We try to remember but it is difficult. We need our stories, our legacy of resistance. The storyteller has returned with good news: the gestures of courage are repeated from age to age, a legacy passed on in the dream, the blood, the collective memory. Even if we forget, even if the stories are taken away again, something in us will remember when the time comes. It is a mystery but it's true. The gestures of courage are repeated from age to age. Consider for example, the nonviolent tactic of providing sanctuary:

- In 1300 BC, male babies were condemned to death by law. An Egyptian princess and a Hebrew slave mother crossed ethnic and class lines to conspire to break the law. Women's hands reached through the bull-rushes, pulled a baby to safety, sheltered him from the pharaoh's wrath, from the soldiers' blades. This is the ancient art of providing sanctuary, the gesture of creating a safe place in a violent world. The women were brave, clever, and creative in their resistance to the insanity of their day.
- In 1844, a Quaker farmer put a candle in her window as a sign that her farm was a stop on the secret Underground Railroad. Late that night she hid a black mother and her baby in a barn until the slave-hunters had passed.
- in 1944 Germany, a Protestant woman watched as Nazis goose-stepped past her house. Every time she heard a siren she held her breath. An entire Jewish family was hiding in her attic.
- in 1984, a young volunteer opened the door of a battered-women's shelter to a dispirited woman and her fussing baby. She found milk for the baby and tea for the mother and led them to a room where they would be safe for the night.
- In 1987, an Iowan church woman pulled over into the parking lot and opened her car door to the frightened, young "illegal alien" from Guatemala she had agreed to carry to the next safe house. She was playing her part in the sanctuary movement, the "underground railroad" of the 1980s.

The gesture is sanctuary, an ancient art of protection and resistance to unjust authority. It is easy to imagine certain familiar gestures being repeated by generations of women lifting spoonfuls of food to babies' mouths, placing cool hands on damp, feverish foreheads. The gestures are familiar and ancient. Less familiar but just as ancient are the gestures of resistance to oppression and yet they are part of our legacy. There is power in these stories. There is power in remembering them.

The Women are Watching

On a cold, misty November day in 1984, over 1000 women marched through the streets of New York City in the "Not In Our Name" demonstration in preparation for a civil disobedience action the next day on Wall Street. They sang to the accompaniment of drums and bells, carried huge puppets and banners, chanted, and danced. They passed out leaflets to the onlookers and pointed accusing fingers at the headquarters of corporations that manufactured nuclear weapons and at banks that did business with the white South African government. "We don't want war! Don't call a war in our name!" the women shouted. "Get out of South Africa! Divest now! Don't do business with apartheid in our name! Not in our name! Not in our name!"

Toward the front of the march that day was a small group of women, each of whom carried a tall pole, and on the top of each pole was attached a decorative eye made of cardboard and construction paper. "The women are watching!" the marchers called out. The cardboard eyes looked over the heads of the other marchers, over the heads in the onlooking crowds. The eyes led the way, turning their hard stare toward the headquarters of institutions which had financed oppressive governments, manufactured nuclear weapons, been unfair to their workers, displaced low-income communities, or endorsed racist or sexist policies. The eyes were turned toward these institutions while the marchers chanted, "The women are watching! The women are watching!"[6]

Seeing what we are not supposed to see, recognizing what we are not supposed to name, making the invisible visible – these are acts of defiance, courage, resistance. The women who watch do not cast down their eyes or try to spare embarrassment by politely looking away as women have been trained to do. They see what no one is supposed to see. By watching, they say to the greedy and warmongering, "We know who you are. We know what you're doing."

In her poem "A Song for Gorgons," feminist, pacifist, activist author Barbara Deming pondered the myth of the Gorgons, the snake-haired sisters of Greek mythology who personified women's rage. According to the myth, anyone who met their furious stare would be turned to stone. But in Barbara's retelling of the myth, a woman who dares to meet the Gorgons' stare will turn, not to stone, but to her natural self, with her own fury writhing awake. And it is, for Barbara, women's insightful fury that can save us all. Her poem celebrates "The truth-hissing wide-open-eyed rude / Glare of our faces" with which we can see truth and unmask ties. Women can help men to see the truth too, so that together we can bring an end to the patriarchal world order which distorts all our lives.

> I sing this song for those with eyes that start,
> With curls that hiss.
> Our slandered wrath is our truth, and –
> If we honor this –
> Can deal not death but healing.[7]

Mothers of the Disappeared

In Argentina, the mothers were watching with a wide open-eyed rude glare that helped bring down a death-dealing kingdom. Ever since the military coup in 1976, their children and their children's children had been disappearing. They disappeared if they raised their fists, raised their voices, raised their eyebrows. They disappeared if they joined a union, sang freedom songs, were seen with the wrong people in the wrong place at the wrong time. And occasionally they disappeared even if they had done nothing at all. Heavy footsteps came at night, muffled screams, and then nothing – no bodies, no proof of torture, no world outrage.

For the bewildered families of the "disappeared" there was neither word of assurance nor word of bad news. With no word there could be no funerals, no closure, no coming to terms, no time to grieve or heal. There was only time to wonder, hope, pray, and wait and wait and wait. The mothers' children were silently disappearing and no one was supposed to see a thing. They should look the other way if they knew what was good for them.

Every day many of the mothers of the disappeared went to the Ministry of the Interior in Buenos Aires seeking information from the officials. The mothers waited in long, barren corridors. When a woman finally met with an official, she was told that her case would be "processed" but that, in all likelihood, her missing child had run off, had abandoned the family, was having a secret affair someplace, or was a terrorist who'd been executed by other terrorists. The officials smirked and told the mother to go home. Still, the mothers went day after day and waited in the long corridors. One day an official smirked when he dismissed Azucena De Vicenti. She was a sad and aging woman, well into her sixties. Her suffering was not his concern. But that day Azucena De Vicenti was angry. As she passed the other waiting, anxious mothers on her way out, she muttered, "It's not here that we ought to be – it's the Plaza de Mayo. And when there's enough of us, we'll go to the Casa Rosada and see the president about our children who are missing."[8]

And that is how it all began.

The next Saturday, April 13, 1977, 14 women left their homes to do the bravest thing they had ever done. At a time when all public demonstrations were forbidden, they had decided to stand together as witnesses to the disappearance of their children. They came separately to the Plaza de Mayo carrying only their identity cards and coins for the bus, and wearing flat shoes in case they had to run. Only after several years were they able to look back at that day with a sense of humor, joking about the first lesson they had learned – that even in the heart of the most vicious dictatorship, no one cares if you demonstrate on a Saturday afternoon in a deserted square where no one is around to see you.

After that, the women decided to gather on Thursday afternoons when the Plaza was crowded. From that time on, they walked every week in a slow-moving circle around the square carrying pictures of their lost loved ones. Their numbers grew as daughters, sisters, and grandmothers of the disappeared joined the circle. People began calling them "the Mothers of the Plaza" or sometimes *las locos de la Plaza* – "the mad women." The women were watching and making their witness a public act of defiance against the military regime. When they realized that the newspapers were afraid to write about their action, they got together enough money to buy an advertisement. It appeared, against great odds and despite efforts by the military to stop it, in *La Prensa* on October 5, 1977. Above pictures of 237 "disappeared" and the names of their mothers was the headline, "We Do Not Ask for Anything More than the Truth."

Ten days after the advertisement appeared, several hundred women carried a petition with 24,000 signatures to the congress building demanding that the government investigate the disappearances.

The police repression which followed was severe. Hundreds of people were harassed, arrested, and detained during the month, including American and British journalists who tried to interview some of the Mothers. Still, the women refused to hide their actions. Every Thursday, two or three hundred women would gather to walk around the Plaza.

On other afternoons the Mothers held open meetings. Many desperate people came seeking information about loved ones who had disappeared. The Mothers were no longer looking for their individual sons or daughters: they were seeking each others's children and the truth about what had happened to the children of Argentina.

At some point during the fall of 1977, a young man named "Gustavo" began coming regularly to the meetings, seeking information about his disappeared brother and helping the women in whatever way he could. A sweet-faced, blue-eyed blond in his mid-twenties, sincere, friendly, generous, and compassionate, Gustavo seemed to be every mother's dream child.

Then in December, two days before another advertisement was to be published, this time in La Nación, nine of the women left a planning meeting by a side door and walked directly into a trap. Five or six men, one of them armed with a machine gun, had been lying in wait for the women. The men had been well informed. They demanded the money the Mothers of the Plaza had collected for the advertisement and forced the women into a car. The women disappeared forever. Two days later three more women disappeared; one of them was Azucena De Vicenti.

There was no doubt that young Gustavo had orchestrated the whole maneuver. His real name turned out to be Alfredo Astiz, later recognized as one of the most notorious kidnappers and torturers in ESMA, the Navy Mechanics School in Buenos Aires where an estimated 5,000 people were imprisoned and tortured, and of whom only an estimated 200 survived. Astiz's nickname was "the blond angel."

The Thursday following the kidnapping, only 40 women came to the Plaza; even some of these stayed hidden in the shadows. When the Mothers of the Plaza called a press conference, only four journalists dared attend, all of them foreigners.

Throughout 1978 the Mothers tried to maintain a presence in the Plaza, to let Argentina and the rest of the world know that the women were still watching, still watching despite great odds, still watching. But the police violence against them was great and each week a few women were arrested. By the beginning of 1979, the Mothers of the Plaza were finding it almost impossible to endure the violence. Each Thursday they met in the shadows, hurried across the square and quickly formed their small circle for a few minutes before the police closed in. Finally, even that became impossible.

No doubt the military men felt smug then as they chuckled over their afternoon cocktails; it seemed that guns, billy clubs, tear gas, and terror could defeat even the Mothers of the Plaza. Little did they know that in churches around the city the Mothers continued to gather.

Every meeting was illegal and dangerous but the women had found a way. They entered the dark sanctuaries as women do in cities all over the world every day. Some lit candles and knelt before little altars murmuring special prayers, and then they found a place in the pews to rest and pray. There was nothing unusual in this.

What the authorities couldn't see was that the women in the churches, sometimes numbering over 100, were passing notes to each other as their heads were bowed. These were "meetings" at which decisions were made without a word spoken aloud.

It must have been a great surprise to the authorities when, seemingly out of nowhere, the Mothers of the Plaza stepped out of the darkened churches in May 1979. Determined to formalize their structure, they held elections, legally registered as an association and opened a bank account with some of the financial support which began to come in from around the world. In 1980, they rented an office on Uruguay Street and opened the House of the Mothers. They even started publishing their own bulletin and within several years counted their membership in the thousands.

The women returned to the Plaza. They wore flat shoes and white scarves embroidered with the names or initials of the relatives they were seeking. They came to the Plaza carrying photos of the "disappeared." Some days after walking the circle, several women would leave the square, take a megaphone down a side street and each tell her personal story. They had learned that it was easier for people to understand the horror of one missing child than it was to grasp the picture of thousands who had "disappeared."

The police met the women in even greater numbers than before and the women continued to face tear gas, nightsticks, and arrest. But something had changed. The Mothers of the Plaza were determined that they'd never again retreat into silence and shadows. Their visible courage was contagious. Onlookers who had been too afraid to stop long enough to acknowledge the women now stood still to applaud the Mothers as they circled the square.

Argentina's bloody military regime could not hide from the eyes of the Mothers of the Plaza de Mayo. The women were watching and the world was watching them. With their persistence they inspired women in other countries (such as the mothers of El Salvador and Guatemala) where children were disappearing. And they helped bring the day in December 1993 when the people of Argentina inaugurated President Raul Alfonsin as the head of a democratic government.

No More Hiroshimas

"No more Hiroshima!"
"No more Nagasaki!"
"Women for peace!"

Over 2,000 chanting women marched through Tokyo's commercial district on December 6, 1981, just as they had marched in December 1980. The women marched again in remembrance of the day Japan had bombed Pearl Harbor. They followed a banner which declared, "We will not allow the way to war!"

The women were publicly remembering and calling on others in their country to remember with them. Theirs had been the only nation to suffer the wartime devastation of atomic bombings. Even as they marched, the disfigured atomic holocaust survivors called *hibakusha* women were suffering from radiation-caused cancers and from ostracism by other Japanese citizens.

The women were remembering, and they were watching in shared rage and despair the increasing militarization of their beautiful Japan, a nation which had made so much progress in transforming its national spirit from warlike to peace-seeking. Wasn't Japan the only industrialized nation whose constitution, written and adopted after defeat in the Second World War, renounced war? Hadn't Japan's government boldly affirmed a three-point antinuclear principle in 1968 by vowing never to manufacture, possess, or store nuclear weapons? Hadn't Japan managed to keep its military spending to under 1 percent of its gross national product and concentrated its citizens' brainpower on designing and producing nonmilitary consumer products? Hadn't it set an example for other nations of the world that peace could be a financially healthy investment? Was all this to be lost?

The women who gathered on December 6, 1981 were watching. They knew that all the good intentions of maintaining a peace-loving Japan were being undermined, that men were preparing for war in the very shadow of Mount Fuji. The United States, which had occupied Japan at the end of the Second World War had never really left, some said. It had signed a security act with Japan in the 1960s which permitted installation of US military bases and was now spending $2 billion per year to maintain its operations there. And suddenly, in 1981, there was no doubt that Japan's peace consciousness had eroded. A "hawkish" prime minister had come to power and the Liberal Democratic Party was leaning far to the right. There was serious talk of revising the constitution and even of reinstituting a conscription system. The "Self-Defense Force" had grown into the seventh largest army in the world. Twenty-four nuclear power plants were operating in Japan, with more being constructed, all of them producing plutonium which could be used to manufacture nuclear weapons.

Now, too, rumors were spreading throughout the population that the United States had brought nuclear weapons to its bases in Okinawa and to its submarines that cruised Japan's waters, and planned to bring Tomahawk cruise missiles tipped with nuclear warheads to its Iwakuni base on Japan's mainland. For its part, the United States would neither confirm nor deny the presence of nuclear weapons in Japan.

The women were watching. They had been watching a long time, and in the spring of 1981 they intensified their campaign to let their government know they were watching. Women workers took to the streets, collecting 2 million signatures against the increasing militarization of Japan. Many pledged that, even if the prisons should become "filled with mammas and grandmas," they would stop the draft before it started. All spring long, women, gathered to voice their concerns – at the Rally to Build Peace with Women's Votes, at the Women's Symposium for Thinking of the Constitution, and later, at the Women's Rally Never to Allow an Undesirable Amendment of the Constitution.

That spring, too, 6,000 working women came to Meiji Park, Tokyo in the pouring rain to attend a demonstration with a very long name – the Central Rally of Women for a Ban on Adverse Revision of the Japanese Constitution and for the Establishment of Peace. Women from the Housewives Association, the Socialist Party, the 20,000-member Japan Women's Council, the Japanese Women's Caucus against War, and the Women's Bureau of the General Council of Trade Unions of Japan joined together in a campaign of witnessing to the increased militarization.

The year of intense antiwar activity by women concluded with the December 6 demonstration in Tokyo. They chanted as they marched, "No more Hiroshima! No more Nagasaki! Women for peace! Women for peace!" In an effort to encourage solidarity with women's antiwar movements in other countries, the Japanese Women's Caucus Against War invited London–based peace activist and writer Leonie Caldecott to speak briefly during that day's rally about women's initiatives in the European peace movement. Caldecott spoke on a platform with Japanese peace activists who stood, one after the other, to give sincere, carefully crafted messages.

Suddenly, a group of rough peasant women took the stage. They were dressed in cotton trousers and jackets and wide straw hats. Several of the women held a banner while one of their group spoke. The speech was angry and passionate. The crowd stirred. These were the Shibokusa women who lived at the foot of Mount Fuji, two hours by bus from sophisticated Tokyo.

The Shibokusa women, mostly in their fifties and sixties, had been watching military maneuvers in the shadow of the mountain for many years. They had made it their business to watch and disrupt the military exercises conducted there by Japan's young warriors, warriors not so different from those of an earlier time, a time which had brought immeasurable suffering to Japan. The women remembered.

They had watched the young soldiers parade and practice killing on land that did not belong to them. For centuries, that land at the foot of Mount Fuji had been cultivated by hard-working farmers. They had worked the poor land, managing to grow radishes and beans. The people had also started a silkworm industry there. But in 1936, the Japanese army took over the land – and began using it for military drills, and after the Second World War the US army moved in. The San Francisco Peace Treaty was signed in 1952 between Japan and the United States, and the farmers hoped that the land would be returned to the people, but the Japanese government continued to use the land for its "self- defense" exercises. The local farmers protested and a few concessions were made, but the state didn't leave. Eventually the men went off to cities to look for work. The women stayed. The women watched, and they helped create a resistance movement in Japan, helped fight for their land rights and against all preparations for war. When others got discouraged, these women sustained the spirit of resistance. They remembered Hiroshima and Nagasaki. They remembered when the land at the foot of the beautiful Mount Fuji had been used to grow food.

During an interview with Leonie Caldecott, the Shibokusa women explained:

> We are not clever. Most of us have hardly been educated at all. But we are strong because we are close to the earth, and we know what matters. Our conviction that the military is wrong is unshakeable. We are the strongest women in Japan! And we want other women to be like us.[9]

It is their intention to be a mischievous, bothersome, embarrassing presence at the military base. They create secret paths leading from their cottages to the center of the military exercise areas. In groups of ten or less, they sometimes crawl along the paths startling the soldiers, plant scarecrows here and there, sit in a circle to sing and clap, or stand to point and laugh at the soldiers. They always ignore direct orders to go away.

Theirs has been a long struggle. Once, in 1970, 1,000 riot police came to evict them from their cottages. The women dressed for death that day. They realized that the struggle was their whole life, the journey was their home. The people in the nearby town sometimes treat the women with contempt. Of less concern to the women are their frequent arrests. When they are arrested, the grinning Shibokusa women refuse to give their names or any information. They laugh and say they are too old to remember who they are. The Shibokusa women, by their own reckoning the "strongest women in Japan," witness for peace with their lives. They are watching, watching, taking care "that the third atom bomb never comes."[10]

Deadly rain gathers poison from the sky,
And the fish carry death
In the depths of the sea,
Fishing boats are idle, their owners are blind,
Deadly harvest of two atom bombs.
Then land and sea folk
You must watch and take care
That the third atom bomb never comes.
– Ishigi Astu, "Furusato" (English verse by Ewen MacColl)[11]

Greenham Common

The women at the Greenham Common peace camp were also watching. They saw what they were not supposed to see and made the invisible visible. The women began their presence at Greenham Common in England in 1981, watching each of the nine gates at the US Air Force base where ground-launched cruise missiles were deployed in November 1983 in preparation for the Third World War.

Except for the nine miles of barbed wire fence surrounding low-lying bunkers and missile silos, it might have been easy to overlook the missile base in the gray mist and the lush green countryside. This is just what the peace camp women didn't want to happen, so thousands of women would sometimes show up to encircle the base. They hung photos of their mothers or children on the wire fence, creating little yam webs as a symbol that everything is connected in a fragile and precious web of life. They sang and banged pots and pans. One time, 50,000 women "embraced the base." They held mirrors up to the fence to reflect its death-dealing energy back on itself. It was as though the women were answering the myth of the Gorgons by saying to the missile base patriarchs, "It is not our glance but your own that will turn you to stone."

Between these expansive media events, small handfuls of women persisted. They played host to the constant stream of supporters from around the world who visited the camp every day. Sometimes they did nothing but wait and watch, and sometimes they tore open great holes in the fence with wire cutters, or went over the top of the fence, entering the base either to damage whatever equipment they could or to illustrate just how inadequate the security is at the nuclear missile base. Once, at dawn on January 1, 1983, 44 women climbed the fence and danced in a great circle on top of a missile silo.

It is very hard to make the threat of nuclear war tangible. It is too big, terrible, unthinkable. Real estate agents complained that property values around the base had dropped dramatically, not because of the ugly barbed wire that grew where silver birches once did, but because of the presence of the peace camp women.

While the missiles were deployed, the women made it their business to monitor and expose the missile system, which was supposed to be very secret, if not invisible. Cruise missiles are small and designed to be launched from mobile launch points. If a nuclear alert was given, the missiles were to be taken from the silos and put in a truck caravan which would carry the missiles to a firing point somewhere in the countryside.

In preparation for an actual alert, the trucks were sent out for practice runs that function partly to make nuclear war, or the thought of it, a matter of routine for the young men hired to do the job. But a caravan of 20 trucks is not really invisible even if camouflaged. How, the women wondered, would an enemy know that any movement of trucks from the base is merely a dress rehearsal for the Third World War and not opening night? And was it really safe to have these mammoth 50-foot trucks designed for US highways traveling along the narrow, winding English roads, trucks presumably carrying a massive cargo of death on a nighttime practice run?

The peace camp women observed other eerie late-night practice runs at Greenham. Every so often a siren sounded. Nearby, in the prosperous town of Newbury, the wives and children of the US military men were gotten out of bed, herded onto buses and raced to the "safety" of the nuclear bunkers inside the base. The children were terrified, crying, wondering if this was real, if the end had come. The British police who opened the gates for the Americans have no such bunkers. There were no plans to protect them in case of a nuclear exchange.

The peace camp women watched the cruise missiles. During the deployment, women stood at the gates of the base in nightly vigils, tracking the movements of the missile carriers. They stood in rain and snow, enduring the abusive taunts of the soldiers, watching for the invisible. Whenever the gates would open and a convoy rumbled past, they would blow whistles into the night to awaken the women at the other gates, then find phones to alert nearby towns. Other women would race for their cars and spend the night charting the course of the convoy, tracking every inch of its movements. The women painted slogans on the sides of the trucks and published their findings about the convoys' routes and hiding places.

The women saw what they were not supposed to see, forced the invisible out into the open. The women were watching.

Notes

1   Excerpts reprinted from McAllister, Pam *You Can't Kill the Spirit*. (Philadelphia, Pa.: New Society Publishers, 1988).
2   Barbara Deming, *Remembering Who We Are*.: Pagoda Publishers, pp. 187–8.
3   Deming, cited in June Meyerding, ed., *We Are All Part of One Another: A Barbara Deming Reader* (Philadelphia: New Society Publishers, 1985) pp. 177–8.
4   Barbara Deming *Prisons That Could Not Hold: Prison Notes 1964*. (San Francisco: Spinster's Ink, 1985) p. 213.
5   Boston: Porter Sargent Publishers, 1973.

6   "Not In Our Name," *Off Our Backs*, vol. 14, no. 12 (Jan. 1985), p. 8.

7   Deming, Barbara. "A Song for Gorgons." In Pam McAllister, ed., *Reweaving the Web of Life: Feminism and Nonviolence* (Philadelphia: New Society, 1982).

8   Simpson, John, and Jana Bennett. *The Disappeared and the Mothers of the Plaza: The Story of the 11,000 Argentinians Who Vanished* (New York: St. Martin's Press, 1985).

9   Caldecott, Leonie. "At the Foot of the Mountain: The Shibokusa Women of Kita Fuji." In Lynne Jones, ed., *Keeping the Peace: A Women's Peace Handbook*. (London: Women's Press, 1983).

10 Astu, Ishigi. "Furusato." In Student Peace Union, ed., *Songs for Peace: 100 Songs of The Peace Movement* (New York: Oak, 1966).

11 Ibid.

PART II
The Middle East

Introduction

We begin our regional survey of nonviolence with what many would consider the most unlikely part of the world: the Middle East. While terror, repression, and war have dominated Western media coverage of that region, there are other images as well: of hundreds of Christian and Muslim women marching together through the streets of Beirut demanding an end to Lebanon's sectarian violence; of thousands of Israelis and Palestinians holding hands to encircle the entire Old City of Jerusalem for the cause of peace and self-determination for both peoples; of Saudi women driving cars through the streets of Riyadh in open defiance of the kingdom's ban on female drivers.

With the United States and other Western powers pouring billions of dollars-worth of sophisticated armaments into the region and providing repressive governments and occupying armies with military and economic aid, it may be too simplistic to blame the militarism and authoritarianism of the Middle East on cultural or religious factors. Indeed, the need for nonviolent action in the Middle East may be no less than the need for nonviolent action in the United States and other Western countries in opposition to those governments' policies which help sustain the region's violent and undemocratic status quo.

Co-editor Stephen Zunes, in his overview of nonviolent struggles in the Middle East and North Africa argues that, despite Western stereotypes to the contrary, certain aspects of Islamic culture are quite consistent with the practice of nonviolent action even though the concept of nonviolence per se may not be widely supported. Indeed, as Zunes observes, a number of the most significant nonviolent struggles this century have taken place in Islamic societies of the Middle East and North Africa.

Souad Dajani, a Palestinian American sociologist, describes the role of nonviolent action in the *intifada*, the 1987–93 movement by the Palestinians to resist Israeli occupation. She puts forward an assessment of the movement's successes and failures, along with the very real limitations for authentic self-determination within the current peace process, which has usurped the popular initiatives for peace through the nonviolent action of Palestinians and sympathetic Israelis prior to the signing of the Oslo Accords.

3

Unarmed Resistance in the Middle East and North Africa

Stephen Zunes

Introduction

Despite the stereotype of the Middle East as an area of violent conflict, the region also has an impressive and growing tradition of nonviolent resistance and other unarmed challenges to authoritarianism. The term "nonviolent action" is not highly regarded among those in unarmed Middle Eastern resistance movements, in part because its Arabic translation of the term connotes passivity and because the chief Arab advocates for its use have tended to be among the tiny minority of Arab Christians who identify as pacifists and their Western pacifist supporters. Yet while the term understandably may not have widespread acceptance and while few may explicitly refer to these movements as largely nonviolent campaigns, in practice most of the actions fall under the rubric of nonviolent action.[1]

The Middle East has seen more than its share of violence, in large part due to foreign invaders and authoritarian regimes. However, Middle Eastern peoples have not historically been more violent than those in other parts of the world. Despite Western stereotypes to the contrary, the dramatic spread of Islam in the seventh century was not as much through Arab militarism as the absence of formidable opposition. More often than not, the way was open to them. Indeed, the Arabs of that period had little military professionalism, techniques, or organization. Their generals tended to be merchants, poets, or tribal chieftains. Their culture did not have the militaristic caste tradition of the Spartans, Prussians, Janissaries, or Karalis, nor did they build up a military organization comparable to other empires as the Greeks, Romans, Byzantines, or Persians.[2]

Part of this perception in the West of Islamic militarism is based on confusion over the concept of *jihad*. Rather than a holy war in the sense often conceptualized in the West, *jihad*

stands for the total struggle which a Muslim makes in his lifetime. It starts
from the effort which he makes to improve his personal character to the total
sacrifice of self and resources which he renders for the establishment of Allah's
authority on earth.[3]

Thus, *jihad* – which relates to an overall struggle – is distinct from *qital* –
the fight. When a *jihad* must take the form of a *qital* is debatable, but belief
in *jihad* does not presuppose the use of violence in the quest of a just
society. It has been said that the term "militant Islam" is redundant, given
Islam's inherent dedication to struggle for justice. Militancy, however, does
not necessitate militarism. And struggle does not necessitate violence.
According to Khalid Kishtainy,

> The many references in the Quran to jihad convey different meanings depen-
> dent upon the kind of effort required. The term "jihad" can mean persuasion
> and argument, fulfillment of God's will, service to religion, or fighting in the
> defense of Islam. The Prophet himself seems to have laid more emphasis on the
> peaceful side of jihad, as in his saying "Pilgrimage is one of the highest forms
> of jihad" and "some of the men of learning are mujahidin."[4]

Indeed, Abd Rabboh, in his study of the linguistic roots and derivatives of
jihad, concludes that "None of the meanings discussed implies that jihad is
a synonym of war or fighting."[5]

One of the great strengths in Islam and Middle Eastern cultures which
makes unarmed insurrections possible is the belief in a social contract
between a ruler and subject. This was stated explicitly by Muhammad's
successor Abu Bakr al-Siddiq when he said "Obey me as long as I obey God
in my rule. If I disobey him, you will owe me no obedience." Such a pledge
was reiterated by successive caliphs, such as Imam Ali, who stated that "No
obedience is allowed to any creature in his disobedience of the Creator."
Indeed, most Middle Eastern scholars have firmly supported the right of the
people to depose an unjust ruler.[6] The decision to refuse one's cooperation
is a crucial step in building a nonviolent movement.

Nonviolence in North Africa

Some of the most impressive cases of nonviolent resistance has come in
North Africa. The 1919 revolution in Egypt consisted of months of civil
disobedience against the British occupation, centered in Cairo and Alexan-
dria, and strikes by students and lawyers, as well as postal, telegraph, tram,
and railway workers, and, eventually, Egyptian government personnel. The
result of this nonviolent movement was the British recognition of limited
Egyptian independence.

Recent years have seen nonviolent insurrections against military-dominated governments in Mali and Niger, the former being successful in

restoring the country to democracy. Despite scattered and well-publicized cases of armed resistance by Islamic forces against the military government in Algeria, much of the resistance movement, particularly in the early months following the January 1992 coup, were nonviolent in character.

The repressive 16 year rule of Jafaar Nimeiry in Sudan was ended during the spring of 1985 following two weeks of largely nonviolent demonstrations in the capital of Khartoum and the neighboring city of Omdurman. A general strike called by trade unions and professional organizations paralyzed the country and the democracy movement received active support from a cross-section of the population, including the business community. Despite thousands of arrests and scores of shootings, the protests continued. While there was some rioting, most of the protests were peaceful. By April 5, even the judiciary had joined what was referred to as a "civil rebellion." Radio stations were shut down and the airport was closed to prevent Nimeiry, who had been visiting the United States (a major supporter of the regime), from returning home. The military then seized power in a bloodless coup on April 6 but popular demands soon led to the establishment of a civilian government followed by democratic elections, which resulted in a popularly elected government that remained in power for another four years.[7]

Despite a history of repressive colonialism and military rule, Pakistan has witnessed impressive examples of nonviolent resistance. The Pathans of the Northwest Frontier, a traditional warrior people, were among the most effective participants in the nonviolent anticolonial struggle against the British – Mohandas Gandhi referred to them as his best "nonviolent soldiers."[8] Khan Abdul Ghaffir Khan, known as the "frontier Gandhi", organized a group called Khudai Khidmatgar, or "Servants of God", which grew into the thousands and played an integral part in the independence movement, particularly in the early 1930s.

Not only are there such cases of unarmed insurgencies against existing regimes in power, but there is a case of such a successful movement existing within a nationalist movement prior to the formal seizure of power. The Polisario Front, the nationalist movement of Western Sahara seeking to reclaim their country from Moroccan occupation, has ruled up to 170,000 Sahrawis in refugee camps in the desert of southwestern Algeria since the exodus following the 1975 invasion. While Polisario guerrillas waged an armed struggle against Morocco, the Front set up a sophisticated governmental structure in exile independent of Algerian control, calling itself the Sahrawi Arab Democratic Republic (SADR), and which included a network of health care centers, cottage industries, agricultural projects, and distribution systems which have won praise from international development agencies. Though Morocco occupies most of the territory, the majority of this sparsely populated country lives in these camps under Polisario control.[9]

Despite these impressive structures which have insured a high degree of economic and social democracy, actual political democracy for most of this period was limited. Many Sahrawis felt there was too much domination by one element of the Polisario and serious discrepancies between the movement's egalitarian line and the political reality. On the political level, the Polisario's executive committee made all the real decisions despite the facade of participatory democracy; many of the local political leaders were hand-picked. There were a series of work stoppages and protests in 1988 as democrats pressed for liberalization. Hardliners resisted, arresting democratic opposition leaders. Still facing stiff opposition from the population through ongoing nonviolent resistance, the SADR went through several governments that autumn, but still failed to satisfy the population. Due to continued protests, however, the democrats won a series of victories during 1990–1, and now essentially hold power. The June 1991 Polisario Congress, the largest ever and the first to include substantial representation from outside the camps, was dominated by democrats. Among other radical reforms, the executive committee and Politburo were replaced by a national secretariat with key positions held by reformers. There is now a new and more democratic constitution and an independent human rights commission.

Undoubtedly the already existing social and economic democracy made possible the transition to political democracy. Yet given the isolation of the camps and the monopoly of the armed force in the hands of the Polisario elite, a more active policy of repression would have likely been attempted had the leadership thought it would work. Indeed, it may be the first time that such a serious division within a national liberation movement was resolved through nonviolent action, avoiding disintegration into armed factions or establishing a new rival liberation organization. By avoiding splitting the movement on the eve of the United Nations-sponsored referendum which should shortly determine the fate of the disputed territory, it gives the Polisario a much stronger chance of liberating their territory, albeit through the ballot box.

The Iranian Revolution

Through mass arms transfers from the United States, Shah Mohammed Reza Pahlavi built one of the most powerful armed forces ever seen in the Middle East. His American-trained secret police, the SAVAK, had been thought to have successfully terrorized the population into submission through widespread killings, torture, and mass detentions. However, open resistance began in 1977, when exiled opposition leader Ayatollah Ruhollah Khomeini called for strikes, boycotts, tax refusal, and other forms of noncooperation with the Shah's regime.

Such resistance was met by brutal repression from the government. The pace of the resistance accelerated as massacres of civilians would be met by larger demonstrations following the Islamic 40 day mourning period. In

October and November 1978, a series of strikes by workers including hospital employees and journalists paralyzed the country. The crisis deepened when oil workers struck at the end of October, demanding the release of political prisoners, costing the government $60 million a day. A general strike on November 6 paralyzed the country. Under enormous pressure, oil workers returned to work, but continued to stage a series of slowdowns. Later in the month, the Shah's nightly speeches would be interrupted when workers cut off the electricity at precisely the time of his scheduled addresses. Massive protests filled the streets in major cities throughout December, as oil workers walked out again and an ongoing general strike closed the refineries and the central bank. Despite large- scale massacres by royalist troops acting against unarmed demonstrators, their numbers increased. The Shah fled on January 16, 1979 and Ayatollah Khomeini returned from exile two weeks later. He appointed Mehdi Bazargan prime minister, thus establishing a parallel government to challenge the Shah's appointed prime minister Shapur Bahktiar. With the loyalty of the vast majority clearly with the new Islamic government, Bahktiar resigned on February 11.

Despite the bloody image of the revolution and the authoritarianism and militarism of the Islamic Republic which followed, there was a clear commitment to keep the actual insurrection unarmed. Protestors were told by the leadership of the resistance to try to win over the troops rather than attack them; indeed, thousands of troops deserted, some in the middle of confrontations with crowds. The mobilization of the masses by clandestinely smuggled audio-cassette tapes led Abolhassan Sadegh, an official with the Ministry of National Guidance, to note how "Tape cassettes are stronger than fighter planes."[10] Ayatollah Khomeini's speeches, circulated through such covert methods, emphasized the power of unarmed resistance and noncooperation, stating that " the clenched fists of freedom fighters can crush the tanks and guns of the oppressors"[11] There was little of the violent activities normally associated with armed revolutions such as shooting soldiers, setting fires to government buildings, or looting and sacking. Such incidents which did occur were unorganized and spontaneous and did not have the support of the leadership of the movement.

The central value of martyrdom in Shi'ite Islam made it possible so that, despite savage repression under the Shah – which led to as many as 20,000 deaths at the hands of his army and secret police – the opposition could mobilize popular resistance rather than allow it to be crushed or to force it into a self-defeating armed confrontation against the government's vast military forces. The emphasis was to "save Islam by *our* blood." Indeed, there are interesting parallels between the early Islamic figure Imam Hossein's emphasis on martyrdom with Gandhian tradition of self-sacrifice.[12]

Once in power, the Islamic regime proved to abandon its nonviolent methodology, particularly in the period after its dramatic shift to the right in the spring of 1981. However, there was a clear recognition of the utilitarian advantages of nonviolent methods by the Islamic opposition while out of power which made their victory possible.

Golani Druze

When Israel seized the Golan Heights of southwestern Syria in 1967, it forced most of the population to flee. However, five villages populated by Druze remained. The Israelis sought to gradually annex the territory, and began pressuring the Druze to accept Israeli identification cards. The population resisted. In December 1981, when the Israelis formally extended direct administration over the territory, they began an attempt to systematically coerce the population into accepting Israeli citizenship. The Druze began a nonviolent campaign, including a general strike, peaceful demonstrations, and violating curfews. They systematically ignored military restrictions against fraternization between villages and public demonstrations. Children and adults eagerly sought arrest and many engaged in a "reverse strike," installing a sewer pipeline which the occupation forces had refused to support. As many as 15,000 Israeli troops occupied the Golan, imposing a 43–day state of siege, destroying homes, arresting hundreds of people and shooting suspects, but the Israelis finally ended their insistence that the Druze accept Israeli citizenship. Furthermore, they promised not to conscript Golani Druze into the army, allow them to open economic relations with their fellow Syrians across the armistice line, and to no longer interfere with Druze civil, water, and land rights. When the Israelis refused to live up to these promises, mass protests and civil disobedience continued.

It forced the Israelis to compromise further. Palestinian attorney Jonathan Kuttab, in his account of the nonviolent Druze campaign, observed, "The [Israeli] soldiers were really being torn apart, because they couldn't handle that type of nonviolence."[13] Scott Kennedy similarly noted that

> Israeli soldiers generally function so effectively, at least in part, because of the widespread conviction that they are acting out of genuine security needs of their fellow Israelis and because so many of the situations in which they are stationed give them cause to fear for their own lives. In face of a disciplined unarmed civilian population, which threatened neither Israeli security, nor the lives of the individual soldiers, the morale and discipline of Israeli soldiers began to break down. According to several reports, the division commander complained that the Golan situation was ruining some of his best soldiers.[14]

The successes of this resistance effort inspired Palestinians, also living under Israeli occupation, to rethink their previous reliance on armed struggle by exiled guerilla groups, and to consider the efficacy of unarmed resistance in the West Bank and Gaza. Within a few years, the *intifada* had begun.

Palestine

The still-incomplete struggle for national self-determination for the Palestinians, after little progress during years of armed struggle, including terrorism, against Israel, made signficant gains in the late 1980s and early 1990s as the result of the shift towards largely nonviolent methods during the *intifada*, the uprising in the Israeli-occupied West Bank and the Gaza Strip.

Palestinians have engaged in such forms of unarmed resistance for decades, including the general strikes of the 1930s against Zionist immigration. Hundreds of such actions and campaigns over the past half-century have been documented by the Palestinian Center for the Study of Nonviolence.[15] Many of the tactics of the *intifada* were not new, but they brought this form of struggle to new heights in terms of its scope and role as a calculated strategy of resistance.[16]

Despite well-publicized incidents of stone-throwing and the murder of collaborators, the bulk of the *intifada* was nonviolent, including peaceful demonstrations, strikes, boycotts, tax refusal, occupations, blockades, and the creation of alternative institutions.

After decades of focusing on military means for the liberation of Palestine, far greater progress has been made as a result of the *intifada*, which has explicitly endorsed the use of nonmilitary means of resistance. Indeed, the Palestine Liberation Organization, after having de-emphasized the armed struggle for a number of years, formally renounced it in 1988.

In addition, within its first year, the *intifada* forced Jordan to give up its nominal administrative authority over the West Bank and to endorse Palestinian self-determination to an unprecedented degree, and exerted substantial influence in popular opinion throughout the Arab world to force some often unresponsive regimes to once again take the Palestinian question seriously. The intifada forced the PLO to take the political initiative, including the declaration of independence in December 1988, which led to a number of diplomatic successes, including recognition of the PLO as a negotiating partner by Israel and the United States.

The Palestinian population was mobilized and empowered to an unprecedented degree during the *intifada* and the Israelis were faced with their most intractable opposition ever. As Nafez Assaily of the Palestinian Center for the Study of Nonviolence described the situation in 1989, "In 1967 they defeated the armies of three countries in six days, but they [are yet to] defeat the intifada..."[17]

Given that the Palestinian people were united in their desire for national self-determination, that most accepted – at least provisionally – the establishment of an independent Palestinian state alongside Israel, and that most of the world community supported such a two-state solution, the obstacles to Palestinian statehood clearly rested upon the policies of Israel and its international supporters, principally the United States government.

Therefore, it had long been argued that a successful strategy for the national liberation of the Palestinian people must involve the following:

- the maximal utilization of the overwhelming numerical majority of Palestinians within the occupied territories to the advantage of the liberation struggle against Israeli forces;
- the creation of sufficient negative ramifications within Israeli society resulting from its occupation policy to make the costs of continued occupation outweigh its benefits;
- a usurpation in the morale of major segments within the Israeli occupation forces to such a degree that they can no longer reliably serve as the enforcement mechanism for continued Israeli rule;
- the creation of sufficient sympathy for the Palestinian cause in the United States and other Western nations which currently provide the necessary economic, military, and diplomatic support for continued Israeli occupation so that such support can no longer be guaranteed.

The calculated decision by leaders of the Palestinian resistance to the use of unarmed methods against Israeli occupation authorities made major progress towards fulfilling these criteria. Furthermore, the noncooperation with the occupation authorities initially led to an unprecedented degree of cooperation between the Palestinian population in the occupied territories, those living in Israel proper, and those in the Palestinian diaspora. It was hoped that the power of such tactics could eventually force an end to the Israeli occupation, not by driving Israeli forces out physically, but by making Palestinian society ungovernable by anyone but the Palestinians themselves. Indeed, it is this recognition which led to the Israeli concessions obtained in the September 1993 agreement. It is perhaps significant that as the main arena shifted away from popular nonviolence resistance to US-led diplomacy interspersed with acts of terrorism, that the optimism for Palestinian statehood has faded.

While Gene Sharp and others have stressed the key role of noncooperation, the ultimate failure of the *intifada* suggests that there were other factors than Palestinian acquiescence which made the Israeli occupation possible. As Andrew Rigby, in his study of Palestinian nonviolent resistance, noted "Israel wants to rule over the *land* of Palestine. It does not want the *people*."[18]

Israel

With strong democratic institutions for its Jewish citizens and a proportional representation system in the Knesset, there have been ample opportunities for dissenting political voices to be heard through existing political channels. Yet the failure of normal political channels to halt successive Israeli governments from pursuing ongoing occupations of neighboring countries, human rights violations, and the bombing and shelling of concentrations of Arab civilian targets has forced many Israelis to engage in a series of nonviolent actions to challenge policies which they considered to be morally unjust and contrary to their country's long-term security interests.

Over 400,000 Israelis – over one-tenth of the country's entire population – demonstrated against Israel's 1982 invasion of Lebanon and its responsibility for massacres in Palestinian refugee camps. Other peace demonstrations have routinely drawn tens of thousands of participants. Women in Black have held ongoing vigils against the occupation despite widespread harassment from rightist opponents and have inspired Israeli feminists to address larger questions or sexism and patriarchy within Israel's highly militarized society. Scores of leading Israeli intellectuals risked arrest by meeting with officials of the Palestine Liberation Organisation when such meetings were deemed illegal. Thousands of Israelis soldiers have joined the Yesh G'vul movement, refusing to serve in the occupied territories; hundreds have served jail sentences for their defiance. Other Israelis have joined with Palestinians in joint protests against Israeli occupation forces, including occupations of land seized to build illegal Jewish settlements on confiscated Arab land, resulting in hundreds of beatings and arrests.

These Israeli nonviolent activists have included both committed Zionists as well as non-Zionists and have built links with the Jewish diaspora in the United States and elsewhere to make dissenting Israeli voices more visible. Despite periodic efforts at censorship, alternative media outlets and cultural workers have served to boldly challenge Israeli government policies. This persistence has forced the Israeli government to confront its left-wing critics, though the large-scale economic, military and political support from the United States has enabled the Israeli government to weather the negative diplomatic and economic repercussions it might otherwise face from its ongoing violations of human rights and international law. With greater political freedom to operate than dissidents in most Middle Eastern states, however, nonviolent activists in Israel will continue to have an impact in challenging government policies. The US-backed Israeli interpretation of the Oslo framework has effectively neutralized ongoing Palestinian nonviolent resistance; it has placed the bulk of the population under the non-contiguous control of the Palestinian Authority, while the Israelis control most the land. As a result, perhaps the best hope of advancing a just and peaceful solution resides in the ability of progressive Israelis to mobilize their resistance to their government's occupation policies.

Conclusion

The peoples of the Middle East and North Africa are recognizing alternative strategies for achieving political goals against entrenched and repressive governments. With the failure of warfare to attain such goals as human rights and economic justice, or even national freedom for the Palestinians, unarmed insurrections may still offer hope for real political change. The carnage in Algeria and repression in Egypt has demonstrated the limits of internal armed resistance. The many years of futile armed resistance by the Palestinians against Israeli occupation and the disastrous deployment of conventional Arab armies against Israel demonstrated the difficulty in challenging Western-backed client states militarily. The overwhelming military response by the United States against Saddam Hussein's military challenges has shown the futility of challenging Western powers militarily.

Yet, popular sentiment for challenging autocratic regimes, occupying armies and Western imperialism remains as strong as ever. The limited but significant success of nonviolent action in North Africa and the Middle East raises the hope that the injustices which have led to the rise of violent and extremist movements might be addressed increasingly through the power of nonviolent action.

Notes

1 Palestinian American sociologist Souad Dajani prefers to use of the term "civil resistance". Her studies emphasize that the nonviolent components of the Palestinian resistance was not based on a Gandhian ethic but simply because it worked.

2 Khalid Kishtainy, "Violent and Nonviolent Struggle in Arab History." In Ralph E. Crow, Philip Grant, and Saad E. Ibrahim, eds., *Arab Nonviolent Political Struggle in the Middle East* (Boulder: Lynne Rienner Publishers, 1990), pp. 9–10.

3 Shamim A. Siqdiqi, "Islam vs. Terrorism", New York: Forum for Islamic Work, 1987.

4 Kishtainy, "Violent and Nonviolent Struggle," p. 14.

5 Abd al-Hafiz Abd Rabbuh, *Falssfat al Jihad* (Beirut, 1984), p. 28, cited in Kishtainy "Violent and Nonviolent Struggle," p. 14

6 Ibid., p. 18

7 These democratically elected governments proved highly unstable and were overthrown in June 1989 by hardline Islamic military officers.

8 Joan Bondurant, *Conquest of Violence*, (Berkeley: University of California Press, rev. ed., 1965), pp. 131–44. See also Pyaralel, *A Pilgrimage of Peace: Gandhi and the Frontier Gandhi Among N.W.F. Pathans*, (Ahmedabad, India: Navajivan, 1950).

9 For a detailed description and analysis of the internal workings of the Polisario refugee camps, see my article "Participatory Democracy in the Sahara: A Study of Polisario Self-Governance." In *Scandinavian Journal for Development Alternatives* vol. VII; nos. 2–3, June–September 1988, pp. 141–56. In hindsight, parts of my analysis dealing with the actual level of political democracy at that time appears to have been premature in light of subsequent events.

10 Lynne Shivers, "Inside the Iranian Revolution." In David Albert, *Tell the American People: Perspectives on the Iranian Revolution*, (Philadelphia: New Society Publishers, 1980), p. 66.
11 Ibid.
12 Ibid.
13 Scott Kennedy, "The Druze of the Golan: A Case of Non-violent Resistance, *Journal of Palestine Studies* vol. XIII, no. 2 (Winter 1984), p. 49.
14 Ibid.
15 For more information, contact the Palestinian Center for the Study of Non-violence, P.O. Box 19543, Jerusalem, via Israel.
16 See Souad Dajani, *Eyes Without Country: Searching for a Palestinian Strategy of Liberation*, (Philadelphia: Temple University Press, 1995). See also Johan Galtung's *Nonviolence and Israel/Palestine*, (Honolulu: University of Hawaii Press, 1989) and Philip Grant's "Nonviolent Political Struggle in the Occupied Territories" in Crow, et. al., *Arab Nonviolent Political Struggle*.
17 Cited in Donna Ainsworth, "Resistance in the West Bank and Gaza", *The Newsletter for Interfaith Council for Peace and Justice*, Feb. 1989, p. 1.
18 Andrew Rigby, *Living the Intifada*, (London: Zed Books, 1991), pp. 195–6.

4

Nonviolent Resistance in the Occupied Territories: A Critical Reevaluation

Souad Dajani

The peace talks between Israel and the Arab states, including Palestinian representatives, that opened in Madrid in October 1991 signaled a new phase in the ongoing attempts to achieve a peaceful resolution to the conflict in the Middle East. That these direct negotiations could take place at that time attests to the strategic reevaluation that was conducted by all parties – particularly by the Palestinians – in the aftermath of the Gulf War. The defeat of Iraq at the hands of US-led forces led the Palestinians to conclude that the US held the key to peace in the region. Palestinians would have to trust their fate to the Americans, and sit at the table with Israel to negotiate an end to its occupation of Palestinian lands. Behind this apparent change in strategy lay the *intifada*, the Palestinian uprising that was launched in December 1987 in the Occupied West Bank and Gaza Strip.

Despite the waxing and waning of this uprising over the years, and despite successive changes in its form and emphasis, the momentum created by the *intifada* had a direct impact on subsequent developments, including the peace process. It was as a result of the *intifada* that Israel's continued occupation of the West Bank and Gaza Strip captured the attention of the international community and brought pressure to bear on Israel to address this issue.

This chapter examines the origins, methods, and impact of the *intifada*. It assesses its effect, as a largely nonviolent civilian struggle, in contributing to efforts to achieve a just and peaceful settlement of the Palestinian–Israeli conflict, based on the rights of both peoples to national independence and statehood.

Background

The Palestinian *intifada* first broke out in the Gaza Strip on December 9, 1987, before spreading to encompass virtually the whole of the Occupied

West Bank and Gaza Strip. Unlike earlier forms of resistance in these areas, the Palestinian *intifada* was distinguished by its universality across the Occupied Territories and by its largely nonviolent character. Its launching at that time, and the particular forms it took over the intervening years, can properly be located within the context of the preceding 21 years of Israeli occupation.

Israel captured the West Bank and Gaza Strip during the 1967 June War. These were the last remaining areas of the original Mandate Palestine that fell under Jordanian and Egyptian control respectively following the establishment of the State of Israel in 1948.

From the outset, Israel instituted policies that were aimed at seizing control of the lands and resources of these areas and integrating them economically into Israel. At the same time, Israeli policy was directed at preventing the emergence of any independent development initiatives on the part of the indigenous Palestinian population. The two processes of integration and dependence took various forms and were backed by a series of military orders, laws, and regulations that facilitated their realization.[1] A military administration was immediately imposed on these areas and remained in force until 1981, when it was nominally replaced by a civilian administration. Even then, however, the military administration, directly accountable to the Israeli minister of defense, retained ultimate responsibility for these areas. Of far-reaching impact was the drive to acquire lands in the Occupied Territories. Immediately following the 1967 War, tens of thousands of Palestinian were driven from their homeland, and thousands of Palestinian homes were destroyed, including several villages that were completely destroyed.[2] The Israeli authorities issued a whole series of laws and military orders (some modeled on those that were in effect in Israel proper) that enabled them to expropriate large tracts of Arab lands and evict the original Palestinian inhabitants, in order to make way for the establishment of Jewish settlements.[3]

Thousands of newly dispossessed Palestinians – who, as a consequence of these land expropriations lost their traditional means of livelihood – were increasingly forced into cheap wage-labor in the Israeli-dominated economy. This was particularly true in the Gaza Strip, which, as a result of a set of unique historical and structural circumstances, was severely affected by the Israeli occupation.[4] For both regions, however, the process of forced proletarianization, the exploitative and humiliating conditions suffered by Arab workers in Israel, as well as the situation of continued dependence on Israel, had a profound effect on Palestinian society, and later, on Palestinian resistance to occupation.

Economic integration of the Occupied Territories into Israel proceeded in other ways. These included marginalization and disintegration of indigenous Palestinian structures, and a virtually complete suppression of all Palestinian efforts to develop their own society and express their national identity. For example, Israel assumed control over decision-making and planning even within Palestinian municipal boundaries and on lands remaining in Palestinian hands. Israel issued laws to regulate virtually every area of life, including such activities as water consumption, the digging of wells, the planting of fruit trees and crops, and the construction of roads and houses.

Israel also intervened at various times to suppress the functions of official Palestinian municipalities. In 1982, for example, most of the Palestinian municipalities were dissolved and Palestinian mayors were replaced by Israeli officials. All aspects of administration, including budgets, spending, development, provision of services, and others, fell under Israeli control. It was not until 1985 that Arab mayors were once again appointed to municipal posts; however, the Israeli military administration kept full authority over the legislative and administrative processes in these areas. In effect, the Israeli authorities barred any development projects that would strengthen indigenous Palestinian structures and enable the Palestinian community to become self-sufficient.[5]

The Israeli authorities issued legislation and measures in other areas that were designed to control and suppress all expressions of national identity. For example, Israel passed a number of laws that defined "security violations" in the Occupied Territories. These ranged from making a "V" sign, to raising the Palestinian flag or exhibiting the colors of the flag, possessing certain literature, holding demonstrations and other activities.[6] Sanctions against individuals were supplemented by punishment of whole communities. This occurred even in cases where only one individual was guilty of a particular violation, and/or where this individual had neither been charged nor tried. This is known as collective punishment, which is prohibited under international law, but which Israel continued to practice quite liberally throughout the years of occupation and particularly in the years since the *intifada*. Related measures of collective punishment include blowing up houses, imposing curfews, declaring closed areas, uprooting trees, and, conducting mass arrests. Well over 1,400 military orders were issued in the Occupied Territories that controlled virtually every aspect of Palestinian existence in these areas. It is for this reason that observers have referred to this occupation as the "iron fist," rather than the "benign occupation," as the Israel authorities have been wont to characterize their rule.

It is not really necessary, therefore, to go far beyond the Occupied Territories themselves to locate the origins of the *intifada*. Palestinians have always resented this occupation and have been intent on ending it. In fact, Palestinian opposition and resistance to Israel's rule began very early in the occupation. As one study notes, each year since 1983 an average of 3,000 "incidents" were reported in these areas. Over the first 20 years of occupation, some 20,000 Palestinians had been detained on "security charges."[7] The difference between earlier resistance and the *intifada* lies mainly in the pervasiveness of the latter throughout the whole of the Occupied Areas, and the degree of organization, determination, solidarity, and unity that characterized the uprising, especially during its first two years.

Given these trends, Palestinians generally blamed Israel for its intransigence and its unwillingness to reach a political settlement to the conflict. Frustration with an on-again, off-again political process had been accumulating for years. As the daily hardships of life under occupation multiplied, and the world seemed to them increasingly ignorant or indifferent to their plight, Palestinians reached a point where they were to say, "enough is enough," and take matters into their own hands to change the situation. This development also coincided with a shift in the Palestine Liberation Organization's (PLO) strategy, to refocus attention on resistance from within the Occupied Territories, a policy that began in earnest after the PLO's evacuation from Lebanon in 1982. Between then and the outbreak of the *intifada* in 1987, Palestinians under occupation were gearing up and preparing for their new role within a broad-based mass movement.

The foundations and impetus for this movement had already been laid back in the 1970s, when Palestinians began to embark on a course of mobilization and participation within the framework of a variety of grassroots organizations. Popular committees were established in many sectors in response to the restrictions placed against the functioning of official institutions. In areas such as health care, agricultural relief, voluntary work, and women's issues, these grassroots committees quickly attracted the support of the local communities in which they were located, and helped to mobilize the population politically around issues of daily concern. These grassroots committees later became the basis for the proliferation of the local popular committees that first emerged to administer the *intifada*.

One essential condition for the emergence of a mass movement in the Occupied Territories rested on the tacit support given it by the PLO outside. Although the PLO may have been caught off-guard by the precise timing of the *intifada*, there is little doubt that this organization had long been preparing for precisely such a civilian struggle by the people under occupation themselves.[8] While the PLO continued to embody the whole Palestinian national struggle, and as such remained responsible for charting the overall strategy, the population inside the Occupied Territories was granted responsibility for formulating and implementing the tactical steps of the *intifada*.

The *Intifada* as Palestinian Civilian Resistance Against the Occupation

As the first two years of the *intifada* closed with the struggle against the Israeli occupation still in full force, it came even closer to fulfilling the literal meaning contained in the term, "to shake up" or "to shake off." In reality, the *intifada* shook up both Palestinian society itself under occupation and the

Israeli occupying regime against which it was launched. The sustained use of direct action and generally nonviolent resistance had two main thrusts: To render the Occupied Palestinian Territories nongovernable by Israel and thus to unlink these areas from their dependence on Israel; and, to establish indigenous social structures that would serve as the foundations of the future Palestinian state. In the event, the *intifada* had both a positive and negative impact on both the Palestinian community and on Israel. The following paragraphs outline some of these processes.[9]

1   The impact of the Intifada on Palestinian society

Although the *intifada* was ostensibly a struggle of an oppressed people to throw off its oppressors, the dynamics engendered by this experience of resistance caused a momentum that challenged social relationships and behaviors within Palestinian society itself. The very act of resistance transformed the resistors. As Palestinians tested the limits of the power they could pit against their opponent, they were alternately empowered and frustrated. This, in turn, created a situation that was never static, and Palestinians found themselves constantly in the process of redefining their priorities, objectives, and the techniques of their struggle. This process proved to be both a source of strength as well as weakness for the Palestinians. On the one hand, they could continuously innovate and use methods that would keep their opponent, Israel, off balance and confused. But sacrificing strategy to tactics proved costly: Palestinians eventually found themselves simply responding to Israeli measures as they occurred, or expending energy trying to maintain cohesion and unity within their own communities. Frustrations and setbacks were interpreted as failures; and while moments of empowerment brought euphoria, they also brought deep demoralization and resentment with the lack of political progress. Inevitably, strains and conflicts were turned inside the Palestinian community and took the form of factional infighting, increased violence, and, crucially, the backlash against women.

It is important to pause for a moment to examine the role of women during the *intifada*. Much has been written about their activism and participation, and the challenge they posed to traditional patriarchal values and prevailing notions concerning appropriate roles for women.[10] Palestinian women had always been active in the national struggle, and their participation during the *intifada* was, in some ways, an extension of their increased politicization over the years. Women especially benefited from the widespread mobilization that took place within the grassroots committees from the mid-1970s, and used the skills they gained to contribute at various levels during the uprising. What was different during the *intifada*, was the extent of their participation, and the degree to which women assumed responsible public roles in their communities. At the same time, Palestinian women began questioning their role in the national struggle, and for perhaps the first time since the occupation, they began to articulate publicly the need for a separate women's agenda beyond the goals of the overall national movement. Openly describing themselves as "feminists," women activists pointed to the necessity of theorizing about the character of a future Palestinian state, and to take the necessary measures to ensure that a "civil code" would be in place to guarantee democracy and equality for all.[11] Women's increased activism during the *intifada* earned them the wrath of some of the extremist religious groups, who tended to blame Palestinian defeats on the departure from tradition and religion.

Hamas (the Islamic Resistance Movement) is perhaps the best known of these groups. It flourished mainly in the Gaza Strip, where conditions of life under occupation and during the *intifada* were particularly harsh, making its message there especially appealing. Hamas gained many supporters, especially after the Gulf War, because it was able to meet the needs of many of the residents for support, food, medical care, and the like. Its message was compelling in view of the perceived failure of the secular PLO to achieve any political gains. Hamas appealed to the familiar and to tradition, and this resonated among the weary, demoralized, and disillusioned Palestinian population. Inevitably, Hamas came to pose a danger within Palestinian society itself, in its attempts to democratize, liberalize, and concentrate its energies on the construction of the institutions and agencies of the forthcoming Palestinian state.

The roots of the organization of the *intifada*, therefore, can be traced directly to the creation and expansion of the grassroots committees since the mid-1970s. Palestinian participants in these committees were quickly able to adopt their roles and functions in view of the emerging needs of the uprising. It was these derivatives of the grassroots committees at the local level that were active in implementing the instructions issued by the Unified Leadership of the Uprising, the body that was formed early in the uprising to chart the tactics of the *intifada*.[12]

Over time, overt demonstrations and stone-throwing confrontations gradually receded in the Occupied Territories. This did not, however, signal an end to the uprising, and restructuring within the Palestinian community proceeded behind the scenes. Local and popular committees proliferated into ever-widening spheres. They attracted the participation of large numbers of Palestinians, and branched out into specific functions. The role of these committees became especially pronounced with the cut-off of aid and funding to regular institutions due to the Gulf crisis. Examples abound of women activists who defied curfew orders and risked their lives to enter into closed areas. Members of medical relief committees likewise violated curfews to enter into camps and other areas where residents were in desperate need of medical care, especially after long sieges or after particularly brutal confrontations with Israeli soldiers or settlers. In many cases, the medical treatment provided by these committees would be the only type of care received by youth who were beaten or injured by Israeli soldiers.

During the first two years of the *intifada*, such local committees were characterized by an impressive degree of organization and solidarity. With their support, and with the services they managed to provide, Palestinians were able to continue to participate in the uprising. Given their predominantly underground and unofficial character, activists in these committees remained a rather elusive target for the Israeli authorities – in spite of Israeli action to declare these organizations illegal. With time, however, stringent Israeli measures, such as widespread tax raids, curfews, closing off of whole communities, and other measures that were designed to put obstacles in the way of collective action, caused Palestinian participation at the community level to wane. This situation was exacerbated by the serious problem of collaborators; individuals who were paid and even armed by Israel, whose task was to infiltrate the Palestinian community and identify nationalist activists. These activists in turn, frequently became the victims of Israeli death squads.[13]

By the second year of the *intifada*, the popular committees were no longer able to sustain their earlier appeal. The population under occupation was growing increasingly tired of the burden of strikes and "civil disobedience" – as the Palestinians of the Occupied Territories described their campaign.[14] Meantime, whole areas and sectors began to defy calls for strikes and demonstrations, and competing groups began to vie for control of the streets. Yet even with these setbacks, this organizational restructuring of the Palestinian community during the *intifada* had a significant impact both on the Palestinians themselves and on Israel. For once, Palestinians indicated *en masse* that they were unwilling to cooperate with the Israeli occupation regime, and that they were determined to "disobey" Israeli rule and establish their own institutions.[15]

It was these acts of defiance that caused Israel to react with particular severity against the Palestinian popular committees: between March and August 1988, the bulk of these committees had been outlawed and many of their members detained or imprisoned. In further action against these and *intifada* – related activities in general, Israel escalated its use of "collective punishment," a practice which, ironically, may have in some cases coalesced Palestinian resistance against the occupation regime. As the *intifada* wore on, Israel instituted methods of selective punishment that took the form of massive tax raids against specific individuals or communities, the imposition of curfews, travel bans, and other measures that were designed to isolate Palestinian communities from each other and break the collective will of that particular community to resist, thus to forestall any further mobilization and action against the occupation.

It is worth underscoring the largely nonviolent character of this *intifada*. Stone-throwing demonstrations and individual armed attacks against selective Israeli targets notwithstanding, the *intifada* was consciously and deliberately envisioned as an organized and universal unarmed civilian struggle against the Israeli occupation. As to whether or not nonviolent means of resistance could put enough pressure on Israel to withdraw from the Occupied Territories, this question should be considered in light of the impact of the *intifada* on Israeli society and politics in general, and on the international community at large.[16] Clearly, scenes that became quite famous during the *intifada*, of stone- throwing Palestinian youth pitted against armed and often brutal Israeli soldiers, helped to change the image of Palestinians from "terrorists" to a people with a legitimate national cause.

Inside the Palestinian community, reliance on largely nonviolent methods of struggle gave Palestinians a sense of their own power, and of the dynamics of this type of action. They learned that through such action they could manipulate Israeli power to backfire against itself. Palestinians engaged in various methods of nonviolent action; ranging from protests and demonstrations, to actions that established their non-cooperation with the Israeli regime, to those that were clearly designed to help establish indigenous alternatives to the occupation and that would serve as an infrastructural basis of the future Palestinian state.[17]

The *intifada* proved to be a double-edged sword. Strengthening and transforming the Palestinian community in the service of the national cause was to some extent outweighed by the degree of violence and repression to which Palestinians were subjected. As the *intifada* wore on, this population became increasingly weary and demoralized, and anxiously awaited some measure of hope from abroad. The situation generally persisted between the outbreak of the Gulf War and the beginning of the Arab/Israeli peace talks in October 1991.

2   The impact of the Intifada on Israel

Israel was clearly stunned and confused by the *intifada*. Here was a case of organized and sustained civilian action in the Occupied Territories that was unprecedented in the history of the occupation. Israel was immediately put on the defensive, confused about how to respond as it strained to contain the *intifada* at least cost to itself. Initially, Palestinian nonviolent action allowed them to retain the initiative in their own hands, and, in a classical case of jujitsu, to force the excessive Israeli power to backfire against itself. Israel then decided to respond with military might, regardless of the damage to its image in the rest of the world.

In their book on the *intifada*, Ze'ev Schiff and Ehud Ya'ari raise the important point that the uprising overturned prevailing notions of security in Israel.[18] Many Israeli Jews had tended to regard the Occupied Territories as indispensable to their security. These areas provided strategic depth and a geographical buffer between themselves and the Arab world. Yet the *intifada* erupted right in their own backyard, on land that was ostensibly under their control, and by a population that had become largely invisible to them over the years. Israelis were shocked into rethinking their assumptions about the security of their state. Some came to realize that occupying another people would neither guarantee peace nor security. Others came to the opposite conclusion, and were convinced that Israel should never relinquish these lands, and must do everything in its power to prevent the emergence of a Palestinian state.

Another set of concerns emerged with the Gulf War, where once again, the presumed links between land and security became painfully clear. Iraq's launching of Scud missiles into Israel reinforced the view of some that territorial depth was imperative. Others countered that the nature of modern warfare rendered territorial issues irrelevant. Although the lines were not clearly drawn between the left and the right in Israel, or between the army and the public over this issue, most Israelis apparently missed the point that the Palestinians had been trying to underscore all along: namely that a state of war remains possible because of the absence of a just peace, and that Israel may do better to eliminate the political reasons for war – at the heart of which lies the Palestinian issue.

In the final analysis, the success of the *intifada* should be evaluated in terms of its impact on Israel. Although this uprising did not cause it to withdraw from the Occupied Areas, the *intifada* did incur some direct (as well as indirect) costs to Israel that warrant serious attention. The *intifada* also contributed to some changes in the structures of relations between Israel and the Palestinians.

The impact of the *intifada* on Israel could be examined at three levels: the Israeli army, the Israeli public, and the Israeli government. Although each of these sectors was affected in a different way by the uprising, it is clear that the *intifada* did have a discernible impact on Israel.

3 The impact of the intifada on the Israeli army

Costs of the *intifada* to the Israeli military were both moral and economic. Early in the uprising Israeli officials voiced their concerns about these issues and tried to adopt measures to address them. Essentially, the problem boiled down to the dilemma of pitting a well-equipped and trained army against a largely nonviolent civilian population. Questions of morale, concerns about excessive violence corrupting the occupier, fears of dissent or disobedience, concerns over the decline in standards of training and preparedness, all commanded Israeli attention. In fact, many in the army did question their role in the Occupied Territories, and some expressed overt resentment at being placed in an untenable position being called upon to suppress by military might a population whose concerns should be properly addressed through political means.[19] While violence against Palestinians continued to escalate, some in the army began to feel more uncomfortable with their role, sometimes to the point of refusing to serve in the Occupied Territories altogether.[20]

Such developments were encouraging, and indicated the impact of the *intifada* on the Israeli forces. But they did not result in any serious dissent within the army nor did they precipitate a political crisis within Israel itself over the appropriate role of the army in this situation. Periodic reevaluation by Israeli officials of their military tactics in the Occupied Territories simply reinforced the social distance between the occupier and occupied, and made it difficult for Israeli soldiers to come to empathize with the local population and their cause.[21] Palestinians have themselves contributed to widening the social distance by using more violent methods in their attacks against Israelis. Ultimately, the indiscriminate and deliberate force used against Palestinians by Israeli soldiers and police created a situation of mutual hatred and distrust. This was exacerbated for Palestinians by such Israeli measures as its use of assassination units – Israelis dressed as women or Arabs who penetrated Palestinian communities and frequently killed in cold blood those they defined as "wanted" Palestinians – and their (Palestinian) perception that the commanders in the field, as well as the system of justice in Israel, condoned these practices.

4   The Impact of the intifada on the Israeli Government and Public

The Israeli government and public constitute a second level at which the impact of the *intifada* may be analyzed. Though these do comprise distinct spheres, they are addressed together here.

Since Palestinian encounters with Israeli civilians inside Israel were relatively infrequent and indirect, the dynamics of the *intifada* and the processes by which Palestinian direct action could effect change at this level operated differently than they did at the level of the army or the other branches of the occupation regime.

Palestinian tactics during the *intifada* vis-à-vis the Israeli public concentrated on trying to affect public perceptions of the Palestinians. Palestinians anticipated that after learning more about their struggle and being reassured of their willingness to coexist peacefully in two states, the Israeli public would in turn exert pressure on its government to withdraw from the Occupied Territories. Palestinian tactics at this level were, therefore, directed at polarizing Israel from within and widening any existing splits in its government and society over the issue of occupation. Although Palestinians were aware that they did possess certain leverage to manipulate the struggle in their favor, they did not articulate any specific strategy to organize activities at this level, and tended to rely on the indirect pressure generated by the *intifada*.

The Israeli peace movement was one sector that was significantly affected by Palestinian resistance, and was jolted out of the lethargy that had characterized it since the 1982 invasion of Lebanon. Joint Israeli–Palestinian efforts increased during the early period of the *intifada* and were evident among key sectors of the population: medical personnel, journalists, writers, prisoner support groups, women, and others. Some joint efforts had been in existence for years; as for example, the Committee to Confront the Iron Fist, which was an umbrella group for a variety of other groups. Since its formation in the early 1980s, this committee continued to protest the harshness of Israeli rule in the Occupied Territories.[22] Other committees were organized around more specific concerns: for example, the Committee for Solidarity with Birzeit University, and the Family Reunification Committee. The significance of these and other joint efforts was that they brought into focus Israel's claim to respect the rule of law and its adherence to democratic principles. For some Israelis, the defense of Palestinians became linked, directly or indirectly, to the struggle for democracy in Israel itself. For example, the West Jerusalem based Alternative Information Center, run by Michael Warchawski, was raided by the Israeli authorities in February 1987, and later closed down; its publications, documents, and equipment all confiscated and the director himself detained. Through its newsletter and publications, this center had been active in documenting and publishing information about Israel's repressive policy in the Occupied Territories.[23]

Over 50 Israeli peace groups were created or reemerged during the *intifada*; many mobilized around the goal of ending the occupation. These groups have been active in working on different fronts within Israeli society, such as in organizing marches and demonstrations, counseling and advising soldiers who refuse to serve in the Occupied Territories, providing support networks for Palestinian activists, and others.[24] For example, a coalition of about 20 peace groups organized a march and rally on June 4, 1988 in Tel Aviv that drew an estimated 10,000 people.[25] One of the more militant and active groups formed during the *intifada* was The 21st Year, which as of June 1988 had over 1,500 members.[26] In its "Covenant for the Struggle Against the Occupation," this group articulated its main objective as achieving Israel's withdrawal from the Occupied Territories.[27] What is interesting to note about The 21st Year is that it advocated direct action to secure its goals: Some of the proposed actions bordered on civil disobedience, as illustrated by its affirmation "not to obey any military order or command ordering us to take part in acts of repression or in policing the Occupied Territories." Both The 21st Year and Yesh Gvul ("There is a Limit") are noteworthy among this new genre of peace activism in Israel, in that their political action campaigns focused on the army. Unlike Palestinian action in this regard, members of these groups were in a position to work directly within the army. Palestinians could contribute to these efforts by wielding their struggle effectively in a manner that would enhance the impact of such groups. In this respect – as far as resistance in the Occupied Territories was perceived as a struggle of a civilian population against an occupying army – so would the prospects of success of these groups be enhanced. Violent acts by Palestinians, however, would beget the opposite effect, as Israelis, including army personnel, coalesced in fear and hatred, and, hence, in opposition to political concessions.

The *intifada* had a significant impact on Israel even within the ranks of staunchly Zionist groups, where disaffection with the occupation increased. One group, "End the Occupation," was also established during the uprising and included among its ranks some dedicated Zionist supporters. Its members were concerned that Israel was being harmed by its continued occupation of the West Bank and Gaza Strip. As such, they concluded that it would be in Israel's long-term interests to give up these territories. Some of their concerns stemmed from the perceived "demographic threat": the fear of a large Arab minority existing in their midst. Other concerns related to their interest in reaching a solution that would guarantee their security within a "Jewish State."

On the whole, the *intifada* did initially succeed in drawing the lines between different poles in Israeli society, although this did not ultimately result in any significant policy changes, nor in the victory of the position of the progressive groups. On the contrary, the effect of the *intifada* on Israel dissipated over the years, as Israelis became convinced that the "costs" were within acceptable limits and that they could live with this uprising. The Gulf War only strengthened this perception and reinforced the position of the right in Israel, making Israelis in general less willing to compromise or arrive at a solution that would address the national rights of Palestinians. These positions continued up to the time of the peace talks that began in Madrid in October 1991.[28] Even the "moderate" government of Yitzhak Rabin, elected to power in June 1992, did not envision a solution that would go far beyond granting limited "autonomy" to the population under occupation. The outlines of a long-term solution in this scenario remained unclear, though ostensibly these would lead to Israeli withdrawal from some unspecified areas of land.

The End of the *Intifada*

Since its inception, the *intifada* was based on the principle of the non-use of lethal weapons, and on a full escalation of the "campaign of civil disobedience". However, adherence to nonviolent methods was never totally uniform nor disciplined. While practicing a variety of nonviolent methods, Palestinians under occupation did not appear to recognize the feasibility of nonviolent civilian resistance as a strategy in itself.[29] Nor were they familiar with the dynamics of this type of struggle or the mechanisms by which it operates.

A fundamental consideration in preparing for nonviolent resistance is to adopt tactics and methods both in view of the ability and willingness of the Palestinians to carry them out, and in view of their expected impact on Israel. These factors underscore a basic strategic question that was left unaddressed during the "civil disobedience" campaign: that is, on whose terms the struggle would be fought. While in the early days of the *intifada*, Israel was clearly confounded by the intensity, pervasiveness, and discipline of popular Palestinian nonviolent resistance. Later stages witnessed Israel taking the initiative in anticipating Palestinian moves and striking at their nascent structures.

Lacking a coherent strategy to organize the *intifada*, and allowing the struggle to escalate or degenerate into indiscriminate use of violent means, posed the danger of Palestinian resistance spinning out of control, and eventually backfiring against the Palestinians' own community. This is indeed what happened, which also explains some of the backlash that this uprising caused within Palestinian society. One such consequence relates to how the *intifada* began to divide the Palestinian community from within and pit factions and sectors of the population against each other. These developments threatened to destroy all the gains that Palestinians had made over the earlier months, both the social gains pertaining to their own unity and purpose, as well as the political gains, in so far as increasing debate and dissent in Israel over the issue of continued occupation.

In the event, some Palestinians would come to see the *intifada* and its reliance on largely nonviolent methods as merely a phase, one tried and failed, and, therefore, one that would need to be supplanted by more "effective" violent means. Others interpreted this type of action (without necessarily using its terminology) as a kind of supportive activity that took place behind the scenes, falling somewhere between "diplomatic and political efforts" and "armed struggle."[30]

Five years after the launching of the *intifada*, Palestinians under occupation were under no illusion that independence would come any day now. They realized that a combination of their efforts, along with the external influence of the PLO and the intervention of the international community, would ultimately be needed to bring about a just settlement.

The opening of the Madrid Conference in 1991, and the ensuing meetings between Israeli and Palestinian negotiators throughout most of 1992 and 1993, focused on political and diplomatic initiatives to address the conflict. For a while, *intifada*-related activities persisted behind the scenes, both in the form of daily confrontations with Israeli forces, as well as in efforts to create alternative Palestinian structures and organizations. Meantime, the Palestinian population under occupation was becoming increasingly weary, frustrated, and divided over the appropriate courses of action. Violent attacks against Israeli soldiers and civilians escalated during this period, as did the severity of Israeli sanctions and reprisals.

The task for Palestinians remained: To formulate a strategy that would at once unify and protect their own society and, more importantly, dislodge the Israeli occupation. That was the challenge that lay ahead.

Post-*Intifada* Developments

Though overtaken by events in the region, the *intifada* remains a powerful example of the largely nonviolent civilian resistance of an oppressed people in their struggle for liberation. However, the signing of various accords between Israel and the Palestinians, beginning with the Declaration of Principles (DOP) on September 13, 1993, introduced unforeseen qualitative changes to policy-making and conflict resolution in the Israeli–Palestinian conflict.

Since the DOP, four additional accords have been signed by Israel and the Palestinians. These include: the Cairo Agreements of May 4, 1994, that installed interim self-rule in the Gaza Strip and Jericho; the "early empowerment" agreements, of August 29, 1994; the Israeli–Palestinian Interim Agreement on the West Bank and Gaza Strip, of September 28, 1995, the Protocol Concerning the Redeployment in Hebron, of January 15, 1997, and the Wye River Memorandum of October 23, 1998.

Yet by 1999, and as the five-year interim phase specified in these accords was nearing its end, peace seemed increasingly remote. Israel was stalling in its implementation of provisions of the accords that called for the transfer of additional areas of the West Bank and Gaza Strip to the Palestine Authority, and was instead accelerating the pace of settlement expansion, and intensifying its economic and social strangulation of Palestinian areas. Palestinians, in turn, interpreted Israeli moves as creating "facts" on the ground in advance of negotiations over final status issues.[31] Their anxieties were also heightened by a mounting perception that Yasser Arafat had signed a deal that left the occupation intact while transferring to the Palestine Authority and its police the role previously performed by Israeli forces. In Israel, a spate of Palestinian suicide bombings – with the main casualties being Israeli civilians – caused Israeli public opinion to turn against the "peace process." This shift was used by Prime Minister Benjamin Netanyahu as a reason for halting further "concessions."

By 1999, even the most optimistic observers concluded that Palestinians needed to reexamine their calculations, and reevaluate the provisions of these accords in light of their overall struggle for national independence. Some of the central considerations emerging from these accords include the following:

1 The inside becoming outside and the outside becoming inside

By virtue of the DOP and later accords, the roles of the Israeli occupation regime and the PLO/PA (Palestine Authority) were reversed. Israeli forces "redeployed" from the most populous Palestinian areas in the West Bank and Gaza Strip (Area A), transferring administrative control over the population to the PA. The PA, in turn, carried out its mandate with escalating corruption, violence, and repression, and was consequently viewed by Palestinians as an unprincipled and ineffectual stooge of Israel. Arafat himself, as head of the PA, was also seen as having succumbed to Israel's dictates.[32] In Palestinian eyes, self-rule became nothing more than a euphemistic term designed to mask the substitution of direct Israeli control by an indigenous Palestinian authority, in whose hands would fall the responsibility for maintaining internal "law and order" on Israel's behalf.[33]

Palestinians did not submit passively. For example, in early January 1995, the noted Gaza physician Haidar Abd al-Shafi proposed the establishment of a new Movement for Democracy.[34] By focusing on the mobilization and unification of Palestinians and the revitalization of their grassroots institutions – reminiscent of mobilization during the *intifada* – his initiative was designed to raise Palestinian consciousness about democracy and the need to struggle against proposals and actions (be they Israeli or Palestinian) which stood in the way of the achievement of Palestinian independence. Other Palestinians continued working at the grassroots level in their various spheres of influence – and if they did not succeed in achieving tangible gains, they attempted at least to prevent the further erosion of Palestinian civil liberties and independence of action – for example, in indigenous health initiatives, in the burgeoning Palestinian media, and among human rights groups.

2   Economic and political constraints

The accords signed by Israel and the PLO/PA appeared to serve dominant Israeli political and economic interests by essentially sidestepping the political issue of Israeli occupation in favor of self-rule for the Palestinians, within the context of continued Israeli control of territory and resources.

As specified in the DOP and subsequent agreements, the PA was delegated civil authorities and capacities for limited economic improvement, but was denied the political authority necessary for independent economic development. Vital sectors such as land and water, both essential for economic development, remained under Israeli control throughout the interim stages.

As an illustration, Area A, which comprised the eight heavily populated Palestinian areas transferred to Palestinian self-rule, totaled only 9 percent of the area of the Occupied Territories. This contrasted with Area B (about 19 percent) in which the PA enjoyed very limited jurisdictional authority within the scattered Palestinian towns and villages, and the remaining Area C (about 71 percent), that included major Jewish settlements, over which Israel retained exclusive control. Israel remained responsible for overall security, land, water, borders, and Jewish settlements, throughout the whole of the West Bank and Gaza Strip, including the "Greater Jerusalem" area.

Independent economic initiatives were strictly regulated by the provisions of these accords, by the military orders that remained in force, and by the day to day actions of Israeli officials. For example, the prolonged closure of Palestinian areas first put in place in March 1993, was expanded not only to prevent Palestinians from traveling into East Jerusalem and Israel, or between the Gaza Strip and the West Bank, but to prevent Palestinians from traveling outside their immediate villages or towns, even to contiguous Palestinian areas. This ban caused a virtual economic collapse in some communities, as not only were people prevented from reaching their places of work, education, and worship, but the import and export of goods and raw materials to and from these areas were also banned.[35]

The economic repercussions of the agreements were experienced very differently within the Palestinian community. Particularly hard hit were the poor and the refugees (a majority in the Gaza Strip). Closures, curfews, and the denial of work permits often resulted in an unemployment rate of 65 percent or more in the Gaza Strip, and have left hundreds of thousands of Palestinians destitute.[36]

The terms of the Accords placed Palestinians in an untenable position. While outward forms of democracy, such as elections, were allowed as legitimate avenues for expressing democratic choices, acts that demonstrated active resistance were outlawed. In effect, the PA appeared to be reproducing Israeli definitions of legal action, in which the mechanisms and external manifestations of "democracy" would be permitted, while those acts that challenged the economic underpinnings and the political power of the newly formed Palestinian authority were forbidden. Moreover, the PA was expected to carry out with the strictest determination and efficacy, Israel's commands that it crack down on "terrorists" (that is, virtually all Islamist and other dissident groups).

For many Palestinians, the economic (class) costs and the political (civil and national) costs of the Accords became increasingly transparent. Not only did their dreams of an independent state fail to materialize, but the emerging entity, still dependent on Israel, was being ruled by a group of people that was quickly enriching itself and benefiting from this rule. Some Palestinians did attempt to challenge the oppressive conditions under which they lived. A number of nonviolent campaigns were launched against the PA itself, comparable to those used earlier against the Israeli occupation. For example, Palestinians went on strikes and demonstrations to press for the complete release of political prisoners. They engaged in protests against the repression by Palestinian officials and police. Some Palestinians even predicted that a mini-*intifada* would erupt against the PA itself if it continued to behave as an ineffectual, brutal, and repressive instrument of larger Israeli control.

3   Leaving the Israeli occupation intact

From all indications, the signing of the various accords enabled Israel to reach a less costly "accommodation" with the Palestinians than had previously been foreseen, especially during the heyday of the *intifada*. With an Israeli occupation regime left intact and administered in part by a Palestinian authority, Israel, especially in its dominant classes, could reap the benefits of these accords without incurring the costs of an unwanted domination over another people. This position seemed reinforced by the international community, led by the US, that essentially regarded the "peace process" as an opportunity for the two protagonists to "negotiate" between themselves – in total (or deliberate) disregard of the striking asymmetry in power between occupier and occupied.

Despite many proposals emanating from Israel during the interim period, all concurred on one essential point: There would be no complete withdrawal from the West Bank and no dismantling of major existing settlements.[37] There was ample evidence of Israeli plans to retain control of most of the occupied areas. One was the drive to continue with settlement-building, including in East Jerusalem, along with the attendant roads and infrastructure. This settlement drive went on unabated despite clear references in the DOP that settlements were part of final status issues that would need to be negotiated between the two parties.[38]

Taken together the permanent closure of Jerusalem and the effective division of the West Bank into three disjointed areas administered by the PA; the bantustanization of populated Palestinian centers; the creation of bypass roads for settlers only crisscrossing the occupied areas; the concentrated rings of settlements around Jerusalem as a harbinger of formal annexation; the ever salient presence of the Israeli army even within the self-rule areas; and the inability or refusal by the international community (led by the US) to put pressure on Israel to fulfill the terms of the accords it signed, all signaled to Palestinians that they were to be permanently barred from establishing a sovereign and independent Palestinian state.

Summary

One aim of this essay is to evaluate the effectiveness of Palestinian civilian mobilization and resistance during the *intifada*. Though that struggle did not win Palestinians the independence they sought, and indeed, appears to have backfired in recent years, the struggle is not over. More than ever, Palestinians need to protect not only the legitimacy of their national claims, but their very presence on the lands of their birth. They will have to resist authoritarian control in any form – be it that of the Palestine Authority or the Israeli occupiers. Nonviolent civilian resistance and civil and democratic liberties appear inextricably linked in such a struggle; one that will need to be waged until the Israeli occupation is totally withdrawn and a fully independent Palestinian state is founded on principles of equality and justice.[39]

Notes

1 See for example, Sheila Ryan, "Israeli Economic Policy in the Occupied Territories," *MERIP Reports*, no. 24, (January 1974), pp. 3–24; and Abdullah Abu Ayyash, "Israeli Planning Policy in the Occupied Territories," *Journal of Palestine Studies*, vol. XI, no.1 (41) (Autumn 1981), pp. 111–24.

2 See National Lawyers Guild Report, *Treatment of Palestinians in the Israeli-Occupied West Bank and Gaza* (New York: National Lawyers Guild, 1978); "Report of the Secretary-General U Thant on Mr. Gussing's mission in the Occupied Territories, September 15, 1967." In Ann Lesch, "Israeli Settlements in the Occupied Territories, *Journal of Palestine Studies*, vol. VIII, no.2, (Winter 1979). pp. 100–47 (Part I); Ann Lesch, "Israeli Deportation of Palestinians from the West Bank and Gaza Strip, 1967–1978," *Journal of Palestine Studies*, vol. VIII, no. 3, (Spring 1979) pp. 81–112 (Part II); *The Arabs Under Israeli Occupation*, Beirut, The Institute of Palestine Studies, 1977, p. 14; and, Felicia Langer, "Four Years of Occupation," *New Perspectives*, vol. 1, no. 2, (August 1971), p. 32.

3 For a comprehensive review of these laws, see Raja Shehadeh, *Occupier's Law* (Washington, D.C.: Institute of Palestine Studies, 1985). By the time of the *intifada*, over 52 percent of West Bank lands and over one-third of the Gaza Strip had been confiscated by Israel. A report by Peace Now, *A Summary of Government Activities in the Settlements during 1991*, dated January 22, 1992, documented a total of 157 Israeli settlements in the Occupied Territories. The total population of these settlements, including East Jerusalem (and the "Greater Jerusalem" area) was estimated at 250,000. Despite Rabin's election promise to restrict settlement building, especially of those defined as "political" settlements, this activity continued. According to one Israeli journalist, Orit Galili, who quotes Peace Now sources, "only 6% of the land of the West Bank and Gaza Strip is defined by the [Israeli] Administration of Inhabited Areas as being under Palestinian control"; *Haaretz*, December 1, 1992, trans. and repr. in Israel Shahak's *Translations from the Hebrew Press: The Situation in the Fifth Year of the intifada*. The Occupied Territories are 94 percent Palestinian Arab. (By 1996, the total number of Israeli settlements had risen to 300, and the number of settlers to 313,000; see *Report on Israeli Settlement in the Occupied Territories*, vol. 7, no. 4, (July–August 1997), p. 3.)

4 Before the *intifada*, some 46 percent of the Gaza Strip labor force, compared to about 30 percent of that of the West Bank worked in Israel. For more on this and conditions in general in the Gaza Strip see Sara Roy, *The Gaza Strip Survey*. West Bank Data Base Project (Boulder, Colorado: Westview Press, 1986).

5 Over the years, Israel arrested and deported many activist Palestinians, including municipal officials, professionals, and, others who were engaged in attempts to resist Israeli encroachments on their lands and to develop their own institutions and communities.

6   See for example, Raja Shehadeh and Jonathan Kuttab, *The West Bank and the Rule of Law* (New York: International Commission of Jurists, 1980); esp. Appendix, "Military Proclamation No. 101 (as amended by Order No. 718) Concerning the prohibition of incitement and adverse propaganda;" dated August 27, 1967, pp. 126–8. Based on Israeli definitions, "terrorist activities" for which Palestinians are liable to be arrested, comprise anything from writing slogans on walls, singing nationalist songs, making a "V" (victory) sign, displaying the colors of the Palestinian flag in any combination or form, burning tires, throwing stones, demonstrating, making nationalist statements to gatherings of over ten people, and other clearly nonviolent acts; see Michal Schwartz, "Israeli untouchables: Criminals are those who talk to Palestinians," *The Jordan Times*, November 10, 1986, repr. from, *The Middle East International*; and, Karen White, "Torture, Perjury and Palestinian Children," *The Washington Report on Middle East Affairs*, February 1988, p. 9.

7   This amounts to almost half a million Palestinians who had been arrested or detained for these reasons; see Meron Benvenisti, The West Bank Data Base Project, *1987 Report. Demographic, economic, legal, social and political developments in the West Bank* (Boulder, Colorado, Westview Press, 1987), p. 40.

8   See for example, Helena Cobban, "Gunless in Gaza," *World Monitor*, vol. 3, no. 3, (March 1990), p. 64. I lived in Cyprus during 1984–5, where many of the PLO institutions had relocated after their evacuation from Beirut. I can confirm that as early as 1984, the PLO was commissioning studies and formulating detailed plans and strategies on the feasibility of a campaign of nonviolent civilian resistance in the Occupied Territories. What this author learned, from people closely affiliated to these projects, was that they were undertaken at the specific request of Abu-Jihad. Early in the *intifada*, around January or February 1988, a publication began circulating in the Occupied Territories that was also attributed to Abu-Jihad. In it are clearly spelled out the elements and conditions for a successful "civil disobedience" campaign in the Occupied Territories, and the need to escalate this movement to encompass the whole of the West Bank and Gaza Strip (Arabic, n.d.). Many Palestinians are of the opinion that Abu Jihad was assassinated by the Israelis (in April 1988) precisely because of his strategic planning for the use of nonviolent civilian resistance in the Occupied Territories.

9   For a full discussion of the *intifada* and the context in the Occupied Territories, see Souad Dajani, *Eyes Without Country: Searching for a Palestinian Strategy of Liberation* (Philadelphia, PA: Temple University Press, 1994).

10 See for example, Suha Sabbagh and Ghada Talhami (eds.) *Images and Reality: Palestinian Women Under Occupation and in the Diaspora* (Washington, D.C., Institute of Arab Women's Studies, 1990); Orayb Aref Najjar, *Portraits of Palestinian Women* (Salt Lake City, Utah: University of Utah Press, 1992); Philippa Strum, *The Women are Marching – The Second Sex and the Palestinian Revolution* (New York: Lawrence Hill Books, 1992); Kitty Warnock, *Land Before Honor: Palestinian Women in the Occupied Territories* (New York: Monthly Review Press, 1990); and publications in English of the Women's Work Committees and Working Women's Committees in the Occupied Territories.

11 Palestinian women especially feared becoming "another Algeria." They were concerned that their gains over the long years of struggle would be taken away

from them, and that their society would replicate patriarchal structures and traditions found in the surrounding Arab states. They were especially concerned with issues of "personal status " (marriage, divorce, inheritance, and the like) which in the Arab world are regulated by religious laws, and have proved rather discriminatory against women. Hence their struggle to have civil codes in place prior to liberation.

12   The UNLU, formed in January 1988, comprised representatives of the four major factions of the PLO in the Occupied Territories and Islamic Jihad.

13   The undercover units, as they are known, were reported by Palestinians quite early in the *intifada*; see, for example, Yizhar Be'er, "'Death Squads' in the Occupied Territories?" In *Kol Ha'ir*, October 21, 1988, trans. Israel Shahak and repr. in *Journal of Palestine Studies*, vol. XVIII, no. 2 (70) (Winter 1989), pp. 163–6. Later, their activities were documented by Israeli civil rights groups and others. For a comprehensive account of their operation, see Palestine Human Rights Information Center, *Targeting to Kill: Israel's Undercover Units* (Chicago, Illinois: PHRIC, 1992).

14   One popular form of protest was the "general strike," during which all activities were brought to a halt for the day. While this tactic may have symbolized Palestinians' defiance and their refusal to obey the occupation authorities, in reality, it was they – Palestinians – who suffered most. While they closed down their schools and shops, and for the most part stayed indoors, Israeli soldiers would roam the streets unhindered, or take the day off themselves, to lounge around and read magazines (as I personally witnessed them do during a general strike day in Ramallah in October 1989).

15   Examples of such alternative efforts were the "victory gardens," where Palestinians started growing their own vegetables on nearby plots of land; or the education committees that held classes for students in peoples' homes, or in churches or mosques, when the Israeli authorities closed down schools.

16   The impact of the *intifada* on the international community is not addressed here.

17   For more on these classical methods of nonviolent action and the mechanisms by which they operate, see Gene Sharp, *The Politics of Nonviolent Action* (Boston: Porter Sargent, 1973) (three vols). Implicit in Palestinian efforts was the realization that Israeli Jews would not be likely to change their views of Palestinians ("conversion"), but rather that Palestinians would need to exert pressure to cause Israel to reach some kind of "accommodation" with them, and withdraw from these territories.

18   Ze'ev Schiff and Ehud Ya'ari, *Intifada: The Palestinian Uprising – Israel's Third Front* (New York: Simon and Schuster, 1989), p. 168.

19   *The Jerusalem Post* and other Israeli papers carried a number of articles on the role of the army in the Occupied Territories, for example *The Jerusalem Post*, International Edition, February 27, 1988, p. 3.

20   One report notes that by the seventh month of the *intifada*, some 600 reservists had refused to serve (Israel does not allow conscientious objection); see *The Jerusalem Post*, International Edition, January 9, 1988. In another vein, in March 1988, an estimated 2,000 reservists were reported to have urged then Prime Minister Itzhak Shamir to "favor the way of peace"; *Al-Fajr*, March 13, 1988 quotes an article from *Haaretz* to the effect that 96 of these were "high ranking army reserve officers."

21   Imposing economic sieges, curfews, tax raids, closures of whole areas, and the
     like, as well as army attacks from afar, such as in their use of pebble-throwing
     machines, helicopters, and launching missiles directly at Palestinian homes
     (which gained popularity since late 1992) guaranteed the maintenance of this
     social distance and the perpetuation of mutual hostility and fear.

22   Irene Ertugul, "Working Together for Peace," *Middle East International*, Jan-
     uary 9, 1987, p. 16.

23   The Center was later reopened and resumed its publications. For more infor-
     mation on this Center, see ibid., and *Al-Fajr*, February 27, 1987, and March 29,
     1987.

24   One noteworthy group in Israel was Women in Black, whose members stood
     for an hour each week to protest the occupation. Many Women in Black
     groups were later organized in large US cities. For more on Women in
     Black, see, *Al-Fajr*, April 3, 1988, p. 9; and, *Israel Scene*, April/May 1990,
     supplement with *Jerusalem Post* international edition, May 1990. For personal
     interviews with Israeli women activists and a comprehensive listing of various
     Israeli peace groups, see Deena Hurwitz (ed.), *Walking the Red Line: Israelis in
     Search of Justice for Palestine* (Philadelphia, PA: New Society Publishers,
     1992).

25   For more on the peace movement in Israel and its activities during the *intifada*,
     see Peretz Kidron, "Revival of the Peace Movement," *Middle East Interna-
     tional*, June 11, 1988, p. 9.

26   See *Jerusalem Post* international edition, June 11, 1988, and *Israel Scene*,
     April/May 1990 supplement with *The Jerusalem Post* international edition,
     May 1990.

27   Published in Jerusalem, n.d. Also reprinted in *Tikkun*, June–July 1988.

28   By the time of the Gulf War, international censure against Israel that had been
     more pronounced earlier in the uprising had largely lost its edge. Meanwhile, a
     large influx of Soviet Jews to Israel, increased settlement activity in the Occu-
     pied Areas, the guarantee of continued aid and support from the US, all
     converged to reassure Israelis, and preclude any significant pressure being
     applied to cause it to change its stance.

29   For more on strategic possibilities, see Souad Dajani, *Eyes Without Country*.

30   For example, Sari Nuseibeh, a Palestinian professor at Birzeit University and a
     prominent political figure, apparently viewed the *intifada* as a strategy that was
     ultimately designed to culminate in political initiatives. Among these is the
     establishment of a provisional government to realize the earlier Palestine
     National Council (PNC) declaration of Palestinian statehood; see *Middle
     East International*, no. 365 (December 15, 1989), pp. 16–18. Similarly, Pales-
     tinian journalist Daoud Kuttab wrote about the choices available to Palestin-
     ians: either to "escalate" into total civil disobedience, or to resort to some form
     of armed "action," ibid., p. 15.

31   As specified in the agreements, "final status" issues include Jerusalem, refugees,
     security, Jewish settlements, borders, and the like.

32   For example, a 17,000-member-strong Palestinian police force, along with the
     seven or so layers of "security" forces under Arafat, were entrusted with
     the task of quelling opposition to the peace process and with cracking down
     on "extremists." More ominous yet to Palestinians was the creation of a State
     Security Court to deal with such suspects. Decried by human rights activists,

but praised by Israel and the US, these courts functioned as military tribunals where deliberation and sentencing are done in secret, without oversight by any civil law, see Israel Shahak, "Before and After the Massacre of November 18, 1994." *Report No. 147*, (December 4, 1994) (mimeo); and Israel Shahak, "The Secret and Uniformed Police Forces of the Palestinian Authority." *Report No. 151*, (March 3, 1995) (mimeo). Arafat exhibited his power and dictatorial rule by closing or banning the publication of newspapers, interfering in institutional elections, issuing arrest warrants against political dissidents, appointing and/or removing people from official positions, and monopolizing the disbursement of development funds. For more on the actions of the PA, including corruption, economic monopolies organized by various ministers, and other developments, see *The Palestine Report*, a weekly news brief published by the Jerusalem Media and Communication Center (JMCC), Jerusalem.

33 Israel Shahak, "The Secret and Uniformed Police Forces," "Before and After the Massacre of November 18, 1994," December 4, 1994 (mimeo); and Joel Singer, "The Declaration of Principles on Interim Self-Government Arrangements." *Justice*. no. 1, (February 1994), pp. 4–14. Singer was Legal Advisor of the Israeli Ministry of Foreign Affairs. He leaves no room for doubt concerning Israel's overall interests in the Occupied Territories and the advantages it accrued by signing the DOP.

34 Lamis Andoni, "New Opposition Movement," *Middle East International*. no. 492, January 20, 1995. None of these indigenous efforts proved powerful enough to seriously challenge Arafat's authoritarian rule.

35 Closure has been regarded as one of the most serious and least discussed aspects of the "peace process." For a comprehensive discussion of the closures and their impact, see Sara Roy, "The Palestinian Economy After Oslo," *Current History*, January 1998. For more on closure, see *Palestine Human Rights Information Center* (PHRIC), "Two Years of Closure: The Most Severe Collective Human Rights Violation Against the Palestinian People in Occupied Palestine Next to the Israeli Military Occupation on June 5, 1967," April 9, 1995.

36 As was the case throughout the occupation, the economic dependence of the West Bank and Gaza Strip did not decrease with the implementation of "self-rule." With little independent indigenous productive enterprises of their own, an estimated 80 percent of Palestinian exports still went to Israel, and 90 percent of imports to these territories came from Israel (from which – combined the Palestinian economy derived its gross domestic product (GDP). With prolonged closures, with the drastic cut in the number of Palestinian workers allowed into Israel (down from about 120,000 before 1993 to less than 60,000 in 1996), with the loss of revenues to the PA, and with a host of other restrictions on Palestinian movement and investment, the Palestinian economy was losing about US $6 million per *day*; see comments by Oussamma Kanaan, Desk Economist for the West bank and Gaza Strip at the International Monetary Fund (IMF), in The Center for Policy Analysis on Palestine, *Newsletter*, vol. V, no. 5, (September/October 1997), p. 2. Many Palestinians, particularly in the impoverished Gaza Strip, were going hungry and unable to feed their families.

37 Israel Shahak, "Political Situation in Israel at the End of 1994." *Report No. 148*, December 30, 1994 (mimeo). See also *The Christian Science Monitor*,

December 6, 1994; and *Report on Israeli Settlement in the Occupied Territories*, March 1995. This issue notes that despite a "settlement freeze," Israel planned 30,000 new housing units over the next three years. In the Gaza Strip, with its approximately 6,000 Jewish settlers, despite self-rule, Israel remained in control of 65 percent of the lands. For updates of these trends throughout the interim period, see the monthly publication *Report on Israeli Settlement in the Occupied Territories*. For the text of the DOP and other accords, as well as for documents and statements from Israeli officials, see the Israeli Ministry of Foreign Affairs web site on the internet.

38 Under Prime Minister Netanyahu, Israeli officials began talking about bypassing interim stages altogether and accelerating "negotiations" toward a final solution. Other proposals suggested tying some "concessions" on interim self-rule (such as building a Palestinian seaport and airport in the Gaza Strip) with progress on final status issues. In the event, neither Israel nor the US anticipated more than another 10 percent or so of the West Bank and Gaza Strip territories would be transferred to the Palestinians. Whatever Palestinian "entities" would finally emerge, all would preclude independent statehood.

39 Though beyond the scope of this paper, it should be noted that there have been signs of new thinking among some Palestinians, and concerned Israelis, Americans (Jews and others). Most have concurred on the point that Oslo "is dead," and that the ways in which the DOP and other accords have been implemented have, for all intents and purposes, erased the "Green Line" between Israel and the territories. Rejecting "apartheid" as both immoral and untenable, the only remaining solution would have to be based on some form of binationalism for Jews and Arabs in all of Israeli-held Palestine. Some of this thinking has centered around reevaluating "normalization" of relations between various Arab and North African countries and Israel, until real progress has been made on the Israeli–Palestinian conflict. Others have focused on reintroducing the idea of binationalism in the discourse, especially in the US, as the only viable long-term solution; see writings by Edward Said and Marc Ellis, among others.

PART III

Europe

Introduction

In the late 1970s, Georgetown University political scientist Jeane Kirkpatrick, soon thereafter United States ambassador to the United Nations, justified US aid to repressive right-wing governments battling leftist insurgencies on the grounds that, while authoritarian governments of the right could be reformed, totalitarian governments of the left were essentially permanently ensconced.[1] Indeed, according to the conventional wisdom of the time, the best that supporters of democracy could hope for was that communism would be contained through hundreds of thousands of American troops stationed in Western Europe, backed by hundreds of billions of dollars-worth of sophisticated military equipment, as well as a nuclear deterrent force. Further to the right, there were some who sought to revive the Truman era belief in the possibility of a "roll-back" of communist control of Eastern Europe, but here, too, it was assumed to be possible only through the use of military force.

The reality was that communism in Eastern Europe fell in large part through the power of nonviolent action by the Eastern Europeans themselves. For years, there were small-scale nonviolent movements on such issues as peace, environmental, and human rights; there was dissident theater as well as underground publications, or *samizdat*. Yet the open defiance of the system through a massive nonviolent movement commenced in 1980, when Polish shipyard workers in Gdansk – supported by dissident intellectuals, farmers and workers from across the country – formed Solidarity, the first free trade union in the communist world. While the imposition of martial law at the end of 1981 forced Solidarity underground, clandestine organizing continued until, in 1989, the Polish people forced the military regime to lift many of its repressive measures and allow for elections which Solidarity and its allies won. Within months, massive nonviolent movements brought down the communist regimes in neighboring East Germany and Czechoslovakia. communist dictatorships in Hungary, Bulgaria, and Yugoslavia – and eventually Albania – also collapsed; only in Romania was the regime overthrown through violence. Lee Smithey and Lester Kurtz examine these movements in "We Have Bare Hands: Nonviolent Movements in the Soviet Bloc."

Meanwhile, the Baltic states of Lithuania, Latvia, and Estonia, under Soviet rule since the 1930s, renewed their struggle for independence. In Lithuania, unarmed demonstrators faced down Soviet tanks, created alternative institutions and waged a nonviolent struggle against enormous odds, resulting in independence in early 1991, the first successful freedom struggle within the Soviet empire.

In August of 1991, a hardline communist coup in the Soviet Union was met by thousands of Russians taking to the streets in opposition. Facing down tanks in the streets of Moscow, the demonstrators forced the coup leaders to surrender within days, culminating in a series of events which led to the breakup of the Soviet Union and the end of communist rule.

The fall of communism did not result in the end of Eastern Europe's problems, however. Indeed, ethnic violence, corruption, economic inequality, massive unemployment, and the vestiges of authoritarian rule continue to plague the region. Along with the proliferation of problems has come the proliferation of nonviolent action. Much of this has been in the form of small-scale struggles dealing with specific local issues, yet there have also been movements for freedom as significant as those of the previous decade. In the former Yugoslavia, pro-democracy activists in Serbia challenged the autocratic rule of Slobodan Milošević during the winter of 1996–97 and dramatic acts of nonviolent reconciliation have taken place in war-torn Bosnia and elsewhere.

For more than eight years, a dramatic nonviolent movement went forward in Kosovo, the once-autonomous region within Serbia, where the Albanian majority is battled Serbian occupation. Though eclipsed by an upsurge of armed resistance in early 1998 and the NATO intervention the following year, the massive resistance and the formation of a parallel government and educational institutions by the 90 percent Albanian majority constituted one of the most impressive acts of nonviolent resistance in recent decades.

It is perhaps not surprising, in this region of unprecedented and dramatic changes, that nonviolent action is being taken so seriously. Indeed, a number of small Eastern European countries are considering substantially reducing or even abolishing their armed forces in favor of nonviolent civilian defense. For example, in Slovenia, which broke from Yugoslavia in a largely nonviolent independence struggle in 1991, the defense minister is a former peace activist who spearheaded efforts for Slovenian demilitarization. When old paradigms regarding the structure of the state and the economic system are brought into question, so then are the old paradigms assuming the necessity and inevitability of violence for political ends.

Meanwhile, an impressive tradition of nonviolent resistance continues in the historically democratic parts of the continent. Western Europe is widely considered to have a healthy and well- functioning political culture, due to its high levels of education, economic prosperity, and strong representative democracy. Yet parliamentary democracies, even those with proportional representation, are not always capable of taking the interests of the population above the imperatives of political, military, and economic elites. As a result, nonviolent action has remained an important factor in Western European politics. When European democracy has been threatened, nonviolent action has played an important role in its defense, such as in the overthrow of the Greek junta in 1974 and the 1974 "Carnation revolution" in Portugal.

French politics have long been shaped by massive nonviolent action. The student/worker uprising of May 1968 came close to causing the downfall of the Fifth Republic. During the past decade, strikes and blockades by students, farmers, industrial workers, and government employees have paralyzed the country for days at a time, often successfully forcing the government to change its policies.

During the 1970s, movements against nuclear power challenged, with varying degrees of success, the energy policies of several Western European countries. During the 1980s, the United States announced the stationing of nuclear missiles in several Western European countries, leading to massive protests involving hundreds of thousands of people at a time, large-scale acts of civil disobedience, and the proliferation of women's "peace camps" outside US military bases.

Despite, or perhaps because of its totalitarian and militaristic legacy, the center of the development of nonviolent theory and practice in Western Europe has been in the Federal Republic of Germany. Matthew Lyons explores the origins of the organized nonviolent resistance movements of Germany in the 1970s and early 1980s in "The Grassroots Movement in Germany." Key segments of the movement later evolved into the Green Party.

While violence from terrorists and the resurgent far-right in Western Europe has received widespread publicity, less well- known is the dramatic nonviolent response from the population in the face of such threats. Following attacks by Basque terrorists in Spain and by anti-immigrant rightists in Germany, hundreds of thousands of people have mobilized within days for mass demonstrations in a powerful witness against the violence. In the 1970s, the "peace women" of Northern Ireland led mass marches of Catholics and Protestants against the violence between extremists on both the Republican and Unionist side, one of a series of nonviolent reconciliation efforts which have helped bring the peace process forward.

Whether in old democracies or new ones, stable political cultures or societies wrought with conflict, nonviolent action in Europe has played an important role. Rather than threatening representative government, as some critics have alleged, nonviolent action may be an important factor in insuring its functioning, its vitality, and perhaps even its survival.

Note

1 Jeane Kirkpatrick, "Dictatorships and Double Standards," *Commentary*, November 1979.

5

The Grassroots Movement in Germany, 1972–1985

Matthew Lyons

Introduction

In September 1972, a man from the West German city of Augsburg chains himself to a street sign in central Barcelona. He carries signs protesting the Spanish government's persecution of conscientious objectors. His arrest and jailing for three months draws widespread attention to the international protest campaign. A few months later, the maximum penalty for conscientious objection in Spain is reduced from 18 years to 3–8 years.

In October and November 1983, tens of thousands of demonstrators across the Federal Republic of Germany (FRG) blockade military bases and government facilities to protest plans to deploy US cruise and Pershing II missiles in West Germany. In Bremerhaven, 3,000 blockaders hold their ground against violent attacks by the police. In Bonn, 5,000 blockaders "besiege" the Bundestag (federal parliament) as it debates formal acceptance of the missiles. Despite massive protests, the Bundestag approves deployment, and the first Pershings arrive immediately.

Each of these actions was informed by a doctrine of nonviolent civil disobedience. In 1972, the concept of nonviolent civil disobedience was little known in the FRG. Twelve years later, it had become a central factor in West German politics, widely endorsed and used by the peace movement, the largest social movement in postwar German history.

In this chapter I will examine the connecting thread between the actions in Barcelona and Bonn: a very small loose alliance of nonviolent action groups known as the "Grassroots" network. This network formed in the early 1970s around the newspaper *Grassroots Revolution (Graswurzelrevolution)*, which advocated using nonviolent action to transform society along anarchist or libertarian-socialist lines. Grassroots groups formed in a number of cities, mostly among university students and other young intellectuals. In 1980 most of these groups formed the Federation of Nonviolent Action Groups (FOGA), as a focus for the grassroots network.

For many years the Grassroots groups were the only organizations in the FRG that combined direct action with the philosophy of nonviolent revolution. Although the Grassroots network never encompassed more than a few thousand sympathizers, and a few hundred people at its activist "core," it played a key role in the ecology and peace movements of the 1970s and 1980s.

The importance of the Grassroots groups to these movements is little known – not only in the United States but in the FRG as well. Repeatedly Grassroots groups utilized innovative tactics and campaigns which have later been picked up by many others:

- They were the first leftist organizations in the Federal Republic to join the movement against nuclear power and to develop alliances with citizens' initiative groups.[1]
- They were among the first groups for conscientious objectors to advocate "total" objection: the refusal of civilian alternative service.[2]
- They were the first organizations outside the Protestant church to cultivate ties with the independent peace groups in the GDR.[3]
- They were the first groups to combine theories of nonviolent "social defense" with direct action.[4]
- They introduced the principles of the affinity group and consensus process to the West German ecology and peace movements.
- They pioneered with a variety of political tactics, including boycotts and blockades, and played key roles in organizing major nonviolent actions such as those at Wyhl (1974), Gorleben (1980), Grossengstingen (1982), and the Fulda Gap (1984).

An Overview of Grassroots Philosophy

The Grassroots network is a part of the broad spectrum of political initiatives or "new social movements" which developed in the Federal Republic after the collapse of the student movement of the 1960s. "Undogmatic" leftists and Spontis (spontaneous leftists) continued the SDS (Socialist German Student League) tradition of loose organization and an archo- Marxist theory. "Dogmatic" leftists formed sectarian Leninist groups, called "K-Groups," and underground guerrilla organizations such as the Red Army Fraction (RAF). The feminist movement developed from a base among women who rejected the sexism within the student left. Other groups such as gay men, young people, and foreign workers from Turkey and other Mediterranean countries, organized against the oppression they faced. Farmers and people from the urban middle class organized citizen initiative groups against nuclear power and other ecological threats. The counter-culture "alternative" movement ranged from vegetarian food crops and self-managed business to spiritual groups such as the Anthroposophists and Rajnishis. A house squatters movement developed, which was strongly influenced by punk culture and by anarchist militants known as "autonomists" (*Autonomen*).[5]

The Grassroots network was formed by radical Christians and libertarian socialists orientated toward antimilitarist work and interested in nonviolent revolution. They drew ideas and examples from pacifists such as a Leo Tolstoy, Mohandas Gandhi, and Martin Luther King, and anarchists such as Mikhail Bakunin, Peter Kropotkin, and Gustav Landauer. With the growth of the ecology movement, Grassroots activists also turned their attention to radical critiques of industrial technology, such as those of Lewis Mumford and Ivan Ilich.

There are important affinities between the principles of anarchism, nonviolence, and radical ecology, which were reflected in the Grassroots network. Like many other radical-pacifist organizations, Grassroots groups opposed not only direct, physical violence such as war but also "structural violence" in the form of social hierarchies, psychological oppression, and the subjugation of nature. Many Grassroots analyses treated capitalism and the state as the twin structures that unify and maintain structural violence throughout the society in the West. Grassroots activists also rejected the then-existing "socialist" models such as the USSR or China, arguing that these states perpetrated militarism, social hierarchy, and ecological destruction in more centralized forms.

Grassroots critiques of existing "socialism" went deeper than the specifics of Soviet or Maoist rule to challenge the principles of Marxism itself. In parallel ways, anarchism, radical ecology, and pacifism all break radically with the Marxist principle that freedom is "dialectically" rooted in its opposite. Radical pacifists reject the claim that armed struggle will lead to a society free of violence. Anarchists argue that the "transitional" workers' state will perpetuate itself – not "wither away" into communism. Radical ecologists reject Marx's belief that human emancipation can be built upon technological "mastery of nature." All three philosophies argue that freedom can only be created through a consistent, unified process.[6]

Anarchist and pacifist philosophies, in particular, converge in the argument that political means and ends are intrinsically linked. Forms of action and organization are not simply "tools" which can be used interchangeably for various ends, but a pathway which influences and shapes the political directions themselves. In order to work toward a "nonviolent, non-hierarchical society," which *Grassroots Revolution* stated as its goal, Grassroots groups have endeavored to develop nonviolent forms of action and non-hierarchical modes of organization.

Concepts of nonviolent action differed within the network, reflecting – in part – differences between the religious and anarchist traditions. Grassroots activists agreed that political action should avoid endangering other people physically, but most maintained that nonviolence involves more than simply the avoidance of violence. They endorsed forms of action both legal (such as demonstrations and boycotts) and illegal (civil disobedience actions such as blockades and occupations). Under certain circumstances most Grassroots activists also endorsed attacks on property (sometimes called "violence against things") if they did not endanger people directly or indirectly.

Grassroots nonviolent action, the network emphasized, as being participatory in the sense that people acted for themselves rather than delegating their political voices through elected "representatives." The network's forms of organization were designed to emphasize collective participation, local autonomy, and decentralization. Each group in the network made decisions for itself, and within each group decisions were reached by a consensus of all its participants. Political work generally was local and regional.

The Network's Social Base

While the network advocated "grassroots" politics rooted in the broad community participation, it remained sharply limited in size and social composition. Although the network was never clearly delineated, its approximate size remained relatively constant at a few hundred "core" activists and a few thousand sympathizers and supporters. Throughout the network's history it predominantly attracted university students, along with some high-school students and other young intellectuals: in general, young Germans from educated middle-class backgrounds. Men outnumbered women by perhaps two to one.[7]

This narrow social base held certain advantages for the network. The flexibility of student life made it easier for many Grassroots activists to devote time and energy to political work. Similarity of background made it easier for group members to get to know one another and to become close friends more easily and quickly than might have occurred in a broader coalition. Integration of political work and personal support within the group was a widespread, implicit part of Grassroots philosophy, but it was inconsistently applied in practice. A strong focus on intellectual debate within many groups left little room to deal with personal feelings or experiences. This made it difficult for newcomers, particularly women. Both women and men commented that it took them several months in a Grassroots group before they were able to follow the discussions.[8]

The predominance of students has also made continuity difficult: students often disperse during university vacations, move from city to city relatively frequently, and most dropped out of the Grassroots network after completing their degrees, creating a higher turnover rate in the membership of many groups. This made it hard for Grassroots groups to develop long-term perspectives on their work.

In many other ways, the political style and focus of Grassroots groups both reflected and perpetuated the network's social base. For example, many (if not most) men in the Grassroots network were conscientious

objectors. The threat of conscription made militarism an immediate, personal concern for them. This accounted, in part, for the network's emphasis
on antimilitarist work and for the predominance of men in the network.
Opposition to military (and civilian) compulsory service, a specific form of
structural violence affecting men, was thus a key source of continuity in the
Grassroots network.

However, the Grassroots network largely focused on the "universal"
aspects of oppression: the structural violence that pervades society and
affects all social groups (e.g. militarism). Ironically, this may have limited
the network's appeal. The network paid less attention to the forms of
structural violence which target specific oppressed groups in society.
Women in Grassroots groups sometimes pushed them successfully to
focus on sexism, as in a campaign initiated in the late 1970s against the
extension of military conscription to women. But the network as a whole
did not consistently oppose sexism either outside or inside the network.
Other forms of oppression, such as racism, class oppression, heterosexism,
and anti-Semitism, were acknowledged as problems in society, but were
never a major focus of the network's attention or energy.

The emphasis on opposing structural forms of violence in general, and
militarism in particular, rather than the oppression of specific social groups,
reflected the privileged position of the Grassroots activist majority: university educated, middle- class men. For these activists, other forms of oppression may have seemed less immediate, or even invisible. Treating structural
violence as "universal" often reinforces this.

Grassroots activists' "universalistic" approach to oppression was reflected
in their own system of organization. The activists tended to assume, in
practice, that hierarchy within a political group was mainly a matter of
formal structures. The network's "nonhierarchical" forms of organization
were designed to encourage equal participation. But unless combined with
antihierarchical measures designed to counter specific oppressive dynamics,
they tended to leave much of the informal power in the hands of middle-class
student men. This made participation difficult for some groups, such as
women, and helped to exclude others, such as working-class people.

Nonviolent Action or Anarchist Theory?

These problems in the Grassroots network's responses to social oppression
pointed to hidden complexities underlying Grassroots philosophy. The
relation between anarchism and nonviolence in Grassroots philosophy is
also complicated for other reasons. Although both nonviolence and anarchism were important for the network, it would be an exaggeration to say
that the network synthesized the two. The Grassroots network had no
unified program or analysis, and *Grassroots Revolution*'s consistently
anarchist orientation did not fully represent the network as a whole.

Some Grassroots activists rejected anarchism in favor of reforming the state apparatus. A larger number had no clear position on the subject.

Commitment to nonviolence, rather than to anarchist goals, was what held the network together, and action rather than theory was its focal point. Even among Grassroots activists who consider themselves nonviolent anarchists, most have become interested in anarchism through nonviolence, seldom in the reverse. Many Grassroots groups were known simply as "nonviolent action groups" and in working with other organizations they usually kept silent about revolution. *Grassroots Revolution* provided a forum for political discussion, including theoretical analysis, but the majority of Grassroots groups devoted most of their efforts to relatively limited goals such as ending nuclear power or opposing military conscription. Many Grassroots activists, in fact, treated political theory with disinterest, skepticism, or even suspicion.[9]

This tension, too, reflected the social backgrounds of Grassroots network members, such as the large number of conscientious objectors. In the process of applying for state recognition as a conscientious objector, or in some cases refusing to apply for civilian alternative service, the conscientious objector must carefully examine his personal beliefs about violence. Thus nonviolence became a concern with personal immediacy in a way that an anarchist vision often does not.

The predominance of students within Grassroots groups affected their attitudes toward political theory and action in complex ways. On the one hand, the university trains students in many fields to feel comfortable using theory and to discuss society in abstract, analytic terms. This has been reflected in West German student politics since the SDS discussion groups of the early 1960s. But the university structures, and the atmosphere within large sections of the left, encouraged an approach to theory, which is sterile, "objective," and divorced from other spheres of life. This led some students to reject the theoretical analysis entirely as incompatible with concrete political action. This "actionism" was a recurrent problem within the Grassroots movement.

The priority that the Grassroots movement placed on nonviolent action before revolutionary goals influenced its relations with other organizations. It facilitated contact and cooperation with citizen-initiated groups, which focused on specific reforms and often included many people suspicious of radicalism. However, it helped to isolate the Grassroots movement from other libertarian-socialist groups, many of whom dismissed nonviolent action as bourgeois-reformist.

Spearheading Nonviolent Action

The Grassroots network was able to play an important role in propagating nonviolent action because it stepped into a political vacuum. Although earlier movements, such as the student movement of the 1960s, had used nonviolent *techniques*, groups committed to nonviolent action were virtually unknown in the Federal Republic before the 1970s. A few other organizations, such as the Fellowship of Reconciliation (FOR), and independent peace researchers such as Theodor Ebert, played important roles in spreading the ideas of nonviolence, but the Grassroots network turned these ideas into action earlier and more consistently than did other groups.

In the social movements of the 1970s, several factors made it difficult for the network to win broader support for nonviolent action. The major peace organizations, and other groups committed to centralized political organization and to seeking mass appeal, regarded the nonviolent action (especially civil disobedience) of small, autonomous groups with suspicion. Many people, especially other leftists, identified nonviolence with "passive resistance", and therefore considered it less effective than violence. Within the antinuclear movement during the mid-1970s, "militant" leftists systematically worked to escalate political demonstrations into physical combat with the police. Frequent actions by terrorist groups and wide-reaching police repression during this period also fostered a violent political atmosphere. Thus Grassroots antimilitarist work in the 1970s was largely isolated from the major peace organizations, while in the ecology movement, where Grassroots activists often worked as part of larger coalitions, they clashed repeatedly with the "militants" over principles of political work.

The collapse of several Leninist groups and urban guerrilla organizations in the late 1970s opened the door for greater discussion of nonviolent action. This shift was represented, and to some extent aided, by the emergence of the Green Party, which inscribed both nonviolence and "grassroots democracy" (*Basisdemokratie*) at the top of its program. In the early 1980s, and in the seventies, the Grassroots groups took the lead in developing nonviolent forms of action.[10]

During the peace movement of 1982–3, the "nonviolent action movement" briefly exploded far beyond previous dimensions. Thousands of nonviolent action groups and affinity groups formed across the Federal Republic, and tens of thousands of people took part in civil disobedience actions, mostly blockades. In part this growth in activity represented an important success for the Grassroots network. But as nonviolent action spread, much of its political content was lost or radically diluted. Most of the people who rushed to take part in civil disobedience had little or no understanding of Grassroots philosophy: to them nonviolent action meant only a specific technique (the blockade) which could be applied mechanically. When the technique failed to stop the deployment of cruise and Pershing II missiles in November, 1983, most of the new activists quickly became disillusioned and dropped out.

These events pointed to the basic questions of self-definition which Grassroots activists never fully resolved. Did the network encompass all who identified themselves as supporters of nonviolence, or only those committed to a radical vision of nonviolent revolution? Ironically, the term "Grassroots", implying a broad community-based movement, had come to be associated with a specific, if loosely defined, political perspective. "Nonviolent action group," meanwhile, became a label used by many organizations outside the Grassroots movement.

Another central question was the network's strategy for social change. In both ecology and peace movements, Grassroots groups tended to seek a mediator role between contingents seeking reform and those advocating revolution. In part, this allowed the network to hedge its own internal political differences over long-term goals. But to some extent, the role of mediator was also a conscious, active choice. Nonviolent civil disobedience, it was perhaps hoped, could serve as a bridge: at the least, it could provide a tactical compromise between approaches favored by other radicals and by reformists, thus enabling them to work together. Ideally, it would go further, and push both liberals and militant leftists to question their own political assumptions about means and ends.

"Creative tension" between the radical and liberal tendencies plays an important, positive role in many social movements. Mediating between the two can thus be an effective approach to take, particularly for a small group with limited resources, such as the Grassroots network, and can be readily justified on both reformist and revolutionary grounds. We need to be careful, however, not to read too much into the Grassroots network's actions. If the mediator "strategy" became important, it was mainly an ad hoc strategy, guided by a mixture of external forces, unspoken preferences, and conscious analysis.

And as the events of 1982–3 in particular showed, the mediator approach was only successful in practice. During the "blockade boom" period, many Grassroots groups proved to be concerned to differentiate themselves more from militant leftists than from liberal reformers. While the pages of *Grassroots Revolution* maintained a revolutionary tone, Grassroots activists found that nonviolent action was easily watered down in a broader coalition. It was often heavily susceptible to co-optation by established liberal organizations, and to some extent by the State itself. This alienated many leftist groups, and contributed to the defeat of the peace movement.

It would be wrong to consider this process either inevitable or a result solely of mistakes made by the Grassroots network. With the "Fulda Gap" actions of 1984, Grassroots groups showed that it was still possible to use nonviolent action to push the movement in a more radical direction. But this limited success did not erase the major difficulties involved in developing a radical strategy of nonviolent action.

The Grassroots Network and West German Politics

A study of the Grassroots network also points to several broader issues that were central to the West German Left and to West German politics in general. I cannot address all of these issues in detail, but I will briefly outline some of the more salient ones, which include the following:

- Historical discontinuity on the left
- The legacy of Nazism and war
- The role of students and politics
- Political violence
- The new social movements
- The "change of values" (Inglehart's thesis)
- The emergence of the Green Party

Nazism destroyed Germany's radical movements of the early twentieth century creating a major historical break in leftist politics. Efforts to recreate a radical current in politics after the end of the Second World War were stifled for two decades by the occupying powers, by the authoritarian tendencies of the West German State, and by the climate of Cold War anti-Communism. This blight did not end until the growth of the student movement and the Extra-Parliamentary Opposition (APO) in the mid- and late 1960s.[11] Like many other leftist groups in West Germany, the Grassroots network sought to define itself by looking outward to movements in other countries, and backward to political currents of the pre-Nazi era.

The legacy of Nazism and war has itself been a central reference point for many popular movements in the FRG. APO, in the 1960s, convinced itself as a belated anti-Fascist resistance to a state which had never been effectively de-Nazified and to a society in which the socioeconomic roots of Fascism persisted. In the early 1980s the "independent" wing of the peace movement (including Grassroots activists) used the slogan "from protest to resistance" as a rallying cry, implicitly laying claim to the anti-Fascist heritage.

The Grassroots network's philosophy of nonviolence, its emphasis on anti-militarism, and its opposition to political hierarchy all reflected a reaction against the memory of Nazism. As members of the Göttingen Nonviolent Action group wrote in 1978, "The superiority of anarchism over other political theories is, for us, that there can be no anarchist concentration camps."[12]

Like APO, the Grassroots network predominantly included university students and other young intellectuals. Unlike APO, however, Grassroots groups did not focus on their own youth as a point of political identity; their social critiques did not single out their parents' generation. By the mid-1970s, people of many different ages were politically active in the new social movements – thus the young people in the Grassroots network found themselves less isolated than their activist counterparts years before.

The political use of violence became a critical issue for the West German left in the 1970s, with the continued rise in "street violence" in leftist confrontations with the police (e.g. antinuclear demonstrations, the squatters movement), and particularly with the emergence of terrorist groups which claimed to be revolutionary, such as the Red Army Faction (RAF). Some commentators (such as the former RAF member Horst Mahler) have suggested that the terrorist experience was closely tied to the unresolved Nazi legacy; both rooted in a "traumatic, moralistic" reaction against it, and drawing on some of the political attitudes and traditions that it left behind.[13]

Obviously, Grassroots activists sharply distinguished themselves from users and supporters of political violence. In some cases they defined terrorists and themselves as "opposite poles" on the Left. The issue particularly influenced Grassroots work within the ecology movement and contributed to the network's isolation from other leftist organizations. At the same time, the network worked hard to offer an alternative to political violence, and in some cases was able to persuade other leftist groups to take a nonviolent approach.

The emergence of ecology, women's alternative, peace, and other movements beginning in the early 1970s greatly expanded the sphere of political action in the Federal Republic. If the movements of the 1960s helped to break the dependence on traditional party politics, and pioneered new issues and forms of the action, the new social movements that followed continued in the process. Feminists, for example, expanded the definitions of politics by addressing issues in women's personal lives as matters of political power. Citizen initiatives brought a new kind of participatory politics to thousands of nonradical, middle-class people.[14]

Grassroots activists themselves pointed to this shift as an important new political opportunity.

> Because the resistance has had to organize itself outside the political parties, it has developed a new quality. The Easter March of nuclear weapons opponents [in the early 1960s], the student movement, and the citizen initiatives are stages of a process of liberation from bureaucracy...New values such as autonomy, self-determination, self responsibility are developing,

while, they argued, basic structures of society are more and more called into question.[15] Much of the Grassroots network's efforts were an attempt to further this process.

The phrases in the Grassroots pamphlet quoted above about "new values" seem to echo the claims of socialist Ronald Inglehart, whose ideas won favor in explaining the FRG's resurgent political activism. Inglehart argued that increasing satisfaction of material needs, plus rising levels of formal education, led to a shift from "materialist" to "post-materialist" values among young, middle-class adults in Western industrialized countries. Materialistic values mainly include economic security and physical protection. "Post-materialistic" values include: desires for community, self-esteem, a greater voice in decision-making, and an aesthetic and intellectual satisfaction.[16]

Inglehart's hypothesis accords with the new social movement's focus on the "reproductive sphere" (as distinct from the productive sphere): energy, health, housing, education, etc. And it accords, more specifically, with the social composition of the Grassroots network.

Elim Papadakis, however, challenged Inglehart's distinction between material and postmaterial needs, and pointed out that "post-materialists may in fact be pursuing materialist goals in a different guise." The widespread participation of university students and graduates in the new social movements may, in fact, have reflected their fear of unemployment, due to shrinking job opportunities in the public service sector, as much as it did any "shift in values."[17]

In the 1980s much of the scholarship on the FRG's new social movements focused on development of the Green Party, founded as a national party in 1979–80. Several authors refer to a "Green movement" encompassing the wide range of groups from which the Greens have drawn much of their support. I question this usage, which implies a teleological relationship between a social movement base and the political party that grew out of it. Grassroots activists, who frequently criticized the Green's participation in parliament as a retreat into traditional politics, would object to being labeled part of a "Green movement." But the Green Party has provided a new kind of political voice to members of the new social movements, and it has brought together a tough range of activists, issues, and organizations more successfully than anyone else. Beginning in October 1998, the Greens became part of the federal government's ruling coalition, as junior partners to the Social Democrats.

It is also true that the Grassroots network contributed to the development of the Green Party. In its promotion of nonviolent action, its commitment to participatory democracy, its radical approach to ecological issues, and its efforts to bridge divisions between citizen initiatives and the Left, the Grassroots network anticipated the Green Party by several years, and influenced it – directly or indirectly. The network functioned both as an external critic and as a political partner of the Greens: sometimes challenging the Greens' political decisions, sometimes offering new ideas and forms of action (especially within the peace movement) which the Greens later came to support.

Conclusion

The Grassroots network became a small but influential segment, first of the ecology movement, then of the peace movement. Its contributions must be weighed in the context of the limitations it faced: a narrow social base, small size, limited resources, a high turnover rate, and the difficulty of coordinating local groups. And as a proponent of radical nonviolent action, the Grassroots network was practically starting from scratch. There were few political examples or experienced activists close at hand. Thus, many of the forms of action and organization which the network introduced – such as nonviolence training, affinity groups, and the consensus process – were "imported" from other countries, particularly the United States. Thus, too, the network initially focused on the internal campaigns which had little direct connection to problems in the Federal Republic.

But when the Grassroots groups turned their attention closer to home – to the struggle against nuclear power – they were brought directly into coalitions with other groups. Here they began to have an important impact. In both the ecology and peace movements, Grassroots groups continuously sought to develop a wider base of understanding, support, and participation for nonviolent action. They defended nonviolence against sections to the Left which rejected its principles and also against liberal and "traditional" groups which equated nonviolence with legality or the avoidance of conflict. At the same time, Grassroots activists sought to work together with both of these other political currents, sometimes moving closer to one, sometimes the other. Their "mediator" role was partially a political choice, partly a reflection of the network's own internal tensions and lack of consensus on many political issues.

The Grassroots network always included some activists with an anarchist orientation, some with a radical Christian orientation, others with a mixture of both, and many with no clear position politically. And Grassroots activists struggled with their own differing conceptions of nonviolence and social change. They argued about voluntary suffering, about forms of political organization, about symbolism versus direct action, and about the relative weight of persuasion and pressure from below. Some attempted to make feminism a more central part of Grassroots politics but they found little support. Rarely were these conflicts "resolved"; they recurred as new situations arose, new members joined and older ones left the network, and new activities were initiated.

As Gunter Saathoff noted in the conclusion of his 1980 dissertation on the Grassroots network, Grassroots groups' influence in propagating nonviolent action must be viewed skeptically for two reasons. First, other factors influenced the ecology (and peace) movements to use nonviolent action. The military strength of the police and the failure of violent confrontation made some organizations (such as the Communist League, or KB) more amenable to nonviolence for purely tactical reasons. And other groups besides the Grassroots network – such as the citizen initiative federation (the BBU), and later the Greens – began to advocate nonviolence as well. The BBU's magazine in particular had for several years a close relationship to Grassroots perspectives. Its editors included Michael Schroeren and Manuel Walther, both nonviolent anarchists and former editors of *Grassroots Revolution*.[18]

But if external forces made tactical "nonviolence" attractive by default, and larger organizations endorsed the concept of nonviolent action, it was still the Grassroots groups who set the example, who gave the concept concrete form and vitality. In campaign after campaign, action after action, it was the Grassroots activists who provided the key ideas, who offered the training, or who did the initial organizing.

Saathoff's second point was that the Grassroots influence in larger movements was "purchased at the cost of radicalism."[19] Grassroots groups propagated their nonviolent *means*, but seldom their nonhierarchical *ends* – despite their own claim that the means and ends were indissoluble. This dynamic persisted in the peace movement of the 1980s and contributed to the movement's decline.

It may be, however, that Grassroots activists had to choose between limited influence and no influence at all: if they had been more forceful about their radical goals, they might have simply lost the ear of citizens initiatives and local peace groups. And while the network did not often have a strong radical presence in public, it never completely abandoned its radical orientation. The Fulda Gap action showed that the Grassroots network would not simply be coopted but would try to learn from its mistakes and apply political pressure in different directions.

Finally, it should not be forgotten that nonviolent action often constituted a radicalizing step in itself. The blockade actions of 1982–3, for example, taught large numbers of people that they could choose to break the law for political reasons, something which none of them had ever done before. Civil disobedience was often framed as a way to symbolically "withdraw one's loyalties from the state." These were not necessarily revolutionary steps but they served as powerful counterweights to the conscription and passivity which the government sought to impose on the population.

Recently someone asked me, "What is the most important thing we can learn from the Grassroots network?" I answered, "That a small group of people, with a clear perspective on what is possible, a commitment to what they consider important, and the patience to stick to the task, can accomplish a surprising amount. They can become a pivotal force."

The story of the Klatsschmohn Group is perhaps the most vivid example. This West Berlin Grassroots group, which included about 12 members, formed to address the lack of direction that the ecology movement was experiencing in the late 1970s. They set themselves the task to develop a new concept of nonviolent political action for the movement, based on the example of the Seabrook, New Hampshire occupation of 1977. The group spent one year in preparatory work: four months in the USA learning about nonviolent activism and then another year evaluating and applying what they had learned. The affinity group/speakers council model of organization which they brought back was first used at Grossengstingen in 1982, and in scores of other actions. Thus a concept of political organization used by tens of thousands of people can be traced to the work of this group of 12.[20]

We need not romanticize the Grassroots network in order to appreciate its strengths. Throughout the 13-year period considered in this study,

Grassroots activists repeatedly brought new ideas and fresh energy to important political struggles. With their commitment to nonviolent civil disobedience, to radical ecology and antimilitarism, and to grassroots democracy, they expanded the sphere of political possibility in the Federal Republic of Germany.

Notes

1 Gunther Saathoff, "Graswurzelrevolution': Praxis, Theorie und Oranisation des gewaltfreien Anarchisums in der Bundesrepublik 1972–1980." Thesis, University of Marburg, 1980, p. 40.

2 Saathoff, " Graswurzelrevolution," pp. 55–6.

3 Klaus Wolschner, "Wir sind nicht untereineander loyal": Die westliche Friedensbewegung und "Schwerter zu Pflugscharen," *Kirche im Socialismus*, no. 5 (1982). See also the special issue of *Grassroots Revolution* on the Warsaw Pact (January/February, 1984).

4 See for example *Grassroots Revolution*, no. 56 (1982), a special issue on social defense (Soziale Verteidigung).

5 For a brief overview of these movements, see Joseph Huber, *Wer soll das alles andern* (Berlin: Rotbuch Verlag, 1981). On the "alternative" movement, see Wolfgang Kraushaar, ed., *Autonomie oder Getto?* (Frankfurt-am-Main: Verlag Neue Kritik, 1978).

6 On the convergence of radical-ecologist and anarchist critiques of Marxism, see Murray Bookchin, *Toward an Ecological Society* (Montreal: Black Rose Books, 1980).

7 Saathoff, "Graswurzelrevolution," p. 156, estimated a two-to-one male–female ratio in 1980.

8 Interviews with Diter Kannenberg (Gottingen, July 15, 1985), and Cony Brinckmann (Gottigen, July 16, 1985)

9 On ambivalence within the Grassroots network towards radical theory, see Saathoff, "Graswurzelrevolution," pp. 157–60.

10 On the shift from the 1970s to 1980s, Ulrich Wohland's comments have been particularly helpful to me. (Interview, Heidelberg, July 26, 1985.)

11 See William Graf, *The German Left Since 1945* (New York: The Oleander Press, 1976).

12 Gewaltfreie Aktion Gottingen, *Feldzugue fur ein sauberes Deutschland* (Gottingen, 1978), p. 13.

13 See Luciana Castellina, "Terrorism in West Germany: Interview with Horst Mahler, *Socialist Review* no. 39 (May–June 1978) pp. 118–23; and Albrecht Wellmer, "Terrorism and Social Criticism," *Telos* no. 48 (Summer 1981) pp. 65–78.

14 See Elim Papadakis, *The Green Movement in West Germany* (New York: St. Martin's Press, 1984) pp. 9–11.

15 "Feldzuge, für ein sanberes Deutschland." (Gottingen: Gewaltfreie Aktion Gottingen, 1977), 8. Note: All translations from German-language sources are mine unless otherwise indicated.

16 See Ronald Inglehart, "Value Priorities and Socio-Economic Change." In S. Barnes and M. Kaase et al., *Political Action: Mass Participation in Five*

Western Democracies (Beverly Hills: Sage Publications 1979); and Inglehart, *The Silent Revolution* (Princeton,: Princeton University Press 1977).

17 Papadakis, "The Green Alternative: Interpretations of Social Protest and Political Action in West Germany," *Australian Journal of Politics and History*, no. 323 (1986) esp. pp. 443–6; Elim Papadakis, *The Green Movement in West Germany*, p. 155

18 Saathoff, "Graswurzelrevolution," pp. 272–3.

19 Ibid pp. 274–5.

20 Interviews with Dieter Rau (August 15, 1985), Benjamin Putter (July 9, 1985).

6

"We Have Bare Hands"[1]: Nonviolent Social Movements in the Soviet Bloc

Lee Smithey and Lester R. Kurtz

We live in an age in which humans have developed the capacity to destroy life on earth but also in which an unprecedented elaboration of nonviolent action, theory, and philosophy has taken place (Kurtz 1995; Sharp 1973). In the most dramatic example of this development nonviolent social movements contributed to the transformation of the former USSR between 1988 and 1991.[2] Those nonviolent insurgencies were probably not sufficient conditions for the collapse of the Soviet empire and the end of the Cold War, but may well have been necessary. Indeed, it is hard to imagine any armed insurgency against the Soviet bloc having been successful in the late 1980s. Surely any attempt by an armed group to confront any of the Central and East European countries, let alone the Soviet Union itself, would no doubt have been immediately crushed by overwhelming military force. Nonviolent insurrection, however, was not so easily countered by the state; in fact, efforts to suppress nonviolent demonstrations by force back-fired on officials and led to increased support for the dissidents, a dynamic we are calling the "paradox of repression."

A comprehensive treatment of the revolutions in Eastern Europe cannot be provided here, but we will provide a brief overview and an analysis of the salience of nonviolent methods to the success of the Soviet revolutions. Empires rise and fall; what is unique about this case is the nature of its demise: The Soviet empire was defeated not by foreign invaders or a military coup, but rather by a series of nonviolent populist insurgencies. The 1988–91 revolutions were a culmination of an awakening in which citizens became increasingly vocal in expressing their grievances and insisting on governmental reforms. As the threat of armed intervention by Soviet troops in Warsaw Pact countries declined, communist regimes made more and more concessions to popular citizens' groups, finally consenting to free elections that predictably ousted the ruling elites. In this chapter, we contend that one cannot understand the transformation of revolutions without considering both the role of nonviolent social movements in them and the broader history of nonviolent resistance worldwide in recent decades. We will discuss three particularly important features of nonviolent social movements: parallel institutions, nonviolent methods, and the paradox of repression.

Nonviolent Action and Nonviolent Social Movements

Nonviolent action has been used in conflicts for centuries, but it has been most widely used in the twentieth century. The strategic use of nonviolent action that Mohandas K. Gandhi exemplified has been diffused globally by scholars and activists. His nonviolent techniques in the India Freedom movement contributed to the withdrawal of the British Empire from India and dealt a blow to the entire colonial system. His principled yet highly strategic use of nonviolent methods became the model for disenfranchised groups around the world, employing nonviolent methods to resist corrupt political regimes. Gene Sharp's (1973) three-volume systematization of strategic nonviolent action, *The Politics of Nonviolent Action,* has served as a guide for activists everywhere, including those in the Soviet bloc.

The overview that follows uses data from "on the ground" accounts in Central and Eastern Europe and the USSR, such as reports by journalists, activists, and other eye-witnesses who provide narratives of the resistance and the context in which resistance occurred.[3] We have incorporated biographical and autobiographical materials that provide an inside view on the revolutions. This approach is, of course, a tentative compromise in lieu of the sort of intensive multinational study that involves interviews with activists and governmental officials, as well as research in movement and official archives.

The Revolutions

Poland

The political transformations in Central and Eastern European unfolded one after another in the late 1980s. The momentum began in Poland, where Solidarity, the trade union opposition party, had been gathering strength for several years. Pope John Paul II's visit to his homeland of Poland in 1979 is widely considered a critical turning point in that country's transformation. The Pope's visit drew enormous crowds, and inspired the people toward greater self-determination. Only one year later, workers went on strike at the Lenin Shipyards in Gdansk, and an electrician named Lech Wałesa formed a committee of workers and intellectuals who challenged the government on a range of issues. As a result of the negotiations, Solidarity was allowed to organize legally.

In December 1981, however, General Wojciech Jaruzelski declared martial law and arrested Solidarity leaders. Solidarity supporters held large demonstrations protesting the state of martial law, and after one year of internment, Wałesa was released and martial law was suspended though many restrictions remained. Workers across the nation went on strike again in April and May, 1988. Solidarity struggled to manage the second wave of strikes in August, and as a result, was able to pressure the government into negotiations and regain their legal status (Stokes 1993). The Central Committee of the communist Polish United Workers' Party (PUWP) accepted Solidarity's proposals for political pluralism, and on February 6, 1989, the "Round Table Talks" opened between the PUWP, Solidarity, and other parties and civic organizations. These negotiations led to constitutional adjustments, a new system of government, the formation of a coalition government, and the election of Lech Wałesa to the post of president in December 1990.

Hungary

Almost simultaneously, Hungary was experiencing its own transformation. Like Poland, reform within the communist apparatus accounted for substantial progress toward Hungary's transition to democracy. However, as in Poland and all of the other Soviet bloc countries, the communist reformers found themselves outpaced by the forces of opposition. Reformers such as Károly Grosz and Imre Poszgay were trying to steer Hungary to economic and political safety without entirely ejecting the Communist Party. While they worked to control the reform process, opposition groups were organizing and mobilizing. On March 15, 100,000 Hungarians carried out a powerful symbolic march passing six historical locations that referred to previous Hungarian revolutions (Stokes 1993).

Then, on June 16, 1989, a more powerful and symbolic celebration was held to commemorate the death of Imre Nagy, a Hungarian communist prime minister who had supported the revolution in 1956. Shortly after the 1988 strikes in Poland, Hungarian demonstrators commemorating the death of Nagy were violently dispersed by police despite the recent moves toward pluralism that had been allowed by Károly Grosz's administration.[4] The government had agreed to allow Nagy's relatives to rebury his remains and those of his revolutionary associates. By agreeing to Nagy's political rehabilitation, the Communist Party hoped to benefit from the popular energy that was generated through the affair. In the event, opposition leaders took the opportunity to speak out boldly against the status quo, and the funeral turned out to be a critical turning point in the efforts to transform Hungary. Viktor Orban,[5] a representative of the Young Democrats even compared Nagy's funeral to Pope John Paul II's first pilgrimage to Poland (Garton Ash 1990: 55).

Negotiations similar to Poland's Round Table began three days before Nagy's funeral. The meetings consisted of leaders from a collection of opposition groups organized as the Opposition Round Table with leaders of the communist Hungarian Socialist Worker's Party. The negotiations led to a set of proposed constitutional amendments that were passed by Hungary's parliament on October 18, 1989. In these amendments, Hungary became "an independent, democratic legal state in which the values of bourgeois democracy and democratic socialism prevail in equal measures. All power belongs to the people, which they exercise directly and through the elected representatives of popular sovereignty" (quoted in Stokes 1993: 135). When the new parliament was elected, the communists, both reformers and hard-liners, fared poorly, leaving the opposition leaders to take the helm of Hungary's new republic.

East Germany

Changes occurring in Hungary had a critical effect on the precipitous transformations underway in the German Democratic Republic (GDR). The decision to dismantle Hungary's border fences in May 1989 facilitated the exodus of East Germans to the West. At first, refugees collected on Hungary's border with Austria, and on September 11, when Hungarian authorities opened the border, 10,000 crossed in one day. Young East Germans were, in effect, voting with their feet and attempting to emigrate by the thousands. By the end of October, 50,000 East Germans had left for the west via Hungary, Prague, or Warsaw (Garton Ash 1990: 66). Once Czechoslovakia closed its border with Hungary, refugees began packing the West German embassy in Prague. On two occasions, October 1 and October 4–5, the East German government allowed trains of refugees (approximately 16,500 in total) to pass from Czechoslovakia through East Germany into West Germany. On the second occasion, additional trains transported 800 refugees west from the West German embassy in Budapest. Thousands of East Germans lined the route, and many tried to get on the trains (Darnton 1991: 69; New York Times 1991: 156–8). The permission for passage was an attempt to placate East Germans and ensure the success of the events celebrating the fortieth anniversary of the German Democratic Republic on October 6. However, to Soviet leader Mikhail Gorbachev, who attended the celebration, it was clear that East Germany was out of control (Gorbachev 1995).

The sizable demonstrations which were held across East Germany forced many in the regime to recognize the seriousness of the situation. East German communist leader Erich Honecker, for his part, seemed oblivious to the need for reform and ordered a "Chinese solution" for the demonstrations that were being held in Leipzig. For weeks, demonstrators had been congregating on Karl-Marx Platz on Mondays after "prayers for peace" at the Church of St. Nicholas; by the time Honecker ordered that the demonstrators be attacked, their numbers had grown to 70,000 (Garton Ash 1991: 67). Fortunately, Kurt Masur, the director of the local orchestra; Bend-Lutz Lange, a cabaret artist; and, a priest named Peter Zimmerman joined three local party leaders in appealing for nonviolence. The appeal was broadcast in churches and over loudspeakers, and the police action was canceled (Darnton 1991: 98–9; Garton Ash 1991: 68).[6]

Honecker resigned on October 18 leaving Egon Krenz to take his place as the leader of the Communist Party. Still, no less than 500,000 people demonstrated in East Berlin on November 4, and demonstrations were being held in other cities such as Dresden (*New York Times* 1991: 171) and, two days later, 500,000 people attended the weekly Leipzig demonstration. The growing demonstrations culminated in a "nonviolent explosion" (Garton Ash 1991: 68) on November 9 as East German authorities agreed to let a few people pass through the Berlin Wall (Darnton 1991). The trickle became a flood, and, without any preparation by the East German government, the Berlin Wall became redundant. The Communist Party's Central Committee immediately responded with a program intended to address citizens' now obvious concerns. The prologue to the program read, "A revolutionary people's movement has brought into motion a process of great change. The renewal of society is on the agenda" (New York Times 1991: 175). Apparently, the GDR's program of renewal was not sufficient. Less than one year later, on October 3, 1990, Germany became a reunified nation.[7]

Czechoslovakia

The political transformations that occurred in East Germany and Czechoslovakia were the most precipitous among the East European nations. They were more dramatic, rapid, and could more easily be referred to as "revolutions" or, in the case of Czechoslovakia, the "velvet revolution." The Czech opposition, noting that nonviolent resistance against communist regimes had been successful in Poland after ten years, in Hungary after ten months, and in East Germany after ten weeks, thought perhaps it would take Czechoslovakia "only ten days" (Garton Ash, 1990: 78). They were not far from being correct.

On November 17, 1989, a group of students in Prague gathered to commemorate the fiftieth anniversary of the death of Jan Opletal, a student who had been murdered by the Nazis. After the ceremony, they marched to Wenceslas Square where they were met by security forces. The students offered flowers to the police and held their hands in the air while reciting

"We have bare hands," but the police still moved against the students without discretion, using their truncheons. As Garton Ash (1990: 80) puts it, "This was the spark that set Czechoslovakia alight."

This phase of popular unrest was initiated by students, but its momentum was picked up by other activist organizations, especially Charter 77, a group of artists and long-time dissidents (Kriesova 1993). Civic Forum was established on November 20 from several dissident groups, and it assumed leadership of the resistance movement from its headquarters in the Magic Lantern Theater in Prague. After one week of continuous demonstrations by hundreds of thousands of people in Prague and negotiations between Civic Forum and the Communist Party, the Politburo and the party's Central Committee resigned. The following day, a Saturday, over 500,000 people gathered near the Letna football stadium for the largest rally yet held. Also, on Monday, November 27, a two-hour general strike was carried out. Only 23 days had passed since the students' demonstrations, when President Husak had sworn in a new federal government, and when he had resigned (Garton Ash 1990). Vaclav Havel, the peoples' conscience and inspiration, was installed as the new president of the Czechoslovak Socialist Republic on December 29, 1989.

Romania

Romania constituted a radical departure from the predominantly violence-free revolutions in other Soviet bloc countries, in that armed force played a significant role in the downfall of the communist regime. There were still some important nonviolent components, however.

Historically, President Nicolae Ceauşescu had ruled by means of harsh and effective security forces, and he did not hesitate to use those forces against his own citizenry as the notion of change reached Romania. On December 17, 1989, 97 peaceful demonstrators protesting the forced relocation of a reformist ethnic Hungarian minister were killed in Timisoara. Two days later, as demonstrations continued, a massive general strike was carried out that brought Timisoara to a standstill (Stokes 1993: 163). One week later, as more demonstrators honored the deaths of their fellow citizens, the security forces and army opened fire on a crowd of 100,000 people. One hundred and sixty people were killed (*New York Times* 1991: 333). However, soon after the Timisoara massacre, the regular army defected to the defense of the citizens and fighting ensued with the Securitate, Ceauşescu's highly trained security force (Stokes 1993: 163–4). On December 23, Ceauşescu and his wife were captured and immediately tried by the newly formed National Salvation Front government. They were convicted of genocide and executed in front of a firing squad on Christmas Day. The fighting diminished once the Ceauşescus were killed, and a Council of National Salvation took over as the new government.

It is noteworthy that Romania was economically and politically more isolated than other Central and Eastern European nations. As a result, Ceauşescu may have felt less pressure from outside forces, such as Gorbachev's encouragement toward reforms (*New York Times* 1991: 229; Stokes 1991: 160). Additionally, the Romanian regime probably felt less pressure from the West and had been isolated from the diffusion of nonviolent methodology that had occurred in other European nations. Consequently, there was a great deal of bloodshed before Ceauşescu was ousted.

The Baltic States

The Baltic States of Lithuania, Estonia, and Latvia represent a unique approach to reform among the Soviet bloc nations. As opposed to civil opposition groups, the national governments within these countries served as the instruments of opposition against Soviet control and influence. Unlike other Central and Eastern European nations, where dissidents led organizations into negotiations with Communist Party leaders, the state apparatus in the Baltics resolved to secede from the USSR. Lithuania led the way with a parliamentary council declaring on August 21, 1989 that the Soviet annexation of Lithuania in 1940 was void. Two days later, 2 million people joined hands in Lithuania, Estonia, and Latvia to signal their desire for their respective sovereignties. The Lithuanian parliament continued to express its intentions to Moscow through political channels and set about undermining the Communist Party's monopoly by legalizing rival political parties. Estonia made a similar move on December 7 in striking Article Six of its constitution which had ensured the privileged position of the Communist Party in national politics (*New York Times* 1991: 314).

As Lithuania seemed intent on secession, Gorbachev was equally concerned that the USSR should not disintegrate like its East European satellites. In January 1990, he traveled through Lithuania in an attempt to persuade Lithuanians to remain within the Soviet Union. Two months later, Gorbachev resorted to placing pressure on Lithuania by demanding that $33 billion be paid in the event that the Baltic country seceded. The Lithuanian parliament did in fact vote unanimously to declare its independence on March 11, 1990, and Gorbachev responded by sending paratroopers and tanks into Lithuania and placing an embargo on oil and other supplies. Under pressure, the new Lithuanian government eventually suspended all laws that had been instituted since the secession and postponed its independence. However, the government later renewed its declaration of independence, and Estonia and Latvia followed Lithuania's lead, declaring independence respectively on August 20 and 21, 1991.

Despite the fact that parliaments were the primary political actors in the Baltic States' efforts to secede from the Soviet Union, there were also instances of mass nonviolent action. There was the early "joining of hands" in each of the Baltic states. One day before Gorbachev visited Lithuania, "tens of thousands" of Lithuanians gathered in Vilnius chanting "Freedom." "Speaker after speaker acknowledged that one goal of the demonstration, which was called by the popular political organization Sajudis, was to show through the Soviet and foreign press that an over-whelming majority of Lithuanians support the call for independence" (Oleszczuk 1990: 351). Like the political transitions across Eastern Europe, change proceeded from "above" and "below" in Lithuania.

USSR

The wave of dissent that swept Central and Eastern Europe culminated in the fall of the central Communist Party system in the USSR. Gorbachev, though he had clearly deferred to popular desires for independence in Central and Eastern Europe, was not prepared for the same to occur in the USSR. He intended instead that perestroika and glasnost run their course leading to a reformed communist system. The leadership of the politically privileged Communist Party would carry out a new Marxism that Gorbachev called "humane socialism" (*New York Times* 1991: 262).

However, it became apparent that, like their Baltic neighbors, Soviet citizens in Russia desired changes in their own government. Nationalist movements were similarly developing in Moldavia, Georgia, Ukraine, Uzbekistan, Kazakhstan, and Tadzhikistan. In some of these regions, such as Armenia and Azerbaijan, ethnic violence was breaking out (Smith 1990: 295). Against this background of increasing entropy, 50,000 or more people demonstrated in Moscow on February 25, 1990 to express their disappointment in Gorbachev and the Communist Party and to promote pro-democracy candidates for the Russian parliament. According to news reports, the authorities attempted to suppress the rally by threatening bloodshed, and the Russian Orthodox Church requested that people stay in their homes (*New York Times* 1991: 375).

Over the course of one year, a rift widened between the central Soviet government and the national Russian government. Gorbachev was pro-vided additional emergency powers by the Soviet parliament and was re-elected as head of the Communist Party. At the same time, Boris Yeltsin assumed the presidency of Russia and left the Communist Party soon after the Russian parliament declared that its laws took priority over Soviet laws. The Russian parliament even went so far as to refuse to pay its usual share of the Soviet budget. The rift between Russia and the Soviet government expressed itself most blatantly during the coup attempt launched on Mon-day, August 19, 1991 by the hardline "State Committee for the State of Emergency" (*New York Times* 1991: 520).

During the coup, Gorbachev was removed from power and placed under house arrest while the new self-proclaimed leadership moved troops into

Moscow, banned protest meetings and closed independent newspapers. Yeltsin immediately opposed the putschists. Addressing a crowd from atop an armored vehicle, he called for a general strike to be held the following day at which he addressed a crowd of 20,000, while another 2,000 people had gathered at Leningrad's city hall where they were addressed by Mayor Sobchak. By evening in Moscow, 25,000 people had arrived at the Russian Government building, and many began building barricades and pledging to remain in defense of the parliament building (*New York Times* 1991: 517–25). Citizens created a ring around the building while government leaders inside prepared for battle with the Soviet troops that were not already defecting to the people. At one point in the middle of the day, more than 30,000 people had gathered outside the parliament building. Yeltsin instructed the crowd: "The military has become a weapon in the hands of the putschists. Therefore, we should also support the military and maintain order and discipline in contact with them" (*New York Times* 1991: 532). Some violence did occur during the second night of the coup when molotov cocktails were thrown at military vehicles, and three people were killed by armored carrier movements.

During the third day of the coup, the State Committee for the State of Emergency relented, and the coup collapsed. Gorbachev returned to Moscow congratulating Yeltsin and those who engaged in the nonviolent resistance for their success. The coup leaders had found it impossible to carry out their plans for a new Soviet government because popular resistance had been widespread in Moscow and Leningrad and military units had defected to the point that the coup leaders could not rally the political or logistical resources necessary to meet their goals.

Nonviolent Action

A comprehensive catalog of nonviolent action in the former Soviet bloc is beyond the scope of the current chapter, but several key features were particularly salient. First, it is important to recognize that most of the nonviolent action was not spontaneous, but it was cultivated and promoted outside of the state with the help of what activists and scholars call "parallel institutions" in the civil society: cultural institutions, civic organizations, and the church. Second, the resistance usually took the form of nonviolent protest, though there were some instances of nonviolent non-cooperation such as strikes. Third, what we are calling the "paradox of repression" was the primary conflict dynamic that made nonviolent action successful in the Soviet bloc. Some communist leaders recognized the folly of suppressing citizens through physical force while others carried out suppressive measures and found that they only fueled the determination of opposition activists. We will begin by addressing parallel institutions since their development tends to precede nonviolent action and the paradox of repression.

Parallel institutions

Successful social movements generally develop an infrastructure that serves to recruit, train, encourage, and mobilize activists Regardless of the types of methods used in opposing a central government, movement activists construct alternative or autonomous "spaces" in which opposition frames and strategies can be disseminated. In each of the Soviet bloc countries, non-violent resistance operated from alternative spaces, notably the Church, the Academy, the cultural community, and the media.

The creation and utilization of public space is not, of course, entirely unique to nonviolent action, but it is crucial, especially if one acknowledges that ideas are important for the motivation and cohesion of any resistance (Weigel 1992; Snow et al.). Nonviolent resistance is no exception. In fact, effective education in the principles of nonviolent action is important because of the discipline that nonviolent action requires. Parallel institutions preserve not only a spirit of resistance but ideologies that complement nonviolent action.

The Church The Church has often played a crucial role in nurturing courage and a spirit of resistance by providing time and space in which nonviolent resistance can be planned and carried out, due to the fact that it possesses vast institutional resources, cultural capital, and a Polish pope (Weigel 1992). Indeed, it was the only major institution in civil society to which the communist state was initially forced to grant some autonomy. In Poland, thousands of Catholic catechetical centers were established, in which as Weigel (1992: 113) claims, "many of those [Solidarity] consciences were first found, and the final revolution gestated". Other Polish programs included "Oasis" summer camps for families which later became the "Light and Life" movement that promoted the nonviolent principle of living "as if" Poland were truly free. Three hundred thousand Polish youth took part in the movement from the mid-1970s to the late 1980s.

Father Jerzy Popieluszko, who was martyred by the state for his dissidence, had already served as a chaplain to the striking workers of Warsaw when he began a monthly "Mass for the Fatherland." During these services, the priest spoke openly about human rights and nonviolent resistance. His homilies attracted Poles by the thousands, and he continually reminded the nation that it would have to decide whether or not to live "as if" it were free. When Popieluszko was killed by state security officers, mourners occupied his church by the thousands for ten days.

In East Germany, most resistance emerged from the Protestant church (*New York Times* 1991: 226). For Protestant Slovakians, the most common type of protest was pilgrimage. Five hundred thousand people went on pilgrimages in 1988, and one particular pilgrimage to Levoca involved 100,000 people (*New York Times* 1991: 312).

Cultural and Academic Institutions   These also played a critical role in the development of nonviolent social movements. In Czechoslovakia, the "Velvet Revolution" began when students used school buildings and resources to organize demonstrations and disseminate information about the "massacre" that police perpetuated against demonstrators on November 17, 1989. Once Civic Forum picked up the momentum initiated by the students, the artistic community in Czechoslovakia volunteered time and a wide range of resources (Garton Ash 1990; Stokes 1993). For instance, Vaclav Havel and other dissidents led their nonviolent campaign from the basement of a local theater called "The Magic Lantern." Other theater owners offered their spaces as forums for debate and showed videos of the violent suppression of students. Similarly, the Polish Student Theater played an important role in the early stages of the development of an opposition movement in Poland (Goldfarb 1980).

A similar phenomenon occurred in the East German city of Leipzig, where discussions and demonstrations were conducted in various nongovernmental public spaces as Robert Darnton (1991: 100) observes:

> The Gewandhaus, the opera, and the university surrounding Karl Marx Platz, where the demonstrations begin, constitute a new public space in opposition to the actual town hall, farther down the ring of boulevards. Together with the churches, they represent the only institutions around which public life can form. In a system where the Party has monopolized power, politics has taken refuge in the sphere of culture, and legitimacy has shifted to the intellectuals – ministers, musicians, actors, writers, and professors, or at least a few dissident professors in the lower ranks of the faculty.

Darnton expresses the way in which alternative institutions may parallel official ones. The opera house and the university took on some of the functions of the town hall; the parallel institutions thus oppose official structures and may even make them redundant.

Media   Finally, one can hardly overestimate the importance of the media to the success of nonviolent resistance in the Soviet bloc; indeed they constitute a structural element crucial to the success of the insurgencies. An assortment of media sources were used as parallel institutions to disseminate new ideology that contradicted the conventional communist Rhetoric. For decades, the Communist regimes strove to maintain strict control over the media, both the institutional and the underground media. Yet, despite the censorship policies, there were some sources of critical journalism that managed to survive alongside the legal communist ones. Over the years, the Polish Catholic church's press *Tygodnik Powszechny* (Universal Weekly) and the Catholic intellectual month *Znak* (Sign) managed to publish high-quality material that reflected the Polish situation in a fair and critical light despite harassment by the State (Monticone 1986; Weigel 1992).

In other countries, underground or *samizdat* materials made their way into the hands of citizens and encouraged ideological shifts that undergirded nonviolent action. In Hungary Laszlo Rajk, who operated a "samizdat boutique" in his apartment, supplied intellectual dissidents with unofficial literature (Stokes 1993: 89). Over many years, these sorts of activities educated future dissidents and provided coherence to the movements that later confronted communist regimes.

Gorbachev's glasnost policies and modern media technology meant that oppositional material could finally be found not only in underground sources, but through officially sanctioned media outlets. As censorship was relaxed in the name of "openness," newspapers offered critical analyses that resonated strongly with their readers. Garton Ash (1990) describes Czechoslovakian enthusiasm for the new journalism: "At six o'clock in the morning on Wenceslas Square you saw a line of hundreds of people waiting patiently in the freezing mist. They were waiting to buy a copy of the Socialist Party newspaper, *Svobodne Slovo* (The Free Word), which was the first to carry accurate reports of the demonstrations and Forum statements (Garton Ash 1990: 91). Other newspapers such as *Lidova Demokracie* (People's Democracy) and *Mlada Fronta* (Young Front) followed (Kriseova 1993); the more citizens learned about the state of their political circumstances and the opposition, the less their fear inhibited them.

Television technology proved to be at least as effective as print media. A picture truly is worth a thousand words, and both opposition and communist leaders knew it. According to Jacek Kuron, during the Polish Round Table negotiations, one party leader said, "'We'll give you the Zomo (riot police) before we give you the TV.' 'And he's quite right,' commented Kuron, 'I'd much rather have the TV'" (Garton Ash 1990: 26). As it turned out, after the Round Table talks, Solidarity was allowed one half-hour of weekly television broadcast time, one hour of weekly radio time, a daily national newspaper, and a regional weekly newspaper (*New York Times* 1991: 35).

Images broadcast on television and radio provided citizens and activists with current information on the political situations in their respective countries and the potentials of nonviolent protest. Television broadcasts of Imre Nagy's funeral electrified Hungary, and as Garton Ash (1990: 15) points out, the movement was conducted in the media as much as on the streets. In Romania, even the brief image of citizens waving their fists at Ceauşescu and his wife were enough to awaken the population at large (Stokes 1993: 165).

Neighboring countries also learned from each other's experiences through television; East Germans learned of the Polish and Hungarian situations from daily West German television broadcasts (Garton Ash 1990: 66). Most East Germans only learned of their own Neues Forum (New Forum) when the GDR denounced the organization and West German media reported the story (*New York Times* 1991: 168). In each of these instances, the media or other parallel institutions provided ideological, material, or informational resources that aided the mobilization of citizens to effective nonviolent action.

Nonviolent Protest

Perhaps the most popular and well-known form of nonviolent action is nonviolent protest. Methods that fall into this category are used to alter the opinion of an opponent or a third party about the bases of conflict such as actionists' grievances (Sharp 1973). The collective expression of popular will can be powerfully persuasive, especially when opponents interpret the protest as symbolic of a real withdrawal of consent. The effect is maximized when activists incorporate creative variations of protest that directly address the issues at hand and resonate with opponents. The use of nonviolent protest was widespread in Central and Eastern Europe and the USSR, and many rallies incorporated the use of creative conflict symbols to communicate a frame alignment between the movements, goals and widespread grievances in civil society. The fact that agents of the state sometimes responded violently partially testifies to the effectiveness of the method. We will return to the issue of repression later, but first let us demonstrate some of the ways in which citizens adapted nonviolent protest to their needs.

Hungary

The official funeral of Imre Nagy in Budapest, Hungary on June 16, 1989 was an effective symbolic event that raised national awareness of the potential for opposition. Nagy was a communist politician who served twice as Hungary's premier in the 1950s and provoked Russian military intervention when he introduced liberal policies and weakened Hungary's ties with other Warsaw Pact nations (Garton Ash 1990). He was consequently hanged on June 16, 1956, but his official state funeral was not held until 33 years later. Two hundred and fifty thousand people attended the ceremony in 1989. Despite attempts by the Communist Party to co-opt the event, popular opposition was expressed through speeches from the podium and through the creative use of symbols by those in attendance. As in 1956, insurgents cut out the hammer and sickle from their flags, leaving holes in their centers. Opposition leaders spoke in open criticism of communist leaders in attendance while the event was carried live on national television (Garton Ash 1990; *New York Times* 1991: 133–136).

East Germany

Citizens in East Germany attended massive rallies in the country's major cities. During the summer and autumn months of 1989, people gathered weekly on Mondays at Karl-Marx Platz in Leipzig, East Germany following "prayers for peace" in the nearby Church of St. Nicholas. The demonstrations were initially small and were often violently dispersed by the police, but by October, the protesters' numbers had mushroomed to approximately 20,000 people. On the day after Gorbachev left East Germany, having attended the GDR's fortieth anniversary celebrations, 50,000–70,000 people attended the demonstration on Karl-Marx Platz. Garton Ash (1990: 67) describes the event as a critical turning point in the East German revolution: "They sung the Internationale and demanded the legalization of the recently founded 'citizens' initiative', New Forum. The police were baffled, and in places peacefully overwhelmed." After speeches, the demonstrators walked through the city carrying candles and banners. The demonstrations grew even larger as the Communist Party's crisis worsened, and by November 6, 500,000 people were attending the weekly demonstration (Darnton 1991).

Czechoslovakia

Some of the most dramatic protests were conducted in Czechoslovakia. Petition signing campaigns grew into regular public demonstrations, often in Wenceslas Square, where thousands of Czechoslovakians listened to addresses by Vaclav Havel and other opposition leaders. The rallies were highly charged events, and many observers have commented on the way in which the crowds developed a collective voice that often spoke in unison and answered those addressing the crowd (Kriseova 1993; *New York Times* 1991: 305).

> The crowd answered the speakers, talked back to them. Often I wondered where the genius of the crowd was located, who led it, and who thought up its slogans. Was there one person who was the first to shout a slogan, and then the others joined in; or did these words and sentences arise in many minds simultaneously? Perhaps there was some kind of higher direction the crowd was listening to, instructions that were simultaneously whispered into thousands and hundreds of thousands of ears. It was a miracle; I can offer no explanations. (Kriseova 1993: 250)

Regardless of who organized the collective voice, it apparently left a significant impression on observers and contributed to a collective effervescence (Durkheim [1912] 1965: 241–2) and the perception that supernatural powers were at work (Garton Ash 1990: 128; Kriseova 1993). The effect aided citizens in overcoming their fear of retaliation by authorities. One can imagine that the authorities observed such protests with a certain awe. When communist prime minister Ladislav Adamec addressed cheering crowds at the Letna playing fields in Czechoslovakia, they soon turned against him with protests of "Too late, too late!" when he began reverting to the old communist rhetoric (Kriseova 1993). Nonviolent protests such as this one were a form of public discourse with authorities, and the collective voice carried substantial political power, what Havel (1990) calls "the power of the powerless."

Other examples of symbolic protest include the stopping of clock hands positioned at five minutes before midnight as a sign that "time is up for the Communist Party" in Czechoslovakia (*New York Times* 1991: 256). Many of these nonviolent protests were highly effective at communicating popular grievances. However, protest was not the only nonviolent method used in the Soviet bloc.

Nonviolent Non-cooperation & Nonviolent Intervention

Sharp (1973) specifies two main methods besides nonviolent protest and persuasion: nonviolent non-cooperation and nonviolent intervention, methods less common than protest in the Soviet bloc, but significant elements in the resistance. In noncooperation, activists intentionally withdraw their usual cooperation with a regime (Sharp 1973: 183), resulting in a breach in the normal operation of day to day life; the classic example is the strike.

One might argue that workers' strikes and the creation of the opposition party, Solidarity, marked the beginning of the end for communists in Poland. In Czechoslovakia, Romania, and Russia protesters successfully orchestrated general strikes. Massive nonviolent noncooperation occurred in East Germany when thousands of young, skilled East Germans fled across Hungary's border with Austria or took refuge in West German embassies. East Germany hemorrhaged, losing citizens who otherwise contributed significantly to the routine operation of the country. In Lithuania, it was the parliament who planned to use noncooperation strategically in the event that the Soviet army overran the country. In an extraordinary resolution, the parliament declared that "In the event a regime of active occupation is introduced, citizens of the Republic of Lithuania are asked to adhere to principles of disobedience, non-violent resistance, and political and social non-cooperation as the primary means of struggle for independence" (quoted in Roberts 1991: 29). Lithuanians were not forced to carry out the campaign, perhaps because the declaration itself served as a deterrent to the deployment of Soviet troops. Still, it is noteworthy that a state government opted to promote nonviolent methods as opposed to violent methods such as guerrilla actions.

Nonviolent intervention

Nonviolent intervention is more proactive than protest or noncooperation; activists deliberately interrupt a targeted institution or activity rather than simply withdrawing cooperation or voicing protest (Sharp 1973: 357–8). In both Romania and Russia, unarmed citizens surrounded opposition head-quarters to deter attacks by armed state-controlled military forces. Russians created a human ring around the Russian Parliament building to protect it, and in another instance blocked armored personnel carriers at Manezh Square (*New York Times* 1991: 525, 531). In Romania, activists considered it imperative that Free Romanian Television's Studio 4 not be taken, since it had become the heart of the opposition movement. Consequently, thou-sands of students intervened and surrounded the station to ensure that its broadcasts continued.[8]

The most spectacular event in the 1989 revolutions was also a form of nonviolent intervention: the fall of the Berlin Wall. On November 9 a Politburo spokesman casually announced a "vaguely worded addendum to a new set of rules for permanent emigration" (Stokes 1993: 141). The new rule promised citizens prompt permission for trips abroad, but the spokesman did not know if the rule applied to West Berlin. East Germans decided to intervene and test the rule. They congregated at the wall, and eventually convinced border officers to let people pass without authoriza-tion. The trickle quickly became a flood and Germans began defiantly dismantling the wall piece by piece (Stokes 1993: 141). East Germans used both nonviolent noncooperation and nonviolent intervention, but throughout the Soviet bloc these methods were used infrequently.

Paradox of Repression

One of the core dynamics of nonviolent action lies in the *paradox of repression*: in an asymmetrical conflict, when the opponent representing the status quo uses force (psychological, physical, economic, or otherwise) to repress its nonviolent opponents, the repression often ironically weakens the regime's authority and strengthens the opposition. Public opinion is likely to turn against the repressive regime. Paradoxically, the more the regime applies force, the more citizens and third parties are likely to become disaffected, sometimes to such an extreme that the regime disin-tegrates from internal dissent. Sharp's (1973) notion of nonviolent action as a form of "political *jiu-jitsu*" is an example of how the paradox of repres-sion works. Like the techniques of many martial arts, employing the para-dox of repression causes an oppressor's use of force to rebound and become counterproductive.

The paradox of repression was perhaps the defining element of nonvio-lent conflict in the Soviet bloc revolts, partly because Gorbachev under-stood its importance. In order for his perestroika and glasnost programs to be successful, he could not afford to sacrifice any portion of the Soviet system's popular legitimacy. Gorbachev intended to rally the support of citizens, to motivate them toward carrying out the sort of work and sacrifices required to pull the Soviet economy out of its slump, thus renewing faith in the Communist Party and the Soviet system. Gorbachev's reforms required popular support, and he knew that repression of Soviet bloc citizens would delegitimize the regime.

There is also reason to believe that other communist leaders experienced a sense of revulsion toward the prospect of repression. Perhaps a turning point in the opposition to the Soviet regime was an incident in Tbilisi, Georgia, when troops opened fire on peaceful demonstrators. Public opposition to the action was swift and negative. When military force was finally used in Moscow by communist authorities attempting to unseat Gorbachev in a coup, the very few deaths that did occur triggered a local and global reaction.

One explanation for the coup's collapse was shared both by Prime Minister Valentin Pavlov, one of the participants, and by Alexander Yakovlev. Both said that the Emergency Committee's most stupid mistake was deploying troops and tanks in Moscow. Without that, the resistance would have been much less focused and the overall impression much more one of business as usual, and of course there would not have been the deaths of three young men on the night of August 20, which horrified the country, the world, and probably even the plotters themselves (Palazchenko 1997: 314–15). The emergency committee's military strategy had backfired horribly and crippled their coup.

East German leaders experienced the same bind when Erich Honecker decreed a "Chinese solution" to the massive protests in Leipzig and East Berlin. Pressured by the hemorrhage of emigration and the obvious level of popular discontent, Honecker decided that the country's youth had to be restrained; extreme means would be used against the protesters just as Chinese forces had opened fire on demonstrators in Tiananmen Square. Some of Honecker's advisors saw the futility in such a strategy, however; Erich Mielke, the tough 82–year-old security chief reportedly told Mr. Honecker, "Erich, we can't beat up hundreds of thousands of people" (*New York Times* 1991: 219). Given the choice of supporting a crudely oppressive regime or nonviolent demonstrators, several members of the Politburo began to express sympathies with the latter. The issue of repression in Leipzig was a final step toward Erich Honecker's resignation.

The violent actions of police towards student protesters in Prague on November 17, 1989 provide an excellent example of the paradox of repression. Students had organized a demonstration to commemorate the death of Jan Opletal, a Czech student martyred by the Nazis. After the program, 1,500 of the students marched toward Wenceslas square where riot police in Narodni Avenue confronted the students who were singing, handing out flowers, and carrying candles. The police moved against the demonstrators with tear gas, truncheons, and attack dogs (Garton Ash 1990: 80; Kriesova 1993: 245). The next day, activists in the cultural community began organizing and Civic Forum took over the momentum that had been initiated by the students. The effectiveness of nonviolent action and repression in Narodni Avenue can be attributed to the fact that many people witnessed the event. The attack of the riot police was caught on videotape, and the footage was duplicated and shown in Prague Theaters. Students even carried the tapes out into rural areas attempting to gather support for the resistance being conducted in Prague (Kriseova 1993). In this way, the paradox of repression was magnified as greater numbers of people witnessed, and in a sense experienced, the repression from a distance.

One particular manifestation of the paradox of repression occurs when military personnel become disaffected with serving as instruments or tools of repression (Sharp 1973). When military personnel are ordered to move against nonviolent demonstrators, they may find the psychological costs of repression too great and may refuse to carry out orders against popular opposition. On August 20, 1991, for example, the coup leaders in Moscow ordered a unit of troops to storm the Russian parliament building where citizens had gathered for its defense. The soldiers simply refused to follow the orders, and Gorbachev subsequently referred to them as heroes (Palazchenko 1997: 314). After deaths in Vilnius and Riga, Soviet commanders in the Baltics also declared that they would not give orders to shoot citizens. Likewise, deaths in Tbilisi provoked military commanders to insist that the army should not be used as a domestic police force (Reddaway 1993). These examples demonstrate the centrality of the paradox of repression to the Soviet bloc revolutions. Nonviolent action was successful in part because communist authorities were profoundly affected by the potential repercussions of repression.

The Relevance of Nonviolent Action[9]

In the course of presenting preliminary drafts of this chapter at professional meetings, we have found that some scholars de- emphasize the relevance of nonviolent action in the Soviet bloc, arguing instead that economic and political crises precipitated the transitions to democracy and free market economies. According to this thesis, the Soviet systems were self-limiting and their failures bred discontent not only among the general populace but also among the elites. Elites encouraged reforms when they saw the writing on the wall warning that the Soviet system was inefficient to the point of collapse. By participating in semi-controlled transitions elites could position themselves favorably in the new market economies. They might thus retain their positions of leadership and reap the benefits of power (Misztal 1993). When nonintervention policies were put into effect, with Gorbachev making it clear that Soviet troops would not be used to prop up communist regimes, progressive leaders seized the opportunity and reforms proliferated.

According to this line of argument, activists in opposition groups sensed the same opportunities and organized nonviolent protests ensued, but their actions were secondary causes of reform. Some scholars thus suggest that the combination of political and economic crises plus the willingness of communist leaders to pursue radical reforms makes popular nonviolent action increasingly irrelevant.

We agree with Adam Roberts' (1991: 31) assertion that "There can be no pretense that civil resistance alone and in splendid isolation brought about the dramatic changes...The best overall explanation of the process is probably to be found in words attributed to Napoleon: 'All Empires die of indigestion'" Gorbachev, addressing the Communist Party Central Committee, identified a similar Soviet problem:

> Where there is delay in dealing with overripe problems, excesses are inevitable. What is taking place in socialist countries is the logical outcome of a certain stage of development which makes the peoples of these countries aware of the need for change. This is the result of internal development, the result of choice by peoples themselves...We proceed from the fact that any nation has the right to decide its fate itself, including the choice of a system, ways, the pace and methods of its development (*New York Times* 1991: 320).

Gorbachev attributes changes to both system problems *and* popular will. Certainly, economic and political malaise contributed heavily to the environment in which the sweeping changes of the late 1980s occurred (Misztal 1993). However, it is also difficult to discount the role of nonviolent action as a catalyst that accelerated changes (Reddaway 1993). We believe that a combination of Soviet reforms led by Gorbachev *and* effective nonviolent action precipitated the rapid disintegration of the Soviet bloc.

In fact, there was change proceeding both from "above" and "below." Some communist elites promoted reform policies which allowed the growth of popular opposition which in turn precipitated further reform. Garton Ash (1990: 14) has accordingly called the transitions in the Soviet bloc "refolutions":

> Even in Poland and Hungary, what was happening could still hardly be described as a revolution. It was in fact, a mixture of reform and revolution. At the time, I called it 'refolution.' There was a strong and essential element of change 'from above', led by an enlightened minority in the still ruling communist parties. But there was also a vital element of popular pressure 'from below.' In Hungary, there was rather more of the former, in Poland of the latter, yet in both countries the story was that of an interaction between the two."

The fall of Soviet regimes was the result of an interaction between state-level reforms and popular resistance. Often, the lion's share of credit falls to Gorbachev and his policies of perestroika and glasnost. However, we would like to preserve a place for popular nonviolent action and its important contribution to the fall of communist regimes.

The argument that nonviolent social movements did not play a significant role suffers from at least three deficiencies. First, it fails to see nonviolent opposition as a long-term project that extends decades into the past. The 1989 revolutions did not erupt spontaneously but were the result of decades of unrest, during which mobilized movements fueled by the bold acts of dissidents, led to the cultivation of a robust civil society throughout the Soviet bloc. Second, it fails to acknowledge the global nature of nonviolent action and nonviolent movements, especially given modern media technology. Vaclav Havel appreciated both of these notions:

> And we ask: Where did young people who had never known another system get their longing for truth, their love of freedom, their political imagination, their civic courage and civic responsibility? How did their parents, precisely the generation thought to have been lost, join them? How is it possible that so many people immediately understood what to do and that none of them needed any advice or instructions?...Naturally we too had to pay for our present-day freedom. Many of our citizens died in prison in the 1950s. Many were executed. Thousands of human lives were destroyed. Hundreds of thousands of talented people were driven abroad...Those who fought against totalitarianism during the war were also persecuted...Nobody who paid in one way or another for our freedom could be forgotten....But we should also not forget that other nations paid an even harsher price for their present freedom, and paid indirectly for ours as well. All human suffering concerns each human being.... Without changes in the Soviet Union, Poland, Hungary and the German Democratic Republic, what happened here could hardly have taken place, and certainly not in such a calm and peaceful way. (Havel 1990: 279)

Traditions of opposition, however small, were maintained in various Central and Eastern European countries by intellectuals and activists. Many who led opposition at the end of the 1980s had honed their skills in political, union, peace, nuclear, and environmental movements in the 1970s and early 1980s (Morton and Landy 1988; New York Times 1991: 168; Smith 1990: 12).

Third, the skeptics' view of nonviolent action often assumes that successful nonviolent action is the kind that coerces the opponent into submission, whereas the preferable outcome within nonviolent theory is the conversion of the opponent. Part of the subtle power of nonviolent resistance is that it facilitates efforts to persuade opponents to accommodate activists. Sometimes opponents' world views are even altered. Victory does not require that the opponent be taken away kicking and screaming; compromise and accommodation may also be acceptable. In the Soviet bloc, flexibility on the part of communist leaders often reflected the ability of popular movements to persuade *and* coerce leaders toward reform.

Time

One central theme of this book is the diffusion of nonviolent methods across time and space. Indeed an historical perspective is essential because nonviolent resistance in Central and Eastern Europe began long before 1988 (Roberts 1991: 34). Resistance had been offered on various occasions and was often firmly put down. While these historical repressions are often viewed as unqualified failures, they have served a purpose through the paradox of repression. The suppression of opposition movements by Soviet forces left a mark on the collective memories of Central and Eastern European societies. The limited "failures" of earlier nonviolent action in Czechoslovakia, Poland, and Hungary thus became symbols around which contemporary protest in the 1980s was constructed.

In Czechoslovakia, for example, the protest of Jan Palach became highly relevant to nonviolent protest 20 years after his death. Palach was a young philosophy student at Prague University when Russian tanks were sent into Czechoslovakia as a response to the Prague Spring. In protest over the invasion, Palach martyred himself by self-immolation on January 16, 1969. He died three days later and more than half a million people attended his funeral in Prague while additional memorial services were held across the country (Sharp 1973). Twenty years after Palach's protests, civic organizations arranged demonstrations to commemorate his death. The police insisted that the crowd disperse and charged with truncheons. Eda Kriseova (1993: 235),[10] described the importance of the event:

> The proud authorities would not allow people to honor the memory of a dead man, and by this they had done more to revive his memory than Havel could have if he had spoken, and perhaps more than a new human torch could have done, if one had been lit. Face to face with truncheons, people felt even closer to Jan Palach, who had intended his death to be a warning against this kind of violence. As if by a miracle, the years all merged together.

Whether or not Palach's protest was purely nonviolent is debatable, but the paradox of repression is clearly in effect and his death precipitated non-violent protest. Hungary's posthumous tribute to Nagy and other dissidents of the 1956 Hungarian Revolution, demonstrates the historical link between 1989 and earlier nonviolent protest was not used in historical isolation.

Nonviolent demonstrations were often powerful because they drew on traditions of opposition. Even when historical opposition was violent, contemporary movements were able to capitalize on the paradox of repression for their nonviolent protests. Visions of Jan Palach's self-immolation and Nagy's execution during periods of Soviet intervention were revived in the public conscience and used with effect in the 1980s. The tradition of opposition on which nonviolent action relies is much broader than one might expect by looking only at the nonviolent action that was temporally proximate to the fall of communist regimes.

The Pope's visit to Poland in 1979 occurred over ten years before the Polish United Worker's Party dissolved, but his tour of the country set the stage for the revolutions that followed. One decade before the Communist Party disbanded, Karol Wojtyla made his first official pilgrimage to Poland as Pope John Paul II. He delivered 32 sermons to 13 million Poles and laid the groundwork for resistance and eventually the formation of Solidarity (Weigel 1992: 131, 133). The Pope boldly criticized communism and prepared the people to make choices about opposition: "The real danger for both sides – for the Church and for the other side, call it what you will – is the man who does not take a risk and accept a challenge, who does not listen to his deepest convictions, to his inner truth, but who only wants to fit somehow, to float in conformity, moving from left to right as the wind blows" (Weigel 1992: 132). These papal masses were in themselves an act of nonviolent protest, since communist governments across Central and Eastern Europe were openly hostile to religious institutions.

At the Pope's most acclaimed appearance, on the first day of his visit in Warsaw's Victory Square, thousands of Polish citizens attended and repeatedly interrupted the Pope's sermon, chanting "We want God!" The Pope was reported to reply "People are preaching with me" (Weigel 1992: 132). Adam Michnik called the pilgrimage a "national plebiscite" and Bogdan Szajkowski, a political scientist, referred to it as "a psychological earthquake, an opportunity for mass political catharsis." Garton Ash (1990: 133) saw the Pope's first pilgrimage as a turning point: "Here for the first time, we saw that massive, sustained, yet supremely peaceful and self-disciplined manifestation of social unity, the gentle crowd against the Party-state." Thus, Pope John Paul II's pilgrimage provided a unique context in which Polish citizens could express their discontent with the communist regime.

Before the Pope's pilgrimage, Cardinal Wyszynski's nine-year Great Novena beginning in 1966 served as an exercise in religious solidarity in the midst of a "secular" socialist state. The portrait of the Black Madonna visited every parish in the country and was received with "fervor" and the program developed into a nonviolent competition with the communist leadership. In the final year, Cardinal Wyszynski himself made pilgrimage around the country where he was greeted each time by "tens and hundreds of thousands." The state countered with a forged book of the Cardinal's sermons. The Church and the state also engaged in a symbolic battle of banners. The Catholic authorities had decided to hang banners in the nation's streets to celebrate the approaching millennium of the Church. The state responded to each successive banner with its own banner (Weigel 1992). After the Pope's pilgrimage, his mantel was taken up by Father Jerzy Popieluszko, other resistance priests, and the intellectual left.

In order to appreciate the full effect of nonviolent opposition in the latter half of the 1980s, one must recognize that nonviolent opposition had been the writing on the wall for many years in Central and Eastern European countries, particularly in those among the first to move away from communism. Gorbachev and Krenz both recognized the powerful relationship between the historical withdrawal of consent in East Germany and the current manifestations that were being expressed through nonviolent protest: "We agreed that it would be naive to reduce the political crisis in his country to the developments of the past few months: in reality, the problems had been accumulating for years... Mass exodus to 'the West', a growing tide of demonstrations, civil disobedience, and open threats against the authorities threatened a peaceful settlement of the crisis" (Gorbachev 1995: 526). In summary, nonviolent resistance was not confined to the latter years of the Soviet bloc, it had been wearing away at the hegemony of communist regimes while at the same time developing a history of resistance that served as a foundation during the final revolutions.

Space

Nonviolent protests outside of the Soviet bloc contributed to the revolutions within, and those within Central and Eastern Europe contributed to one another. Certainly Gorbachev's decision not to send in troops to crush insurgencies encouraged those who were already flooding out of East Germany, those who would participate in rallies in Czechoslovakia and Romania, and reforming politicians in the Baltic States. However, nonviolent action in non-Soviet countries not only facilitated nonviolent movements in Eastern Europe but also helped to produce Soviet nonintervention policies. Gorbachev's positive encounters with students in China profoundly affected his reaction to China's suppression of demonstrators. During the height of the student protest in Tiananmen Square, Gorbachev visited China and intentionally sought contact with the Chinese dissident Jiang Zemin. On one occasion, his motorcade came across a student demonstration:

> We stopped, got out of our cars, and shook hands. The demonstrators maintained perfect order and themselves organized a living corridor, through which we calmly drove with our guard behind us. In short, our diverse contacts with Chinese youth confirmed for me that I had acted correctly in deciding not to postpone my visit to China, even though some of our comrades had wondered whether the student demonstrations in Beijing might not interfere with its successful conduct.

On June 4, 1989, army and police forces entered Tiananmen Square to remove student demonstrators who had been protesting nonviolently for seven weeks. Gorbachev issued a statement of regret that "combined noninterference... with a sincere interest in the stable development... along the path of reform and openness with civil peace and non-violence" (Gorbachev 1995: 493).

According to Yan Jia Qi (1992), former head of the Beijing Academy of Political Sciences, it was ironically the Tienanmen massacre that made it possible for insurgents to be successful in the Soviet bloc, because it demonstrated to Gorbachev the moral and political problems of using brutal repression to put down popular protests. On October 25, 1989, Gennady Gerasimov, a foreign ministry spokesman, announced that the Soviet Union did not have the right to interfere in the political affairs of Central and Eastern European countries. He explained that the policy was reminiscent of Frank Sinatra's song "I Did it My Way." The Soviet bloc countries would be allowed to do it their way.

Shortly before the announcement of the "Sinatra Doctrine," Gorbachev visited East Germany where citizens were expressing their desire to go their own way as well. As with his visit to China, Gorbachev encountered activists and demonstrators when he attended events commemorating the fortieth anniversary of the GDR in early October 1989. Erich Honecker, the long-time Communist leader of East Germany, had invited Gorbachev to the ceremonies, and while he was there, East German citizens appealed to him for help in reforming their situation. Gorbachev narrates his experience and thoughts in his memoirs:

> I left Berlin with mixed feelings. The image of that enormous stream of humanity, the thousands of German boys and girls – healthy, strong, welcoming, thirsting for changes – had made an impression on me that instilled hope and optimism. But there was something else, too. In my memory there remained the cautious, concentrated faces of the SED leadership each of whom, it seemed, was preparing to make his decision... I returned to Moscow in a state of alarm. The country reminded me of an overheated boiler with the lid tightly closed. The danger was there for everyone to see, and subsequent events vindicated my premonitions. The crisis reached its breaking point only two weeks later... Thank God, the new East German leadership had the courage and enough common sense to refrain from trying to quench the popular unrest in blood. I believe that the Soviet position had also contributed to this; the East German leaders realized that Soviet troops would not leave their barracks under any circumstances (1995: 526).

Not only did the Tienanmen movement affect Gorbachev, his response facilitated further nonviolent action throughout the Soviet bloc in the following months.

Additional research is needed into the broader diffusion of nonviolent techniques over time and space; nonviolent movements around the world influenced political culture in the Soviet bloc long before the 1989 revolutions. For example, Soviet news agencies loved to broadcast footage of the American civil rights movement as a form of anti-American propaganda. Ironically, the broadcasts may have educated their own activists in the potential of nonviolent protest and other techniques.

Conversion and coercion

Sometimes, the effectiveness of nonviolent action is downplayed on the grounds that Communist leaders were simply "giving in." Some think nonviolent action is only effective when it is obvious that communist leaders were clearly forced from power once they simply had no more options. However, it is important to realize that nonviolent action can produce multiple results, including what Sharp (1973) calls conversion, accommodation, and nonviolent coercion. In conversion, an opponent's will is transformed such that the opponent desires to meet the requests of the nonviolent activist. Accommodation, a combination of conversion and coercion, occurs when the opponent's will is not entirely transformed, but the opponent is compelled to grant concessions. Nonviolent coercion results when a regime's ability to function is sufficiently crippled by the withdrawal of consent that the regime is forced to concede by default.

Coercion, was rarely the final result of nonviolent action in the Soviet bloc. Nicolae Ceauşescu was clearly coerced, even to the point of execution, but the means of his removal were considerably more violent than in any of the other East European countries. His regime was finally swept away only after intense fighting between Ceauşescu's security forces and army units. Certainly, there were individual incidents in which communist leaders felt constrained by nonviolent techniques. As we have already noted, repression was, at times, simply not an option due to the mere volume of nonviolent demonstrators or the unwillingness of military and police commanders to carry out orders. Overall though, none of the regimes, outside of Ceauşescu's, were suddenly dragged away kicking and screaming, but perhaps only grumbling.

Conversion was also rare. Most communist regimes were replaced through democratic elections, and their high-ranking leaders were forced to resign. However, the Baltic state governments remained intact because there government officials themselves acted as agents of the people in opposition to the central government in Moscow. In Poland, Jaruzelski, a prominent leader, remained in office, though his election was sanctioned by Solidarity. When Jaruzelski resigned as president to make way for Wałesa, he expressed his conversion offering public apologies for decisions he had made over the years (*New York Times* 1991: 510–11).

Instead of pure conversion or coercion, most of the communist regimes in the Soviet bloc made a series of accommodations in the form of increasing political freedoms and negotiations that eventually eroded their ability to maintain their ascendancy. It might appear that communist leaders were simply "giving in" when, instead, their actions were a chain of partly coerced concessions offered to civic opposition organizations such as Solidarity, Civic Forum, and New Forum. Thus, Gorbachev intended that the Communist Party retain authority in Soviet life, but the accommodations he made in terms of glasnost and the Sinatra Doctrine eventually led to the disintegration of the USSR from above and below.

A willingness by regimes to offer concessions in the face of nonviolent action does not necessarily diminish the effectiveness of the action. To measure the success of nonviolent action only in terms of coercion would mean discounting a key element of nonviolent action. Such a move would, as this book suggests, be a mistake. Accommodation and even conversion can be a direct result of nonviolent action. For other communist leaders, nonviolent protest was the political writing on the wall, and many such leaders should be given credit for recognizing the importance of the people's voices. In summary, the effectiveness of nonviolent action can be varied, subtle, and elusive, and should not be dismissed too hastily.

Conclusion

The Soviet bloc revolutions that culminated in 1989 and 1990 were extraordinary, primarily nonviolent transitions, a fact that is especially notable given that they occurred within the jurisdiction of one of the world's greatest military superpowers. Once communist regimes at the periphery began to collapse, very little time passed before the core, in Moscow, was also faltering. There was considerable variation between the national revolutions across a number of dimensions (political, economic, geographical, historical, civic, religious), but in other ways they were also remarkably similar and interconnected.

The presence of nonviolent social movements was one of the common denominators shared by each country. Social movements developed their own particular histories and programs of action, but they also shared features such as their strategies. First, nonviolent social movements developed within institutions such as the Christian Church, cultural organizations, and various media that provided resources for the development and dissemination of nonviolent philosophy and strategies. This resource mobilization was fundamental to the execution of nonviolent action.

Second, nonviolent protest involving large crowds was the most common form of nonviolent actions, and protesters often used creative and thought-provoking conflict symbols to communicate their will. In other instances, insurgents employed nonviolent non-cooperation and nonviolent intervention to draw the attention of authorities and pressure them to make concessions. Third, these methods were largely successful as a function of the paradox of repression. Nonviolent social movements took advantage of the principle whereby regimes' attempts at repression backfired, magnifying popular discontent, delegitimating the regime, and further mobilizing opposition movements.

In this chapter, we have contended that nonviolent social movements were a highly significant factor (among others) in the demise of communist regimes. Some scholars of the revolutions claim that the movements were relatively insignificant and isolated events when compared with problems in the political and economic systems. Before one dismisses nonviolent social movements as isolated events, however, one should consider them within their broader historical and geographical contexts. Popular protest seems to have appeared almost spontaneously at the end of the 1980s, but movements that were active between 1988 and 1991 drew upon traditions of nonviolent opposition that extended decades into the past.

We have also argued that nonviolent action, properly understood, was effective in persuading and coercing communist elites. Many communist authorities were compelled to accommodate the oppositions' demands in the face of massive nonviolent protests. Some concessions were made grudgingly. Others were granted willingly by communist leaders who saw in the protests the massive withdrawal of consent and the inevitability of change.

To summarize, the nonviolent revolutions in the Soviet bloc are another expression of the proliferation of nonviolent social movements in this century. We have identified fundamental features of nonviolent struggle while, at the same time, appreciating the diversity of circumstances in which the revolutions occurred and the forms the revolutions assumed. Our goal has been to provide a general account of the Soviet bloc revolutions in hopes of provoking further research into the dynamics and execution of nonviolent action. These revolutions provide a wealth of case studies, and more specific inquiries will help to clear up debates about the relevance of nonviolent action in facilitating peaceful social change.

Notes

1 Czechoslovakian students chanted "We have bare hands" during the pivotal demonstration on November 17, 1989 that marked the beginning of the "Velvet Revolution."
2 We will be paying particular attention to Poland, Hungary, Czechoslovakia, East Germany, Romania, the Baltic States, and Russia.
3 The compilation of New York Times (1991) articles assembled in The Collapse of Communism have been especially useful. This book will be cited throughout this chapter as (New York Times 1991).
4 Grosz replaced Janos Kadar, who, while still clinging to the ascendancy of the Communist Party, had instituted some economic reforms and allowed reformers to develop (Stokes 1993).
5 On May 24, 1998, the Hungarian Civic Party won the most seats in parliamentary elections, making Victor Orban the new prime minister.
6 Other accounts suggest that Egon Krenz took the initiative in canceling the police operation (New York Times) or that Masur and his colleagues contacted Krenz (Anderson 1990).
7 Ironically, New Forum, the opposition organization that received the lion's share of popular support, never intended the reunification of Germany. Instead, they envisioned a reformed socialist East Germany.

8 The defense of opposition buildings in Russia and Romania are instances in which mixed methods were used. Defenders of the Russian parliament building had a limited number of small firearms and molotov cocktails. Free Romanian Television's Studio 4 was being protected by army personnel.

9 For another analysis of nonviolent action in the Soviet bloc, see Adam Roberts's "Civil Resistance in the East European and Soviet Revolutions."

10 Vaclav Havel's authorized biographer.

References

Ackerman, Peter, and Christopher Kruegler. 1994. *Strategic Nonviolent Conflict: The Dynamics of People Power in the Twentieth Century*. Westport Connecticut: Praeger.

Anderson, Edith. 1990. "Town Mice and Country Mice: The East German Revolution" in Brinton and Rinzler.

Brinton William M., and Alan Rinzler. 1990. *Without Force or Lies: Voices from the Revolution of Central Europe in 1989–1990*. San Francisco: Mercury House.

Csicsery, George Paul 1990. "The Siege of Nogradi Street, Budapest, 1989." In Brinton and Rinzler.

Darnton, Robert. 1991. *Berlin Journal: 1989–1990*. New York: W. W. Norton & Company.

Durkheim, Emile. [1912] 1965. *The Elementary Forms of the Religious Life*. New York: The Free Press.

Garton Ash, Timothy. 1990. *The Magic Lantern: The Revolutions of '89 Witnessed in Warsaw, Budapest, Berlin, and Prague*. New York: Random House.

Goldfarb, Jeffrey. 1980. *The Persistence of Freedom: The Sociological Implications of Polish Student Theater*. Boulder: Westview.

Gorbachev, Mikhail. 1995. *Memoirs*. New York: Doubleday.

Havel, Vaclav. 1990. "The Power of the Powerless." In Brinton and Rinzler.

Kerblay, Basile. 1989. *Gorbachev's Russia*. New York: Pantheon Books.

Kriseova, Eda. 1993. *Vaclav Havel: The Authorized Biography*. New York: St. Martin's Press.

Kurtz, Lester. 1995. *Gods in the Global Village: The World's Religions in Sociological Perspective*. Thousand Oaks, Calif: Pine Forge Press.

Misztal, Barbara A. 1993. "Understanding Political Change in Eastern Europe: A Sociological Perspective." *Sociology*. 27 (3): 451–70.

Monticone, Ronald C. 1986. *The Catholic Church in Communist Poland 1945–1985: Forty Years of Church–State Relations*. Boulder: East European Monographs.

Morton, Brian, and Joanne Landy. 1988. "East European Activists Test Glasnost." *Bulletin of the Atomic Scientists*, (May 1988), 44 (4): 18–26.

New York Times. 1991. *The Collapse of Communism*. Bernard Gwertzman and Michael T. Kaufman. New York: Times Books.

Oleszczuk, Thomas A. 1990. "The Peaceful Revolution in Lithuania." In Brinton and Rinzler.

Palazchenko, Pavel. 1997. *My Years with Gorbachev and Shevardnadze: The Memoir of a Soviet Interpreter*. University Park, Pa: Pennsylvania State University Press.

Reddaway, Peter. 1993. "The Role of Popular Discontent" *National Interest*. (Spring 1993), 32. 57–64.

Roberts, Adam. 1991. *Civil Resistance in the East European and Soviet Revolutions*. Cambridge: Albert Einstein Institution.

Sharp, Gene. 1973. *The Politics of Nonviolent Action*. 3 vols. Boston: Porter Sargent.

Smith, Hedrick. 1990. *The New Russians*. London: Hutchinson.

Snow, David A., E. Barle Rochford, Jr., Steven K. Worden, and Robert D. Benford. "Frame Alignment Process, Micromobilization and Movement Participation," *American Sociological Review*, 51: 464–81.

Stokes, Gale. 1993. *The Walls Came Tumbling Down: The Collapse of Communism in Eastern Europe*. New York: Oxford University Press.

Walesa, Lech. 1991. *The Struggle and the Triumph*. New York: Arcade Publishing.

Weigel, George. 1992. *The Final Revolution: The Resistance Church and the Collapse of Communism*. New York: Oxford University Press.

Yan Jia Qi. 1992. Interview by the author.

PART IV

Asia

Introduction

The world's largest continent has seen the largest numbers of nonviolent campaigns of recent years. Nonviolent movements in 1989 and 1990 were instrumental in the downfall of the Communist government of Mongolia, the military government in Bangladesh and autocratic monarchical control in Nepal. Largely nonviolent campaigns in the mid-1980s forced a phased democratization by autocratic governments in South Korea and Taiwan. In 1983, in Pakistan, a large-scale nonviolent resistance movement nearly toppled the dictatorship of Zia al-Huq in the face of severe repression. With the return of exiled pro-democracy leader Benazir Bhutto from exile in 1986, a renewed series of nonviolent actions eventually led to free elections in 1988.

Thailand has an impressive history of nonviolent resistance. In 1973, a student-led uprising led to the collapse of the military dictatorship and several years of democratic rule, interrupted by a military coup in 1976 which targeted the universities during the bloody takeover. Subsequent nonviolent campaigns led to a democratic opening in the 1980s. In this section, Thai political scientist Chaiwat Satha-Anand talks about the 1992 pro-democracy uprising in Bangkok against the military dominated Thai government as illustrated through the artistry of postcards commemorating the event, a powerful example of the importance of imagery in nonviolent struggles.

One of the most well-publicized successful nonviolent movements in recent decades was the overthrow of the Marcos dictatorship in the Philippines in 1986. Stephen Zunes' article "People Power in the Philippines" describes the dramatic events leading up to the dictator's ousting, as well as the years of less well-known nonviolent struggle leading up to those dramatic days in Manila.

The best-known unsuccessful mass nonviolent movement was the pro-democracy campaign in China during the spring of 1989, which culminated in the June 4 massacre in Tiananmen Square. The resistance campaign, which took place over seven weeks, included not just the students, but sizable sectors of industrial workers and the intelligentsia. The mobilization paralyzed the government, spread to cities and towns throughout the country, included perhaps the largest hunger strike in history and captured the attention of virtually the entire world. Despite virtually no formal understanding of the history, theory, or practice of nonviolent action and despite very weak organization, this spontaneous movement seriously threatened the very foundations of the communist regime. Indeed, it is unlikely the government would have risked the alienation of major segments of its population and the international community by slaughtering thousands of unarmed civilians had they not calculated that they were under serious challenge.

A similarly dramatic nonviolent uprising in Burma was suppressed in 1987–8. Under the leadership of Nobel Peace Prize winner Aung San Suu Kyi and international solidarity efforts, the struggle for freedom continues. Rather than continuing to respond to savage repression with violence, ethnic guerrillas – who have been waging a largely futile armed resistance for decades – have now begun to explore the possibility of adopting nonviolent resistance as well. Michael Beer of Nonviolence International, who has engaged in nonviolence training with a variety of Burmese dissidents, describes the interplay between the nonviolent resistance and armed ethnic guerrillas in the countryside.

As Asia has become an increasingly important actor in the global economy, often as a source of cheap and exploited labor kept in check by autocratic regimes, the role of nonviolent action will continue to play an important role, as witnessed in the spectacular unarmed uprising which toppled the brutal 33-year old Suharto dictatorship. In Indonesia, Malaysia, and elsewhere, nonviolent movements continue to press for greater democratization as well as demand that the crony capitalism and uneven economic development strategies of recent decades which have brought on the current economic crisis are replaced by more equitable and sustainable development.

7

The Origins of People Power in the Philippines

Stephen Zunes

Introduction

Well over a decade after the eyes of the world were fixed upon the masses in the Philippine capital, the overthrow of the Marcos dictatorship remains one of the world's more remarkable nonviolent uprisings. Despite more than a dozen similar successful movements during subsequent years in South Asia, Africa, and Eastern Europe, the Philippine "people power" revolution remains one of the most impressive in terms of the numbers of people involved, the level of nonviolent discipline and the way it captured the imagination of observers around the world.

President Ferdinand Marcos, who had ruled under dictatorial powers since 1972, had ordered a snap election in February 1986 as a means of legitimizing his control. When it became apparent that the election had effectively been stolen, the opposition called for a massive campaign of civil disobedience. However, in the international media, quotes were placed around the word "nonviolent," implying a dubious assessment, or at the least a skeptical outlook, of the strategy or its significance. Even after Marcos fled, there was difficulty in the foreign press in describing exactly what happened. An editorial in *Asiaweek* noted that "political scientists will have to come up with new words to describe the four-days' wonder that convulsed Manila...the whole phenomenon...fits no standard category."[1] Similarly, on the left, there was widespread skepticism over the prospects of success, prompting Cory Aquino to state that "Those who are prepared to support armed struggles for liberation elsewhere discredit themselves if they obscure the nature of what we are doing peacefully here."[2]

While there have been a sizable number of published accounts of those remarkable 77 hours, there has been relatively little analysis of the fact that the successful use of nonviolent action in the overthrow of the Marcos regime was not wholly spontaneous, but a culmination of years of preparation for such an uprising through the training of Filipinos, both in the years preceding the uprising as well as during the hours of the uprising itself, in the methods of nonviolent resistance. The motivation for the use of non-violence was based on both ethical principles which eschewed the use of violence, as well as a pragmatic view that nonviolence would be more effective than armed struggle in challenging the government. This is particularly significant in light of the Marcos government's ability and willingness to use great amounts of force against a well-organized armed resistance movement during that same period, the Communist Party of the Philippines' New Peoples Army (NPA).

Many observers had ruled out nonviolence in circumstances such as those in the Philippines, citing episodes like the Escalante Massacre in September 1985. It was a classic nonviolent action: 10,000 farmers and their families, protesting their conditions in the sugar plantations, marching peacefully into a town in the Negros Occidental province. They barricaded a portion of a major thoroughfare, gathered, and linked arms in front of the public market, only to be met by gunfire from soldiers. The official death toll was listed at 27, though the actual figure was probably much higher. Some argued at the time that this incident demonstrated the futility of nonviolent forms of resistance against a regime as ruthless as that of Marcos.

However, advocates of nonviolent action, including those in the Philippines, never claimed there would be no casualties in such a movement. To rule out the use of nonviolence because people get killed is no more logical than ruling out armed resistance for the same reason. Challenging an oppressive authoritarian regime is a hazardous activity whatever the method. The key variable is not whether people get killed, but how the suffering of those challenging the regime can be used in the context of the overall struggle. The Escalante Massacre helped mobilize popular resistance against Marcos far more than an encounter between the NPA and government forces, with similar casualties, would have done. Indeed, the tragedy at Escalante appears to have been an important chapter in the loss of legitimacy of the Marcos regime in the eyes of the Filipino people. For in calculating the chances for success in a nonviolent action campaign, the key variable is not the material strength of the opposition so much as the lack of support for the regime.

Despite incidents like the one in Escalante, there are limits to the brutality that even a toughened military can inflict. Exiled Filipino social scientist Francisco Nemenzo prophesied in 1985,

> Once tens of thousands have congregated and their passions aroused, they will gain the courage to march out in open defiance of the riot police. It requires the utmost violence to diffuse large and angry crowds. From the standpoint of the authorities, this poses an extremely delicate question: will the soldiers always obey an order to open fire? It is one thing to shoot peasants in some God-forsaken village and another to massacre middle class dissenters while the whole world is watching.[3]

Fortunately for the Philippine opposition, the whole world *was* watching during the events in February, which took place almost exclusively in Manila, which – in addition to being the national capital – is also the communications center of the country. As will be noted later, this was a major factor in the success of the movement.

The Power of Nonviolent Action

Advocates of a nonviolent strategy in the Philippines for the overthrow of Marcos differed from those advocating a military victory through armed struggle: the advocates of nonviolence argued that their greatest hope for victory lay not in defeating government troops in a long series of battles culminating with the storming of Malacanang Palace, but through withdrawing sufficient support for the regime so that Malacanang became the only part of the country over which Marcos maintained effective control. In contrast to armed struggle against the dictatorial regime, whose greatest strength lay in the armed forces, the events of that February demonstrated the efficacy of attacking where the opponent is weakest, in this case, in popular support.

According to one pamphlet from the Filipino nonviolent campaign

> Let us ... be clear on the nature of political power. The power wielded by those who govern is not intrinsic to them. The power and authority that the 'rulers' wield comes from the people, the society which they govern. No ruler has power beyond that which the people allow and consent the 'ruler' to use over them.
>
> ... Since Mr. Marcos would not seem to yield graciously, we, the sovereign people, must act to deny him the support, the resources, the personal skills and expertise that continues to enable him to inflict his violence and injustice upon us.
>
> ... In this system, no government can continue to function without the support of the people. The principal resource [*sic*] are the people themselves; their allegiance, their transforming skills, their administrative skills, the natural resources of the country.[4]

American sociologist and radical Quaker activist George Lakey outlined five stages of a theoretical nonviolent revolution,[5] which appear to have been borne out by events in the Philippines:

1 *Cultural preparation* during much of the martial law period, cadres from the Catholic Church and leftist organizations became involved in grassroots organizing and consciousness-raising among the peasantry and urban poor, developing an analysis of the ills in Philippine society, a vision of what a liberated society would look like, and strategies on how to get there. Similar efforts were going on among students and other elements in the middle class opposition.

2 *Organization building* this was seen most evidently in the development of the sectoral opposition, vast networks of decentralized popular organizations based among various interest groups and geographical areas. Not trusting either the elite-dominated traditional parties nor the Communist-led military or civilian front organizations, there was a strong movement for the development of popular grassroots organizations that would respond directly to local concerns.

3 *Propaganda of the deed* these were public demonstrations of opposition which were used to empower the population and serve notice to Marcos and those in authority that there was organized opposition to his rule that could make its presence felt. The importance of this strategy was that it challenged the mythology of omnipotent power by the governmental and military authorities, and thus helped mobilize the population into the realization that they could, in fact, resist. Such tactics included "people's strikes" (*welgang bayan*) and other forms of nonviolent resistance. (A number of cases will be described below.)

4 *Massive noncooperation* the kind of widespread resistance which makes it difficult to govern, as witnessed by the events of February which brought down the Marcos regime. While President Marcos was nominally in control, and was even sworn in for another term of office, the level of public noncooperation to his emergency edicts made it quite clear that was no longer in charge of the country. The instruments of power, such as the Philippine armed forces, were no longer under his command.

5 *Parallel institutions* these can include, on a local level, the establishment of rural cooperatives separate from government control and the establishment of alternative educational institutions, as was being developed throughout the Philippines during and after the martial law period, particularly in urban slums and areas of traditionally high peasant activism, such as Mindanao and central Luzon. The forming of a parallel nongovernment election commission (NAMFREL) proved to be a pivotal institutional alternative in the movement, which culminated with the formation of a parallel government and the swearing in of Cory Aquino as president while Marcos still held claim to power.

These five stages do not necessarily follow in neat chronological order. As with the Philippine case, there were elements where each stage occurred simultaneously. The stages can perhaps be best envisioned as a conch-shaped spiral with openings into each chamber rather than as a neat linear diagram.[6]

The Roots of Nonviolent Resistance in the Philippines

Nonviolent resistance has been used extensively in the Philippines, as it has in most countries where there has been opposition to illegitimate authority.

Such traditions go back as far as Spanish colonial times. The nonviolent movement in the Philippines was, as such, two movements: that of the poorer elements of the population, often assisted by the radical clergy and laity, organizing on immediate local concerns that were part of the desire for radical change in Filipino society; and secondly, that of the middle class opposition, backed by the Church hierarchy, which became fully mobilized only after the assassination of Benigno Aquino in 1983.

Unlike the middle-class movements, which were centered in Manila during the final two years of Marcos's rule, the more radical nonviolent movements had a longstanding presence throughout the Philippines. Most of these were never well-reported outside the country, in part because unlike organizational efforts by the NPA and its civilian front organizations which stress the use of the cadre from a disciplined Communist Party structure, these nonviolent campaigns were far more decentralized and thus less prone to develop an elaborate propaganda apparatus. Much of the organizational structure was based on affinity groups, small units of activists with a degree of autonomy but closely linked with similar groups involved in a particular campaign. (Such organizational units had their first appearance with Spanish anarchists in the 1930s and were seen more recently in nonviolent action campaigns against the construction of nuclear power plants in the United States.)[7] In addition, villages where many of the groups organized were remote and were not often frequented by major media, particularly the foreign press. Being based largely on local issues and finding it advantageous to spread their message by word-of-mouth through sympathetic peasants, rather than forcing a premature showdown brought on by embarrassing publicity, also played a role in the relative lack of awareness to those outside the Philippines. The early campaigns were focused on specific local issues, with challenging but obtainable goals. As these early efforts proved successful and the confidence and numbers in the movements grew, they aimed toward higher goals.

During these campaigns, representatives of the religious and secular organizations leading the movements would be responsible for the training of activists. As with most nonviolent campaigns worldwide, there was great emphasis on training those taking part in an action in order to insure discipline and effective tactics. There was extensive use of role-playing and other training methods to prepare the activists for various contingencies. Organizers would suggest creative actions that would be militant enough to discourage what they referred to as "leftist adventurism" but modest enough so as not to alienate elements of the population they were trying to reach. These organizers would have a year or two of on-the-job training before branching out to share their skills over a broader area. Despite the use of experienced organizers and trainers from the outside, those in local areas had ultimate control over the issues to be addressed and would participate in the negotiations with officials and businessmen targeted by the campaigns.[8]

In addition, during the martial law period there began the development of consumer collectives similar to Gandhian ashrams. These small cooperatives began developing production and marketing methods in an effort to build an indigenous economy outside of the transnational institutions which dominate the Philippine economy. These collectives also spearheaded initiatives in "appropriate technology" to counter the imported capital-intensive development schemes of the Marcos governments in such areas as agriculture, energy production, and manufacturing.[9]

By 1984, opposition leader José Diokno was developing plans for a sustained nonviolent campaign that would grow out of the boycott movement of the assembly elections through the Coalition for the Restoration of Democracy (CORD). Though the decision by many opposition activists to participate in the elections suspended a widespread campaign, it paved the ground for future organization of nonviolent action and resulted in the forming of the Bagong Alyasang Makabayan (Bayan), which had a mandate to engage in a broad range of "nonviolent struggle on a nationwide scale such as massive rallies, demonstrations, marches, general strikes, *welgang bayan* and other forms of protest" to promote basic change through issue-based politics.[10]

This leftist alliance of approximately 500 grassroots organizations, with a total membership approaching 1.5 million, organized several successful *welgang bayan* throughout the country. Beginning in October 1984 in Davao City and other major urban areas, and continuing throughout 1985, these massive nonviolent actions periodically paralyzed major urban areas. These included simultaneous strikes by transport workers and other labor groups, walkouts by professionals, student boycotts, and demonstrations which shut down industry and commerce. These urban strikes soon expanded to province-wide actions which built on local issues to include outright opposition to the Marcos regime and American neo-colonialism. More militant disruptions were planned following the elections, which Bayan officially boycotted, though many individual members actively took part in the Aquino campaign.

Part of the power of the *welgang bayans* were their multi-sectoral nature, crossing class and ethnic lines. Bayan leaders were explicit that these *welgang bayans* were "test runs" of the kind of general strike that would eventually bring down the government.[11] An important element was confidence- building by the Philippine masses, demonstrating that despite years of repression, they had the collective power to temporarily shut down an entire city or province. In addition to indicating to the government the extent of popular opposition to the regime, such actions also played a crucial role in building confidence among the populace opposed to Marcos's rule. They created a kind of praxis which could serve to raise the consciousness of those participating to an understanding that even a powerful ruler like Marcos was vulnerable if enough people organized and overcame intimidation by the government's repressive mechanisms.

As far back as early 1971, students at the University of the Philippines (UP) engaged in what amounted to a precursor of the *welgang bayan*, when human barricades were set up around the UP campus as part of a nonviolent protest against oil price hikes and other grievances. Though initiated by students, they were soon joined by young people from surrounding neighborhoods and a large number of workers as well. Fishermen and peasants from surrounding provinces sent food. Unlike the territorial nature of the UP uprising (nicknamed the "Diliman Republic"), the policy of the *welgang bayan* was not to attempt to defend a particular area when faced with violent dispersal, but to retreat in a manner similar to guerrilla forces. Another difference was while the Diliman Commune was largely spontaneous, the *welgang bayans* were generally well-planned and publicized in advance.[12]

The first major *welgang bayans* were in Davao City in the southern part of the country. Organized by CORD-Mindanao and the Nationalist Alliance, with the support of a variety of labor, professional, student, and community groups, the general strikes in October and November 1984 focused on increases in gas and oil prices and the murder of activist Alex Orcullo, with demands expanding to include "the dismantling of the US-Marcos dictatorship."[13] Thousands of protestors built barricades along the main highway, some of which were right next to military checkpoints. The strike in some areas was as much as 95 percent effective.[14]

In December 1984, a *welgang bayan* in Bataan shut down 80 percent of the transportation in the entire province as thousands of people took over the streets. In February, 1985, Mindanao's Center for Nationalist Trade Unions staged a one-day general strike which joined 140,000 workers in 187 unions in protest at the killing of union leaders which brought both factories and plantations to a standstill.[15]

Given the successes of these and other actions, Bayan and other resistance groups grew bolder, expanding the geographical boundaries of the general strikes. On May 2–3, 1985, there was a massive *welgang bayan* throughout Mindanao, which, according to Philippine Armed Forces regional commander General Dionisio Tangatue, paralyzed two-thirds of the island.[16] Davao City and Iligan City were effectively shut down. The strike also crippled Pagadian in Zamboanga del Sur, Dipolog in Zamboanga del Norte, Ozamis in Misamis Occidental, and General Santos in South Cotabato. Several smaller towns were affected as well. Most people stayed at home, but tens of thousands took part in rallies, marches, and barricades. The lengthy list of demands included an increase in the minimum wage; a rollback in prices for fertilizers, feed grains, and other agricultural inputs; an end to repressive taxation; a reduction of prices on basic commodities and utilities; a cessation of "development" programs which bypassed human needs; an end to foreign control of Philippine fishing grounds; investigations into a recent series of political killings; the repeal of repressive laws; the demilitarization of Mindanao; and the dismantling of US military installations.[17]

One of the more notable *welgang bayans* took place over the controversial nuclear power plant under construction on the Bataan Peninsula, believed by many experts to be potentially one of the most dangerous nuclear facilities in the world, being located on the slope of the Natib Volcano near seven geological fault lines. In addition to safety concerns, there was widespread opposition to what were perceived as the misplaced economic priorities of the Philippine government in moving ahead with this $2 billion facility, made possible in part by US Export–Import Bank loans and an apparent $35 million bribe by the Westinghouse Corporation, the manufacturer of the facility, made to Marcos through an intermediary.[18]

There was a widespread grassroots campaign against the facility during the early 1980s, despite the arrest, torture, and killing of several prominent organizers by government forces. In 1985, the movement linked up with Philippine nuclear disarmament advocates to form the Nuclear Free Philippines Coalition, which in turn was linked to international campaigns for a Nuclear Free Pacific.[19] These efforts were necessarily tied into the campaign against the US military bases, which included tactical nuclear weapons on certain ships and aircraft. Inspired by actions of the New Zealand government and by the nuclear-free constitution in Belau, the Philippines' nearest neighbor to the east, this movement garnered both grass roots and intellectual support.

There were a series of large-scale nonviolent actions against the plant, the largest taking place June 18–20, 1985. A *welgang bayan* called against the government's nuclear energy policy was organized by 22 regional and national organizations. On the first day of the action, 10,000 people rallied against the plant. In addition, there was a strike by transport workers which paralyzed the province, disrupting the major bus lines to and from Manila, and effectively shutting down transportation in nine of the province's eleven major towns. Classes were suspended as a result of a student boycott, and stores and businesses were closed. Most significantly, 6,000 workers from the Bataan Export Processing Zones, representing 29 of the 34 factories, walked out *en masse* and joined the general strike. Thousands more came to join the protests from nearby provinces in contingents of marchers and by motorcade, including representatives of women's groups and professional organizations in Metro Manila. An estimated 4,000 local residents offered support, providing food and water to the marchers and erecting barricades against soldiers sent in to stop the march, which proceeded through the heavy rains of a tropical storm.[20]

Despite harassment and threats by police, a nonviolent discipline was maintained. The government sent in agents provocateurs, who hurled stones and tried to encourage a violent confrontation which would have provoked the police into stiffer counter measures, a clear demonstration that the government preferred to engage an opposition movement using violent methods than one with a strong nonviolent discipline. In Pilar, a light tank ran into a crowd, resulting in several injuries, but government forces were unable to use force effectively against the marchers in most situations. At one point, a threatened assault by armored personnel carriers was thwarted by demonstrators strategically placing large stones against the treads of the military vehicles. There were a number of arrests, and virtually all protestors were searched and photographed by the military before it was over, but 20,000 marchers managed to arrive at their destination in Balanga in the final day of the action. For nearly three days, the normal activity of the entire province had been halted by a sustained nonviolent campaign.[21] This action rivaled the efforts of better publicized protests against nuclear energy in West Germany, the United States, and other industrialized democracies of that era in its magnitude, a feat made all the more impressive given the repressive nature of the Marcos government.

Nonviolent action such as this was not just undertaken by urban workers, but by rural peasants as well. In February 1985, 7,500 peasants from the Alliance of Central Luzon Farmers marched on Manila, demanding lower interest rates, a rollback in fertilizer prices, and other economic issues, though it was clear that the long-term strategy was to challenge the entire land ownership system. They staged a nine-day sit-in in front of the Agriculture Ministry. When their camp was attacked and leader Jaime Tadeo arrested, they regrouped on the University of the Philippines campus and held their ground until Tadeo was released.

There were many forms of nonviolent action that were spontaneous and did not make the news. Peasants across the country resisted demands by the government to join the paramilitary "Civilian Home Defense Forces" (as well as demands to join the NPA). There were numerous cases of hundreds of villagers marching to their town hall to successfully demand the release of a fellow villager recently arrested without charge. Nor were all forms of nonviolence active or public, such as the 1981 election boycott, in which millions – most of them quietly – defied martial law requirements to vote in what clearly was to be a rigged election.

The Middle Class Joins the Nonviolent Movement

The embracing of nonviolent action by middle-class opponents began in earnest at the funeral of democratic opposition leader Benigno Aquino, assassinated at the airport upon his return from exile in August 1983. Massive demonstrations in the financial district of Makati, showered with ticker-tape, were in sharp contrast to the protest in the cities and towns of the rural Philippines and in Metro Manila's less affluent areas where nonviolent resistance had once been centered. While segments of the poor majority did take part in some of these demonstrations, it was also apparent that the perceived need to escalate the opposition to the Marcos regime had reached even the relatively comfortable segments of society.

This paralleled the growing disillusionment among the Filipino elite over the Marcos dictatorship. Outside of those who lost out of the normal rotation of power among the Filipino elites, many of the better-off elements of society welcomed martial law as a means of countering the growing unrest, nationalist sentiment, and radical economic demands from below. Yet the corruption, arbitrariness, and general incompetence of the Marcos regime was clearly taking its toll among some of these erstwhile allies, most of whom had been so only reluctantly.

While most of the brutality of the martial law period was directed towards radical opponents, Marcos was clearly not averse to using force against elite opponents as well. Some responded with petitioning and mild criticism. Others chose exile. However, with traditional outlets closed off, there appeared to be few options.

Much of the new-found interest in nonviolence, especially in the Catholic Church, can be traced to the influence of nonviolent organizations outside the country. Since the 1920s, activists affiliated with the International Fellowship of Reconciliation (IFOR), an ecumenical pacifist organization, had made extended visits to the Philippines.[22] Starting in 1984, IFOR led workshops on active nonviolence throughout the Philippines. French activist Jean Goss-Mayer and his Austrian wife, Hildegard, along with Americans Richard Deats and Stefan Merken, organized these training sessions for a score of Catholic and Protestant bishops, along with hundreds of other clergy, nuns, and lay people, which included representatives of the Aquino family.[23] Though their commitment to nonviolence was premised on spiritual faith, the bulk of the agenda was centered on practical uses of nonviolent action to resist dictatorship.[24]

A Philippine chapter of the Fellowship of Reconciliation, known as Aksyon Para sa Kapayapaan at Katarungan (AKKAPKA), was founded that year. During the next several months, it organized more than 40 seminars on active nonviolence in 30 provinces. An estimated 1,500 people took part in these seminars, many lasting three full days, including people who would become major figures in the February 1986 uprising. Topics covered included sessions on "Awareness of Violence," including both personal and structural forms; "Awareness of Responses," which compared passivity, counter-violence and active nonviolence; "Humanistic" and "Biblical" bases of nonviolence; and, the preparation, analysis, strategy, and tactics of active nonviolence. Also included in these workshops were testimonies on and the histories of active nonviolence in the Philippines and elsewhere, strategy sessions, an examination of the Philippine Church and opposition groups and their possible role in a nonviolent struggle, role playing, and a daily liturgy.[25]

AKKAPKA also set up tent cities for prayer, fasting, and nonviolence training in ten cities in the period immediately prior to the election and in the weeks that followed.[26] There they led short seminars on active non-violence and strategy sessions on civil disobedience. The tent cities were opened to the public as a gathering place for inspiration and information sharing. A wide range of people, including charismatics and soldiers, who had little previous interest in the active opposition to Marcos, came to the tent cities for information.

The growing awareness of the power of nonviolent action allowed many Filipinos, aware of the need for social change but anxious about the prospects of armed struggle, to become activists. This was particularly evident within the Catholic Church, where strong ethical objections to killing precluded for many an embrace of violent methods of change. There were seminars among Philippine clergy and theologians on nonviolence, inspired in part by similar discussions elsewhere. The work of Catholic lay leader and Nobel Peace Prize winner Adolfo Perez-Esquivel of Argentina and his counterparts in Brazil, such as Archbishop Dom Helder Camara; the lengthy section on nonviolent alternatives to war in the United States bishops' pastoral letter on the nuclear arms race; the support of the Polish Church for the nonviolent action campaigns of Solidarity, and similar activities by Catholics worldwide were also an inspiration.

It would be a mistake, however, to attribute the openness of Filipinos to nonviolent action on purely religious considerations. While Christians, on average, are more likely to accept nonviolence as a tactic than nonbelievers due to its consistency with Christian theological teachings, many more were able to recognize its tactical utility. Most of those involved in nonviolent actions, both before and during the Marcos overthrow, had not been exposed, directly or indirectly, to the religious-oriented nonviolence training of AKKAPKA, and it is highly unlikely that most of them considered themselves pacifist in orientation. It appears, then, that most of the nonviolent activists favored nonviolence on largely pragmatic grounds. As with similar struggles elsewhere, there was probably an awareness that soldiers were far less likely to shoot into an unarmed crowd of demonstrators than they were to fire at dissidents who were shooting back. Related to this would be an understanding that most Filipino soldiers were poor conscripts whose real interests were not with Marcos, but with those seeking his overthrow, and who could possibly be persuaded to abandon their role as enforcers of an unjust order. Another factor was that the middle class, business people, and others who were just beginning to defect from the Marcos camp, would be far more likely to support a nonviolent movement than one of armed resistance.[27] As with most major conflicts in the Philippines, many activists were concerned about perceptions in the United States: based on US reactions to other Third World insurgencies, there was undoubtedly also an awareness that Americans would be far more supportive of nonviolent forms of resistance against Marcos than of those by force of arms, which could be identified with the NPA and possibly lead to direct US military intervention in support of the Marcos regime.

The Filipinos coined the term *alaydangal* for the nonviolent protests, which is the Tagalog expression for "to offer dignity." Many of the religious-based advocates of nonviolent action were inspired by the Gandhian principles of *satyagraha*, or "truth force", which was based on the premise of nonviolent witnesses converting those in oppressive roles to an understanding of the injustice of which they were a part. Yet not all nonviolent action is based on the premise of conversion; there can also be a coercive element to some nonviolent strategies, created by withholding support from and/or disrupting the administration sufficiently for a government or system to no longer function. It is significant that when Filipinos spoke of nonviolence they referred to "active nonviolence," or "ANV," to distinguish it from a "turn the other cheek" brand of New Testament pacifism or other forms of passive nonviolence.

In the spectrum of approaches to nonviolent struggle in the Philippines there were, on one side, those who embraced nonviolence as a conscious philosophy, inspired by Gandhian and Christian pacifist beliefs that nonviolence was more than a tactic, but part of an entire belief system. On the other side, there were those who used nonviolent tactics on purely pragmatic grounds, who recognized the power of nonviolence as a coercive measure not qualitatively different from the force of arms. Many in the latter group did not even consciously consider their activities as "nonviolent"; they were just another form of struggle. While literature from the radical wing of the movement, the pro-Communist National Democratic Front (NDF) tended to embrace nonviolence on purely utilitarian grounds, and the literature of middle-class church and lay activists tended to identify with the more ethically based approach, these differing views on nonviolence did not necessarily parallel the ideological spectrum.

The appeal of nonviolent action in the Philippine context lay in that it united both leftists (outside the NPA) and many conservatives in active opposition to Marcos. To the left, it provided an effective confrontational tactic against the Marcos regime and the social and economic forces behind it. To the more conservative opposition, especially those in the church hierarchy, it left open the possibility of reconciliation. For the clerics, then, active nonviolence offered a militant resistance strategy free from rigid Marxist dialectics and the emphasis on class struggle. Even Cardinal Ricardo Vidal of Cebu, generally thought of as one of the more conservative Catholic leaders in the Philippines, attended three nonviolence training programs during 1985, and endorsed active nonviolence.[28]

This constituted an important shift from only a few years earlier. In October 1979, the Catholic Bishops' Conference of the Philippines issued a major "Exhortation Against Violence," criticizing those who take up arms in revolutionary struggle. Two years later, 17 of the bishops issued their own caveat which encouraged the hierarchy to focus their opposition to violence on the government as well as revolutionary forces. In addition, these bishops noted that

> not many of the bishops, it seems, are prepared to back nonviolent methods of fighting violence, especially the violence of the government. This makes for

confusion among the people – and for the suspicion that the bishops' nonviolent stance is actually a vote for the violent status quo. The Church must hence begin coming up with more definite programs of countering the violence of the day...[29]

Cardinal Jaime Sin of Manila attributed the Goss-Mayers in particular with the training of opposition leaders in nonviolent resistance.[30] Outside of the Christian Base Communities, the Church did not start teaching nonviolent resistance before 1985, and only then took up this political role reluctantly.[31] According to Richard Deats, a Methodist clergyman from the United States who had lived for more than a decade in the Philippines

> The importance of the Goss-Mayer's seminars were that they were able to reach a large number of Filipinos with a radical message of social change depending not upon violence, not upon a Marxist analysis, but depending upon the resources they had in their own faith. Not justifying but deeply and analytically looking at the structures of violence and oppression that keep the people in chains and calling the participants to mobilize their forces to bring about the liberation of the people.[32]

The Goss-Mayers were leaders among Catholic pacifists for more than 30 years. They represented IFOR in Eastern Europe, lobbied at the Second Vatican Council for an endorsement of nonviolent peacemaking, and were successful in receiving the first official church endorsement of the option of conscientious objection to war. Between 1962 and 1977, they worked largely in Latin America teaching revolutionary nonviolence, greatly influencing such human rights activists as Esquivel and Camara.[33]

For many years, Benigno Aquino (Ninoy) was considered part of the political establishment, as – like many other Filipino leaders – had his family before him. During his time in prison, however, he was said to have experienced a "genuine religious conversion,"[34] embraced active nonviolence, and was radicalized. His main inspiration, he later said, was Mahatma Gandhi, Dietrich Bonhoeffer, and the Gospels. This greatly influenced his wife Corazón Aquino (Cory) as well, and subsequently, while neither could be considered part of the left, they were no longer simply part of the traditional politics. Following Ninoy's assassination, many of his supporters, including his brother Agapito (Butz), seriously considered turning to armed struggle in order to overthrow the Marcos regime. However, both Ninoy's mother and Cory insisted on a nonviolent response. While Butz and others seriously questioned the utility of nonviolence under such circumstances, they were won over by apparently convincing arguments on the potential of sustained nonviolent resistance.[35]

Ninoy was talking openly about leading a Gandhian struggle to overthrow Marcos in the months prior to his ill-fated return to the Philippines. He had stated that his travels in Asia, Africa, and Latin America had convinced him that the costs of armed struggle were too great in terms of loss of life, damage to a nation's infrastructure and the chances of building post-revolutionary reconciliation.[36] His exact plan of action will never be known.

The Election Campaign

Following the widespread fraud in the 1984 parliamentary elections, there were months of nonviolent protests, such as marches, rallies, group jogging, and other efforts. Two seven-day marches converging on Manila from the north and south involved an estimated 70,000 protestors.[37] It was clear that if the 1986 election pitting Marcos against Cory Aquino was going to allow for a truly democratic transition, there needed to be widespread nonviolent challenges to the government.

During the 1986 election campaign, there were numerous episodes of nonviolent resistance throughout the country. Inspired by her husband's conversion to active nonviolence, Cory Aquino, from the outset of her campaign, made it clear that she would not permit the kinds of violent attacks and retaliations against her opponents as had frequently occurred in Philippine politics. The theme of nonviolence came up repeatedly in her speeches, encouraging people to overcome their fear and exercise their power to stand up to the seemingly omnipotent state and armed forces. Most nonviolent actions during the campaign were defensive in nature, such as the human barricades protecting pro-Aquino speakers from attacks by government goon squads. Some nonviolent activists took the offensive, as with an incident on January 27 when a dozen Filipina feminists disrupted a KBL press conference at the Manila Hotel and seized the microphone to challenge the sexism of the Marcos government, including the president's recent statement that "women should confine their preachings to the bedroom."[38]

The most powerful uses of nonviolent direct action in the campaign were in the activities of the National Movement for Free Elections in the Philippines (NAMFREL), which sent an estimated 500,000 volunteers,[39] largely consisting of priests, seminarians, and nuns, to cover the most sensitive and vulnerable precincts in an effort to minimize violence and electoral fraud. Unlike the Aquino campaign itself, which was rather disorganized and chaotic, NAMFREL displayed strong organization and discipline, in part through their training sessions during the period leading up to election day. AKKAPKA activists met with NAMFREL leader José Concepción to share contacts across the country in their nonviolent network that might assist NAMFREL. Many NAMFREL volunteers took part in AKKAPKA training seminars. Trainers in nonviolent action led NAMFREL volunteers in role plays involving ballot box snatching, irregularities in vote counting, and other scenarios which in fact occurred throughout the country on election day. These actions were at great personal risk: there were 93 deaths on election day alone, a number of them NAMFREL volunteers.

The use of NAMFREL was not just aimed against Marcos, but also against the left, which was insisting that there was absolutely no hope of there being a free and fair election. NAMFREL was seen as the one hope to prevent a Marcos victory – or at least to make its unfairness obvious enough so as to negate such a victory – and to thus prevent the leadership of the opposition to be seized by radical forces.

While the efforts of NAMFREL certainly did not prevent fraud, it drastically limited its scope. More importantly, it provided an opportunity for the world to understand the extent of the cheating, and to demonstrate the determination of the Filipino people that the elections be fair. Similarly, the highly visible walkout on February 9 by 30 of the 400 COMELEC workers over the government's doctoring of vote tallies, also at considerable personal risk, helped focus attention on the extent to which the election was stolen, and allowed for increased domestic and international pressure that Marcos should resign.

Plans for Nonviolent Resistance in Response to Election Fraud

For months there had been tentative plans circulating within the Aquino campaign to force Marcos out of office by means of nonviolent civil disobedience, should the election results be rigged. As far back as mid-December, there had been meetings between Cory, AKKAPKA activists, Cardinal Sin, and some bishops on plans for a civil disobedience campaign if this should happen. Learning that the Goss-Mayers were in the country for a brief visit in early February, Cory called them in for a meeting to discuss strategies and set them up with follow-up meetings with several bishops.[40] When it became apparent that the Filipino National Assembly would ratify Marcos's fraudulent election victory, approximately 250 activists, mostly those involved in the Aquino election campaign, met in Manila on February 13 to finalize a plan of action. Included were campaign regulars, AKKAPKA activists, and some Bayan supporters. They divided into working groups of about a dozen each to "assess the pulse of the Filipino people," discuss ideas for enforcing Cory's electoral mandate through nonviolent action, and pass on specific messages from her.

A number of ideas were discussed, including one encouraged by Butz and others (inspired by the scene from the 1982 movie *Gandhi* depicting the 1930 raid on the Dharasana Salt Works) where waves of nonviolent activists would descend on Malacanang Palace and keep on marching however many were gunned down. Other proposals were much less ambitious. Finally, a seven-point program was approved.

The plans for the nonviolent campaign, announced at a rally on February 16 which drew over one million people, were far more modest than many anticipated, although a gradual escalation was promised if responses to the initial phase were good. The seven-point program included the following:

1   a general work stoppage on February 26, the day after Marcos's planned inauguration;
2   a withdrawal of funds from seven banks controlled by Marcos's cronies;
3   a boycott of media controlled by the government or by Marcos's cronies;
4   a delay in payments of electric and water bills;
5   a boycott of products of the San Miguel corporation and its subsidiaries, controlled by Marcos and his cronies;
6   following a nightly broadcast by Cory, a 15-minute noise barrage (a tactic borrowed from Latin America);
7   whatever other forms of nonviolent resistance that people might find appropriate.

While many expressed disappointment at how limited the initial stages of the campaign appeared, the boycotts began to show their effect even before they were formally organized. (The exception appears to have been the targeting of the popular beer, San Miguel, which even many anti-Marcos partisans felt they could not do without. Many others, however, particularly women, concerned with the growing problem of alcoholism, strongly supported its inclusion.)

In a Third World country such as the Philippines, where the financial situation is so precarious and support of the middle class is so crucial in order to maintain a minimum of government functions, even such modest tactics can threaten a regime's stability. The cash-starved utilities can not stay in business very long if ratepayers refuse to pay their bills. Wealthy Filipinos began to panic and started to shift large amounts of personal savings out of the country,[41] dramatically escalating a trend that had been taking place for the previous two years. For an economy already in serious decline, these seemingly modest forms of nonviolent resistance advocated by the Aquino camp appeared to be on the verge of causing major repercussions.

As a result, Marcos threatened greater use of his power, which many interpreted as a prelude to the reimposition of the martial law which had been in effect between 1971 and 1981, as a response to the threatened civil disobedience campaign. In contrast to the more militant nonviolent campaigns previously led by the increasingly leftist Bayan and other radical groups, an important strategy of this largely middle-class movement was the use of family and other ties to convince Marcos's government officials to resign.

In anticipation of a crackdown on the press, Aquino's forces set up universities and churches as alternate communications centers. A follow-up meeting was scheduled for February 19 to evaluate the campaign and develop it further.

Meanwhile, the Catholic Bishops Conference of the Philippines had called formally for "active resistance" against the Marcos regime through a "nonviolent struggle for justice."[42] There was disagreement as to whether the carefully worded two-page document was in fact a call for civil disobedience, since the actual words were not specifically included in the statement; this is likely to have been a calculated ambiguity, given the aversion of many in the church hierarchy to getting involved in politics. Most Filipinos interpreted it in the affirmative, however, noting that while the bishops might be unwilling to publicly recommend a particular form of political action, the hierarchy *did* wish to indicate that those who felt called to engage in such actions had their prior approval.

As a result of concerns over possible misinformation about the planned actions by the government, Aquino specifically ordered on February 17 that plans regarding the nonviolent campaign be made only through Veritas radio, a statement which perhaps contributed to the sabotage of the Catholic station by Marcos forces three days later. A phony circular calling for vandalism against the property of Marcos cronies and verbal abuse against Marcos supporters and their families was disavowed by Aquino's organization, stressing that the specific tactics for the civil disobedience campaign be organized from above. The Aquino media bureau warned their supporters against "forms of protest against the Marcos regime not sanctioned by Mrs. Aquino and the newly formed advisory committee on civil disobedience, a group which serves as the clearing house of all acceptable means of nonviolent protest," and that the public should check with the headquarters of "Cory's Crusaders" on the approved methods.[43]

Due to the tendency for governments to treat entire resistance movements as the opposition's most violent and irresponsible elements, there was a strong awareness of the importance of keeping this kind of massive action on a disciplined nonviolent course. Bayan, experienced in such strikes where thousands took to the streets to set up barricades and demonstrate, called on their followers to take to the streets on February 26. By contrast, Aquino encouraged her supporters to stay at home or in churches during the strike. Aquino's insistence that people avoid such public protest may have come both from a concern over a possible outbreak of violence discrediting the movement, as well as from a fear that leftist elements, even if they did remain nonviolent, might seize the leadership of the resistance campaign.

It was here that the different philosophies of nonviolence came into focus. There was concern that Bayan, which had found nonviolence a pragmatic vehicle up to this point, might also find violence pragmatic if they felt on the verge of seizing power. As a result, the insistence on nonviolence of the Aquino campaign repeatedly stressed the need both to separate themselves from any potential violence as well to emphasize their philosophical and ideological differences with the more radical Bayan.

Schools and universities reopened on February 12, after being shut down by presidential decree on January 28 (possibly to limit election-related protests or to allow adequate time for the stuffing of ballot boxes). Before classes fully resumed, however, preparations were being made to support the civil disobedience campaign. By February 18, there was a full-scale walkout by teachers and students in the Metro Manila schools and at the University of the Philippines. The previous day, 2,500 students and employees at the UP gathered on the steps of the College of Arts and Sciences to listen to suggestions on how the university would enforce its part of the civil disobedience campaign. Professor Garcia, advocating the program of civil disobedience and using terms similar to his initial call for nonviolent resistance 16 years earlier, called for "unarmed resistance aimed at disarming an illegitimate government."[44]

On February 19, utilizing a tactic used periodically before, long lines of students flocked to three pro-Marcos banks, opening accounts with minimum deposits and returning soon afterwards to withdraw them, playing havoc with these financial institutions. Also, faculty members took advantage of their widespread use as government consultants in addition to their academic duties, and were resigning government consultancy jobs in "epic proportions," refusing to return to work until ordered by "President Aquino."[45] Despite orders by UP chancellor Ernesto Tabuhara that students and faculty return to classes, their support of the civil disobedience campaigns continued and special "alternative classes" were organized to discuss pressing national issues.[46]

Unions representing workers in mining, manufacturing, and sugar industries met to organize strategies for a series of work stoppages. Similar meetings were held by those in the service industry, along with truckers, stevedores, and bank and hotel workers. The effectiveness of transit strikes in the *welgang bayans* encouraged transportation workers to consider mounting a nationwide work stoppage. The leftist trade union, the May 1 Movement (KMU), endorsed the general strike scheduled for February 26 and called on its 300,000 members to join. There was also tacit support from the Trade Unions of the Philippines (TUPAS) and the Federation of Free Workers. It was clear that a showdown was coming, but few suspected it would come so quickly or dramatically.

The Uprising

When Defense Minister Juan Ponce Enrile and Lt. Gen. Fidel Ramos announced their revolt on February 22, many saw it as an act of desperation. The rebels were badly outnumbered and were holed up in highly vulnerable army bases in the Manila suburbs. Furthermore, President Marcos had weathered other crises, and few people believed he would not be able to survive this one. Originally, Marcos decided to play for time, believing that everything was in his favor. The rebels only had 500 troops at their command, trained primarily in counterterrorism and traditional combat, or, as one Filipino put it, they had "more foreign correspondents than troops."[47] By contrast, Marcos had 10,000 men in the loyal Army Second Division, headquartered just 30 miles north of Manila, that were moving south. In addition, there was the 15,000–man Presidential Security Command, including a Marine unit skilled in hand-to-hand combat as well as a light armored unit equipped with about 30 armored cars and several light tanks.[48]

However, as one American journalist wrote, "Marcos . . . watched incredulously as a desperate mutiny by a handful of soldiers blossomed into a full-scale revolt."[49] What made the difference was not the popularity of the two military leaders, but the organized nonviolent support by hundreds of thousands of Filipinos, "bringing provisions not for combat but for a family picnic."[50] The stage of massive non-cooperation had begun.

There was some initial question by the opposition as to whether the civilian opposition should side with Enrile and Ramos, given their years of active support of the Marcos dictatorship. There was a tendency among some of them to just watch the soldiers shoot it out, or at least to wait for further developments. Butz Aquino, however, recalling Hildegard Goss-Mayer's analysis of the four pillars of the Marcos dictatorship – the government machinery, the US presence, the fear and apathy of the people, and the military – quickly realized that the last major pillar holding up the regime might be crumbling. Thus, he encouraged other opposition leaders to an emergency meeting that night to take advantage of the situation by backing the rebels with the hope of dividing the military. They realized that they should attempt to implement immediately what was to have been the culminating act of a protracted nonviolent campaign: the use of massive noncooperation. (Cory was in Cebu at the time and was not yet aware of the military revolt.) Appealing on Radio Veritas, Butz made a public call for people to gather in the Cubao section for a march on Camp Aguinaldo. By the time they reached the base a little after midnight, there were 20,000 people massing in the streets outside demonstrating their support.[51]

The role of the media was significant. Unlike many authoritarian situations, there had been an active opposition press for at least two years prior to the uprising. The business community and the church establishment, which was funding much of the nongovernment media, had been moving into open opposition following the assassination of Benigno Aquino. Their widespread noncompliance made it difficult for Marcos to enforce his restrictions on the media, though he had more success in controlling the smaller and more radical press. Soon after the uprising got underway, Marcos ordered that all print and broadcast media clear their stories with the information ministry. The order was ignored. It is noteworthy that the few armed encounters between government and rebel forces which occurred during the uprising took place over control of key radio and television stations, underscoring the growing significance of media in modern nonviolent political struggles. Even some of these confrontations, however, such as the rebel takeover of Channel Four, were resolved nonviolently.[52]

The transmitter for Radio Veritas was destroyed by government forces on the second day of the uprising. Soon afterward, Filipina–American announcer June Keithley began using Station DZ RL, broadcasting from a secret location on a frequency close to Veritas, reading messages fed to her from the action calling on people to meet armored columns that were reportedly moving into to the area. Where there were weak spots or incipient conflicts on the front lines, she would call for additional support. The result was that the civilian masses protecting the bases knew they could rely on reinforcements when ranks thinned due to fatigue, or when it appeared that government forces would attempt to penetrate the area.

When Butz first encountered Ramos after the start of the uprising, the general noted that "we need speech writers more than we need food and medicine,"[53] an indication of the centrality of the public appeals in determining the success of the uprising.

Soon after the revolt was announced, the Catholic Church appealed to sympathizers to bring food and other needed supplies to the Defense Ministry, then in rebel hands, an appeal which was responded to in generous measure. In addition, instructions were given over Radio Veritas before it was knocked out of service, and later on the captured television stations, on techniques of nonviolent resistance, including instructions on fraternizing with loyalist soldiers with offers of food and cigarettes to encourage them to defect. There were also instructions on preparation for expected tear gas attacks, encouraging participants to bring lemons, cloths, and pails of water. People were also asked to bring flashlights and transistor radios. These instructions were carried out despite a Marcos declaration of a state of emergency, a dusk-to-dawn curfew, and specific demands that civilians leave the area surrounding the rebel strongholds. As with other successful nonviolent movements, the nonviolent discipline was maintained along with a determination not to be intimidated by such official orders. By the second day, the crowd had swelled to 40,000, among them 7,000 nuns and 5,000 priests and seminarians.[54]

Nicandro Navarette, a labor leader who had been active in AKKAPKA, along with other graduates of the nonviolence training workshops, went from one human barricade to the other assisting the defenders in relevant nonviolent techniques. Those on the front lines were encouraged to link arms and sit down in case of attack. If this became untenable they were encouraged not to run, as it could create panic, but to leave in a deliberate and orderly manner. This advice was taken successfully during later tear gas attacks.

Some of the tactics used were inspired by previous nonviolent struggles. Some of the nonviolent Filipino leaders knew of the resistance in the streets in Czechoslovakia in the face of Soviet tanks, where in contrast to the armed resistance in a similar situation in Hungary 12 years earlier, the invaders did not open fire. (It also took the Soviets a full six months before they could install a puppet regime in Prague compared to only a matter of days in Budapest.) In addition, there were some uniquely Filipino innovations in the confrontation. The use of statues of sacred figures and other religious artifacts played a deterrent role against soldiers who might have had few qualms about running down civilians in their vehicles but who felt a superstitious dread of running a tank over a statue of the Virgin Mary. To encourage the use of such religious symbols, General Ramos, even though a well-known Protestant, appeared on television carrying a statuette of the Madonna.[55]

Though the training in nonviolent action over the years and the discussions of various scenarios by the Aquino forces clearly played a crucial role, there was also some inventiveness on the spot. In addition to the human masses blocking the entrances to the bases, cars and buses were parked in important intersections leading to the area, holes were dug in the street, fallen trees and other miscellaneous debris lay across the roads.[56] Even children insisted on contributing to the effort by leaving their bicycles and other beloved possessions in the street to help block oncoming tanks. In an act reminiscent of anti-Vietnam War protests in the United States, demonstrators tied yellow ribbons, symbolizing the Aquino campaign, onto the bayonets of the soldiers. There was a strong spiritual fervor during those four days, a sense that the participants were caught up in a force stronger than the sum total of their numbers. Many described it as being part of a "miracle of God."[57] Indeed, there were several precipitous incidents which some participants took as signs of divine support, such as a large-scale tear gas attack that was halted when the wind suddenly shifted direction.[58]

It was the human barricades that proved the most formidable: Soon after the initial revolt, Marcos ordered General Fabian Ver to clear the area of civilians by whatever means necessary. A Marine major reported that they were ordered by Brigadier General Tadiar to move on to the camps. Marines under orders to fire into the crowd took aim, broke into tears, and retreated. They then moved onto an adjacent empty field and proceeded no further.[59] According to Col. B. B. Balboa, the deputy Marine commander, Tadiar – under direct orders from Malacanang – demanded that Balboa have his troops fire on the crowd and relayed an order from General Ver that mortar and cannon rounds be fired into Camp Crame regardless of civilians in the way. Balboa protested, on the grounds that his troops would also be likely to resist his orders, but he was ordered to move in anyway. Rather than openly disobey, Balboa stalled for time by claiming they were "trying to get into position."[60]

Meanwhile, Marcos had ordered the air force to attack Camp Crame. Air force jets circled eight times but never opened fire. The pilots later indicated that they realized a bombing attack on this relatively small base would inevitably cause widespread casualties among the civilians in the perimeter area, and refused to attack. At least one pilot was reportedly discouraged by noting that the crowds on the streets below were in the shape of a cross.[61]

Throughout the series of encounters, startled troops were met by gestures of friendship, embraces, food, and cigarettes. Eventually, as police began beating on their shields in time with the anti-Marcos chants, and troops began flashing "L" signs with their hands, symbols of Aquino's Laban Party, it became clear that the crowd's insistence of nonbelligerence towards the government forces was beginning to pay off.

Cardinal Jaime Sin announced over the airwaves,

> I would like to appeal to all our soldiers and our people never to use weapons to hurt any of our countrymen. We shall solve our problems through dialogue and peaceful means.

Defections among armed forces personnel began to escalate.

One significance of this series of events was, contrary to claims by the Reagan Administration and others that Marcos showed his decency by refusing to attack nonviolent civilians, that it was the soldiers in the ranks and lower-level officers who decided not to attack, in direct defiance of their superiors. Similar claims that it was mass defections by whole units across the country, not the nonviolent campaign, which actually resulted in the downfall of Marcos ignores the fact that it was the masses outside the bases which bought Ramos time to contact commanders throughout the country and successfully convince them to join the rebellion.

It may be one of the few times in history where civilians were protecting the military rather than the other way around, and where such large numbers were physically keeping two groups of armed antagonists apart. And the civilian participation grew along with the military revolt; by the fourth day, the numbers outside the rebel base had swelled into the hundreds of thousands.

There were periods when it appeared that the mass action might deteriorate into violence. Monday evening, a group claiming to be members of the NPA moved on to one of the barricades, asking for people to disperse when the Marines approached and an NPA detachment would move in for the attack. Their request was roundly rejected and they were asked to leave. At other checkpoints, a group of armed men claiming they were under orders from Enrile attempted to take control of a barricade controlled by priests and nuns. When it became clear that this was not actually the case, they were similarly prevented from seizing control.

Meanwhile, a Bayan-led crowd assembling at Mendiola Bridge facing Malacanang Palace was threatening to storm through the barricades. Though unarmed, this group was belligerent and ready for confrontation, unlike the atmosphere around the camps, which was far more friendly.

Some young Jesuits and other volunteers played the role of peacekeepers to keep the crowd calm.

Enrile ruled out distributing firearms to the supporters outside the base, steadfastly insisting that, if challenged militarily, the fighting would be done by the rebels themselves. Both he and Ramos no doubt also realized that they and the rebel forces were being protected far more by unarmed supporters than they could be by equivalent numbers of armed supporters. At the same time, Ramos acknowledged that "We have been successful not so much because of our military option but because of people's power."[62]

By the time the Marcos entourage fled on February 25, there were more than 250,000 Filipinos directly surrounding the base, and hundreds of thousands more on the streets demanding the president's ousting. In addition to Aquino's urban middle-class supporters, thousands came in from the slums and from outlying rural areas to join the throng. Participants reported witnessing a number of moving incidents of wealthy businessmen alongside the poor, sharing donated food and drinking from the same cup. In the 77 hours of the uprising, only 16 people were killed, nine of whom died "in a police shootout with a mentally unstable man posing as a rebel military officer."[63] Cardinal Sin noted that the nonviolent action of the masses came not from the ideas of opposition leaders as much as from the way in which it fired the imagination of hundreds of thousands of people. According to Sin, remarking on the discipline of the crowds, "It was amazing. It was two million independent decisions. Each one said, in his heart, 'I will do this,' and they went out."[64]

For nonviolent actions that emerge victorious, there appear to be two major personal factors which contribute to success. The first, which has been most emphasized in this chapter, was individuals' decisions on the maintenance of a nonviolent discipline. The second, but at least as important, was the determination of a sufficient number of people to take part in such an action despite tremendous personal risks. Most participants on the streets outside the camps believed that they were going to be attacked with lethal force. Most acknowledged being quite frightened, but were determined to take part anyway. Under such circumstances, it is evident that the amount of courage to take part in a nonviolent uprising such as this is at least as great as the decision to take up arms. Equally fundamental to the realization, on both ethical or pragmatic grounds, of the importance of maintaining a nonviolent discipline, was the realization that it was worth risking their lives for the cause of democracy.

There is little doubt that the rebellion would have quickly been crushed without the massive nonviolent direct action in support of the dissident troops. In addition, because Enrile and Ramos were dependent on the outpouring of popular support, any attempt by these conservative military leaders to seize power themselves rather than turn things over to Aquino would have faced a well-mobilized popular resistance. Indeed, there are some indications that had Enrile and Ramos succeeded in their coup without the massive outpouring of popular support, Cory would have been included as merely a figurehead leader in a military-civilian junta dominated by Enrile and Ramos.[65] Since civilians protected the coup leaders rather than military officers unilaterally taking action "for the people," the popular civilian elements of Cory Aquino's government, despite internal tensions, had clear leverage over the military.

Also important factor was that the use of nonviolence gave the uprising widespread sympathy in the United States, which limited the options that could be taken by the US government. State Department officials have since acknowledged that the use of nonviolence made intervention on behalf of Marcos virtually impossible, whereas contingency plans existed for intervention in the case of an armed rebellion.[66] Despite widespread evidence of vote fraud, President Reagan maintained his support of the Marcos regime – including continued military assistance – until masses of Filipinos appeared on the streets. The support of the "people's power" movement by the US media and the public at large helped force the US government to end its two decades of support for the Marcos government, which it had maintained through years of corruption, human rights violations, and unpopular governance. US ambassador Stephen Bosworth telephoned Marcos with what he claimed was a direct warning from President Reagan not to use heavy weapons against the rebels.[67]

The Aftermath

An editorial in the *Philippine Daily Express* stated that "a Gandhi-like nonviolent drive became the program, not a platitude."[68] Indeed, it was a powerful statement of the power of massive nonviolent action. Yet the goal of the uprising was the honoring of an electoral mandate, not fundamental social change. It was an urban phenomenon in a largely rural society. It was a largely middle-class movement in a country where most people are desperately poor. It could not be considered a nonviolent revolution, then, but simply a nonviolent revolt or a nonviolent coup.

While other nonviolent campaigns in the Philippines had a much broader constituency, there was little involvement of the left during the uprising itself. Part of the left's distance may have been tactical. There was fear that a visible left presence among the crowd – even a nonviolent one – could provoke the military to attack. Marcos's attempt to discredit the Aquino campaign by linking it to the left was made difficult by the left's boycott of the election, an advantage which might have been jeopardized with their visible presence in the uprising. However, these may just be rationalizations for a major tactical blunder.

NDF leader Edicio de la Torre has acknowledged that the left may have "missed out on history" by not actively supporting the nonviolent uprising. He went on to state that the people achieved a "new, higher level of politicization and national consciousness, not because of the Left, but because of the experience of bringing down a dictator through collective mass action." De la Torre concluded that this experience could be used again against another regime at some future point.[69]

A Jesuit priest shared a story which may be similar to that of many Filipino activists currently reevaluating the methods of struggle. He described his conversation with a young Filipina Communist who had spent many years underground, sharing great pride in how the people had freed themselves from tyranny.

> Her eyes filled with tears as she spoke of her husband and companions who, years ago, died in combat for the Party. She now faults the "movement" for failing to realize and respect the spiritual power that resides in the people... Beyond this was something which the Party could never have anticipated, namely the bond of solidarity that linked the people with the soldiers on both sides.[70]

AKKAPKA, among others, have seen their role subsequently as building a movement based on the nonviolent methods so effective in the overthrow of Marcos to make a revolutionary transformation of society, including radical land reform, replacing the oligarchy with a more democratic social and economic structure, and curbing US influence in the county's affairs. Ramon Pedrosa, a founder and president of the August 21 Movement, has attempted to build a program to reintegrate Communist rebels into society through involvement in nonviolent campaigns for land reform. Training centers have been set up in rural areas for farmers and other advocates of land reform in the use of nonviolent action. In the dozen years since the downfall of Marcos, the underlying social inequities in Filipino society remain, yet nonviolent grass roots movements and have scored a number of important local victories.

The question must be asked as to why such a nonviolent movement succeeded in the Philippines where nonviolent movements elsewhere have so often failed, or never even been attempted. There were a number of characteristics in Philippines society which made a difference. Despite the repressive nature of the Marcos regime, there was a relatively free press and few restrictions on freedom of movement; it was far easier for such a movement to be organized than it would be in a completely totalitarian situation. In addition, the Philippines had much of the world's media attention during the critical hours of the standoff at Camp Crame, which led to the threat of sanctions by the United States, the Marcos government's traditional benefactor. In contrast, a dramatic and large-scale nonviolent uprising against the regime of Pakistani dictator Zia al-Huq in 1983, also a recipient of generous US military and economic assistance, got little media attention, and thus no threatened cut-offs of aid. The revolt was crushed.

In addition, while Filipino governments preceding Marcos were somewhat plutocratic, the country did possess nominally democratic institutions and, more importantly, an expectation that there would be a degree of pluralism in Filipino society. While the colonial period under the United States certainly had negative aspects, the expectation did exist – and institutions did evolve – that insured a representative form of government. Despite conditions which might have earlier led to dictatorial rule – such as the Communist-led rebellion in the 1950s and the negative ramifications of being a dependent Third World economy – the Philippines never became a "banana republic" in the sense that governments came to power and lost power through a series of military coups. The Marcos presidency, despite a certain resemblance to the bureaucratic-authoritarianism of many Latin American states during the same period, was, by contrast, seen as an aberration. Despite years of martial law rule, democracy was seen as the norm. This was certainly not the case in many Third World situations.

Another advantage was the power of the Catholic Church, which, despite a history of supporting the concept of a "just war," also has a strong pacifist tradition, which allowed an openness to nonviolent alternatives. Again, few Third World countries have such an ethical foundation in their society upon which to draw. As the only predominantly independent Christian country in Asia, it is not surprising that the Philippines became a place where such a movement could find fertile ground. In is perhaps significant that the nonviolent pro-democracy movement in South Korea was centered among the Christian minority.

On the other hand, the methods by which the Filipino people overthrew the Marcos dictatorship indicated a growing awareness of an effective and less costly means of forcing change in an era of increasingly brutal counter-insurgency warfare. More importantly, it also demonstrates a kind of popular empowerment that may foretell increasing militant, nonviolent actions by the population to force more fundamental changes in Filipino society and in other Third World nations suffering from the effects of neocolonialism and economic inequality. In the words of Cory Aquino,

> The world saw and recorded a people who knelt in the path of oncoming tanks and subdued with embraces of friendship the battle-hard troops sent out to disperse them. All the world wondered as they witnessed ... a people lift themselves from humiliation to greatest pride.[71]

Notes

1   Editorial, *Asiaweek*, March 10, 1986.
2   Quoted by Virginia Baron, *Fellowship*, (March 1986), 52(3): 3.
3   Francisco Nemenzo, "The Left and the Traditional Opposition." In R. J. May and Francisco Nemenzo, *The Philippines After Marcos* (New York: St. Martin's Press, 1985) p. 61.
4   Jose C. Blanco, SJ *The Role of Nonviolence in Philippine Society*, (Manila: self published pumphlet, 1986) p. 2.

5   George Lakey, *Strategy for a Living Revolution* (New York: Orbis Books, 1973).

6   Lakey's work implies that such a scenario would result in the creation of a truly revolutionary society, presumably one which resembles his own libertarian socialist ideals. Clearly the events in the Philippines were far short of such revolutionary change. One could argue perhaps that the Philippine revolution came so quickly that the time line was telescoped to an extent that the necessary polarization of society needed to invoke such sweeping changes was made impossible.

    While such ideological polarization may be necessary for a truly revolutionary transformation of society, this does not necessarily mean, as some Marxists imply, that the opposition movement therefore will be prone to violence. Often, in the process of the ideological development of the opposition, they will become convinced, rightly or wrongly, that nonviolence was not a practical means of forcing change. However, the radicalization of an opposition group's goals and the tactics they employ to overthrow or usurp the existing regime should be seen as independent variables. Though the shift to armed struggle has often coincided with the development of a more radical ideology, it has not been demonstrated that they are intrinsically linked.

7   For a more detailed account of the use of affinity groups in recent nonviolent action campaigns in the United States, see my article "Seabrook: A Turning Point", *The Progressive*, (Sept. 1978), 42(9): 28–31.

8   Benjamin Bagdion, "People's Power in the Philippines," unpublished TS, 1986.

9   John Miller, "Rural Organization in the Philippines During the Martial Law," unpublished TS, 1984.

10 Quoted by John Miller, "People's Power in the Philippines: The Challenges Ahead," *Nonviolent Activist*, (June 1986).

11 *Peacemaker*, March–June 1985, p.

12 James V. Jazmines, "Mass Politics vs. Elite Politics?" February 2, 1986, unpublished MS, Manila.

13 "Blazing the Way," *Liberation*, (January–February 1985) 28: 6.

14 Ibid.

15 Ibid.

16 Quoted in *Ang Bayan*, May 1985.

17 Ibid.

18 William Branigan, "Marcos Aims at Ex-Rival," *Washington Post*, Jan. 13, 1986, p. A15.

19 *The Mobilizer*, October 1985.

20 Ibid.

21 Miller, "People's Power in the Philippines.

22 Fellowship of Reconciliation, "Nonviolence Wins in the Philippines: A Short History," 1986

23 Ibid., "Letter to Friends and Members of FOR," March 12, 1986

24 AKKAPKA, "Thematic Guide/Seminar Outline" for Seminar Workshop on Active Non-Violence, Level One: Basic Training.

25 Ibid.

26 Fellowship of Reconciliation, "Letter to Friends."

27 For more extensive studies on the use of nonviolence in winning neutrals and potential adversaries to the opposition, see Gene Sharp, *The Politics of Nonviolent Action* (Boston: Porter Sargent, 1973); Martin Oppenheimer, *The Urban Guerilla* (Chicago: Quadrangle Books, 1969); George Lakey, *Powerful Peacemaking: A Strategy for a Living Revolution* (Philadelphia: New Society Publishers, 1986).

28 Interview with Richard Deats, May 14, 1986.

29 Quoted in Earl Martin, "The Philippine Church Amidst Revolution", *Peace Section Newsletter,* Mennonite Central Committee, (September–October 1982), pp.

30 James L. Franklin, "A Prelate Explains 'Revolution of Love,'" *Boston Globe,* June 1, 1986.

31 Ibid.

32 Richard Deats, "The Development of Active Nonviolence in the Philippines," unpublished TS, 1986.

33 Peggy Rosenthal, "The Precarious Road:" Why Nonviolence in the Philippines? *Commonweal,* (June 20, 1986) 113(12): 354–83.

34 Interview with Richard Deats, May 14, 1986.

35 Ibid.

36 Ibid.

37 Douglas Elwood, *Philippine Revolution, 1986: Model of Nonviolent Change* (Quezon City: New Day Publishers, 1986), p. 20.

38 *Veritas*, Feb. 2, 1986.

39 Franklin, "A Prelate explains."

40 Rosenthal, "Nonviolence in the Philippines."

41 Christopher Marris, "The Showdown," *Newsweek*, (March 3, 1986), CVII(9): 41.

42 Cited in Elwood, *Philippine Revolution* p. 4.

43 Quoted in *Manila Times Journal*, Feb. 19, 1986.

44 *Manila Times*, Feb. 18, 1986.

45 FBIS, Hong Kong AFP, Feb. 19, 1986.

46 FBIS, City Maharlika Broadcasting System, Feb. 19, 1986.

47 Monina Allarey Mercado, *People Power: The Philippine Revolution of 1986* (Manila: James B Reuter, S.J., Foundation, 1986), p. 101.

48 *Newsweek*, (March 3, 1986), CVII (9): 33.

49 Harry Anderson, "Cory's people power," *Newsweek*, (March 10, 1986) CVII (10): 18.

50 Mercado, *People Power*, p. 101.

51 Interview with Richard Deats.

52 Elwood, *Philippine Revolution*, p. 9.

53 Ibid.

54 Ibid., p. 8.

55 Interview with Richard Deats.

56 Mercado, *People Power*, pp. 101–2.

57 Ibid.

58 Ibid., p. 102.

59 FBIS, Hong Kong AFP, Feb. 23, 1986.

60 Quoted in Interview with Richard Deats.

61 Ibid.

62 Anderson, "Cory's People Power," *Newsweek*, March 10, 1986 CVII(10): 36.

63 FBIS, FEBC, Feb. 28, 1986.
64 Quoted in *Boston Globe*, June 1, 1986.
65 *Ang Kaipunan*, March 6, 1986.
66 Interview with knowledgeable State Department official, March 1986.
67 Mercado, *People Power*, p. 102.
68 *Philippine Daily Express*, Feb. 27, 1986.
69 Manila *Business Day*, Feb. 27, 1986.
70 Fr. George Brady, *Los Angeles Times*, Feb. 18, 1986.
71 *Newsweek*, March 10, 1986, CVII(10).

8

Imagery in the 1992 Nonviolent Uprising in Thailand

Chaiwat Satha-Anand

A Brief Account of the May Event

The most recent campaign for democracy in Thailand began on April 7, 1992 when a veteran, though lesser-known, politician by the name of Khun Charlard Vorachat staged a hunger strike. People began to campaign around the place where he first sat through his solitary campaign, which was near the Thai parliament, situated next to the Bangkok zoo. The general objective of the campaign, which democratic support groups took part in organizing, was for Thailand to become democratic, a demand translated into the election of a prime minister. Thailand had been under the rule of a military-dominated government that had seized power in February of the previous year. This demand for greater democracy, in turn, became more specific in the public cry for the removal of General Suchinda Kraprayoon from the office of prime minister. The means by which the campaign proposed to realize its objective was primarily non-violent demonstration.

For security reasons, the organizers of the campaign decided to move the demonstrators, whose numbers filled the whole street separating the Parliament from the zoo. The people moved to Sanam Luang, a huge ground next to Thammasat University once used mainly for a wonderful Sunday market and in the 1970s for political gatherings. The Campaign at Sanam Luang (literally "royal lawn") had a particular quality: in addition to the entertaining mood of the crowds and the presence of mobile food stalls and drink vendors, perhaps characteristic of the fun-loving Thais, participants in the campaign were visibly different from those who took part in campaigns in the 1970s. Many of them participated after office hours. They would park their cars, some of them Mercedes, walk over to Sanam Luang and in their designer clothing, with cellular phones by their sides, sit down on mats, and listen to streams of speakers, opposition political party members, and democratic activists, speak about the problems of democracy in their country.

On May 4, Maj. Gen. Chamlong Srimuang, a former military commander and Bangkok governor, who later became Palang Dharma Party leader,
announced that he would "fast until death". A devout Buddhist and confirmed vegetarian, who was awarded the prestigious Magsaysay prize
among other things, he was prepared to maintain his fast until
Suchinda resigned from office. He gave himself seven days. The limited
time scale rendered the conflict more acute, with much more public participation, resulting in extensive media attention. During the next seven days of
vigorous campaigning, the number of participants grew significantly, especially in the evenings, and went down as the night were on. On May 8,
Chamlong decided to move the crowds, despite disagreement among some
campaign organizers, to Raj Damnoen Road, a major avenue close by that
was often used by demonstrators during the turbulent 1970s. At the height
of the campaign, Chamlong asked permission from the demonstrators to
give up his fast because, he reasoned, the movement needed a leader and he
could no longer perform his task properly while continuing to fast. They
agreed, but it was a move which many considered to have a negative effect
on his legitimacy as an honest, Buddhist-orientated leader. Confrontation
with the police commandos, who by now had cordoned off the area joining
Raj Damnoen and Pan Fah Bridge, almost took place. Finally Chamlong
was able to disperse the crowd when the Speaker of the House agreed to
persuade all political parties to amend the constitution, thus making it
impossible for an elected person to become a prime minister, among other
things. The people went home on the understanding that they would be
back again on May 15 to hold the coalition parties to their word. As it
turned out, senior government party members did not honor the promise
made between their people and the Speaker of the House. On May 15,
hundreds of thousands gathered. I felt at the time that violence was around
the corner and we tried to do what we could under the circumstances. In
response to this threat, the Peace Information Center published 10,000
copies of a small pamphlet called "19 Secrets of Nonviolence" and distrib-
uted them among demonstrators.
These "19 Secrets" are as follows:

Seven Ideas   conflicts are normal in society and in life; in conflict no one is
completely right or wrong; conflicts can be solved when all sides cooperate;
everyone is equally human – even those who are seen to be brutish – and
they can also be touched by love and compassion; "the enemies" are not
people or groups but narrow-mindedness, love of power, and greed; means
used should correspond with ends desired, if democracy is wanted; nonviolence is the way because it is based on voluntary participation; and lastly,
power does not come from weapons, but it based on consent and obedience.
Five Practical Principles   we are in search of justice and reconciliation, not
victory; walk and speak with compassion; try to purify the mind and be free

from self-interest; deal with friends and oppositions with kindness; and abstain from violence in actions, words, and minds.

Three Special Characteristics nonviolence is an effective way to deal with conflict which will liberate us from the vicious cycle of violence; it is the use of social, economic, and political power for the transformation of society; and it is a way whereby everyone can empower him/herself.

Four Limitations success in using nonviolent actions is not guaranteed; there is no guarantee that nonviolent actions will not be met with violence; effectiveness of nonviolent actions depends on practitioners' preparedness; and lastly, if nonviolent actions are used together with violence, the former's legitimacy will be decreased, while the legitimacy of the violent suppression of the opposition will increase.

The sight and sounds of violence cast their shadow over Bangkok until May 20, by which time there had been 52 official deaths and 177 people had gone missing.[1] The violent suppression of unarmed and largely non-violent demonstrators was well captured by the world media. Due to internal and international pressures, Suchinda later resigned and Anand Panyarachun returned to be the prime minister. Another national election was held on September 13, 1992. Chuan Leepai, a civilian with 23 years of experience in parliamentary politics in the Democrat Party, became head of a coalition government comprising all the parties opposing the Suchinda government during the May incident. I will now proceed to the discussion of nonviolent practices during the campaign.

Looking at Nonviolent Practices during May 1992 through Postcards of the Time

It seems appropriate to begin this part of the paper with an explanation of why I chose to use a set of postcards as representations of nonviolent practices during the May 1992 uprising. Representation is a way of re-presenting something, in this case a political event. In the process of representation, some things will be present and others will be absent. Since this is true in all forms of representation, this set of postcards, unlike photographs or VDO pictures, certainly has a clear advantage. Due to the fact that they are paintings by a Thai artist, they do not pretend to re-present the event from an objective point of view, as it happened, but rather as the memory of the event when fused with the artist's imagination.

Moreover, this set of postcards is explicit about its message on nonviolence and democracy. From the set of seven, the words "nonviolence" and "demo-cracy" figure prominently in four of the postcards. In addition, money earned from selling these postcards would, in particular, be used to fund the interna-tional women's conference in putting an end to violence in Bangkok, held on November 25–9, 1992. Naphas Assawachaicharn, the woman artist whose first name appears as a signature in all postcards and whose full name can be found on the other side, together with the name of her group, the Sarn Fan (Weaving the Dreams), which called this set of postcards "A Flower's Diary of Democracy." It is also important to emphasize that these are real postcards, with space to fill senders' names and addresses as well as a corner for postage stamps. Although words appearing in these postcards are both in Thai and English, the Thai captions and their English renditions are in small prints and hardly readable. Yet in all but one of them, the main messages are in English. The intention is that these nonviolent messages should travel and that their nonviolent messages should reach either to the Thais who know English or foreign friends of Thailand or both. In any case the choice of using English indicates the extent to which the Thai artists are aware of the significance of international influences.

Postcard 1 Democracy and "People's Power" are promoted by this postcard, featuring "flowers of democracy."

First postcard

This can be seen as the cover of "the text." The title is given in Thai which means "A Flower Diary of Democracy." The main character is called "a flower of democracy," who looks like a feminine yellow sunflower, with a headband which reads "People's Power." Perhaps unconsciously the "flower" links herself with another recent nonviolent victory: the February 1986 Philippines uprising. Both the term and the yellow color used seem to point in that direction. It should also be noted that the flower is also a blossoming and happy one.

Second postcard

The two singers are playing their guitars and singing to the joy of the campaign participants, in whose hands appear two banners: "Give me liberty and democracy." The main word, "nonviolence" does not look like another banner but a bright sign joining both banners. It seems to suggest that the way to both the liberty and democracy that the people want can be attained through nonviolence.

The use of singing in nonviolent campaigns is quite common. This method of nonviolent protest can be found in the Finnish disobedience

Postcard 2   Nonviolence is extolled as the means for achieving liberty and democracy.

movement against the tsar's autocratic imposition of the conscription law of July 1901, to the singing of "Nkosi Sikelel' I Afrika" by a large crowd protesting against the arrest of their South African resistance leaders in December 1956,[2] to the recent occasion of 20,000 Estonians singing around the clock for 24 hours. But what this postcard also depicts is that there are real, popular singers who joined forces with the people. The names of Add Carabao, a well-known "songs for life" singer and Aristman, a popular teenage idol came to mind. People like them participated fully in the campaign. In fact, some of them also wrote protest songs which were banned by some radio stations but later used by some young and sympathetic DJs, when the demonstrators were brutally suppressed by the military, in order to uplift the morale and maintain the strength of the public.

Third postcard

The message: "No More Dictatorship," is quite clear. The other banner also indicates that the military is perceived as "the Mafia."[3] Nonviolence posters are also visible in the background. There are a number of things which can be read from this postcard. First the number of people is important. While the military's estimate of the number of people who fought peacefully was decidedly small – 60,000 according to the leader of the now-

Postcard 3 This postcard indicates that the power of nonviolent mobilization is more powerful than military mobilization.

defunct NPKC[4] – in fact people of all ages (note the little flowers), genders and classes, numbering anywhere from 250,000 to 500,000 participated in the campaign. Second, while the moon looks at the people with a soft smile, there is darkness surrounding the monument at the back. That monument is called "democracy monument." Most political campaigns would consider it a landmark and it has its own history to tell.

The monument was built after the 1932 revolution. Structurally, it has four wings and each is 24 feet high. In the center is a small dome-like room with six gates, each decorated with classical Thai swords pointing downward. The height of this little classical room is three meters, with the constitution, originally painted black and now gold, on the Thai ceremonial bowl normally used when something is to be given to the King. Around the base of the monument, 75 cannons can be found. All these figures have symbolic meanings. The number 24 signifies the date of the June 1932 revolution. The number three signifies the month. It is three because during that time January was yet to be considered the first month of the year. The Thai New Year was in April. The number 75 signifies the last two digits of the BE year of the revolution: 2475. The six ancient swords signify the six principles of the Rassadorn Group who sparked the revolution. They are: independence, public safety, economic well-being, equal rights to all citizens, freedom, and better education to all.[5] This could be seen as a "deep reading" into the esoteric meaning of the monument, which is in turn depicted with few details on the postcard.

The Third postcard has the largest number of people in it. What is interesting is what had happened before the event in the postcard took place. The people gathered at Sanam Luang and the organizers decided to move the gathering to another place. The reason given for it was for safety of the crowd. In moving the crowd, nonviolent methods of protest shifted from the protest meeting, held in an open area with easy accesses in all directions, to a march, and then to a show of nonviolent intervention when the crowds occupied the area, including road space, surrounding the monument. There are two points that I wish to discuss here, both of which related to nonviolent techniques. I will use one of the most basic human needs and its corresponding facilities as an illustration.

Fourth postcard

In this postcard, the flower is seen speaking to someone using a cellular phone. She is surrounded by five others with headbands which read: "peace," "non-violence," "love," "democracy," and "freedom." There are two points which need to be elaborated. First cellular phones in Thailand are not cheap. A phone like that can cost anywhere from US $1,200 to US $3,000, depending on its functions and utilities. This would mean that they belong to the middle class or upper class. Although the notion of the Thai middle class is still quite problematic, it can be argued that they are the

Postcard 4 The Thai insurgency, as shown here, involved middle-class participants and the use of modern communications such as cellular telephones.

beneficiaries of the process of economic development who, on the one hand, should support the existing political order but on the other, due to their education, economic standing, and sense of empowerment, should be quite confident in criticizing government leaders.[6] As a group of people with money, they can practice nonviolent action by withdrawing their financial support from financial institutions that appear to support the military establishment.[7] Indeed, more and more people decided to withdraw their money from the Thai Military Bank. Though the amount of money withdrawn was never disclosed, such nonviolent action did create an impact to the extent that the bank's chairperson had to come out and deny any link to the military, which itself was a significant attempt to dissociate themselves from Suchinda and his military allies and also socially weaken him somewhat. One bank executive came out and even proposed that the bank change its name to something unrelated to the military. The banker's concern would seem to support Sharp's thesis of the fragility of established power and the extent to which it depends on social sources.[8] In addition, unlike nonviolent campaigns by the poor, due to their economic strength, the middle class can sustain the nonviolent campaigns longer and can thus cause serious damage to the support system of the dictatorial regime. It should also be noted that of the list of some 45 to 52 people killed,[9] based on their occupations, very few could be classified as middle-class.

Second, a salient feature of nonviolent practices during the May uprising is the extensive use of modern communication. The cellular phones were used to communicate between the campaign ground and the owner's home bases. Sometimes written political solutions issued by the campaign organizers were read into the phones for the benefit of those who could not attend the rally. In fact the Suchinda government exercised tight control over the media. For example, a Visnews spokesperson in London said their Bangkok office was told that they would not be allowed to transmit footage of an anti-government rally for satellite transmission and CNN had to continue to cover events through telephone reports.[10] It was common knowledge that the telephone lines all over the city were tapped. Nevertheless, due to a different kind of network, using cellular phones was a lot safer because they are more difficult to detect.

Telephones, fax machines, and electronic mails were constantly used to bypass the controlled media system. Fax machines in various offices all over the city were sending rally messages so that others could reproduce them. Fax messages almost flooded the city, a fact which adversely affected the communication and information collection of the nonviolent campaigners. The security force could not effectively locate the sources of these alternative accounts of the democratic campaign. The military reportedly had to order 20 "fax detection machines" from the US at the time. In addition, electronic mails helped establish a swift exchange of information both inside the country and with friends abroad. International telephone calls were made to coordinate attempts at bringing international pressure to bear upon the representative regime. In this sense, the spontaneous use of modern communication technology provides alternative communication channels so that the message concerning nonviolent campaigns can be swiftly delivered, wider public support mobilized, and broader actions coordinated. It seems that the modern technologies for person-to-person communication can provide "a stronger basis for nonviolent resistance than one-directional technologies such as television."[11]

Moreover, different professional classes withdrew their support from the military of their own accord. Lecturers from the Faculty of Economics and Political Science, Thammasat University, officially boycotted invitations to teach or give lectures at various military educational institutions. Officials at the foreign ministry were at a loss when receiving an order from their superior to work harder for the better image of the country. A middle-ranking official wrote back to his supervisor that he was at his wit's end how to carry out this order. He believed that there was only one way to protect the image of the country and that was for General Suchinda to resign. Civil servants at the prime minister's office decided to mourn the suppression by dressing for work in black. Medical doctors declared that they would no longer treat military patients after they saw how badly physicians who worked to help the people were treated. Several newspapers were explicit in siding with the democratic protestors. Even a television stationmaster whose work was tightly controlled tried to delay his station broadcast when ordered by the military officer under the emergency situation. He was able to do so by adhering to bureaucratic procedures. Judging the degree to which consent was voluntary withdrawn from the Suchinda government, his collapse was predictable.[12]

Fifth postcard

This postcard depicts a particular portrait. There are five canines, four on the bike with the Thai flag, while the fifth one follows behind with a balloon showing a no-swastika sign. The flower sits in the middle among the four dogs with ribbons on their heads. It seems that these four are females who are leading the male member, the democratic campaigner. I don't think that there were more females than males in the demonstration during the campaign. As a matter of fact, if one looks at the number of women who are still missing, there are 30 out of a total of 177 (or 16.9 percent).[13] According to the nongovernment organizations responsible for the record of those killed and missing during the May event, only one woman was fatally shot. But it should be noted that one of the most important members of the organizing committee, the Confederation for Democracy, which controlled the direction of the movement, especially

Postcard 5 Women were highly visible in the campaign.

during its final phase, is a woman. Teacher Kru Prateep Ungsongtham, a Magsaysay Award recipient, is a dedicated social activist who has spent all her life working for slum people in Bangkok. It could, however, be said that the role of women during this campaign was highly visible; many nonviolent activists who set up their tents to share information on nonviolence among the crowd almost all through the campaign period were women as well.

The other representation in this postcard is the bike itself. During the campaign, motorbike riders, who normally use the bikes to reach their destinations by beating Bangkok's gridlocked traffic, were organized to participated actively in the campaign. The government security forces found these people difficult to pin down because of their speed and mobility. The military later organized a hunter-killer motorbike team to gun them down, especially during the nights of May 18 and 19, when a group of bikers rode around the city vandalizing and destroying traffic lights. Consequently, several innocent motorbike riders who had nothing to do with the rally lost their lives.

Sixth postcard

The caption of this postcard describes the flower's dreams of being able to work with the military in growing the flowers of democracy. This picture

Postcard 6 Traditional Buddhist practices were combined with modern nonviolent training to confront the military in the 1992 Thai uprising.

has double meanings, one embedded in the actuality of what had happened and the other in a reconciliatory wish. When the uprising reached its confrontational phase, the two sides were often separated by a column of concertina wires, if those who were schooled in nonviolence happened to be at the frontline, communication between the two opposing forces would take place. Nonviolent female activists in the field would give flowers to the soldiers who were fully armed. I understand that such action did elicit smiles on the faces of the military. This action has always been strongly emphasized by nonviolent protagonists, because the underlying logic of violence dictates a dehumanizing process, and it is imperative therefore that nonviolent action should be preceded by a conscious rehumanizing effort.[14] Giving flowers as well as food-sharing are crucial in the rehumanizing process. However, the oppressors normally replace the forces that make contacts with protestors with those fresh from the barracks, where the effect of the dehumanization process through indoctrination with false information, among other things, is still strong. These types of soldiers would be less hesitant to kill unarmed protestors.

The dream of the flower is also important because the picture connotes the promise of the future where "the men in green," as they are referred to in the postcard, would work together with others in nurturing democracy. This pulling of the soldiers to the democratic side is also in accordance with nonviolence theory, which maintains that its power is social in nature and therefore can be drawn from all sectors in a given society, civilian and military alike. In fact this dream is not only theoretically sound from a nonviolent perspective, it is also empirically strong because although the military is well organized, nothing would be further from the truth than to assume that it is monolithic. Consequently, there should be among the more than 200,000 soldiers in the country those who support the idea of democracy and do not favor the coup d'état, or the violent suppression of common people. Politically, this message of possible cooperation opens up positive future possibilities instead of hostile closures on the part of the supporters of democracy.

Seventh postcard

Of the whole set of postcards, this final one is the most pronounced in its nonviolent message. There are four flowers sitting in the Buddhist lotus position, separated from the military with their guns by the concertina wires. The faces of the flowers are all in serene mood, and their arms linked to each other. This position is informed by both traditional Buddhist culture and nonviolent training. From within a Thai context, facing someone who sits in a meditative position can have a kind of disarming effect on those brought up in a culture informed by Buddhism. But the sitting itself and the locking of arms, seen from a nonviolent theoretical perspective, make it make difficult for the protestors to be removed. For example, two standing protestors occupying a public space can be pushed away by one soldier. But to remove one sitting protestor, often takes two soldiers to do the job. This would mean that if 100,000 people are sitting tightly together on the street, at least 200,000 soldiers, almost the total number of soldiers in the whole country, will be required to move them. The locking of the arms would also link the protestors together, both physically and psychologically. It should be noted that in some traditions, instead of the eyes being closed, a direct gaze into the eyes being of the oppressors is suggested, in order to reestablish human contact. Here is where cultural context is significant in informing nonviolent theory. A nonviolent practitioner, a former student of mine from Thammasat, sat cross-legged facing the charging soldiers. He did not move but continued to maintain his posture. Those who were afraid and began to run away were said to be shot at, and machine gun butts were used to beat those who tried to crawl away, while the soldiers passed those sitting cross-legged without even giving them a scratch.

I should also add here that a group of devout Buddhists who belonged to the Santi Asoke group also participated in the nonviolent campaign, perhaps due to the group's association with the leadership of the nonviolent campaign, Maj. Gen. Chamlong Srimuang.[15]

Postcard 7 Activists use nonviolent tactics such as food-sharing and giving flowers to soldiers in an effort to demilitarize the military.

Concluding Remarks

I have tried to read nonviolent practices from a small set of postcards, it is only natural that there are many more untold stories. The postcards are obviously mute about violence. But that is, I believe, deliberate on the part of the artist who must have thought that violence is readily represented in other media. The analysis could have been made on other theoretical grounds. For example, the whole set of postcards could be analyzed from a gender perspective where the symbolic nature of the concertina can be discussed. Or the sociological character of the campaign could also be analyzed. Here my purpose is mainly to discuss nonviolent practices as represented in these postcards. After all, as an observer, and not a spectator,[16] gazing from the riverbank at the "floating opera" in the middle of the river,[17] I will be able to observe only fragments of the opera. But it is the nonviolent fragments which I have chosen to discuss.

There may be some who heard the story of these nonviolent practices in the May 1992 uprising in Thailand and felt that what happened was a low-level type of nonviolence. I don't think so, for two basic reasons. First, if the nonviolent image of Tiananmen Square was that lone young man facing the tank, then the image that has emerged from the streets of Bangkok is more complicated. It is a combination of the Buddhist lotus position, and cellular phones with fax machines and e-mail. Nonviolent action in May 1992 was a blend of traditional culture and modern technology which is currently in the hands of the professional and rising middle class. Such a phenomenon was beyond the imagination of the military junta. Right after they came to power in early 1991 they banned all the state enterprise trade unions controlling the water supply and electricity for fear of powerful general strikes. For academics interested in the field of nonviolence research, perhaps, it is this blend of proper and potent chemistry which is needed for nonviolent action in the twenty-first century where a lot more countries may walk along this peculiarly transitional road. True, there is a lack of planning and a general strategy of nonviolence; this needs to be improved. Yet, in its absence, a creative improvisation took place. This suggests that nonviolent practices are natural weapons of the people and instruments of killing are not. Moreover, as a society progresses, the support a sociopolitical system requires from the professional class tends to increase. Thus, this class's power as pillars supporting the established power also increases. As a result, when withdrawn, the power system suffers worse than when dependency on its support was less.

In a way, the May 1992 nonviolent practices in Thailand are more significant that the 1989 Chinese demonstration because the nonviolent character of the former was much more pronounced. Although Chamlong's non-Ghandhian fasting and the burning of three government buildings, which could be the work of agent provocateurs, will not qualify the Thai uprising on a level with as Gandhi's Ahimsa, the campaign was largely nonviolent. In fact throughout the campaign, two "nonviolence cries" were used. They were "Ahimsa" and "Ahosi" – Gandhi's nonviolence and forgiveness. This is significant because, although some would claim that the compaign was a failure because many were killed, I would maintain that it was yet another manifestation of successful nonviolent campaigning to restore democracy. When the government decided to use violence against their own people who were unarmed, it was their failure. Nonviolent actions are used for transformational purposes, and the transformation did take place, especially in terms of popular empowerment.

Notes

1   *Khao Pises*, January 15–21, 1993, pp. 34–5 (In Thai).
2   See more examples in Gene Sharp, *The Politics of Nonviolent Action (Part Two): The Methods of Nonviolent Action* (Boston: Porter Sargent, 1973), pp. 149–52.
3   Perhaps one should be reminded of Charles Tilly's stimulating article: "War-Making and State-Making as Organized Crime" in Peter Evans et al., eds., *Bringing the State Back In* (Cambridge: Cambridge University Press, 1986) as a theoretical ground for this notion.
4   See Air Chief Marshal Kasat Rojananil's special interview in *Manager's Daily*, January 27, 1993, p. 22.
5   See the details in the original document in the Cahi-Anan Smudvanich and Kattiya Kannasutta (comp.) *Documents of Thai politics and Government.* (Bangkok: Social Science Textbook Project and the Social Science Association of Thailand, 1975), p. 211 (In Thai).
6   See also Harold Crouch, *Economic Change, Social Structures and the Political System in Southeast Asia: Philippines Development Compared with the other ASEAN Countries,* (Singapore: Southeast Asia Studies Program, Institute of Southeast Asian studies, 1985), p. 30
7   Such action "by holders of the financial resources" is not new. See Gene Sharp, *The Politics of Nonviolent Action (Part Two): The Methods of Nonviolent Action.* (Boston: Porter Sargent, 1973), pp. 236–7.
8   See Gene Sharp, *The Politics of Nonviolent Action (Part One): Power and Struggle* (Boston: Porter Sargent, 1973).
9   The figures are different because the media believed that 52 were officially killed, the NGO's figure is 45 and the Ministry of Interior's figure is 44.
10 *Ibid.*
11 Brian Martin, "Gene Sharp's Theory of Power, "*Journal of Peace Research.* vol. 26 no. 2 (May 1989), p. 217.
12 See Gene Sharp, *The Politics of Nonviolent Action (Part One),* pp. 25–32.
13 See *Khao Pises*, January 15–21, 1993, p. 35.
14 See a discussion on this point in my "Violence and the Sorcery of Identify," in the Center for the Reconstruction of Human Society, ed., *Global Human Family Looking at the 21st Century.* (Seoul: Kyung Hee University Press, 1987).

15 See a discussion of the relationship between Maj. Gen. Chamlong Srimuang and the Santi Asoke group in Peter A. Jackson, *Buddhism, Legitimization and Conflict: The Political Functions of Urban Thai Buddhism* (Singapore: Institute of Southeast Asian Studies, 1989), pp. 181–9.

16 See the difference between an observer and a spectator in Jonathan Crary, *Techniques of the Observer: On Vision and Modernity in the Nineteenth Century* (Cambridge, Massachusetts: An October Book/MIT Press, 1991), pp. 5–6.

17 See Jon Barth's first novel, *The Floating Opera* (New York, Garden City: Double Day, 1967).

9

Violent and Nonviolent Struggle in Burma: Is a Unified Strategy Workable?

Michael A. Beer

Introduction

Rarely are resistance movements to dictatorships purely nonviolent or violent. In the 1980s and 1990s, violent and nonviolent struggles have coexisted in Burma to oppose the military dictatorship. To prevent the violent forces from contaminating the nonviolent movement, the Burmese resistance tried to strategically separate these struggles geographically, demographically, and politically. A desire for civilian rule and a common foe provided a basis for unified grand strategy. There is often a blend of the two, as seen in recent decades in El Salvador, Nicaragua, Romania, South Africa, and Palestine. Using a chronological approach, this chapter provides an interpretation of selected events to describe the evolution of strategic nonviolent strategy among Burmese pro-democracy forces.

Burma's Plight

The Burmese have experienced two major political problems in recent decades: military rule and ethnic conflict. By 1998, Burma (referred to as Myanmar by the regime) had a population of 46 million people divided into a number of ethnic, linguistic, and religious groups. The Burmese people are ruled by a military junta now known as the State Peace and Development Council (SPDC). Burma is economically poor and civil war has raged almost continuously since 1941. Most of its political history has been either feudal, colonial, or under military rule, with the exception of 14 years of parliamentary democracy between 1948 and 1962.

Sixty-six percent of the population is ethnic Burman, subsistence farmers of rice, and poorly educated. Population growth is faster than its neighbor Bangladesh, despite high infant mortality rates, increasing drug use, poor medical infrastructure, and vast epidemics of malaria and AIDS. Millions of Burmese are internally displaced and 200,000 are refugees. Ethnic minorities such as Shan, Karen, Mon, Kachin, Rakhine, and Chin, live in hilly areas that surround the Burman agricultural heartland. The daily life of ethnic minorities consists of military occupation, forced labor, rape, murder, arbitrary "taxation," and poverty. Many of these ethnic minority lands have been war zones between ethnic minority guerrillas and government soldiers.

Resistance in Burma

For many years, Maoist strategy provided the basis for resistance to the central government. Reinforced by the success of their Chinese and Indochinese neighbors, revolutionaries emphasized guerrilla struggle and an underground civilian resistance. Open resistance by political parties or "above-ground" nonviolent action was eschewed in favor of the Maoist dictum that "power grows out of the barrel of a gun." Burman (mostly Communist) armed resistance was largely contained to Shan State. Meanwhile, Marxist-Leninists, particularly Maoists, predominated in the underground civilian resistance. A variety of ethnic minority groups also adopted Marxist-Leninist organizing strategies in the 1950s and 1960s which they had then mixed with liberal capitalist ideals by the 1980s.

With the exception of student and worker opposition to British rule, Burma never had a history of large-scale nonviolent resistance. That changed in June 1988, when large sectors of the Burman population rose up in opposition to the rule of the military leader Shu Maung (also known as Ne Win). Students led the movement in the capital city, Rangoon, initially against government mistreatment. Government killings led to widespread support for the students. Political demands quickly escalated for democracy and a return to civilian rule. Massive street protests involving hundreds of thousands of people erupted, leading to the resignation of Shu Maung and then two successive replacements. Aung San Suu Kyi emerged as the movement's leader in late July and attempted to enforce, along with Buddhist monks and students, an ethic of nonviolent discipline. By September the government had totally collapsed, but power struggles within the opposition led to a power vacuum which was then filled by a brutal military crackdown killing thousands. Burma was still under military rule but its direction had changed significantly.

The 1988 uprising forced the military to uphold its own rhetoric and carry out parliamentary elections in 1990. The National League for Democracy, led by Aung San Suu Kyi, won a landslide victory. The Junta refused to honor the election results and arrested and intimidated much of the above-ground opposition. Most of the NLD leadership, including Suu Kyi, have suffered long prison terms or house arrest.

The most dramatic change for Burma as a result of this struggle was an end to the country's 26 years of near-total isolation from the world. The people of Burma put into motion policies encouraging international investment, trade, and tourism. However, the military junta used this opening as a means of personal profit by selling off timber, fishing grounds and mining rights to foreigners. Modern technology such as fax machines, computers, and satellite dishes were introduced, although private ownership of these forms of communication are highly restricted by the regime. Foreign goods were imported, although out of the price range of most people. Foreign ideas about economics, politics, human rights, and civil society began to penetrate despite military repression.

The momentum of the 1988 movement continued with the initial legalization of political parties contesting for a promised election in 1990. Open organizing took place despite increasing repression and the banning of more and more groups. The NLD emerged as the leading institution advocating for democracy in Burma.

From 1988 to 1990, more than 10,000 mostly Burman students fled repression to border areas under the control of the ethnic minority armies. Burmans met and learned of the situation of the ethnic minorities for the first time. Mutual understanding from living together may serve as the future basis for ending the civil war. New border coalitions formed. The influx of students also reinvigorated the armed struggle.

Renewed Enthusiasm for Armed Resistance

These students viewed the 1988 uprising as a failure because the military remained in power. Large numbers joined an armed group called the All Burma Student Democratic Front (ABSDF) hoping to replicate their hero Aung San (father of the current opposition leader) who marched into Burma with the Japanese army in 1941 to expel the British. The ethnic minority groups led by their coalition, the National Democratic Front (NDF), viewed the 1988 uprising from the sidelines. They also viewed the 1988 uprising as a failure. They provided sanctuary for the students and were hopeful that new resources would bolster their guerrilla struggles. ABSDF and NDF forces sought to invade their individual states and the country with the help of the masses.

Nonviolent struggle was disparaged by the armed groups. The NDF discouraged seminars and training on nonviolence in liberated areas and discourse had to be couched in language such as "political struggle" or "political defiance." Border forces fretted that education about nonviolence would encourage soldiers to drop their guns and would weaken civilian support for the armed struggles. They equated nonviolence with passivity and weakness and were worried about this as a contaminant to their armed struggle. Students committed to nonviolence fled to neighboring countries where they helped form the international movement.

Problems quickly emerged. The ABSDF had no guns or bullets. They had trained to be students not soldiers. Many drifted to Bangkok or New Delhi or overseas. Ethnic groups such as the Karen National Union (KNU), the Kachin Independence Organization (KIO) and the New Mon State Party (NMSP) could only provide modest assistance that still stretched their resources. It turned out that armed struggle was much more expensive than the students realized. Furthermore, international funding agencies were unwilling to support armed struggle despite their sympathy for the cause.

Meanwhile, the regime moved quickly to raise cash by selling off easily extracted national assets. The Burma army rapidly increased in size to more than 300,000 and more than one billion dollars in weapons were purchased from China. Guerrilla struggle was suffering from a lack of resources, fewer sanctuaries, and an effective strategy for achieving its political goals.

By 1989, Communism as an organizing and resistance ideology collapsed in Burma. Influenced by the Communist collapse of Eastern Europe, the Communist Party of Burma imploded near the Chinese border when its largely ethnic Wa troops mutinied. This accelerated reevaluation of Maoist strategies for revolution and change. Aung San Suu Kyi popularized a modern liberalism and a commitment to Buddhist approaches to resolving conflict. By 1990, those Burmese who had hoped for the United Nations or the armed resistance to liberate Burma turned their hopes to the 1990 election. The landslide results electrified the people and Suu Kyi's gentle approach came to dominate the Burman heartland.

Unity in Being "Against" the Dictatorship

The people of Burma are unified in their hatred for the military dictatorship. It is not surprising that Burmese citizens had diverse reasons for hating the regime. Business people want to stop inept generals from destroying the economy; opposition political parties want the 1990 elections to be honored; ethnic minorities want an end to military occupation and attacks; lawyers oppose the military courts taking over the rule of law; religious leaders want monks released from jail and a resumption of religious examinations; writers want an end to military censorship; workers want a halt to attacks on union organizers, and students, at the time, want the schools reopened. They all have something in common: they wish to replace the SPDC with a government more responsive to their needs.

It is usually not difficult for opposition movements to find agreement on what they are "against." For example, in the winter of 1997 Serbian opponents of President Slobodan Milošević from both the peace and right-wing nationalist movements joined together in a two-month standoff on the streets of Belgrade. These nonviolent demonstrations proved successful in wringing concessions from Milošević, but proved unable to mount an electoral challenge months later when the disparate coalition refused to vote for each other. They could not agree on what or who they were "for." Similar problems plagued the Burmese opposition.

By 1990, newly elected members of parliament escaped to the liberated areas along the Thai and Indian borders to form a government in exile, the National Coalition Government of the Union of Burma (NCGUB). Although the NDF's were excluded, the NCGUB reluctantly supported the NDF chief goal which was a federal system that would recognize some limited autonomy to minority states. Many Burmese feared that these armed groups would seek independence at the first opportunity. Because the exiled nonviolent resistance leaders benefited from the sanctuary provided by the armed groups, they felt pressured to make concessions to the ethnic minorities. This may have been a blessing in disguise as it locked in a commitment (however reluctant) by many Burman exiles to federalism and demands for three-way talks between the NLD, the dictatorship, and the ethnic minorities.

Genuine political alliance could not rest upon the sandy foundation of a common foe. New unity was necessary around serious political goals and leaders. Burmans who fled to border regions made political concessions to the ethnic minorities, but were not in a position to negotiate for the NLD leadership, many of whom were under arrest. The NDF in turn made concessions to the exiled Burmans to support a unified Burma and the results of the 1990 elections (in which they did not participate). Coupled with the enormous 1990 election turnout, NDF support cemented an agreement throughout Burma for a multiparty democratic government. Commitment levels to multiparty democracy varied among ethnic groups, as few minority groups actually practiced democratic internal governance and warlords frequently ruled.

In Burma, there have long been disagreements among the opposition on future policy. However, a temporary unity has been forged around the person of Aung San Suu Kyi. Aung San Suu Kyi has led the main opposition party which won the 1990 election and is a Nobel Peace laureate. Her non-adversarial approach toward all Burmese, including the military, generates widespread support for her, both domestically and internationally. Her father was the best-known leader of the independence struggle against British colonial rule and this provides her with substantial moral authority as well as apparent immunity from physical force by the junta. Her unusual immunity and willingness to speak out publicly has provided coherent leadership for the Burmese people. While receiving endorsement of the NDF member organizations, some have remained suspicious that Aung San Suu Kyi is not fully committed to federalism.

Violence and Nonviolence: Toward a Unified Strategy of Resistance

By 1991, the resistance movements needed a new unified strategy based upon recent NDF concessions to support the results of the 1990 elections and the apparent failure of Maoist armed revolution. Assistance came from American specialists in strategic nonviolent struggle from the Albert Einstein Institution and Nonviolence International. Led by Robert Helvey, this team influenced the border and exiled opposition to create a unified strategy consisting of three components: (1) the Burmese people power; (2) the international community; and (3) the armed resistance forces. Each component had its own function. The Burmese people-power component was to lead the revolution using nonviolent action. The international community component was to provide diplomatic and economic strategies to weaken outside support for the dictatorship. The armed resistance component was to protect the ethnic peoples and activists from Burma military attacks.

The National Council of the Union of Burma (NCUB), a broad-based resistance coalition was formed on the Thai border in August of 1992. This new coalition also formed a Political Defiance Committee to coordinate its nonviolent struggle operations in Burma.

Burmese strategists on the border were more than aware of the contamination of violence in a nonviolent struggle, as demonstrated from a quote from an unpublished Political Defiance Instructor's Manual (*c*.1992):

> VIOLENCE is the most serious contaminant to the success of Political Defiance (nonviolent struggle)...violence by the political defiance organization may give the oppressor the public justification it needs to commit additional atrocities against the public...Political Defiance attempts to move the struggle away from the oppressor's strong points to areas where he is weak. We should never seek to fight on his terms.

Helvey and his colleagues suggested that contamination might be limited to avoid an either/or strategy of violence or nonviolence. Political contaminants were analogous to water contamination in gasoline engines. In a meeting with the PDC in 1992, Helvey said, "Mix a little water with petrol, and the engine would run but performance could be compromised. Too much water and the engine would fail to function. Likewise, mixing a little violence with a nonviolent movement might work but the nonviolent movement could suffer. Too much violence would doom the nonviolent struggle."

The NCUB, the border resistance coalition, conceived a unified strategy to improve the effectiveness of all resistance forces and to reduce contaminants to the primary nonviolent struggle. This involved the separation of armed and nonviolent struggles at most levels.

One of the biggest changes in strategy happened when the military component of the opposition agreed to share and then eventually relinquish its leading role in the revolution. A unified strategy required a more limited role for armed struggle so that contamination of the democracy struggle could be minimized. The first unified strategy gave the armed groups the task of tying down the junta's attention, resources, and troops along the borders, while the NLD led the nonviolent struggle in the cities. The armed struggle moved toward defensive strategies. The NDF gave up plans to invade Rangoon with the ABSDF. They also dropped plans for bombings, assassinations, and terrorist attacks in the cities. The armed groups would stay in ethnic minority areas trying to protect the local populations from what they considered to be genocidal policies.

The armed groups reemphasized the importance of providing safe haven for portions of the nonviolent movement's leadership and underground. Armed groups prioritized communication in and out of Burma by providing guidance for couriers and organizers, and providing protection to forward base camps. Coordinating bodies of armed and unarmed groups were established in liberated areas to plan and coordinate resistance activities. By securing safe space on the border, the nonviolent movement had access to the outside world through Thailand, India, and China.

Another important role for the armed groups was to stall for time. In the past, these groups stalled for time just to survive for another day, now they intended to hold on until a nonviolent uprising threw out the military regime. Preparations for nonviolent struggle can be extensive. Gandhi spent years preparing his Indian citizens for the independence struggle before directly confronting British colonial forces. Because of the successes of nonviolent action and defeats of armed movements, the NDF began to believe in the possibility of success through nonviolence.

New Nonviolent Strategy

A unified strategy called for the nonviolent struggle to take the lead in the revolution. Learning from the events in the 1980s in Eastern Europe, Bangladesh, Thailand, the Philippines, and elsewhere, the people of Burma realized that nonviolent action could more likely triumph than could armed struggle. Aung San Suu Kyi, with her strong commitment to nonviolence, became the paramount opposition leader accepted by most of the people and even the NDF. Underground activists still thrived, but now primarily as adjuncts to the NLD rather than as adjuncts to the NDF or the Communist Party of Burma. Nonviolent struggle in the past had been an underground affair to help the guerrilla struggle. This no longer made any sense. The armed forces of the NDF were too weak, particularly in the cities and heartland. Now nonviolent struggle was primarily "above ground," led by a legal political party.

The Committee for Nonviolent Action in Burma (CNAB) was formed to coordinate the underground resistance from the liberated areas along the India borders. Nonviolent offensives were planned to repeat another major people's uprising. The phased plans were similar to George Lakey's five-step strategy, with efforts beginning with education, then small group organizing, small-scale action, massive noncooperation, and finally takeover.

The NCUB unified strategy clarified an existing separation of groups and division of labor. The NDF and its ethnic minority movements remained in charge of armed struggle. This meant that the ethnically based guerrilla organizations – the Karen National Union, the New Mon State Party, the Kachin Independence Organization, the Karenni National People's Party, the Arakan Liberation Party (ALP), the Chin National Front, and others – were responsible for armed action in their lands. They had the resources, experience, and knowledge necessary to lead the armed actions. However, these groups had no history of involvement with the 1988 uprising and their activists did not work in the NDF, the NLD, or pro-democracy movement.

The nonviolent struggle in Burma has clearly been led by the NLD and its party structure with the secret assistance of many outlawed student, worker, and religious groups. Interestingly, it has shouldered the responsibility for nonviolent struggle upon its party members and elected leaders and has chosen not to call on the people of Burma to resist. This is a bit peculiar and can be explained in at least two ways. First, the NLD wants to act like a responsible political party ready for governance and, second, it feels that as the elected party its duty is to serve the people and not vice versa.

The nonviolent struggle overseas would be led, in part, by the government in exile, the National Coalition Government of the Union of Burma (NCGUB), made up exclusively of elected members of parliament who are scattered in various countries such as Thailand, India, and the United States. A few thousand students who fled abroad also would provide important leadership on the overseas solidarity efforts.

To reduce the contaminant of violence, the nonviolent movement relied on a different population of "soldiers" distinguished by age, gender, and ethnicity. While armed struggle primarily relies on young ethnic minority males aged from 15 to 50, nonviolent struggle as witnessed in the 1988 uprising relied on a much larger percentage of the population. The nonviolent resistance has relied heavily on women, children, and older people, as well as the ethnic Burman. Abroad, the NCGUB, made up of mostly Burman members of parliament, has helped lead the global solidarity movement.

A unified strategy called for geographic separation of armed struggle and nonviolent resistance. Armed struggle would be carried out only in the ethnic states. Burma's populations are relatively homogeneous in their particular ethnic areas, with the notable exception of Shan State, where there are a variety of ethnic minority groups such as the Wa, Kokang, and Palaung. Nonviolent resistance was to limit itself to the heartland and cities. The strategy avoided pouring resources into organizing in free-fire zones where distinctions between combatants and noncombatants quickly becomes blurred. Nonviolent and diplomatic struggle (but not armed struggle) would be used abroad to organize international support.

Each of the three components received separate funding. Funding for the exiled nonviolent groups came from governments such as Norway,

Switzerland, Sweden, the US and Canada, as well as from some private foundations in the West. The NDF financed its armed struggle by collecting taxes from civilians in areas under its control and collecting tariffs from businesses and border trade. They also received funding from ethnic minority allies in the neighboring countries of Thailand and India. The NLD received little outside assistance and collected the bulk of its meager funds through domestic donations.

This new strategy faced a great deal of initial resistance. The armed groups did not want to give up their hopes for a leading role, fearing that their concerns about the treatment of ethnic minorities would be marginalized. The ABSDF did not want to give up their leading role as the vanguard of the Burman revolution. Based upon their own experience, they believed that nonviolent struggle could never succeed in Burma, and foreigners faced the constant refrain, "If only we had more weapons...we could win."

But reality reared its head. The Kachin Independence Organization and Karen National Union suffered major military defeats in 1991 and 1992. Meanwhile, the 1990 election victory of the National League for Democracy (NLD) gave it the leading role in the eyes of the people, and in 1991 Aung San Suu Kyi received the Nobel Peace Prize, vaulting Burma to international attention.

The new strategy gradually took hold over the 1990s. The armed groups gave up their hopes of invading the heartland and moved increasingly to support the political defiance movement. Many of the armed groups signed humiliating "ceasefires" beginning with the KIO in 1993. By 1997, 16 groups out of roughly 25 had signed ceasefires and the remaining ones had lost control of their territories. A few of these groups forced into armistice agreements continued to help the nonviolent resistance but most did not. Nonviolence gained more legitimacy, particularly after Suu Kyi's release from house arrest in 1995. The ABSDF officially abandoned its emphasis on armed struggle in 1997.

The NLD leaders in Burma struggled to survive and were largely removed from the strategic decisions made on the borders in the early 1990s. Power in the resistance shifted back to the NLD inside Burma in 1995 after key leaders were released by the regime. The NLD quickly took the lead by withdrawing its delegation from the regime's constitutional convention and calling for international economic and diplomatic pressure on the regime. Border groups, initiating little independent action, provided support.

People power has yet to defeat the dictatorship in Rangoon. The NLD has declined to mobilize the Burmese citizens to open resistance, with the exception of a weekly rally held after Aung San Suu Kyi's release in 1995 that lasted until 1997. The NLD, however, has successfully stymied the military's plans for a new constitution by boycotting its drafting convention. It has also brought tremendous economic pressure to bear upon the military dictatorship.

Unexpectedly, political defiance became a synonym for underground resistance for the border groups. Similar to the underground strategy of previous years, they still operate on the basis of cells and secrecy. The difference now is that they serve the above-ground nonviolent movement instead of the armed resistance. Political defiance has also served as a term to organize gray areas of action in which, for example, armed escorts are used to escort underground couriers in and out of the country.

The strongest successes of the unified strategy have been overseas. At the UN, resolutions condemning the regime have been passed unanimously on an annual basis. Europe and the US undertook economic and diplomatic sanctions against the junta and foreign donors provided millions of dollars to the pro-democracy movement. The Internet facilitated an impressive citizen's network that led to successful economic boycotts and the withdrawal of multinational corporations such as Apple and Pepsi. The Burmese exiles have raised tens of millions of dollars in funds from foundations to sustain the international and border pro-democracy movement.

In the late 1990s, the ethnic minority groups have lost a great deal of political ground despite a rhetorical concession from the NLD for three-way talks. By relying exclusively on armed struggle to carry their cause of self-determination, they are left with little political muscle after ceasefires and military defeat. Lacking a coherent strategy to deal with the humiliating military defeats of the last several years, the ethnic groups appear now to be dependent upon the Burman pro-democracy nonviolent forces, much as the Burman groups were dependent upon them less than a decade ago. They are now, belatedly, looking at developing civilian nonviolent resistance capabilities.

Conclusion

Burma as a case-study in parallel armed and nonviolent struggle provides uncertain results. Contamination of the nonviolent struggle was partially contained, but the military Junta still uses the existence of ethnic minority military forces to justify its continued authoritarian rule, and the armed struggle influenced the efforts of Burman on the border to overemphasize the importance of revolutionary cells over "above-ground" civil resistance. The strategy of separation of forces consciously reduced the deleterious effects of armed struggle on the NLD and the pro-democracy movement. The Burmese resistance and Aung San Suu Kyi have a sterling global reputation for morally worthwhile political causes. The unified strategy also may have assisted in building trust between the ethnic minorities and the border Burman by encouraging them to collaborate at the strategic and leadership levels. The unified strategy may have saved face for armed groups who needed a transitional way out of their leading (yet failing) role. By relieving them of the leading role in favor of a defensive assisting role, the unified strategy may have served as a helpful transition tool. The demise of military struggle does provide the opportunity for the nonviolent struggle to assume unchallenged leadership of the overall political agenda and strategy of the opposition. No longer is separation of forces necessary for a unified struggle. Ethnic minority groups now have the opportunity to add their resources to the NLD. Unfortunately, until they develop a strong civilian capability, their concerns about self-determination and federal forms of governance are unlikely to be addressed any future government.

The best strategy will never succeed without action. Despite the best efforts of the Burmese opposition leadership, the people of Burma have been unable or unwilling to replicate the mass mobilizations of 1988. There is little doubt that some form of resistance will continue as long as the military remains in power. The question is whether the power of nonviolent action will be more fully recognized by the people of Burma, in the face of the twin challenges of government repression and a failed armed insurgency, to be utilized effectively to restore democracy to that troubled country.

PART V
Africa

Introduction

Despite the widespread impression of the African continent as an area of intractable violent conflict, the region also has an impressive tradition of nonviolent resistance and other unarmed challenges to authoritarianism. Pro-independence movements emerged in the 1950s and 1960s, most notably when Kenneth Kaunda helped lead Zambia to independence in 1965 through his Gandhian-style campaign of civil disobedience. In Namibia, one of Africa's last colonies, the general strike in Ovamboland in the early 1970s against the repressive contract labor system was the key episode in the struggle that finally led to the end of white South African control in 1990.

Nonviolent action also played a major role in the downfall of one-party states in Mali, Malawi, Madagascar, and Benin, among others. Ironically, in Zambia, Kaunda himself was faced with widespread nonviolent resistance in opposition to his one-party rule a generation later. This resulted in an opening up of the political system to the degree that he was forced out of power, and when the successor regime began to demonstrate authoritarian tendencies, Kaunda's followers engaged in nonviolent resistance against the regime of President Frederick Chiluba. Nonviolent campaigns have seriously challenged well-entrenched regimes in Nigeria, Kenya, Gabon, and several other countries. Even in Rwanda and Burundi, where ethnic violence has at times risen to genocidal proportions, large numbers of Hutus and Tutsis, some with support from outside nongovernmental organizations, have engaged in efforts of nonviolent reconciliation in an endeavor to heal their shattered societies.

One component of Nigeria's pro-democracy movement is the struggle of the Ogoni people against the environmental destruction of their homeland by foreign oil companies in alliance with Nigeria's military government. The Ogoni struggle may be emblematic of the kinds of nonviolent movements which will be growing in the future, as issues of indigenous rights, environmental preservation, abuses by multinational corporations, and campaigns of international solidarity all coalesce. Joshua Cooper examines this movement in "The Ogoni Struggle for Human Rights and a Civil Society in Nigeria."

For many years, those skeptical of the efficacy of nonviolence pointed to South Africa as a situation where nonviolence simply would not work. The nature of the apartheid system was such, it was argued, that only armed force could rid the country of its oppression. Yet, as Stephen Zunes writes in this section, even though the anti-apartheid movement was not explicitly or exclusively a nonviolent struggle, it was strikes in key sectors of industry, the establishment of alternative centers of authority in the townships, and other forms of resistance within the country, combined with international sanctions brought on in large part through nonviolent action by anti-apartheid activists in foreign countries, that forced the white minority regime to give up its monopoly of political power.

The growing trends towards democratization in Africa can be directly attributable to the growing awareness of the power of nonviolent action and its effective utilization. However, Africa's greatest problems may not come from dictatorship per se, but from poverty, environmental devastation, ethnic conflict, and other legacies of colonialism. Indeed, there are serious questions as to the significance of democratic governance brought about by nonviolent movements, when most key decisions are made by the International Monetary Fund and other transnational actors. Perhaps the greater appreciation of the power of nonviolence which has arisen from pro-democracy struggles can be used as part of a broader struggle for economic justice. As with the anti-apartheid struggle and the campaign of solidarity with the Ogoni people, however, the Africans may not be able to do it alone. As long as the sources of power that are most responsible for the oppression of Africans today are extra-continental, there needs to be greater awareness of African nonviolent movements worldwide and a willingness to lend support to their efforts.

10

The Ogoni Struggle for Human Rights and a Civil Society in Nigeria

Joshua Cooper

Let me start my search afresh.
One must never scorn a grain of sand or a drop of rain.
That is why I am here. Open those books you are studying, and tell me.
Where can a person girded with a belt of peace find truth and justice in this
country?

(*Ngugi Wa Thiongo*, "Matigari")

Introduction

The Ogoni are a distinct ethnic community of 500,000 indigenous Africans inhabiting one of the most fragile ecosystems in the world. They live in close relationship with the land in the Niger River delta, in one of the most densely populated, economically poor and polluted areas in Nigeria; they constitute only one of the nations of the federal republic's River State. Beginning with British colonialism at the dawn of the nineteenth century, the Ogoni civilization has been repeatedly challenged and assaulted. Throughout the century, multinational corporations and military-backed domestic colonialism have followed in the footsteps of British policies, to promote environmental degradation and genocidal practices against the Ogoni people.

As with many different nations in Africa and other geographical areas occupied through colonial campaigns, the Ogoni were not allowed to exercise their right to self-determination. During decolonization in the 1960s at the time of the Cold War, the act of international colonialism was replaced with internal or neocolonialism by more dominant ethnic groups over others through repressive military regimes. For a majority of the years since Nigerian independence in 1960, the military has ruled; political transitions have come more often through coup d'états than elections. As James Rupert wrote, "The British colonial rulers discouraged any real democracy that might have forced an equitable sharing of the country's earnings."[1]

The Ogoni initiated a different strategy to sever the cycle of colonialism and build a civil society. Their struggle for self-determination offered a model for other nations to organize their resistance efforts. This nonviolent movement for basic human rights through peaceful protest revolutionized politics in Nigeria.

Another important factor in the Ogoni campaign for social change is the inclusion of the environment in the strategy for self-determination. The Ogoni relationship to the land is similar to that of other indigenous peoples around the world, such as the Ainu in Japan and the Yanomami in Brazil challenging current practices of multinational corporations and nation-states. The Ogoni regard the land as a spiritual space for the protection and promotion of the Ogoni culture and language. As Greenpeace International concluded, "The Ogoni...have a long history of preserving their surrounding environment which they regard as sacred."[2]

Noted author and activist Kenule Beeson Saro-Wiwa summarized the indigenous identity in his last book, *A Month and a Day,* "to the Ogoni, the land and the people are one and are expressed as such in our local languages. It emphasizes, to my mind, the close relationship between Ogoni people and their environment."[3] As one nongovernmental organization (NGO) noted after a mission to Ogoni, "The Ogoni have their own distinct culture, in which land was traditionally seen as god and worshiped as such."[4] Another NGO supported such observations about the relationship to the land and its preservation as the providing the basic necessities for existence of the Ogoni people: "Rivers and streams provide water for bathing, drinking and fish for food, so are bound up intricately with the life of the community."[5] Another NGO supports this observation: "People honoured many deities of earth, sky and water, under a supreme God."[6]

This relationship with the land is not reflected in the decision-making of Nigeria's government, which has allowed much of the land to be destroyed in pursuit of profits for the area's oil resources. The results of these policies are witnessed in the great poverty in Ogoni, while the region's wealth is transferred to the Nigerian government and multinational oil companies. The normally pro-business *Wall Street Journal* noted, "Although there are 96 oil wells, two refineries, a petrochemical complex and a fertilizer plant in the 404-square-mile Ogoni area, the sole hospital is an unfinished concrete hut, and the government's schools, unable to pay teachers, are rarely open.".[7] The effects of the oil operations locally are leaky pipelines, gas flarings (causing intense local acid rain), and oil spills. All severely limit the opportunities for economic self-sustainability and political self-determination. While the profits flow out of the delta, human rights violations by the central government have moved in. Internationally recognized human rights are now routinely sacrificed under the altar of the international petroleum market.

Since the early 1990s, the Ogoni have been waging a nonviolent movement against both the largest multinational corporation presence in Nigeria and the dictatorial military government. The nonviolent campaigns inspired by the Ogoni Bill of Rights created people-power movements in different sections of Ogoni society, spearheaded by the Movement for the Survival of the Ogoni People (MOSOP).[8] These indigenous movements have also cooperated with other environmental and human rights organizations such as Greenpeace, Amnesty International, and the Unrepresented Nations and Peoples Organization (UNPO).

The connection between nonviolence, environmental preservation, and indigenous peoples movements has created a coalition of popular forces which has challenged the legacy of colonialism and the current threats posed by multinational corporations such as Royal Dutch/Shell Group and the military regime of Nigeria. To create a culture of human rights and a critical mass of nonviolent political consciousness, MOSOP has advocated in the national, regional, and international arenas a fundamental document – the Ogoni Bill of Rights – based on principles of international human rights law, bringing worldwide attention to a once-obscure movement.

The Nonviolent Struggle

"Aaken, aaken pva Ogoni aaken!"
("Arise, arise, Ogoni people arise!")

There have been important Ogoni movements in existence since the era of British colonialism. One of the first experiments to restore Ogoni national identity was the Central Ogoni Union (COU). It was successful in securing improved conditions during the early years of independence, but only lasted for a decade. The COU, under Paul Birabi, took basic, necessary actions, focusing on education by creating scholarships and building schools; the COU also organized to create a political platform with the Ogoni State Representative Assembly.

The Ogoni derive much of their identity from their relationship with the land and their survival is linked to it. However, for the federal government and foreign oil companies, the land is seen as a profitable resource and the indigenous population an inconvenience. The Royal Dutch Shell Group is one of the largest multinational corporations in the world, with interests in over 3,000 companies and operations in more than 100 countries. Shell's investments in Nigeria account for almost 14 percent of the company's production, the largest in any country outside the United States. Meanwhile, oil sales account for as much as 80 percent of the Nigerian government's total revenues. Therefore, both Shell and the Nigerian government have a strong interest in maintaining the status quo and not disrupting current practices.[9] Indeed, Nigerian oil exports account for about 90 percent of foreign exchange earnings, with over 90 percent of them coming from the Niger River delta.[10]

Ken Saro-Wiwa described the struggle against multinational corporations and the repressive nation-state at the launch of the One Naira Ogoni Survival Fund (ONUSUF):

> Today, the Ogoni people are involved in two grim wars. The first is the thirty-five year old ecological war waged by the multi-national oil companies, Shell and Chevron. In this most sophisticated and unconventional war, no bones are broken, no blood is spilled and no one is maimed. Yet, men, women and children die; flora, fauna and fish perish, the air and water are poisoned, and finally, the land dies. The second war is a political war of tyranny, oppression and greed designed to dispossess the Ogoni people of their rights and their wealth and subject them to abject poverty, slavery, dehumanization and extinction."[11]

Saro-Wiwa summarized the result of the twin challenges, "Taken together, both wars, waged against a defenseless and small people, amount to genocide and are a grave crime against humanity. Pitted against two deadly, greedy, insensitive and powerful enemies, the Ogoni people have refused to yield and are fighting doggedly and heroically for survival. And the war must be won for the alternative to victory is extinction."[12]

The commitment to nonviolent resistance is crucial to the Ogoni movement for self-determination. Beginning with the drafting of the Ogoni Bill of Rights and the subsequent nonviolent campaigns, the Ogoni have been able to light a flame of justice that is burning brighter than the oil flames in Ogoni.

Before 1990, the Ogoni people had not organized a comprehensive strategy of awareness and activism rooted in nonviolence and the leadership had also not been committed to coordinating peaceful protests for social change. With the Ogoni Bill of Rights, however, the demands for economic, social, and environmental justice were established. In twenty points, the Ogoni stated their objective of political autonomy within Nigeria.[13] The power of the words motivated the nonviolent agenda for popular resistance and political reform.

The Ogoni Bill of Rights also issued a strategy to challenge the human rights violations at the national, regional, and international level. This was reinforced with the Addendum to the Ogoni Bill of Rights, where the commitment to nonviolence was reiterated. The Ogoni planned to expose the violations of the Nigerian constitution, the African Charter of Human and Peoples Rights, and the UN Declaration of Human Rights. This revolutionized the nonviolent campaigns pursuing all levels for self-determination, establishing the Movement for the Survival of Ogoni People (MOSOP), and the determination to bring their cause into the international arena.

The initial efforts towards building international cooperation with environmental and human rights NGOs was not successful. As Ken Saro-Wiwa wrote, "I telephoned Greenpeace. 'We don't work in Africa,' was the chilling reply I got. And when I called up Amnesty, I was asked, 'Is anyone dead? Is anyone in gaol?' And when I replied in the negative, I was told nothing could be done."[14] However, Saro-Wiwa continued to knock on the doors of foreign NGOs and governments. On a visit to Germany, he met with the Association of Threatened Peoples which impressed upon him the networking possibility with other human rights NGOs. He was also urged to present the Ogoni issue before a global assembly at the United Nations Working Group on Indigenous Populations and the Subcommission on the Prevention of Discrimination and Protection of Minorities. Saro-Wiwa met extensively with the Unrepresented Nations and Peoples Organization (UNPO) and began to cooperate with them in the compaign for the human rights of the Ogoni through a philosophy and practice of nonviolence.

As Saro-Wiwa wrote, "The UNPO was a real find...I learnt a lot from Michael [van Walt van der Praag] about the ways of the United Nations and its Human Rights Commission, and he patiently guided me on this first contact with the UN. The great appeal of the UNPO for me was its insistence that its members forswear violence in their struggle for local autonomy, self-determination or independence."[15] The UNPO Secretary General Michael van Walt van der Praag noted the positive relationship between UNPO and MOSOP. "There was a lot of news about UNPO being established as the alternative United Nations. He wrote to us, applied for membership and was admitted. Very quickly we helped Ogoni get international attention with CNN. He came frequently to The Hague and we worked on strategy and international contacts. In one year, he became Vice Chair of UNPO."[16]

At the UN meetings, Saro-Wiwa realized that the UN had already spent a decade or more focusing on the plight of indigenous peoples. He also gained valuable knowledge about the UN Decade for Indigenous People and the Year of Indigenous People in 1993. Both would be excellent platforms to build international solidarity for the launch of MOSOP's nonviolent civil disobedience campaign.

As the UNPO secretary general admitted, "In terms of international contacts and coverage, UNPO assisted. However, Saro-Wiwa's own ability and talent made it. UNPO just created that opportunity. All of the media coverage put the issue of Ogoni on the political map."[17] MOSOP and UNPO together strengthened skills and created strategies to raise awareness in Ogoni and around the world. The UNPO was able to work with other international NGOs to create a network to assist MOSOP to reach the aims they had established with the Ogoni Bill of Rights. Another important feature of the nonviolent organizing for social change was also the creation of other organizations in Ogoniland to focus on different aspects of the rights being denied due to the activities of the oil companies and the government.

The environmental arm of the movement was spearheaded by the Ethnic Minority Rights Organization of Africa (EMIROAF). The NGO was rooted in the principles of international human rights law. However, it noted one important premise, that the environment is the first basic human right. EMIROAF maintains that without a safe environment, individuals cannot recognize and receive the other basic human rights enshrined in international human rights law. EMIROAF's main focus is on the environmental protection of the Niger delta region. It also tries to mobilize the local people to protect their immediate environment and has moved beyond Ogoni to other parts of the delta.

By organizing first at the local level on the issue of self-determination in economic and political matters, with the immediate needs of environmental protection, the Ogoni in cooperation with UNPO created an international movement with different NGOs. The earlier efforts of contact that did not result in positive developments for the nonviolent movement were transformed into a working partnership focusing on the environment and human rights. Despite initial reluctance, both Greenpeace and Amnesty International provided important services to assist in the Ogoni nonviolent struggle as it began mobilizing the masses to overcome fear and stand up for their human rights in 1993, the UN International Year of Indigenous People.

MOSOP gained international exposure and the Ogoni were able to coordinate a significant percentage of the population to take action against the injustice of the oil companies and the dictatorship. Before then, the leadership had only been toying with the idea of nonviolent protest in the face of such brutality and destruction.

The coordinated nonviolent action campaign was launched in early 1993, as the Ogoni peacefully protested the environmental devastation in a celebration of the UN Year for Indigenous People. The Ogoni decided on January 4 to celebrate their culture and also to recognize the connection of the Ogoni with the international movement for the human rights of indigenous peoples. The January 4, 1993 march transformed words into action. The green twigs designated as the symbol for the environment were in the hands of the Ogoni people, united in openly demanding their human dignity. Greenpeace went along to bear witness to the peaceful demonstration and also to see the environmental degradation for themselves.

The transformation of words into action also reflected a personal transformation in the minds of the Ogoni movement. Ken Saro-Wiwa noted that as the MOSOP leadership visited the different communities and witnessed nonviolent protests, "The empowerment which had enabled them to stand up against their oppressors at long last was the issue of the day."[18]

Garrick Leton, a MOSOP leader and ex-Chancellor of River State University, addressed a rally of at least 300,000 people explaining the direction of the movement for self-determination, saying, "We are asking for the restoration of our environment, we are asking for the basic necessities of life – water, electricity, education; but above all we are asking for the right to self-determination so that we can be responsible for our resources and our environment."[19]

Over three-fifths of the total population of the Ogoni convened on Bori town to demand their environmental and other crucial civil rights enshrined in international human rights law. As Steve Kreutzman, a former Greenpeace employee and current campaign coordinator for Project Underground, noted, "It was the largest demonstration ever against an oil company and, given the travel restrictions and constant military surveillance the Ogoni face, a remarkable feat of nonviolent organizing. The Movement for the Survival of the Ogoni Peoples (MOSOP) had arrived."[20]

After speaking at different rallies on that historic day, Saro-Wiwa wrote, "The 4th of January was truly a liberation day: a day on which young and old, able and disabled, rich and poor, all of Ogoni came out to reassert themselves and to give notice that the nation had come of age and that it would not accept its destruction passively. We had surmounted the psychological barrier of fear. Ogoni would never be the same again."[21]

While there had been violence before, there was an increase in harassment, human rights violations, and ultimately murder. The World Council of Churches, independent report categorized the repression in Ogoniland in five phases that have resulted in 2,000 Ogoni deaths, 30,000 internally displaced, and thousands more seeking asylum beyond Nigeria.

Even though the Nigerian government had intensified the campaign against the Ogoni, however, the nonviolent actions continued and new organizations were created to build the Ogoni nation. The One Naira Ogoni Survival Fund (ONOSUF) was launched in the immediate after glow of the January 4 march, one month later, when over N700,000 was donated by men, women, and children committed to the vision and values of the Ogoni Bill of Rights and the strategies employed by MOSOP. Candle-lit vigils for self-determination, peaceful protests against Shell construction on pipelines, and boycotting of the presidential election in face of decrees making the demand for autonomy treasonable and punishable by death, were among the forms of nonviolent resistance displayed against widespread and systematic repression.

Indeed, the Nigerian authorities engaged in widespread killings, detentions, and torture against Ogoni activists. Saro-Wiwa was repeatedly arrested, prompting an international campaign for his release. European and North American NGOs supporting Saro-Wiwa were particularly disturbed at the apparent links between Shell and the Nigerian dictatorship in attempts to silence him. Greenpeace exposed a memo leaked from a Shell meeting on community relations and environment which included recommendations that the movements of "key players" in the Nigerian opposition be more "effectively monitored to avoid unpleasant surprises and adversely affect the reputation of the (Shell) Group as a whole." Saro-Wiwa is also mentioned specifically in the document.[22]

Amnesty International adopted Saro-Wiwa and other MOSOP leaders as prisoners of conscience. As the MOSOP leadership was arrested, the movement continued with student and youth wings coordinating peaceful demonstrations. These actions were met with violence by the authorities. There were also some violent clashes between ethnic groups that were widely suspected to have been instigated by Nigerian soldiers. As Amnesty International noted, "Hundreds of Ogoni were reportedly killed in the fighting, and there was evidence implicating the security forces in the killings."[23]

The nonviolent movement continued in the face of intensified oppression and provocation from the authorities, and MOSOP now increased nonviolence training for activists. The government used the ethnic clashes to raid villages active in the resistance and to place key members of the opposition under house arrest or bring them to prison in Port Harcourt. Beginning in May 1994, the Internal Security Task Force began a systematic operation against the Ogoni opposition, with systematic rape, looting, and murder. As many as 1,000 Ogonis were killed and dozens of villages razed. Human Rights Watch/Africa collected testimony of Nigerian soldiers participating in the military campaign, where soldiers were told they were supposed to repel an invasion from Cameroon, only to discover they were being ordered to attack unarmed Ogoni.[24] Greenpeace International also found documents suggesting that the atrocities and human rights violations were planned by the Nigerian military government based on internal "restricted" memos. It noted: "Shell operations [are] still impossible unless ruthless military operations are undertaken for smooth economic activities to commence..." As Greenpeace wrote, "The document goes on to recommend that 400 soldiers undertake 'wasting operations' and 'wasting' Ogoni leaders who are 'especially vocal individuals.'"[25]

As the nonviolent resistance and resulting repression grew, so did international solidarity. While the Ogoni organized in Nigeria, the international community shared their skills in order to increase awareness of the human rights and environmental abuses taking place there. The UNPO cooperated with over a dozen organizations to coordinate World Ogoni Week in 1994.[26]

In the midst of this crackdown, Ken Saro-Wiwa was arrested again on May 21, this time on murder charges. Virtually no independent observers took the charges seriously. According to Amnesty International, "The prosecutions appear to be politically motivated and the proceedings and decisions of the specific tribunal set up specifically to try the cases do not satisfy international standards for fair trial."[27] On top of legal questions raised over the operation of the trial, the intimidation of people involved illustrated the injustice of the proceedings. Gani Fawehinmi, principal defense counsel, had men in military uniforms machine-gun his chambers, resulting in a death and amputation of the limbs of some of the guards. Eventually the defense team withdrew from the case, as noted in Wole Soyinka's, *The Open Sore of a Continent*, "declaring that their continued participation would only give a semblance of legality to a patent circus spectacle."[28] As Michael Bimbaum, Queen's Counsel, observed, "It is clear that there have been several breaches both of the Nigerian Constitution and the International Human Rights instruments, to which Nigeria is a party." Bimbaum made other comments about key witnesses changing their stories from denying seeing a killing to identifying a defendant committing a killing, and also aspects of bribe-taking in exchange for giving false evidence. Another key prosecution witness recanted his statement, claiming he was bribed and forced to sign an already written document. [29] As Charles Suanu Danwi said, "I was promised that after the case in court, I will be given a house in any place in the country a contract from Shell..."[30] Another prosecution witness was recently appointed in early August 1998 to an Independent National Electoral Commission. MOSOP notes that he is a former senior official of the Shell Oil company in Port Harcourt.

Saro-Wiwa and eight other Ogoni activists were hanged in November 1995. International reaction was swift, but limited. Conservative British prime minister John Major referred to it as "a bad verdict, an unjust sentence and now it has been followed by judicial murder."[31] Partial economic sanctions were imposed by the British Commonwealth and other countries against Nigeria, though the only truly effective form of sanctions – against Nigeria's oil exports – has not been included. Meanwhile, human rights groups have launched an international boycott campaign against Shell and Chevron.

Saro-Wiwa's Search for Social Justice

"...a people, no matter how few, who are aware of their rights and determined to reclaim them in a nonviolent manner, cannot be crush by military might."

Ken Saro-Wiwa

Even though Saro-Wiwa was murdered, the Ogoni movement continued. After he was hanged in Port Harcourt, his final words being "Lord take my soul, but the struggle continues," the Ogoni took his words to heart. As Deborah Robinson wrote, "One of the greatest testaments to the ideals and principles that Ken stood for was embodied in Ogoni Day 1996. In the light of increased military presence and Internal Security Task Force orders not to march, 100,000 Ogonis participated in Ogoni Day 1996... The Ogoni have demonstrated, marched and met with international fact-finding missions throughout 1996, even when it was clear that some among them would definitely be arrested, tortured and even killed."[32]

Student groups, such as the National Union of Ogoni Students (NUOS), have practiced nonviolence through persistence and patience. Sunny Kogbo

described the courage of the protests, at the First International Conference/
Training of the Movement for the Survival of the Ogoni People:

> The extinguishing of 'THE AFRICAN SUN' on 10 November, 1995 throwing
> the blacks into a black day, had a reverberating effect on the entire world
> ...On our part, we...organized a massive protest at the Rivers State Uni-
> versity of Science and Technology. This singular activity which was beamed on
> CNN met with unprecedented brutality by the head of the military junta....-
> During the increased oppression, all classes of MOSOP leadership went under-
> ground. But the student as resilient as ever took up the mantle of the struggle.
> This we successfully carried out.[33]

MOSOP still remains an intact organization with offices located in
decision-making capitals around the world. The efforts in Ogoni also
persist even in the face of massive human rights violations. Ledum Mitee,
acting president of MOSOP, said, "MOSOP is very strong, if not stronger.
What has happened is that there have been some changes in strategies to
make the people on the ground less vulnerable to the repression that is
continuing in Ogoni now."[34] Mitee offered some insight to the local and
global strategy, "You know that all Ogoni people are MOSOP, but it is as if
we have created an underground network on how it operates, building
some structural changes where those who are actually doing things on the
ground are not known to the security agents, while the structure internationally is able to become the visible hands and voices of MOSOP. So
internationally we are growing more.[35]
On the January 4, 1997, Mitee issued a statement to his fellow Ogonis:

> I once again salute your courage and spirit of steadfastness. To me, nothing is
> more reassuring than the fact that in spite of these repressive efforts intended
> to silence and intimidate us, we have by our courage, resilience and discipline
> cast out the yoke of crass complacency and passivity that has enslaved many
> an oppressed people. Your courage has demystified the oppressor. Your resi-
> lience in the face of agonies has attracted world attention and deprived the
> oppressor of a slumbering conscience. Your discipline in the face of provoca-
> tion has inspired hope and rewarded faith in non-violence as a weapon for
> fighting oppression. There is no doubt about our ultimate victory.[36]

All of this took place following a difficult year in the face of repression,
with ongoing executions and extra-judicial killings. The Ogoni are essentially under military occupation. Resistance continues, however. Vigils,
peaceful protests, and celebrations of Ogoni culture are ongoing.
The commitment to nonviolence with a long-term perspective toward
peace is stressed by Mitee and MOSOP's vision. As he said about the
struggle for social justice, "[I]t means sustained struggle for justice. Justice
is not something you fight for and get easily...You struggle for it and that
is what Nigerian people must appreciate: that each person should not think

he is too small to make a contribution. Each and every person must know that we must fight if not for ourselves then for generations yet unborn. That is the only way we can go forward."[37]

Saro-Wiwa hoped MOSOP would be a model for other indigenous peoples striving for self-determination. In the immediate aftermath of the first Ogoni Day celebration, he wrote about that possibility for Africa's ethnic nations, "We would be heading for a more democratic system, far from the dictatorships which have ruined the continent, and we might succeed in reordering our societies, undoing Berlin of 1884, so that there would not be so much exploitation at all levels in all parts of the continent."[38]

The message of the Ogoni has been a universal message for self-determination and universal human rights. Saro-Wiwa believed the message and the movement could be adopted by others suffering environmental catastrophes and human rights violations. "I hoped that I had started a movement which might transform Africa. Would the Ogoni revolution be a model for other small, deprived, dispossessed and disappearing peoples? If only we could make it! A large number of communities ready to take their fate into their hands and practice self-reliance, demanding their rights non-violently, would conduce to democracy and more politically developed peoples."[39]

The struggle for the human rights of the Ogoni signifies a significant development in the tradition of nonviolent struggle for self-determination. As Nobel prize-winning Nigerian author Wole Soyinka said at a speech at the United Nations, "The Ogoni movement is impressive because it brought out the entire community – children, women and elders. It is a solitary example of what can be done in the face of extreme circumstances.... It is a model that holds models for other indigenous peoples of the world."[40]

Saro-Wiwa and other Ogoni organized not to only to save their precious land and improve their livelihood but also to begin the process for a better environment and a civil society for all in Nigeria. The idea of the Ogoni Bill of Rights went beyond the artificial borders of Nigeria as a message on nonviolent protest and a model for other indigenous peoples facing extinction. No matter how small a community, if it is aware of its identity, its will to survive can overcome the oppressive obstacles. The indomitable will of the human spirit and its quest for freedom cannot be denied. People's movements for basic human rights constantly protest and stand up in the face of oppression. The force of justice provides spiritual strength for a fearless campaign of nonviolence.

The models provided by different indigenous peoples offer a recipe for moral revolution. From the individual mind to the general masses in an organized movement, the successful transition to the struggle for self-determination is a political attainment of "self," the ability to conquer personal fear, a courageous personal commitment to nonviolence, and a connection with other indigenous peoples in the struggle for the recognition of their human rights. Indigenous peoples have endured conquest, carnage and colonialism. They have survived the policies and practices of missionaries, mercenaries and merchants in their pursuits of profits. The Ogoni continue to create a model for others to challenge those colonial changes imposed upon them. Indigenous people around the world number over 300,000. They make up part of almost every nation-state and these have pursued different policies: from independence, to assimilation, to genocide. Indigenous peoples have been silenced too long; in the twentieth century they began implementing nonviolent strategies to secure their rights to self-determination and other fundamental freedoms. As Ken Saro-Wiwa has observed, "It is bad enough that it is happening a few years [before] the twenty-first century. It will be a disgrace to humanity should it persist one day longer."[41]

The Ogoni have worked collectively with other peoples in Nigeria, Africa, and with the UNPO; this chapter suggests possible future directions in which their struggle might go in the fight to regain their land based on environmental rights and basic inherent human rights documented in international instruments of law. As members of the Unrepresented Nations and Peoples Organization, an international NGO labeled as the alternative UN, the skills and strategies adopted by the Ogoni will serve as a blueprint for future direct action by other member movements.

During the final days before Ken Saro-Wiwa's brutal execution, he claimed, "I'll tell you this, I may be dead, but my ideas will not die.[42] His spirit of struggle will continue to inspire the Ogoni path of nonviolent resistance.

Notes

1   James Rupert, "West Africa's Bumbling Behemoth," *Washington Post*, 10 June 1998.
2   Andrew Rowell, *Shell-Shocked* (Amsterdam: Greenpeace International, 1994), p. 5.
3   Ken Saro-Wiwa. *A Month and a Day* (New York: Penguin Books, 1995), p. 2.
4   The Unrepresented Nations and Peoples Organization. The UNPO Yearbook (The Hague: Kluwer Law International, 1996), p. 499.
5   Rowell, *Shell-Shocked*.
6   Survival International, *Survival for Tribal Peoples: Niger Delta Peoples* (London: Survival International, 1995), p. 1.
7   Geraldine Brooks, "Slick Alliance: Shell's Nigerian Field Produce Few Benefits for Region's Villagers," *Wall Street Journal*, May 6, 1994, p. A1 and A4.
8   While MOSOP receives most of the attention for its nonviolent direct actions, it is also important to note the grassroots work of other organizations such as the Ethnic Minority Rights Organization of Africa (EMIROAF) and the different components of MOSOP such as the National Youth Council of Ogoni People (NYCOP), Federation of Ogoni Women

Organization (FOWA), Council of Ogoni Churches (COC), National Union of Ogoni Students (NUOS), Ogoni Teachers Union (OTU), and Crisis Management Committee (CMC). These affiliate bodies constitute crucial roles in the nonviolent struggle.

9   Rowell, *Shell-Shocked*, p. 6.

10   Survival International, *Survival for Tribal Peoples*.

11   Ken Saro-Wiwa, *Ogoni Moment of Truth* (Port Harcourt, Nigeria: Saros International Publishers, 1994), p. 16.

12   Ibid., p. 17.

13   See Ken Saro-Wiwa's statement to the World Conference on Human Rights, "The Bill called for (a) self- determination for Ogoni people, (b) the control and use of a fair proportion of Ogoni economic resources for Ogoni development, (c) adequate and direct representation as of right in all Nigerian institutions, and (d) the right to protect the Ogoni environment and ecology from further degradation."

14   Ken Saro-Wiwa. *A Month and a Day*, p. 89.

15   Ibid., p. 94.

16   Interview with Michael van Walt van der Praag. Amsterdam, The Netherlands, August 13, 1998.

17   Ibid.

18   Saro-Wiwa, *A Month and a Day*, p. 125.

19   Rowell, *Shell-Shocked*, p. 18.

20   Steve Kreutzmann, "Hired Guns," *These Times*, February 3, 1997, p. 18.

21   Saro-Wiwa, *A Month and a Day*, p. 134.

22   Greenpeace International, "Drop Charges Against Nigerian Human Rights Activist," news release, July 29, 1993.

23   Amnesty International, "Nigeria: Security Forces Attack Ogoni Villages," AI News Service.

24   Human Rights Watch/Africa, "First-Ever Testimony by Nigerian Soldiers on the Military Campaign in Ogoniland," news release March 27, 1995.

25   Greenpeace International, "Greenpeace Demonstrates Outside Shell's London Headquarters; Secret Document Links Shell Oil's Operations to Killings in Nigeria," news release January 16, 1995.

26   The other participating organizations were Greenpeace, Human Rights Watch, International Green Cross, PEN International, European Alliance for Indigenous Peoples (EAIP), Dutch Centre for Indigenous Peoples (NCIV), Both Ends, KWIA (Support Group Indigenous Peoples, Belgium), Ogoni Community Association: UK, League of Ogoni People, USA (LOOP), and Ogoni Support Commission, Geneva.

27   Amnesty International. "Nigeria: The Ogoni Trials and Detention." September 15, 1995, p. 1.

28   Wole Soyinka. *The Open Sore of a Continent* (Oxford: Oxford University Press, 1994), p. 146.

29   Cited in ibid.

30   See "I Lied Against Saro-Wiwa," *The Masses*, Special Edition, February 1995, p. 3.

31   Movement for the Survival of the Ogoni People, "New Electoral Commissioner was Prosecution Witness Against Ken Saro-Wiwa," MOSOP press release, August 7, 1998.

32   Deborah Robinson, *Ogoni: The Struggle Continues* (Geneva: The World Council of Churches, 1996), p. 55.

33   Sunny Kogbo, "The Ogoni Students and MOSOP Struggle," address at the First International Conference/Training of the Movement for the Survival of the Ogoni People at Ghana, November 24, 1997.

34   Soji Akinrinade, "The New MOSOP Strategy," *Newswatch*, August 4, 1997, p. 13.

35   Ibid.

36   Ledum Mitee, "The Ogoni Day Celebrations," January 4, 1997.

37   Akinrinade, The New MOSOP Strategy, p. 14.

38   Saro-Wiwa, *A Month and a Day*, p. 134.

39   Ibid., p. 134.

40   Wole Soyinka, "The Demand for Identity and the Democratic Debate." International Training Center on Human Rights and Peace Teaching 16th International Training Session at the Palais des Nations, 6 July 1998.

41   Ken Saro-Wiwa, "'A Disgrace to Humanity if the Tragedy Persists One Day Longer," *The Independent*, November 12, 1995.

42   Cameron Duodu, "Hanged Activists were Starved," *Observer*, November 19, 1995, p. 24.

11

The Role of Nonviolence in the Downfall of Apartheid

Stephen Zunes

Introduction

Against enormous odds, nonviolent action proved to be a major factor in the downfall of apartheid and the establishment of a democratic black majority government in South Africa. This came despite the fact that movements working for fundamental change had faced unprecedented obstacles. Never had such a powerful and highly industrialized state been overthrown from within. Opponents of apartheid faced a complex web of regulations that produced a rigid stratification system severely limiting dissent by the oppressed majority. Apartheid South Africa defied most traditional political analyses, due to its unique social, political, economic, and strategic position. It practiced one of history's most elaborate systems of internal colonialism, with a white minority composed of less than one-fifth of the population in absolute control. The ruling party was led by racialists who also possessed an unusual level of political sophistication. They controlled some of the world's richest mineral deposits, including one-third of the earth's known gold reserves. A modern military machine stood ready in an area which lacked any other large conventional force. Its internal security system was elaborate and repressive. As a modern industrialized state in an undeveloped region, South Africa created a degree of economic hegemony, despite almost universal nonrecognition of the legitimacy of its government. It was a pariah of international diplomacy, yet economically, and to a lesser extent strategically, was well-integrated into the Western system.

It was this paradoxical situation, of being both extraordinarily powerful as well as highly vulnerable, that gave nonviolent resistance its power. Despite great mineral wealth and an increasing industrial capacity, South Africa's white minority regime found itself dependent on its black majority, its southern African neighbors, and the industrialized West to maintain its repressive political system and its high level of modernization. Indeed, the resistance movement in South Africa has been referred to as "probably the largest grassroots eruption of diverse nonviolent strategies in a single struggle in human history" (Wink 1987: 4). This nonviolent movement, which consisted in both internal resistance and solidarity work outside the country, was largely successful in its strategy, which avoided challenging the South African state where it was strong, and concentrated its attacks on where it was weak. This chapter will examine how unarmed methods of resistance faced these challenges, as well as comparing the history of both violent and nonviolent strategies in South Africa.

While the armed struggle never reached a level which threatened the survival of the regime, the threat of such an armed uprising may have played a role in forcing it to compromise. Yet, as will also be demonstrated below, the regime clearly had the means to forestall a successful uprising for many years to come, whereas the largely nonviolent resistance movement was already causing enormous disruption to the existing order.

The Problems of Armed Struggle

From its inception in 1912, the African National Congress (ANC) was the primary organizational vehicle through which black South Africans pursued their rights. After using largely legal tactics during its first 40 years, the militant youth wing ascended to the leadership in the early 1950s, with an orientation towards nonviolent direct action. The rival Pan Africanist Congress (PAC), founded in 1959, also pursued this strategy until both organizations were banned in the wake of the Sharpeville Massacre of 1960. Subsequently, they advocated various forms of armed resistance until the ANC agreed to a ceasefire during the final stages of talks with the government in 1991. The PAC had largely disintegrated by this point, as a result of government suppression, internal factionalization, and lack of internal and external support. The armed struggle was largely limited to an occasional bombing and intercepted border crossing, which gradually increased in the late 1980s to a rate of three or four attacks every month. Evidence suggests that the armed struggle may have actually harmed the anti-apartheid movement: the bombing campaign by the ANC's armed wing, Umkhonto We Sizwe (Spear of the Nation), in the early 1960s seriously weakened simultaneous nonviolent campaigns, since the government was able to link them to each other in the eyes of the public and thus justify their repression. Not only were most of those involved in the bombing campaign arrested, but the turn to violence was used to justify the rounding-up of many other suspected dissidents as well. Although the ANC explicitly directed their campaign towards property, a number of their trained attackers used their explosives on the homes of progovernment blacks, killing several people, including children. This not only invited further government repression, but resulted in a loss of support by some Africans as well. Given the tendency for those in authority to treat opposition movements by reference to their most violent components, the armed struggle in its early stages probably did more harm than good to the movement against apartheid.

Yet, given the level of repression against nonviolent activists within the country, and the successes of outgunned armed liberation movements elsewhere, there was a widespread belief for most of the 1960s and 1970s that the armed struggle would play a major role in the downfall of apartheid. The problem was that those who dreamed of liberating their country through force of arms faced enormous obstacles.

White South Africa possessed by far the most powerful military machine on the continent. By the early 1980s, it had a rigorously trained operational force of 180,000 men and, with a reserve force constantly replenished through universal white male conscription, it could mobilize nearly half a million troops within a few hours (Leonard 1981: 13). In addition, a cadet program of military training for secondary students would grow to 300,000 within the next few years (ibid.), and every white man and woman was required from adolescence to learn marksmanship. The number of guns per capita for the white population was among the highest in the world, while apart from the 10,000 blacks in special military units and some in the police force, no blacks were allowed to carry firearms under any circumstances. The estimated combined forces of all black African states and liberation movements south of the equator came to less than half that of South Africa. In terms of military equipment, South Africa had an even greater advantage. The South African air force possessed over 875 aircraft, including over 500 combat aircraft, and more than 200 helicopters; the army owned over 260 tanks, 1300 armored cars, over 110 armored personnel carriers, and a large number of self-propelled medium and heavy artillery guns (ibid.: 20). The arsenals of the liberation movements and black African states was limited to small, outdated Western arms and a limited supply of modest-grade Soviet hardware.

Only Angola had major military equipment within its borders, and this was largely in the hands of Cuban forces defending the government from US and South African-backed UNITA rebels. There was little promise of an organized force of African nations launching a successful invasion of South Africa. The Organization of African Unity lacked any coordinated military organization, leadership or general staff, training techniques, or doctrine. Zaire, Ethiopia, and Nigeria, the sub-Saharan states with the largest standing armies, needed their own armed forces for internal control. Nor could Cuba, or other states allied with the black South African cause, be expected to redirect substantial numbers of their troops away from their own national defense needs. Opposition by the United States and other Western states would have prevented any kind of United Nations or other multinational force from being deployed.

Until November 1977, when the mandatory United Nations embargo went into effect, South Africa was the recipient of highly sophisticated weaponry from Israel, France, and other countries. The embargo did not significantly alter the strategic balance, since a large amount of outside arms were getting into the country anyway, and, more importantly, South Africa had by that time become almost self-sufficient militarily. The government was manufacturing its own tanks, mine-clearing vehicles, missiles, and even napalm and nerve gas. No guerrilla movement could hope to combat such a powerful armed force on its own territory effectively, especially when South Africa's preparedness for such an attack was considered. South African forces were being trained by the highly effective Israeli counterinsurgency units (Southern African Committee 1978: 14). In addition, an investigation at that time noted how:

> Five special 'anti-terrorist' training camps have been strategically established for training in camouflage and disguise, the establishment of bases, tracking, field shooting, convoy and ambush drill. The Defense Minister told Parliament that the men were kept informed of counter-measures against the latest terrorist tactics throughout the world. The Air Force has been reorganized for greater mobility and is being integrated with the anti-guerrilla combat forces. An underground air defense radar station has been constructed at Devon in the eastern Transvaal as the nerve center of the northern area's early warning system. Information is fed into computers from radar heads above ground and from various remote satellite stations. Three thousand miles of South Africa's northern borders are reported being patrolled night and day.... An underground radio communications center is [located] at Westlake near Cape Town. Its computer produces on demand a map of the shipping in any selected portion of the ocean. (Adam 1971: 125–6)

In addition, South Africa had:

> augmented its internal production of armaments, established new military bases in the northeastern Transvaal, created a special anti-terrorist police unit and counter-insurgency division within the army, and initiated plans to remove Africans from the border areas and transfer them to villages under military supervision. (Friedland 1983)

The border with Mozambique, the only frontier with sufficient vegetation for cover, had been cleared to a depth of at least one mile, was heavily mined, and was under constant patrol with the assistance of bright floodlights (Gann and Duignan 1978: 53).

Another important factor was the consolidation of the security and intelligence forces under the centralized command of the South African president. This was but one part of the increasing militarization of South African society, in preparation for what many saw as an inevitable armed conflict with black guerrilla movements. There was little question that they would be ready to meet any military challenge in the foreseeable future. The most frightening obstacle to a military victory by armed liberation forces was South Africa's nuclear capability, demonstrated by the apparent nuclear test in September 1979.

Proponents of armed struggle in South Africa pointed to Angola, Mozambique, and Zimbabwe as examples of how an outgunned guerrilla movement need not win the war to achieve liberation: that a war of attrition would be enough to result in the capitulation of the white minority regime. Indeed, the victorious armed struggle in the former Portuguese colonies was the major inspiration for many black South Africans to look favorably on the prospects of a successful armed revolutionary struggle in their own country.

However, several key differences were often overlooked. The white populace in those territories was less than 5 percent of the population, and in each case under a quarter of a million people. South African whites, by contrast, totalled 2.8 million, over 15 percent of the population. There was strong pressure from the colonial power for a settlement with the black majority in their colonies, once they realized that they could not win an unpopular colonial war, which made further resistance by the white minority impossible. White South Africans did not have to yield to the priorities of a "mother country." White South African troops would have been fighting, not for the protection of colonial interests, but for their own livelihood, reducing the chances of the class divisions and low morale which had plagued the Portuguese and others fighting colonial wars. In addition, many Portuguese and white Rhodesians willingly moved to South Africa or returned to their European homelands after liberation. White South Africans, however, had lived in their land for many generations – most Afrikaners traced their ancestry back at least two and a half centuries – and would have nowhere to go. In the face of a violent liberation movement, they would probably have fought to the bitter end. It is likely that the full military might of the South African state would have been unleashed against whole communities, with enormous destructive potential. Many whites on the far right began stockpiling arms for what they saw as an inevitable race war, for which they had an almost messianic commitment to resist to the last Afrikaner.

Also, unlike these former colonies, South Africa was a modern, industrialized state. It was the major industrial power of the continent, if not the southern hemisphere. It was the only country in Africa with major iron and steel industries, advanced engineering facilities, and petrochemical plants. The industrial infrastructure, through its then quasi-governmental administration, was intrinsically linked to the military establishment.

The black townships outside South African cities were designed so that they could be easily cordoned off and subjected to air strikes, making it easy for the military to suppress any armed uprising. While some ANC leaders began to advocate a "peoples' war" of massive armed resistance within the townships in the mid-1980s, such a scenario was never realistic. Unlike Algiers, or other locations of successful urban guerrilla warfare, there was no maze of alleys in which guerrillas could lose those in pursuit. The black townships were built as grids, with wide thoroughfares, making it difficult for a guerrilla to find shelter. In addition, the record of urban guerrilla warfare in the preceding years, as in Uruguay, Brazil, and Argentina, did not offer a very hopeful precedent.

The Bantustans – the small, noncontiguous, remote rural areas set aside by the apartheid system for the black majority – presented basically the same situation on a larger scale. Because of their geographical fragmentation and tight rule by hand-picked elites, they could hardly be ideal bases for guerrilla warfare. There were strong pressures, both internally and externally, on the leadership of the homelands to work with the South African military, and several were cooperating quite closely (Karis 1983–4). In addition, less than 42 percent of the population was male, the majority of these being under 15 or over 65, limiting the number of potential recruits (Johnson 1977: 300). Meanwhile, the four million blacks in white rural areas, laboring primarily as farm hands, were so utterly dependent on their white overlords and geographically separated, that there was little reason to think that they would shift dramatically away from their traditional conservatism and noninvolvement in popular resistance movements, so to be able to contribute to an armed revolution.

Another problem was that the terrain in South Africa was totally unsuitable for guerrilla warfare. The South African countryside mostly consists of open areas of desert and savanna, especially in the strategically important Transvaal, and there were virtually no sanctuaries, such as mountains and jungles, in which to retreat or establish bases of operation. In addition, unlike other countries that experienced successful guerrilla warfare, South Africa was a highly urbanized society, with modern communications and transport facilities, so there would be little opportunity to avoid detection and attack. Guerrilla raids from neighbouring independent states would also have been problematic, since they would have been susceptible to offensive military actions by South African forces. South Africa made frequent attacks in Angola against SWAPO bases and refugee camps during their occupation of Namibia, as well as numerous minor incursions. There were three major attacks deep inside Mozambique during the 1980s, attacking alleged ANC homes and offices. There were also raids during this period into Zambia, Lesotho, and Botswana. It was unlikely that a newly independent Namibia would take the risk of provoking conflict with its giant neighbor, on which it was still dependent. Even the tiny Rhodesian army had been capable of making devastating raids against its neighbours, and the prospect of retaliation made these black states, already in desperate economic shape from previous wars and dependent on South Africa economically, extremely wary about harboring guerrillas. South Africa was financing antigovernment guerrillas in Mozambique and Angola, and there was increasing South African military activity along the borders. Mozambique was forced to sign a peace treaty with South Africa in 1984, as were Swaziland and Lesotho, which severely limited ANC activities.

According to Robert M. Price (1991: 94–5):

through the use of military and economic power, Pretoria sought to create a 'neutral' cordon of African states to its north. Under a regime of South African regional hegemony southern African states would be expected to ... prevent their territory from being used in any manner by the ANC [among others].

No armed guerrilla struggle has ever succeeded without sanctuaries for rest from combat, the provision of food, rearmament, and military training. No sanctuaries existed at this time within easy striking distance of South Africa, and there was little likelihood that any would become available. Even were a neighboring country willing to take the enormous risks necessary to provide sanctuary, there was still the problem of penetrating the heavily guarded border regions, a barrier that the ANC was never able to fully overcome, even before the introduction of highly sophisticated monitoring devices.

Despite increasing numbers of South African blacks leaving the country for military training with the ANC in the late 1970s, the numbers of potential guerrillas was still very small, especially when considering the strength of the South African military and the size of the ANC's objectives. Estimates of ANC military personnel in the early 1980s were never higher than 14,000 (Karis 1983–4). The ANC refused to make a public estimate, presumably because of its embarrassment at the paucity of men under arms. Even taking into account the high ratio of military personnel over insurgents needed to suppress a guerrilla movement, the ANC could hardly have been considered a formidable military threat for many years to come.

Despite 24 years of armed resistance, and large amounts of military aid and training from the Soviet Bloc, the ANC was able to show "little serious military capability" (Uhlig 1986: 170), and, militarily speaking, was referred to as "one of the world's least successful 'liberation movements'" (Lelyveld 1983).

Random terror, as attempted in the Poqo campaign of the early 1960s, or even on a larger and better-coordinated scale, would not have been helpful, either. Terrorism has traditionally united the opposition, often making them more entrenched, while dividing the aggrieved population – in effect, the opposite of nonviolent action. The traditional justification for terrorism, that it would allow the state to reveal its truly repressive nature, certainly did not apply to apartheid South Africa: not only was the repressive nature of the state obvious to any black South African, but their largely nonviolent resistance brought out the repressive apparatus without providing the needed rationalization of curbing terrorism.

It was under these circumstances that the ANC and other resistance organizations in the early 1980s began to seriously question whether armed struggle would be successful. The Soviet Union, the chief military backer of the ANC, had long since joined Western countries in doubting the military capability of the ANC armed wing, now supported a negotiated settlement, and saw continued armed struggle as counterproductive (Price, 1991: 9).

Many South Africans also questioned whether they were willing to subject their country to the mass murder, ecocide, and rampant devastation that occurred in Vietnam. Unlike the Vietnamese, the South African revolutionaries would not have had a terrain favorable for guerrilla warfare or available sanctuaries; nor would their opponent have been in unfamiliar territory, far from supply lines, be acting as proxies for a corrupt regime with little popular support, or have a large antiwar movement with which to contend.

A violent strategy would have led inevitably to spiralling escalation, with the state having the strategic edge at every turn in the foreseeable future. Even had the blacks eventually won, it would have probably left millions dead and a ravaged country. Many skilled whites needed to maintain specialized positions during the interim period before a sufficient number of blacks (denied advancement under apartheid) could take these positions, would be killed or driven into exile. Armed resistance in South Africa would probably have attracted many of the least disciplined elements from African society under apartheid, thus blurring the distinction between revolutionary action and hooliganism. This would have resulted in a widespread debasement of the morals of an entire younger generation of South Africans needed to rebuild their country, a problem which has proved to be difficult enough, even with the relatively limited revolutionary violence that did occur.

There has been a tendency for nonviolent movements to maintain a more democratic and inclusive character than armed movements (Sharp 1980), a factor that many black South Africans undoubtedly considered after years of living under a most undemocratic and exclusivist system. In addition, since a violent struggle would have tended to be directed more against people than a nonviolent struggle, which tends to aim at institutional and systemic targets, there would have been a greater chance of the revolutionary struggle taking on a more destructive racialist orientation.

In addition, as Liddell Hart (1967: 204) observes:

> The habit of violence takes deeper root in irregular warfare than it does in regular warfare. In the latter it is counteracted by the habit of obedience to constituted authority, whereas the former makes a virtue of denying authority and violating rules. It becomes very difficult to rebuild a country and a stable state on such an undermined foundation.

By contrast:

> While the practice of nonviolent resistance is not entirely devoid of such after-effects, they are less damaging, materially and morally. The practice may foster a continuing habit of evasion, but it does not sow the seeds of civil war nor breed terrorists. (ibid)

In addressing the question of what kind of strategy a South African movement for majority rule should consider to maximize its chances of success, Sharp (1980: 163) outlined three major criteria:

1) How to achieve the maximum strength and involvement in the struggle by the non-whites, mainly the Africans.

2) How to split some of the whites from support for the Afrikaner Nationalists and white domination, and move them towards action in support of the non-whites.

3) How to bring the maximum international pressures to bear on the South African government towards change compatible with the self-determination of the South African people as a whole and their future development.

Nonviolent action proved to be the most effective means of achieving those criteria. While maintaining their commitment to pursue armed struggle, both on principle as well as a strategy of disrupting normal operations of the repressive state, the South African opposition reached a clear consensus by the early 1980s that liberation had to be pursued through largely nonviolent methods. Despite the romantic rhetoric of international solidarity groups in the US and elsewhere of a victorious ANC army marching to Pretoria, the ANC never saw armed struggle as the sole or even primary means for bringing down the apartheid regime (Price 1991: 9). Strategic analyst Thomas Karis, writing in 1986 (134), noted that "despite a commitment to 'armed struggle', the ANC has considered sabotage and guerrilla attacks to be only a minor strand in a multifaceted strategy consisting mainly of politically inspired demonstrations, strikes and defiance." By the 1980s, the ANC saw strikes and boycotts as "a main element in the organization's strategy for liberation" (Uhlig 1986: 169–9), emphasizing that the armed struggle was only "one strand" in the fabric or resistance strategies which included civil disobedience (ibid: 170). The ANC even acknowledged that most of its acts of sabotage and small-scale guerrilla attacks were no more than "armed propaganda" (Karis 1986: 112). Indeed, during the anti-Republic Day campaign of 1981, when hundreds of thousands of people took part in protest rallies all around the country, and a successful general strike demonstrated the level to which the opposition could mount a successful mobilization, the ANC launched about a half dozen attacks against strategic targets across the country "as a well-coordinated demonstration of support for a popular campaign of mass resistance" (Frederickse 1987: 39).

It had become apparent by this point that the armed struggle was a means of providing moral support for the unarmed resistance, rather than what many had anticipated as an unarmed resistance being used primarily to support the armed struggle. According to journalist Julie Frederickse:

> While the African National Congress is known for its anti-government guerilla attacks, its leaders also seem wary about any over-emphasis on military rather than political activity. The ANC President's first public statement of 1984 exhorted all South Africans to "create conditions in which the country will become increasingly ungovernable." (Ibid.: 178)

In effect, the ANC recognized that the noncooperation of the people was critical, and that it was the ungovernability of the country by the apartheid regime, and not its physical overthrow, that would end apartheid. Thus, while never formally renouncing armed struggle until the peace process was well under way, there was a growing recognition through the 1980s by the ANC that the largely nonviolent forms of resistance would be the decisive means of overcoming apartheid. Anti-apartheid leader Desmond Tutu, the Anglican Archbishop, who openly declared on several occasions that he was not a pacifist and was open to sanctioning armed resistance if necessary, publicly called upon the ANC to suspend the armed struggle in 1988 (Smuts and Westcott 1991: 135).

The shift to a largely nonviolent strategy, which was concomitant with the decentralization and democratization of the resistance movements, was not the result of an ethical transformation, but was born out of necessity. American theologian Walter Wink, writing in 1987 (80–1), observed:

> Since armed resistance is largely futile, people have taken recourse in nonvio-
> lent means. Nonviolence has even become the preferred method of people who
> have never contemplated absolute pacifism. Because anti-Apartheid leaders are
> arrested almost as soon as they emerge, resistance groups have invented non-
> hierarchical and democratic organizational forms. Means and ends coalesce as
> people create for themselves social instruments for change that already
> embody the better life they seek ahead.

Nonviolent Resistance in South African History

The apartheid system went well beyond segregated public amenities to include the system of grand apartheid, maintained through a policy of influx control, which kept surplus labor and undesirables in the barren Bantustans many miles from the white cities and industrial areas. Squatter settlement by migrants in South Africa, deemed "illegal" by the white minority government, was not just the common Third World phenomenon of rural poor desperately seeking work in the cities, but an act of civil disobedience against one of the fundamental pillars of apartheid. When such settlements were threatened by government bulldozers in the 1980s, multiracial groups would often lie down in front of them, courting arrest (ibid: 93). This resistance against efforts at government repression became both a symbolic and structural defiance against the system. The Urban Institute of South Africa estimated in 1988 that there were as many as 7 million illegal squatters in urban areas (ibid: 125), more than the government could reasonably hope to control.

In Cape Town, District Six, a Coloured neighborhood where 30,000 people whose families had lived there for generations were evicted in 1966 to shantytowns in a distant area, became a no-go zone for prospective white tenants and landowners in the decades that followed due to local opposition (ibid: 92). Campaigns against evictions of Indian families from the white Johannesburg suburb of Pageview in 1979, and of rural blacks from the Ventersdorp area in 1983–4, became national campaigns of resistance (ibid: 115–17). In 1987, migrant mineworkers began bringing their wives into single-sex compounds in defiance of mine management and government regulations (ibid: 94).

In addition, the nonviolent resistance by workers and commuters in the Ciskei bantustan in 1983, centered on a bus fare increase and poor working conditions in factories, which was met with brutal repression by a joint effort of the homeland regime, the South African government, and big business, marked a turning point in delegitimizing the whole grand apartheid scheme, by demonstrating to white South Africans that the homelands policy was based on fear and force, not on a benign mutually-beneficial program of "separate development"' (Frederickse 1987: 111–12). The centrality of the townships became apparent to both the South African government and the ANC following the Soweto uprisings. The whites had to acknowledge that a black urban population was a permanent fixture in South African society and its economy. The white paper which accompanied the Riekert Commission Report emphasized that "black labour represents by far the largest proportion of the total labour force . . . in the so-called 'White area.' " Furthermore, it projected a far greater increase in the black population than for the whites (RSA 1979). This acknowledged the vulnerability of the government and the entire South African economy to strikes and other forms of nonviolent disruption by the black majority.

According to Price:

> The black worker, whose increasing militancy since the Durban strikes of 1973 threatened to undermine South Africa as a haven for multinational investors, and who during the Soweto uprising showed a growing willingness to support radical youth with political strikes, was a township resident. Townships represented both a source of skilled workers, and an enormous untapped domestic market for South Africa's manufactured goods. And the townships, easily accessible to journalists, offered the international media vivid material to reveal the reality of black deprivation in South Africa. (1991: 101)

Nonviolent resistance against white minority rule has a long history in South Africa, going back as far Mohandas Gandhi's nonviolent campaigns in Natal at the turn of the century. A half century later, the 1950s Defiance Campaign, despite its demise, demonstrated the potential of nonviolent action based in the townships in resisting apartheid (Benson 1966: 159): Of the 10,000 volunteers called for, more than 8,500 had gone voluntarily to jail despite the intimidating effect of police action, of dismissal by employers, and the propaganda of the bulk of the press and of the radio; some teachers who had done little before had thrown up their jobs to take part in the Defrance Compaign; the United Nations had been inspired to discuss apartheid and the press of the world had taken the nonwhite challenge to oppression more seriously than ever before.

As Benson (ibid: 151) observed:

> October was the peak of the Campaign. For the first time in the history of modern South Africa, the Africans' militant achievement had kept the initiative hard-won through discipline and self-sacrifice. Only one thing could rob them of such initiative: violence. Violence did indeed break out, and the Campaign was crippled (Sharp 1973: 599). At the peak of the civil disobedience movement, after it had been in motion for about six months, a series of African riots broke out between October 18 and November 9. Six whites were killed and thirty-three Africans. The white dead included a nun who had been missionary doctor to the Africans: her body was spoliated. This contributed to the sensationalism and to feelings that repression was "justified." The precise causes of the riots are not clear. The resistance leaders demanded an enquiry, which the government refused. There was no evidence that the resistance movement was responsible, and there were suggestions that agents provocateurs may have been involved. In any case, the effects of the riots "were to damp down the spirit of resistance."

Zulu Chief and anti-apartheid leader Albert Luthuli (1962: 127–8) added:

> The Defiance Campaign was far too orderly and successful for the Government's liking, and it was growing. ... The challenge of nonviolence was more than they could meet. It robbed them of the initiative. On the other hand, violence by Africans would restore this initiative to them – they then would be able to bring out the guns and the other techniques of intimidation and present themselves as restorers of order. It can not be denied that this is exactly what happened, and at the moment most convenient for the Government. The infiltration of agents provocateurs in both Port Elizabeth and Kimberly is well attested. They kept well clear of the volunteers and the Congress. ... They did their work among irresponsible youngsters. ...

It was all the government needed. The riots and the Defiance Campaign were immediately identified with each other in the white South African imagination. The initiative was with the Government.

It is well known that the Government used its recovered initiative harshly and to the full. The activities of rioters provided the pretext for crushing nonviolent demonstrators. The number of those committing civil disobedience dropped from 2,354 in October to only 280 in November (Kuper 1958: 143). The resistance campaign, for all practical purposes, was at an end.

There were a number of factors leading to this, including the arrests of certain leaders, harsh new penalties against civil disobedience, and the impending general elections, but clearly the riots played a decisive role (ibid: 145). Quite apart from their effect on the resisters, the riots provided the opportunity for the Government to take over the initiative and to assume far-reaching powers with some measure of justification.

It appears that the campaign's successes were limited not because it was nonviolent, but in large part because of the limited violence that did occur. The government refused demands by the resisters that a Judicial Commission of Inquiry be appointed to investigate the causes of the riots, strengthening the belief that the violence was indeed government inspired. The use of agents provocateurs throughout the history of the resistance movement demonstrated that the white minority government did all it could to prevent the black resistance movement, using methods of nonviolence. The government felt threatened by the use of massive, disciplined nonviolent resistance, as demonstrated by its harsh counteractions during the Defiance Campaign and other times when similarly challenged, a phenomenon which Sharp (1973: 110) refers to as "political jiu-jitsu," using the opponent's weight against him.

A major factor in the revitalization of the South African resistance was the Black Consciousness movement, which was launched in the early 1970s, stressing self-reliance and nonviolent resistance. Though inspired in part by Frantz Fanon's ideas of empowerment and conscientization, the Black Consciousness Movement stressed that black pride need not come only through violence. Sam Nolutshungu (1982: 183–4) observed:

> Although Fanon's writings were widely read and his ideas of alienation in colonial society had much influence on many of the theorists of black consciousness, there is little evidence that his ideas on violence were much discussed, and none that they were widely shared. It is nowhere seen as being in itself a mentally liberating process; rather its instrumental role properly comes only when consciousness has been achieved by other means.

Similarly, Gail Gerhart (1978: 285–6), writing about the internal resistance movement of the 1970s, adds:

> The aim of Black Consciousness as an ideology was not to trigger a spontaneous Fanonesque eruption of the masses into violent action, but rather to rebuild and recondition the mind of the oppressed in such a way that eventually they would be ready forcefully to demand what was rightfully theirs.

The late Black Consciousness Movement leader Steve Biko and other internal resistance leaders stressed the need for nonviolence, at least at the early stage of the struggle, and criticized the PAC's "reckless rush to confrontation when circumstance did not favor a black victory" (Gerhart 1978: 285); they similarly criticized armed ANC raids as premature and counterproductive to their work within the country.

Some activists saw the public espousal of nonviolence as a tactical recognition of the need to postpone government repression of the anti-apartheid group's public activities, to be followed by a "second phase" after conscientization, that of armed struggle. Preliminary clandestine committees were set up by black consciousness leaders to explore that possibility, but these were set aside as advances in the internal and largely nonviolent resistance became apparent. There was some pressure from militants both in the leadership and at the grassroots about moving to an active armed resistance, but the tactical advantages of nonviolent resistance, regardless of the sincerity of its initial advocates, had meanwhile won widespread support.

By the 1980s, the ANC and the more traditional nationalist leadership within the country had accepted many aspects of the participatory orientation from the Black Consciousness Movement, and through their mutual support of the United Democratic Front and trade union federations maintained a degree of resilience and unity in the face of the worst repression in South Africa's history. It was during this period that they committed themselves to nonviolent resistance. A mass democratic movement was formed, which included the informal alliance of the ANC, COSATU, UDF, and UDF affiliates, calling for nonracial democracy under the leadership of the ANC. The formation of the UDF in 1983 was significant, in that it was a loose coalition of nearly 700 organizations, including civil associations, trade unions, student groups, youth groups, churches, women's organizations, religious groups, and sports clubs, committed to a "united, democratic South Africa based on the will of the people" and "an end to economic and other forms of exploitation" (Karis 1986: 128). They were able to help coordinate nonviolent resistance campaigns, such as boycotts, strike support, and other issues from local arenas to national support.

The rise of labor militancy was perhaps the most important trend towards successful utilization of nonviolent action. The 1973 strikes in the Durban area demonstrated the vulnerability of crucial sectors of the South African economy to militant actions by black workers. The strike wave spread throughout Natal and beyond; between January and March 1973, approximately 150 firms were struck. Increasing trade union militancy on economic demands, demonstrating (as in the Durban strikes) that they could win, paved the way towards empowering the population to a degree that massive political strikes could succeed. Black working-class support for the 1976 student-led Soweto uprising could be attributed in part to the increasingly precarious position of black workers in the country (Price 1991: 53).

Lodge observed in 1983 (327) the significance of the wave of strikes in the preceding years:

> Their scale, spontaneous character and degree of success made these strikes unique in South Africa's labor history. They had several distinctive features. The strikers refused to elect a leadership, thus immunizing themselves from the effects of victimization and cooption. They avoided all formally constituted representative bodies (there were in any case very few of these). They relied principally on the sharp demonstrative shock of a short withdrawal of labor to

gain concessions from employers rather than entering negotiations or protracted confrontations. The workers stayed in the vicinity of their factories which may have afforded them some protection against police reprisals. The conscious aim of the strikers in almost all cases was to gain better wages.

In addition (Johnson 1977: 187):

> The [1973] strike wave...had more than just economic effects. If anything, indeed, the short-term and partial satisfaction of economic demands merely lifted the threshold of workers' resentment to focus on their wider condition of life.

There was a steady increase in strike activities following 1971, despite occasional downturns in individual years. In 1979, the government allowed Africans to join unions and permitted recognition of both black and multiracial unions. There were still major restrictions on political activities, penalties for illegal strikes were toughened, and government controls were increased. Yet, unions were able to force businesses to enter into negotiations, membership soared, and they began organizing in key sectors of the economy. Over 1,000 black workers were on strike every day by 1982, a number which grew in subsequent years (Frederickse 1987: 22). A half-hour general strike in which 100,000 workers put down their tools in 1982 in protest at the death under torture of a white trade union activist at the hands of government security marked the first such action in over two decades (ibid: 166). The strikes tended to increase in duration, and while the vast majority were over immediate economic issues, a trend emerged by the 1980s towards work stoppages in solidarity with labor struggles elsewhere. The unification of 500,000 workers in 1985 into one union federation, the Congress of South African Trade Unions (COSATU), and its commitment to address concerns beyond the standard bread-and-butter issues marked a turning point in the struggle. Unlike the small isolated black unions that had existed previously, this strong trade union movement helped bring apartheid to its knees.

Another significant development was the increasing community support for striking workers, first made apparent during the 1979–80 strike wave in the Western Cape. The use of consumer boycotts forced major concessions by employers during that period. While boycotts in South Africa go back as far as the successful 1959 ANC-led potato boycott in solidarity with farm workers in the eastern Transvaal (Frederickse 1987: 186), the boycotts of the 1980s were subsequently instigated with increasing frequency. The boycott of red meat resulting from a 1980 strike by meat workers in the Western Cape, the 1981 boycott of Rowntree chocolates during the strike there, and the boycott of National Co-operative Dairies in protest of the dismissal of black workers in 1987 at Clover Dairies in Durban, demonstrated the power of community solidarity (ibid: 27; Smuts and Westcott 1991: 110–11). Thus, strikes by vulnerable independent trade unions, whose workers were mostly unskilled, often migrants, and constantly threatened with unemployment, demonstrated their power through strike support and boycotts from the community. More significantly, these evolved into "long-term, mass-based structures for change in both the workplace and the community" (Frederickse 1987: 27). A particularly good example of this phenomenon was the Sarmcol strike in Natal in 1985, where, following the firing of striking rubber factory workers, the entire region mobilized on their behalf to raise funds, protest, engage in a one-day stay-away and boycott white businesses (Smuts and Westcott 1991: 128–9).

It is noteworthy that the October 1985 ban on media coverage of "unrest" specifically included strikes and boycotts. Yet such labor action escalated still further: in 1987, over 20,000 railway workers struck for over two months, and 340,000 mineworkers struck the Chamber of Mines for three weeks (Smuts and Westcott 1991: 128). In 1989 alone, over 3 million working-days were lost from labor disputes in South Africa (ibid: 129).

The nationwide two-day general strike in 1984, the largest of its kind in South African history up to that point, terrified the government, and many observers see it, along with the government crackdown which followed, as the starting point of the final wave of unrest which brought the regime to the negotiating table:

> as many as 800,000 people refused to go to work and 400,000 students boy-cotted classes. The strike was more than 80 per cent effective among workers from the besieged Vaal townships, and in the east Rand, where heavy industry and organised labour is concentrated. The SASOL (oil-from-coal) and ISCOR (iron and steel) para-statals ground to a halt, despite threats to fire workers who joined the strike. The transport system designed to carry workers to the Transvaal's industrial centre was abandoned ... (Frederickse 1987: 180)

The trade union's foray into the political arena, bolstered by the communities and students, was a stunning success: the stay-away strike had been the most successful in South Africa's history. The combined force of the muscle of organized labor and the back-up of the UDF's affiliated organizations had dealt the government a body blow that sent the politicians, the policy and the army reeling.

To try to halt these challenges, the government imposed a state of emergency in 1985 to curb the dissent. Since violent acts were already illegal, the state of emergency was aimed primarily at curbing the unarmed resistance. According to Wink (1987: 79), "In an eloquent tribute to the power of nonviolence the government had decided, in effect, to treat non-violence as the equivalent of violence." Initially, the restrictions were so comprehensive and the penalties so severe, that this hampered the nonviolent resistance efforts. For example, merely stating an opposition to military conscription, participating in a nonviolent demonstration, criticizing the government or any government official or advocating a boycott, could land one in prison for up to ten years (ibid: 79–80). Yet the state of emergency did not halt the nonviolent movement.

Charges of high treason against UDF leaders were dropped in December (Karis 1986: 128). Indeed, "The imposition of the July 1985 state of emergency was not only a disastrously unsuccessful effort to control the mass uprising, it also galvanized European and American elites into pushing for economic sanctions" (Price 1991: 250). The UDF and the unions had demonstrated the power of nonviolent resistance. Karis (1983: 405) correctly concluded that "black leaders will continue to calculate that mass pressures, including strikes and boycotts, will be more efficacious than violence."

A three-day general strike in June 1988 included more than 3 million workers and pupils, paralyzing industry. More than 1 million participated in a similar stay-away in May 1987, and an August 1989 general strike proved to be the largest in the series, essentially shutting down commerce in Pretoria, Johannesburg, Durban, and East London, and severely crippling industry in the Western Cape (Smuts and Westcott 1991: 125–7).

The rent boycott, based on objections to the poor living conditions, and higher utility rates for black than for white homes, began in the Vaal triangle in August 1984, and spread to 50 townships over the next two years. By September 1986, an estimated 60 percent of the black population was not paying rent. By 1989, the official governments of Soweto and other townships were forced to negotiate (Smuts and Westcott 1991: 26). School boycotts were widespread in the 17 years prior to majority rule, forcing some needed reforms, though the costs of denying much of a generation of blacks their education may have outweighed what was gained (ibid: 30).

In addition to demonstrations, strikes, boycotts, occupations, and other activities, there was an impressive development of alternative institutions, effectively creating a situation of dual power in South Africa, where institutions affecting the daily lives of black South Africans came increasingly to be managed by black South Africans themselves. Civic organizations based in the townships:

> discovered the value of long-term projects in mobilizing community support, such as health and education centers, creches and pre-schools, advice offices, culture clubs, and perhaps most importantly, news media. Newspapers, newsletters and pamphlets [became] a valuable means of consolidating organization, educating the community, and ensuring two-way communication. (Frederickse 1986: 27)

Cooperatives, community clinics, legal resource centers, and similar offices offered places for people to go when existing institutions were clearly inadequate. For example, a group known as OASSA (the Organisation for Appropriate Social Services in South Africa), founded in the Transvaal in 1983, later spreading to Cape Town, Durban, and Pietermaritzburg, offered medical and psychological help to those released from detention and others victimized by state repression (Frederickse 1986: 18). The South African government recognized the power of these young community organizations, or "civics." President P. W. Botha, in justifying a law restricting international financial assistance to community-based organizations, stated: "I say it's subversive to create alternative organizations in South Africa for the education of people, for local government, for proper economic development (Price 1991: 236)" The Kasigo Trust, the country's largest anti-apartheid foundation and a major backer of such alternative institutions, when ordered by the government to disclose all its funding sources, simply refused, on the grounds that it would be used by the government for intelligence-gathering purposes (Smuts and Westcott 1991: 36–7). The trust was supported by the European Community and hundreds of other foreign and domestic funding sources.

These alternative institutions prospered because official institutions were no longer recognized as legitimate. Only 6 percent of the voters cast their ballots in council elections for black townships in the late 1970s after their establishment, well below previous advisory bodies in the 1960s (Price 1991: 132). By the mid-1980s, scores of officially sanctioned local governments in the Black townships collapsed due to massive noncooperation, and the mayors and town councils, in most of these cases, either resigned or were simply ignored. Pro-ANC/UDF alternative governments were established in face of virtual military occupation.

One the most striking examples of this was in the Alexandra Township near Johannesburg, which had a population well over 100,000. The alternative government started at the level of the "yard," where three to five houses, each containing four to five families, shared a courtyard. About six of these yard committees, representing up to 25 families, made up a block committee, which then sent representatives to street committees. All of the street committees formed the Alexandra Action Committee, which became the township's de facto government. With the assistance of a white lawyer, they drew up a local constitution based on participatory democracy and formed their own "peoples' courts," which dealt with matters such as petty theft, family violence, and interfamily disputes. When the Action Committee successfully led a rent strike, the official government cut off water supplies and the cleaning of the communal pit toilets. The Action Committee then simply formed their own committees which took upon these and other jobs themselves (National Public Radio 1987). The rent strikes constituted an overt rejection of the authority of the township councils, making them a major target of state repression (Price 1991: 257).

Not all street and area committees were as democratic and well-functioning as those in Alexandra. Some were composed primarily of self-appointed vigilantes who engaged in undemocratic, violent, and arbitrary forms of control. Yet, in most cases, they did constitute a model of democratic self-governance, where none had ever existed previously, and became a powerful tool of nonviolent resistance to the official government.

Meanwhile, the first general elections based upon the new constitution of 1984, which created a tricameral legislature granting the Coloured and Indian populations their own parliament alongside (though clearly unequal to) the white parliament, but ignoring the black African majority altogether, resulted in an 80 percent boycott by those communities; those who did run were so reviled by their respective constituencies that they were essentially unable to campaign (Frederickse 1986: 147). Dr. Van Zyl Slabbbert, leader of the official opposition Progressive Federal Party (PFP) in the white parliament, resigned from parliament in protest at the disenfranchisement of the majority of South Africans. The result was that the facade of legitimacy of the new constitution was a non-starter.

It was also in the early 1980s that the churches became increasingly outspoken, not just in condemning apartheid as a sin, but in organizing protests in open defiance of apartheid and engaging in nonviolent resistance. Anglican Archbishop Desmond Tutu, who won the 1984 Nobel Peace Prize for his anti-apartheid activism, led the South African Council of Churches (SACC), representing 22 of the nation's leading denominations in ongoing resistance. Having largely failed to support the Defiance Campaign for the 1950s, the church leadership was frequently in the forefront of nonviolent action campaigns in the 1980s. The SACC adopted a resolution in July 1987 which openly questioned the legitimacy of the white minority government, and called on member churches to question their moral obligation to obey apartheid laws. The SACC openly supported the rent boycott, tax resistance, conscientious objection to military service and registering births outside the official race-based system (Smuts and Westcott 1991: 35–6). In addition, individual churches became sanctuaries for squatters whose homes had been demolished and for those sought by the authorities (ibid: 120–1), as well as becoming centers for meetings and offices for anti-apartheid groups.

By the mid- to late 1980s, defiance had reached a point where the government had clearly lost control. At political funerals and elsewhere, the green, black and gold flag of the ANC was unfurled widely despite the ban on such displays (Smuts and Westcott 1991: 55). Schools and other public facilities were renamed by young men with paint brushes after jailed and exiled heroes of the resistance (ibid: 91). Government officials were met by school children who refused to entertain them as a show of opposition (ibid: 123). Universities were faced with in sit-ins in support of black students (ibid: 124). Clergy began to marry mixed-raced couples in defiance of the Prevention of Mixed Marriages Act (ibid: 67), which was finally abolished in 1985. Church preschools and even some state elementary schools began admitting nonwhite students in violation of segregation laws (ibid: 67; Wink 1987: 62). White liberals started boycotting stores which refused to serve all races (Wink 1987: 82).

In February 1989, 300 anti-apartheid activists jailed without charge went on a hunger strike which resulted in the release of hundreds of detainees, and led to substantial limitations on the practice of detention without trial (Smuts and Westcott 1991: 64). Two years earlier, a 40–day public fast by a Buddhist nun from Britain resulted in the release of 250 children from detention (ibid: 66).

The growth in nonviolent resistance culminated in the new Defiance Campaign of 1989, with wave upon wave of illegal multiracial peace marches. These started in Cape Town in September, and spread to Johannesburg, Durban, East London, Grahamstown, Oudsthoorn, Kimberley, King William's Town, Bothshabelo, and Uitenhage, collectively encompassing hundreds of thousands of demonstrators, and effectively neutralizing the state of emergency (Smuts and Westcott 1991: 66). By November, the government allowed an ANC rally of 70,000 to take place in a soccer stadium, to welcome seven released political prisoners (ibid: 111).

There were four major goals of the 1989 campaign: (1) open defiance of the state of emergency to render it ineffective; (2) challenging petty apartheid laws; (3) supporting the rights of black workers by defying antilabour legislation; and, (4) demonstrating the illegitimacy of the tricameral legislative system. The campaign was largely successful, both in making those laws unenforceable, and in rebuilding opposition organizations which had been seriously damaged by the 1986 state of emergency. The alliance between the UDF and COSATU was strengthened and members of the white establishment, ranging from the mayor of Cape Town, business leaders, to leaders of the opposition Democratic Party, joined in the movement (Smuts and Westcott 1991: 45–6).

Actions of this kind, far more than the sporadic armed attacks by the ANC, forced the South African government to recognize that its days were numbered. Price predicted that:

> the precondition for negotiations leading to fundamental political change in South Africa is an extended period of economic decline and political unrest. Over time a situation of economic, physical and psychological deterioration is likely to impact on strategically important constituencies. Support for the political status quo will consequently erode among elements considered vital by the ruling elite, including segments of its security forces. The government's capacity to control will deteriorate as the costs of security escalates beyond the financial capabilities of a deteriorating economy and its self confidence will collapse as the resources and policy options to turn the situation around are perceived as exhausted. This process of decline and disaffection will lead to a gradual shift, over time, toward a position where negotiations for some form of fundamental political change, such as majority rule, is deemed acceptable. (1991: 45–6)

According to anti-apartheid activist Dene Smuts:

> The two historic strands of struggle, violent and nonviolent, were operating simultaneously at the time of the Defiance Campaign of 1989. When nonviolent action coexists with a declared policy of armed struggle, it cannot

approach Gandhian refinement and control. But, with violence on the ground and with the ambiguous goals of negotiation or takeover, nonviolent action in South Africa in the late 1980s – the hunger strikes that ended the mass use of the system of detention without trial, the beach protests that showed up the injustice of segregation and outrageousness of police action – operated on the same premises Martin Luther King described in his Letter from a Birmingham Jail ... [that] "direct action seeks to create such a crisis and foster such tension that a community which has constantly refused to negotiate is forced to confront this issue." (Smuts and Westcott 1991: 9)

Rather than ungovernability of the townships by the white authorities creating liberated zones which would become a beachhead for an armed assault against white South Africa, as many predicted, it was their ungovernability in itself, combined with effective alternative institutions, that helped force the government to recognize the need for negotiations.

Meanwhile, the largely unarmed resistance and the repressive counter-measures against the movement prompted nonviolent resistance movements in the industrialized countries to force sanctions. The existing cultural, academic, and sports boycotts were broadened to include economic sanctions which made a real impact. The British Commonwealth enacted restricted measures in 1986; the US, Japan, Canada, and several European countries enacted a series of sanctions that same year, while international bankers refused to roll over new loans. Several major corporations disinvested and, while their shares were often just bought up by South African firms, it restricted the amount of capital available to promote economic growth. This, combined with the strikes and other forms of economic resistance by the black majority, together with the increasing costs of internal security from both the armed and the far more significant unarmed resistance, led South Africa into the economic crisis which forced many of the country's elites to advocate change.

Reasons for the Success of the Nonviolent Emphasis

The nonviolent struggle in South Africa ultimately proved successful when sufficient numbers were empowered, mobilized, and willing to take the personal risks to challenge the existing order. One complicating factor in the South African struggle had been the use of "bannings," a form of house arrest, and suspended sentences with limits on political activity, against leaders in the resistance movement. In most cases, the leaders abided by these restrictions rather than face years of imprisonment; most of those that did not fled into exile. The political consequence of this submission was quite negative.

Sharp noted that:

One of the objective results of the leaders' choice of accepting these limitations, instead of refusing to comply and going to prison, has been to set an example harmful to future resistance. The ordinary opponent of apartheid is not likely to risk a greater punishment than the leaders are seen to be suffering. Yet willingness to undergo imprisonment and other suffering is a primary requirement of change. (1980: 171)

The increased willingness to defy banning orders in the late 1980s, as evidenced by Winnie Mandela and others, encouraged greater numbers to openly defy the authorities, and created a climate of resistance in the face of government repression. In August 1989, the UDF and other restricted organizations, along with scores of restricted activities, openly "unbanned" themselves in a public march in Cape Town (Smuts and Westcott 1991: 49). As one activist at the time described it:

A remarkable aspect of the 1989 campaign was that many of the organisations and people taking part "unbanned" themselves in order to do so. And not only did the 1989 campaign, unlike that of 1952, take place against the background of a state of emergency – it effectively ended it. (ibid: 45)

An editorial in the *Weekly Argus* during that year noted:

the intimidatory powers of the state have waned; the veneration of the law has diminished with the erosion of the rule of law. Inevitably that meek acquiescence of yesteryear has evaporated and SA is now witnessing an open, deliberate and organised campaign of defiance. (ibid: 37)

Though it is easy to think of apartheid South African society in terms of radical polarization, a model that would tend to support armed struggle as a means of change, the high degree of interdependence, albeit on unfair terms imposed by the ruling white minority, allowed greater latitude for manipulation through nonviolent means than is possible in classically polarized societies. About half of the country's Africans lived in areas allocated to South Africa's whites, including all the ports, major cities, industry, mines, and optimal agricultural land, as did virtually all of the Coloureds and Asians. The white minority existed from day to day with a high level of dependence on the black majority, not just for their high standard of living, but for their very survival. Nonviolent action constituted a more direct challenge to the system of apartheid than did violence.

The black South Africans' overwhelming numerical majority made the use of nonviolent action particularly effective when they started to mobilize in large numbers in the mid-1980s. Nonviolent action, despite its requirements of discipline and bravery in the face of repression, allowed participation by a far greater percentage of the population than would a guerrilla army, thus optimizing the black majority. Sustained nonviolent action created a great deal of unity and militancy among previously noncommitted

Africans, as was witnessed in earlier nonviolent campaigns. The late Zulu chief and ANC leader Albert Luthuli (1962: 64) noted how the 1953 Defiance Campaign "had succeeded in creating among a very large number of Africans the spirit of military defiance. The Campaign itself came to an untimely end, but it left a new climate, and it embraced people far beyond our range of vision." ANC membership jumped from approximately 7,000 at the start of the campaign to over 100,000 towards the end.

Another ANC leader, Walter Sisulu, observed that another nonviolent campaign, the successful 1957 Alexandra township bus boycott, "raised the political consciousness of the people and has brought about a great solidarity and unity among them" (Sharp: 1973: 795).

By contrast, violence often alienates support within the grievance group. This has been apparent in South African history, where the essentially conservative and religious Africans tended to respond negatively or not at all to revolutionary violence. Heribert Adam (1971: 116) reported that Operation Mayebuye, an ANC bombing campaign in the early 1960s, "which aimed at frightening whites into making concessions, instead resulted in a strengthening of the repressive machinery and general discouragement of African militancy closer to general resignative despair that determination to actively resist white domination."

The shift to a largely nonviolent orientation lured white popular opinion away from those seeking continued white domination. Nonviolent action threw the regime off-balance politically. A related factor was that the largely nonviolent struggle of the 1980s made the prospects of living under black majority rule less frightening. Though the prospects of giving up their privileges was not particularly welcomed by most whites, the use of nonviolence by the black majority against their white oppressors was seen as indicative of a tolerant attitude not likely to result in the previously anticipated reprisals upon seizing power. The use of armed struggle as the primary means of resistance, even if white civilian casualties were kept at a minimum, would have led many whites to fear for the worst.

One consequence of the divisions created within the white community was the End Conscription Campaign, which began in the 1970s with white youth opposing South Africa's occupation of Namibia and invasion of Angola, but grew dramatically in the mid-1980s, when the regular armed forces moved into the black townships. As many as 1,000 new, open resisters surfaced in 1989 alone, and thousands more evaded the draft in less public ways. Through the 1980s, an average of 4,000 men failed to report every year for military service (Frederickse 1987: 82). Resistance included voluntary exile, going underground, or voluntarily submitting oneself to arrest and imprisonment for refusal to be drafted into the army. While some were religious pacifists, most resisted on political grounds.

The phenomenon of clearly nonviolent demonstrators being subjected to cruelty and brutality, creating strong dissent within the white minority, had also occurred in earlier nonviolent campaigns. In the 1957 Alexandra township boycott:

> Despite official threats, many European automobile drivers gave rides to the walking African boycotters. On the route the Africans had been systematically intimidated and persecuted by the police. Also, after Sharpeville, unprovoked attacks – including whippings – by police against Africans in the Capetown area during an African strike led to so many European bystanders phoning to report the attacks to Capetown newspapers that the switchboards were jammed; the President of the Cape Chamber of Commerce of Industries, C.F. Regnier, personally pleaded with the Chief of Police, Col. I.P.S. Terblanche, to stop the assaults. (Sharp 1973: 669–70)

The shooting deaths of nonviolent Coloured students on strike in Cape Town in May 1980 produced an outpouring of sympathy for the strikers. Even the second largest white political party, the Progressive Federal Party, complained about the excessive force by the police. By contrast, the PFP strongly supported the January 1981 raid into Mozambique and other incursions by the South African armed forces against alleged armed guerrilla units.

Previously unsympathetic whites actively supported the nonviolent defense of a number of squatter settlements, such as the Crossroads community near Cape Town, threatened with destruction by authorities. Such episodes created a climate of divisiveness within the ruling order which was then exploited by the black resistance. Unfortunately, the slight escalation in armed attacks by the ANC in the early 1980s inhibited this shift. Journalist Julie Frederickse observed:

> When the ANC's attacks were largely confined to the sabotage of township railway lines and raids on black police stations, most whites had been able to dismiss the guerrillas as a few poorly-trained radicals "hurting their own people." But when nineteen whites and blacks were killed by a bomb in the streets of Pretoria in 1983, many white South Africans then readily accepted the government's argument that the ANC was committed to naked terrorism, aimed at civilians. ...The fact that the blast was aimed at the Defense Force Headquarters and half those killed were military personnel was obscured by the media fixation on "the car bomb outrage." (1987: 174)

By contrast, disciplined nonviolence created morale problems within the police and military, rendering them less effective:

> In an effort to crush a strike by Africans which began on March 22, 1960 (the day after the shooting at Sharpeville), police invaded the Nyanga location near Capetown on April 4; for four days they unleashed a reign of terror including extensive whippings of men, use of batons and some shootings and killings. (This was after extensive unprovoked police brutality against Africans elsewhere, which had produced important white protests against the police.) Norman Phillips of the Toronto Star reports the inhibiting effects of non-

retaliation even in this situation: "For sheer sadism, the closest comparison to what happened at Nyanga was when the Gestapo sealed off the Warsaw ghetto and began to annihilate it. Had Nyanga fought back, it, too, would have been wiped out; but the Africans employed nonaggressive tactics that puzzled the police." (Sharp 1973: 585–6)

Armed revolution, in the eyes of the white minority, would have confirmed their worst stereotypes of the Africans as "violent savages," would have reinforced the *laager* mentality, and encouraged whites to resist bitterly and engage in extraordinarily brutal repression. On the other hand, nonviolent action not only challenged the popular image of the "black terrorist," but also that of the "subservient house boy," creating significant attitudinal changes among whites, similar to those that occurred in the American South in the 1960s.

Nonviolent action allowed far greater potential for creating cleavages among the privileged white minority, such as how to respond to the resistance, how long to resist the inevitable changes demanded by the revolutionaries, and at what cost. The importance of maintaining a nonviolent discipline was not lost on leaders of the anti-apartheid movement. Bishop Tutu, in reaction to black attacks against suspected collaborators in 1985, deplored this kind of violence and threatened to leave the country if such tactics were not ended, insisting that "You cannot use methods to gain the goal of liberation that our enemy will use against us" (Smuts and Westcott 1991: 68). When Winnie Mandela, the once-revered wife of imprisoned ANC leader Nelson Mandela, and a prominent anti-apartheid activist in her own right, was found to be sanctioning violent activities, she found herself ostracized by the mass democratic movement (ibid: 96).

The advantages of nonviolence in winning allies went far beyond the potentially enlightened sectors of South Africa's white minority, in that they also extended to the world community. World opinion was of crucial importance. Despite verbal condemnation of its racial policies, the Western industrialized world gave South Africa consistent support over the years in the form of trade, industrial development, technological assistance, infusion of capital, and arms. South Africa would not have become the economic and military power it was without the massive aid it received from the West during 40 years of apartheid rule.

Prior to the imposition of sanctions in the mid-1980s, there was over $13 billion worth of annual trade between South Africa and the West, which, combined with $30 billion in foreign investment, supplied the country with the vast majority of such basic commodities as transportation equipment, electrical equipment and machinery, nuclear technology, telecommunications facilities and services, computer technology, chemicals and related products, paper and manufactures, and other goods essential to the maintenance of South Africa as a modern industrialized state. In addition, the West supported the South African regime through outstanding bank loans and credits totalling $6.5 billion, much of which went to government entities with no restrictions.

When the United Nations Security Council threatened sanctions and other punitive measures against South Africa, the United States, Great Britain, and France, due to their important economic and political interests, cast vetoes. By the mid- to late 1980s, however, thanks to massive non-violent protests in those countries and others by anti-apartheid activists, most industrialized nations imposed sanctions on the apartheid regime. Labor unions, church groups, students, and leftist organisations made business as usual with the apartheid government impossible. This upsurge in solidarity work came as a result of the largely nonviolent resistance in South Africa during the 1980s, and the government repression which resulted. In contrast, had the primary mode of resistance been armed struggle, it is unlikely that the same level of sympathy and the resulting mass mobilization would have been enough to make the sanctions movement so successful.

While some attribute the rioting, such as the Soweto uprising of 1976 and subsequent outbursts of violent township protests in the 1980s, as a key factor in the ending of apartheid, these were probably not decisive. Even as the riots and the repression escalated following the declaration of a state of emergency in 1985, heavy government censorship successfully limited media coverage, and interest in the situation waned. Unlike the concomitant nonviolent campaigns, the rioters were in large part suppressed. Like the youth rebellions in advanced capitalist countries in the 1960s and early 1970s, young militants certainly had a disruptive effect, may have inspired some reforms, and further exposed the repressive machinery of the state; but they did not have the power in themselves to force major structural change. Only when the youthful rebels were able to effectively build an alliance with the black working class was real change possible. The Soweto uprisings of 1976 illustrate this in both ways. Some Zulu migrant workers were used to brutally suppress the student strikes and other actions in August. However, after careful organizing among the workers by striking students, they became largely supportive in the general strike the following month, which led to the most dramatic crisis for the government during that turbulent period. In short, the rioting Soweto youths only began to seriously challenge the white authorities when they stopped rioting, built alliances with workers in the townships, and organized a nonviolent movement.

A resurgence of the student boycotts and protests sprang up among Coloured students in early 1980 in the Western Cape. By keeping their protest primarily nonviolent, and linking their educational demands to national political grievances, this led to the two-day general strike in June, when 70 percent of the workers stayed at home. Police repression was severe – over 60 people were killed in the following week – but it resulted in unprecedented support for the resistance among people of all races (Frederickse 1987: 18–9). When tens of thousands of black students walked out of the classrooms in early 1984, they were met by repression similar to that in the Soweto uprising. Yet not only was the violence more controlled, they were able to involve workers and their communities in their support, and draw up specific demands for educational improvements (ibid: 168).

The wave of violent unrest in the mid-1980s was largely insulated from the white minority community; there was actually less publicity in the white South African media on the unrest than there was in other countries. Often the targets of the rioters were public facilities for Africans, which created rifts within the black populations at a time when unity was of crucial importance. Far more significant, in terms both of building a popular resistance movement and of challenging the state,were the boycotts, strikes, creation of alternative institutions, and other forms of largely nonviolent resistance.

A 1981 study by the American Friends Service Committee (1982: 112) concluded:

> The South African government presents a classic example of bureaucracy, musclebound with arms and ideologically ill-equipped to meet the challenge of massive, nonviolent noncooperation. The government has already demonstrated an inability to use its bludgeoning techniques to foreclose strikes involving even a relatively small geographic area and a relatively small number of workers. What would happen if the black workers, servants, and farm laborers withdrew cooperation on a massive scale in a well-organized nonviolent campaign!
>
> Is it possible that at a certain point, as [Zambian president Kenneth] Kaunda puts it, the oppressor will realize that "he is powerless, in the last resort, to prevent the inevitable because he is trying to fight not an army but an idea, and short of exterminating a whole population he cannot bomb or blast it out of their minds?" The truth of the idea – the releasing of thirty million people to be human – is better served by nonviolent actions which do not deny the basic humanity of the oppressor.

This is exactly what happened in South Africa. And while the struggle was more protracted, more complex, and not as exclusively nonviolent as some similar struggles during this era, it was one of the most significant. It demonstrated that even where so many had given up on nonviolence, key elements of the resistance movement would recognize its power, and utilize unarmed resistance in the successful liberation of their people.

References

Adam, H. 1971. *Modernizing Racial Domination: The Dynamics of South African Politics*. Berkely: University of California Press.

Benson, M. 1966. *South Africa: The Struggle for a Birthright.* Harmondsworth: Penguin Books.

Frederickse, J. 1987. *South Africa: A Different Kind of War.* Boston: Beacon Press.

Gann, L. H., and P. Duignan. 1978. *South Africa: War, Revolution, or Peace.* Stanford: Hoover Institution.

Gerhart, G. 1978. *Black Power in South Africa: The Evolution of an Ideology.* Berkeley: University of California Press.

Johnson, R. W. 1977. *Will South Africa Survive?* New York: Oxford University Press.

Karis, T. 1983–4. "Revolution in the Making: Black Politics in South Africa," *Foreign Affairs*, Winter 1983–84, pp. 378–406.

——, 1986. "Black Politics: The Road to Revolution," In Mark A. Uhlig, ed., *Apartheid in Crisis*, New York: Vantage Books.

Kuper, L. 1958. *Passive Resistance in South Africa.* New Haven: Yale University Press.

Lelyveld, J. 1983. "Black Challenge to Pretoria", *New York Times*, October 12, p. A8.

Leonard, R. 1981. "Mobilizing for Total War," *Southern Africa*, vol. XIX, no. 1, (January/February), pp. 13–15.

Liddell Hart, B. H. 1967. "Lessons From Resistance Movements – Guerrilla and Nonviolent". In Adam Roberts, ed., *The Strategy of Civilian Defense.* Harmondsworth: Penguin, 1969.

Lodge, T. 1983. *Black Politics in South Africa Since 1945.* New York: Longman.

Luthuli, A. 1962. *Let My People Go: An Autobiography.* New York: McGraw Hill.

Marx, Andrew. "Black Consciousness Groups Meet," *Southern Africa*, vol. XIII, no. 7 September/October, 1980, pp. 13–15.

National Public Radio, "All Things Considered", June 3, 1987.

Nolutshungu, S. 1982. *Changing South Africa: Political Considerations,* Manchester: Manchester University Press.

Price, R. M. 1991. The Apartheid State in crisis: *Political Transformation in South Africa, 1975–1990* (New York: Oxford University Press.

Republic of South Africa (RSA). 1979. *Report of the Commission of Inquirty into Legislation Affecting the Utilisation of Manpower* (Reikert Commission Report). Pretoria: South African Government.

Sharp, G. 1973. *Politics of Nonviolent Action.* Boston: Porter Sargent.

—— 1980. *Social Power and Political Freedom.* Boston: Porter Sargent.

Smuts, D., and S. Westcott, eds., 1991. *The Purple Shall Govern: A South African A to Z of Nonviolent Action.* Vol. XI, no. 2 Oxford: Oxford University Press.

Southern African Committee. 1978. "News Briefs", *Southern Africa*, (March 1978), pp. 12–13.

Uhlig, M. A. 1986. "The African National Congress." In Uhlig, ed., *Apartheid in Crisis.* New York: Vantage Books.

Wink, I. W. 1987. *Violence and Nonviolence in South Africa: Jesus' Third Way.* Philadelphia: New Society Publishers.

PART VI

Latin America

Introduction

In Latin America, revolution, change of governments, and even peasant movements are often thought of in terms of armed struggle. Yet Latin American history is replete with nonviolent campaigns. Well over a dozen dictatorship have been overthrown this century through nonviolent movements,[1] the most recent being two dramatic and successful uprisings against successive military regimes in Bolivia in 1977 and 1982 and the ousting of the Duvalier dictatorship in Haiti in 1985. Ron Pagnucco and John McCarthy offer an overview of the role of religious-based organizations in "Advocating Nonviolent Direct Action in Latin America."

In Brazil, Uruguay, and Argentina, and particularly in Chile, nonviolent movements played a significant role in forcing a transition from military rule to democracy. In Argentina and other countries, "Mothers of the Disappeared" defied military authorities in public protests against the kidnapping and murder of young dissidents. In many countries, the Catholic Church played a significant role in challenging military governments; Daniel Zirker examines the role of the Brazilian church in "The Brazilian Church-State Crisis of 1980: Effective Nonviolent Action in a Military Dictatorship."

It is noteworthy that many of the surviving urban guerrillas which had challenged these countries' governments during the 1970s through the use of armed struggle have since renounced violence and continue to work for radical social change through nonviolent means. Some are involved in Church-related organizing efforts among the poor, and 1981 Nobel Peace Prize winner Adolfo Perez-Esquivel has replaced Che Guevara as the model to be followed. Similarly, the decision by many former guerrillas in Colombia to work through the electoral process and the successful negotiated settlement by guerrillas in El Salvador and Guatemala are further indication of the decline of armed resistance as a means of challenging authoritarian and oligarchic rule in Latin America. Indeed, even in the midst of armed revolutionary struggles in those countries, there were impressive mass nonviolent protests. Oftentimes, the protesters were slaughtered; other times, they were able to score remarkable successes which collectively contributed to the willingness of the government to negotiate and compromise.

Despite the Che mystique and the legacy of the Cuban revolution, such revolutions have been the exception rather than the rule. Even with the history of repression and military-led changes in government, there have been relatively few major armed insurgencies in Latin America that have amounted to more than a few hundred ill-fated armed guerrillas with a rather inflated sense of historical importance. Much of the failure of armed struggle in Latin America could be traced to Guevara's thesis that revolutionaries should not wait until all the objective conditions are in place before launching their insurgency, but should create the focal point of insurrection (or *foco*) themselves, thus sparking widespread insurgency.[2] Instead, it now appears that nonviolent struggle building out of popular concerns with active participation by those most immediately affected creates a far more dependable *foco* than an elite band of armed revolutionaries.

The growth in nonviolent movements has also served as a deterrent to possible military efforts to return to power. The most dramatic example of this was in 1986, when right-wing military officers in Argentina staged a rebellion, with their forces seizing barracks in Córdoba, Argentina's second largest city, as well as key military centers just outside the capital of Buenos Aires. More than 1 million people massed on the streets of Buenos Aires as a statement of opposition to the return to military rule. This outpouring of support for democracy led key segments of the military to refrain from joining the uprising and the coup was suppressed shortly thereafter.

While most of Latin America is now under democratic governance, the rise of neo-liberal economics and structural adjustment programs imposed by international economic institutions has created a crisis for the poor, working-class, indigenous peoples and some sectors of the middle class. This has led to the growth of hundreds of grassroots nonviolent campaigns for economic justice.

Perhaps the country hardest hit by these economic changes has been Mexico, where the one-party rule of the Institutional Revolutionary Party (PRI) is under fire for its corruption, autocratic rule, and distorted economic priorities. Nonviolent resistance has spread throughout the country, from Indian peasants in Chiapas, to residents of the poor but oil-rich state of Tabasco, to villagers in the central highlands, to industrial *maquiladores* workers in the north.

There is little question that nonviolent action will continue to play a major role in the struggle for justice throughout the hemisphere.

Notes

1   Patricia Parkman, *Insurrectionary Civic Strikes in Latin America 1931–1961* (Cambridge, Mass.: Albert Einstein Institution, 1990).
2   Regis Debray, *Revolution in the Revolution?* (New York: Grove Press, 1967).

12

Advocating Nonviolent Direct Action in Latin America: The Antecedents and Emergence of SERPAJ

Ronald Pagnucco and John D. McCarthy

The modern world system is characterized by sovereign, territorial nation-states. But while the nation-state may be the most important actor in the world system, there are other important transnational actors that link people with one another across countries and that may have an important influence on the domestic and international behavior of those nation-states.

Historically, religious organizations and churches have been transnational in scope and have been important transnational actors in many circumstances. In the twentieth century the growing interdependence of the world system, driven by developments in communication and transportation technologies among other factors, has facilitated the phenomenal growth of other transnational organizations. In 1909 there were only 176 international nongovernmental organizations (INGOs); by 1985 there were 18,000 (Boulding, 1988). Although the structure and goals of INGOs vary, many focus on fostering international understanding and peace, development, and human rights, and are organized into national sections with local chapters. These organizations provide information on international issues to their members, facilitate international exchanges, and sometimes mobilize their members to take action on common problems (Boulding, 1988; Willetts, 1982a, 1982b). We call INGOs with the aforementioned goals and activities *transnational social movement organizations* (TSMOs). Amnesty International, the Fellowship of Reconciliation (FOR), and Servicio Paz y Justicia en América Latina (SERPAJ-AI.) (Service for Peace and Justice in Latin America), the foci of this essay, are examples of TSMOs.

Such transnational actors, especially those with networks in the resource-rich countries of the North, can play important roles as midwives to developing social movement organizations (SMOs) in the resource-poor South. Churches and TSMOs can provide financial assistance, skilled individuals, bodies of knowledge and experience, and international contacts to resource-poor social justice activists in politically repressive nation-states.

As we shall see, the Protestant and Roman Catholic churches and the Christian pacifist Fellowship of Reconciliation played major roles in the emergence and development of SERPAJ, itself a TSMO. Like the FOR, SERPAJ grew out of a transnational network largely composed of religious activists, many of whom were church professionals. European and U.S. FOR activists, together with indigenous Latin American religious activists, created SERPAJ and developed the philosophy and tactics of nonviolent direct action – a tradition that was, for the most part, absent from Latin America. As we shall see, SERPAJ's transnational web of support was important for its very survival.

Although there are other Latin American groups committed to nonviolence (C. Maciel, unpublished), SERPAJ-AL is without question the most important organized advocate of principled nonviolent direct action in Latin America.[1] Formally constituted in 1974 at a meeting in Medellín, Colombia, its General Coordinator from its founding until 1986 was the internationally famous 1980 Nobel Peace Prize winner, Adolfo Pérez Esquivel. A cadre rather than a membership SMO, SERPAJ acts to coordinate and communicate among groups seeking progressive change, and it provides training in the theory, philosophy, and methods of nonviolence. A faith-based TSMO, with chapters in several Latin American countries and ties with supportive SMOs and churches in Europe and North America, SERPAJ is part of a transnational web of interaction that enables it to mobilize resources beyond the confines of any particular nation- state. Formed out of a transnational network of religious activists, SERPAJ differs from some TSMOs in that it was not the result of "a small number of individuals coming together in order to put pressure on their own government and then later deciding to engage in transnational contacts bypassing the government" (Willetts, 1982: 179).

We will examine how this organization was built, noting especially some important antecedents; how the theory and philosophy of nonviolent direct action, relatively unknown in Latin America, came to be adopted by SERPAJ; and how this small organization was able to survive and successfully advocate human rights while operating under repressive military dictatorships. This chapter begins with a discussion of several theoretical issues central to our analysis of SERPAJ. We then sketch the emergence of the FOR and its work in Latin America and describe the sequence of events that directly led to the founding of SERPAJ. After characterizing its strategy and structure generally, we conclude by illustrating many of our points in an account of the premier SERPAJ chapter, SERPAJ-Argentina.

Until recently a social movement in the Latin American context referred to "large organizations calling upon a nationwide constituency and aiming to influence government policy along the lines of social class" (Lehmann, 1990: 149). However, the last few decades have seen the emergence of many new social movement forms, such as ecclesiastical base communities (*comunidades eclesiales de base*, or CEBs), neighborhood organizations, women's groups, and human rights organizations (Jelín, 1987; Mainwaring and Viola, 1984; Slater, 1985). Both Latin American and North American observers of these new movements have struggled to find ways of under-standing them, realizing, as had their European counterparts, the inadequacy of traditional class-based approaches to explanations. The new social move-ment theory, popular among European and Latin American analysts of move-ments, emphasizes identity transformation; decentralized, participatory movement group structures; and cultural and noninstitutionalized forms of collective action in its framework for investigation (see Jelín, 1985; 1987; Mainwaring and Viola, 1984; Slater, 1985; but see also Eckstein, 1989).

We depend instead on resource mobilization theory (Jenkins, 1983; Zald and McCarthy, 1987), which provides the framework for our analysis of the emergence and development of SERPAJ as a TSMO. We will focus on several factors: preexisting networks and organizations; the religious and political opportunity structures; the sources of tangible resources (i.e., people, finances, meeting space), and intangible resources (skills, commit-ment, legitimacy); the processes by which these resources were coordinated, developed, and mobilized; and the cultural opportunity structure (e.g., the values and beliefs of the population that activists are trying to reach).

We will also examine the processes of tactical choice and tactical diffu-sion by which SERPAJ came to adopt the philosophy and practice of nonviolent direct action, which was relatively unknown in Latin America. Collective actors typically draw upon a rather narrow selection of tactics when they act. Such tactical repertoires (Tilly, 1979) change slowly, with communities sometimes trying new forms while at the same time letting others fall into disuse. Many factors may influence the choice of particular tactics: organizational characteristics, such as degree of formalization and centralization; goals, such as policy change, structural change, or individual transformation; available resources, such as number of members and amount of finances; ideology or belief system; and the political opportunity structure, which includes the institutionalized means of political participa-tion, degree of state repression, and the configuration of political alliances (McAdam, 1982; Tarrow, 1988). There is no scholarly consensus on the role these factors play in tactical choice (see Freeman, 1979; Staggenborg, 1991). However, there is some evidence that faith-based protest groups may be more likely than others to use nonviolent direct action (see Epstein, 1991). This stems from the religious values of personal responsibility, individual transformation, moral witness, and the sacredness of life that many such groups embody (Holsworth, 1989).

Coherent repertoires of tactics that are embedded in abstract webs of justification that rationalize their use and their harmony with one another probably depend more on face-to-face communication and written texts than on the mass media for their diffusion than do the simpler and more easily mimicked tactical elements such as the sit-in (McAdam, 1983). So in our search for clues to the diffusion of the nonviolent direct action repertoire we will be especially alert to transnational communication networks.

Antecedents to SERPAJ

The Fellowship of Reconciliation, a relatively small group of Christian pacifists in the United States and Europe, played an important role in the development of SERPAJ and the spread of the philosophy and techniques of nonviolent action in Latin America. Largely Protestant and not formally a part of any church, the FOR used its international network of ministers, missionaries, and lay people to advocate Christian pacifism and nonviolence in various countries. In the United States during the 1940s, 1950s, and 1960s, some FOR members worked with African American civil rights leaders to develop nonviolent direct action techniques that successfully challenged racial injustices. In the 1960s and 1970s, FOR members, as social movement "midwives," so to speak, brought to Latin America the lessons they learned from the civil rights movement.

The emergence and spread of FOR

The International Fellowship of Reconciliation (IFOR) and its national chapter in the United States, the American Fellowship of Reconciliation (AFOR), both had important roles in the developments that eventually led to the founding of SERPAJ. For many years representatives from both these groups had worked with limited success to plant seeds of the pacifist principles of nonviolent direct action across the nations of Central and South America.

The IFOR had its beginning on the eve of the First World War in Europe, although it was formally established in 1919 at a meeting in Bilthoven, Holland. On August 3, 1914, Friedrich Siegmund-Shultze, the German Kaiser's Christian pacifist chaplain, and Henry Hodgkin, the secretary of foreign mission enterprises for the British Society of Friends (Quakers), made a pledge in a Cologne railroad station to extend the "bonds of Christian love unbroken across the frontier" (quoted in Barton, 1974: 1). Both men had been involved in the Church Peace Union and the World Alliance for Promoting International Friendship through the Churches. In December 1914, through the efforts of Hodgkin, the British Fellowship of Reconciliation, the first national chapter, was born.

The FOR came to America through the efforts of Hodgkin and some of his British associates. Hodgkin was part of a trans-Atlantic church network that facilitated his efforts to organize an American branch. With the help of American pacifist churchmen, such as the Episcopalian priest John Nevin Sayre, the AFOR was founded in November 1915.

In October 1919, 50 Christian pacifists from ten countries, including FOR members from Britain and America, gathered in Bilthoven, Holland, and formally organized the IFOR. The IFOR and AFOR immediately began an energetic campaign of international organizing. The attempts to organize FOR chapters in Latin America were just one part of these efforts.

The founders of the AFOR did not intend to establish a radical, action-oriented group; it began primarily as an informal fellowship of Christian pacifists motivated by spiritual concerns (Barton, 1974). The FOR's first statement of purpose stated that the

> distinctive note of the Fellowship is its repudiation of war and commitment to a way of life creative of brotherhood.... Membership implies such a dedication to the practice of the principle of love as the inviable law of personal relationships and the transforming power of human life that any use or countenance of the war method by those who belong is impossible. (Quoted in Barton, 1974: 3)

Although in the 1920s some FOR leaders began to take an interest in Mohandas K. Gandhi's nonviolent direct action campaigns, most FOR members in the United States and Great Britain continued to have a passive view of nonviolence, eschewing even nonviolent conflict and confrontation (Sharp, 1979). However, several FOR members, including Howard Thurman, Muriel Lester, and Richard Gregg, went to India to learn what Gandhi was doing. They returned as ardent supporters of Gandhi; Gregg's *The Power of Non-Violence* (1934), based on his four-year experience in India, became the bible for such FOR advocates of nonviolent direct action as James Farmer and Rev. Glenn Smiley. It was not until the 1940s that some pacifists in the AFOR began actively experimenting with aggressive nonviolent tactics. With the support of some important AFOR leaders, black FOR member Farmer, a friend of Howard Thurman, helped organize a national interracial nonviolent action organization, the Congress of Racial Equality (CORE), and recruited many local FOR members into the organization (Chatfield, 1971). CORE and some members of the FOR continued to innovate in the use of unruly nonviolent tactics for civil rights. For some FOR members the philosophy and technique of nonviolent action was becoming a central part of the organization's message. The FOR was literally becoming a midwife – assisting the birth of nonviolent collective action as it provided nonviolence trainers and organizers. In 1956 the leader of the Montgomery Improvement Association (MIA), the Rev. Martin Luther King, Jr., sought the assistance of the AFOR's Rev. Smiley and Bayard Rustin as his group planned and implemented the famous Montgomery bus boycott (A. Morris, 1984). Reflecting on his work with Martin Luther King, Jr., Smiley observed that his role was "to carry the mail of the organization [e.g., the FOR] and that mail was the method of nonviolence" (quoted in Morris, 1984: 160). That mail would also be carried to Latin

America. The successful experience of the civil rights movement, the writings of King, and the Latin American organizing efforts of Smiley and other FOR civil rights veterans would play a role in the development of SERPAJ and its adoption of nonviolent direct action.

Early advocacy of nonviolence in Latin America

The AFOR was active in Central and South America as early as 1919. A driving force behind these efforts by AFOR was the Rev. John Nevin Sayre, an Episcopalian priest who helped establish AFOR and IFOR and who was a key leader in both organizations for nearly six decades. According to Sayre's (1961) invaluable summary of FOR activities concerning Latin America from 1919 to 1960, the first South American FOR group was formed in Montevideo, Uruguay, in 1941 through the help of the Methodist church network. At the prompting of FOR member the Rev. Earl Smith, an American Methodist missionary in Montevideo, Sayre arranged for Muriel Lester of London, Travelling Secretary of the IFOR, and Margaret Campbell of the AFOR, to make a South American tour, Smith arranged their schedule. Lester and Campbell held meetings, developed two prayer schools, and had many person-to-person contacts in Peru, Chile, Argentina, and Uruguay. With the help of Smith and the Uruguayan Methodist Bishop Enrique Balloch, Lester and Campbell organized in Montevideo the first South American FOR group. Lester and Campbell then went to Buenos Aires, where they organized another FOR group (Sayre, 1961: 2; see also Deats, 1991).

Other FOR organizers, including Sayre, continued to make short trips to Latin America throughout the 1940s and 1950s. However, all these FOR organizers were Protestant, a number being Methodist, and worked largely through the Protestant church network. While there was a significant and growing Protestant population in Latin America, the countries were overwhelmingly Roman Catholic. Sayre saw the difficulties this might pose for the organization of FOR and reported to the IFOR North American Committee in 1944 after his visit to Mexico: "The outstanding weakness of our position is that we have no Roman Catholic assistance for the planning and development of pacifist work in a predominantly Catholic country Mexico" (Sayre, 1961: 3). Commenting that this statement applies to the FOR throughout Latin America "right up to the present day [February 28, 1961]," (Sayre, 1961: 3), Sayre saw the need to have Roman Catholic organizers sent to Latin America to help recruit Catholics to the FOR and its pacifist message, otherwise the pattern of nearly total Protestant membership in Latin American FOR chapters – a pattern also present in Great Britain and North America – would continue (Sayre, 1961: 7). In his report Sayre recommended that as soon as possible the IFOR send from Europe to Latin America two accomplished Roman Catholic advocates of nonviolence, Jean and Hildegard Goss-Mayr. This was insightful advice, as the Goss-Mayrs went on to play a crucial role in the emergence of SERPAJ. The Goss-Mayrs went to Latin America in 1962; they were the first non-Latin American FOR organizers to make an extended, concerted effort for active nonviolence in Latin America. Although they were executive secretaries of the IFOR, they did not go with the exclusive intention of organizing FOR chapters (although they did organize several), but primarily to try to convert the Roman Catholic Church in Latin America to active nonviolence, which could, in turn, be an instrument for nonviolent liberation of the oppressed in Latin America (Chartier, 1980).

The Goss-Mayrs especially wanted to recruit the clergy to the creed of active nonviolence, believing that their leadership was uniquely important in Latin America. Once recruited, this cadre of priests and ministers would be able to reach people at all levels of society (Goss-Mayr and Goss-Mayr, 1966). The Goss-Mayrs were very aware that, as Europeans and foreigners, their ideas concerning nonviolence could not be imposed from outside; they recognized that all they could do was help sow the seed, give the example and the initiative. From their perspective it was absolutely essential that Latin Americans take leadership roles in the nonviolent movement and adapt nonviolence to the concrete situations in their countries.

The articulated, active nonviolence advocated by the Goss-Mayrs was, indeed, on the whole, relatively new for Latin America, although peasants, Indians, and others had nonviolently resisted oppression for centuries and there had been some nonviolent "civic strikes" attempting to remove dictators from power (see Eckstein, 1989; Parkman, 1990). On the whole, these forms of nonviolent action were pragmatic, not rooted in a philosophy and general strategy of nonviolent direct action. Richard Chartier, a Methodist missionary and FOR member in Argentina from 1959 to 1973, described the Latin American situation:

> For years nonviolence was virtually unknown—restricted to a few familiar with its theory and practice elsewhere—or regarded as alien or irrelevant to the harsh realities of Latin America. For many, it connoted passivism, emphasis on democratic and decent deportment privately and publicly, mild reformism or the resolution of insignificant conflicts. (Chartier, 1980: 9)

Thus, before the Goss-Mayrs came in the 1960s, nonviolence was virtually unknown in Roman Catholic circles (Cornell, 1977). Even those few groups in Latin America committed to nonviolence did not advocate direct action. FOR groups throughout Latin America tended to have a more passive, nonconfrontational view of nonviolence (Chartier, 1980; McManus, 1991a). In this they resembled the orientation of many AFOR members, most notably Sayre. The predominantly Catholic Lanza del Vasto groups throughout Latin America practiced a spiritual nonviolence and "tend[ed] to withdraw themselves from life" (Goss-Mayr and Goss-Mayr, 1962b: 2). The reconceptualization of nonviolence taking place in the United States, largely under the impetus of the civil rights movement, had yet to take place to any significant degree in Latin America.

In the course of their efforts in Latin America, Jean and Hildegard Goss-Mayr interacted person-to-person with bishops, priests, and ministers; spoke in seminaries, both Catholic and Protestant, and in various intellectual and labor groups, both leftist and conservative. They also met with various lay leaders and groups such as Catholic Action, an organization established to promulgate Catholic social teachings that had chapters throughout Latin America and that was especially important in the Brazilian church (Bidegain, 1985; Chartier, 1980). The Goss-Mayrs organized study groups and training seminars on nonviolence and went to groups involved in resistance efforts, such as land occupations and strikes, to talk about nonviolent techniques. Among the bishops and church officials they met with was Dom Helder Cámara, former national chaplain of Brazil's Catholic Action, when he was an auxiliary bishop working with the poor in Rio de Janeiro. According to Cornell (1977) and Chartier (1980), Jean and Hildegard helped convert Cámara to nonviolence through the writings of Martin Luther King. Cámara was to become one of the most prominent nonviolent leaders in Latin America and eventually Archbishop of Recife, Brazil.

However, not everyone was receptive to the Goss-Mayrs' message of active nonviolence. Just War theology, which some used to justify revolution (Goss-Mayr and Goss-Mayr, 1962a), dominated Catholic thought and the Latin American church was becoming polarized between conservatives and leftists. Latin America was in a revolutionary situation. But the Goss-Mayrs worked undeterred, trying to convert conservative and leftist alike to the Gospel message of justice and nonviolence.

Three Stages of SERPAJ's Development

We have seen the important role that the Rev. Earl Smith, Jean and Hildegard Goss-Mayr, and the AFOR and IFOR played in laying the foundations of SERPAJ. We can now investigate the sequence of events that directly led to the founding of SERPAJ. This sequence can be divided into three stages: (1) 1966–1971: outreach and coordination; (2) 1971–1974: the founding of a transitional organization; (3) 1974–1985; the establishment and growth of SERPAJ (see SERPAJ-AL, 1987; Goss-Mayr and Goss-Mayr, 1984; Muñoz, Maciel, and de Souza, 1986). In each of these stages there was significant participation by leaders of various North American and European nonviolent groups as well as Latin Americans. There was also significant participation by church professionals, including the clergy.

Stage 1: outreach and coordination (1966–71)

While the FOR in Latin America had their own limited continental meetings for several years, the first major gathering on nonviolence in Latin America was a FOR "consultation" held in 1966 at Montevideo, Uruguay, followed by a "continental meeting" in 1971 at Alajuela, Costa Rica. These early meetings were "concerned with adopting the intellectual tradition of nonviolence and pacifism received from Europe and the United States" while paying equal attention to the Latin American situation (Antoine, 1983: 8). The Goss-Mayrs and Rev. Earl Smith played important roles in these meetings (Cornell, 1977).

Although the "consultation" at Montevideo was organized by the Latin American FOR, it was supported by other groups. The meeting was largely Protestant, though there was some Roman Catholic involvement. Among those speaking was Lanza del Vasto and AFOR member James Lawson, a Methodist minister and associate of Rev. King, who gave the keynote address on "Nonviolence: The Revolution that Matters." King sent a message of support (see South American Committee of the IFOR, 1966). Among the Latin Americans present was Adolfo Obieta, who in 1973 would help Adolfo Pérez Esquivel start the newsletter *Paz y Justicia*, and FOR member Herberto Sein, a Mexican Quaker who worked with AFOR civil rights veterans Glenn Smiley and Brady Tyson in Justice-Action-Peace Latin America (JAPLA).[2] Significantly, the participants at the meeting resolved to actively reach out to other groups and to collaborate with them if possible. Various organizing efforts were made during this period to spread the message of active nonviolence and to build continental and global ties among advocates of nonviolence. For example, in March 1970, Tyson, a dynamic Methodist minister who had been a missionary in Brazil, an associate of Dr. Martin Luther King, Jr., an SCLC executive board member, and a FOR member, introduced the Rev. Ralph Abernathy, who succeeded King as head of the SCLC, to Dom Helder Cámara in Recife, Brazil. Together Cámara and Abernathy issued the "Declaration of Recife" calling for a worldwide movement of nonviolent protest against the unjust structures that maintain poverty, racism, and war, concluding with the statement that "we look forward to other contacts with each other, and with others of other nations" (Tyson, 1970: 722). During this first stage we see such civil rights movement veterans as Tyson, Smiley, and Lafayette contributing to the nonviolent movement in Latin America through JAPLA. (Tyson would continue to play a role in all three stages.) The Goss-Mayrs, Smith, and others continued their organizing efforts, contributing to the success of the meeting in Alajuela where a new organization that superseded the FOR was founded.

Stage 2: the founding of a transitional organization (1971–3)

The next continental meeting took place in 1971 in Alajuela, Costa Rica. Jean and Hildegard Goss-Mayr helped organize the conference, and, again, international networks were important. Smiley helped with the program, invitations, and financing of the Alajuela meeting (Goss-Mayr and Goss-Mayr, 1971), and he attended the meeting, as did Lafayette, a staff member of SCLC who had been an early leader in SNCC. At this meeting, representatives from groups working nonviolently for change in Latin America, including such church leaders as Dom Helder Cámara, Dom Antonio Fragosa, Msgr. Valencio Cano, and Bishop Federico Pagura, met for the first time (Deming, 1978).

A new Latin American nonviolent organization was born at this meeting. Named "Servicio para la Acción Liberadora en América Latina— Orientación No-Violenta," this continental organization, the precursor of SERPAJ-AL, was comprised of FOR members and others. Smith was chosen to be the coordinator. Servicio was not created to be a mass movement organization, but, rather, a service group that would provide information and help other groups in communication, planning, coordination, and non-violent training (Muñoz, Maciel, and de Souza, 1986). To help fulfil these tasks, Servicio established a newsletter, *Boletin del Servicio para la Acción Liberadora en América Latina Orientación No-Violenta*, with Smith as editor. Organizing and coordinating efforts were expanded, with the goal of developing a stronger continental organization.

Stage 3: the establishment and growth of SERPAJ (1974–85)

It was during the continental meeting at Medellín, Colombia, in 1974 that SERPAJ was formally created. Smith and Hildegard Goss-Mayr organized the meeting. A few months before the meeting, Hildegard made an extensive trip during which she visited almost all of the delegates to the meeting. Both she and Smith raised enough money to pay the travel expenses and living expenses of all who needed help. Richard H. Post of the US War Resisters' League (WRL) wrote an invaluable report on the Medellín meeting (unpublished meeting minutes). Both the IFOR and the WRL were among the endorsers of the meeting. The 1974 meeting had a distinctly Latin American character, and the newly established SERPAJ became a truly Latin American organization.

Only Latin Americans could vote at the meeting. According to Post: "Conscientization was the watchword of the conference. All the delegates were familiar with the works of Paulo Freire, whose classic *Pedagogy of the Oppressed* ... became the conference bible" (Post, n.d.: 2). The churches provided much support; the meeting was held in the major Roman

Catholic seminary in Medellín, and a large number of Latin American church professionals participated:

> The delegates included twelve Catholic clergy – two of them bishops and a third an archbishop – and six Protestant clergy – one [an] active bishop, another a retired bishop. Six of the fourteen women are nuns. Some ten percent are engaged in social service for Indians. About one third are poor tenant farmers (share croppers) or urban industrial workers, all with some experience in non-violent actions but none of them trained in theory. (Post, n.d.: 3)

In all, some 48 delegates from four Central American and eight South American countries participated. Four representatives from the United States and ten European delegates attended, continuing the invaluable transnational connections that would provide increasingly important support for SERPAJ.

The Operational Structure and Strategic Approach of SERPAJ

The basic structure of SERPAJ was established at Medellín. Although there has been continual modification of SERPAJ's structure since its founding, its basic organizational features, as well as its strategic approach, has remained essentially the same throughout the 1970s and 1980s.

SERPAJ is a loosely structured, a relatively decentralized, and an informal transnational organization. The organizational form adopted by SERPAJ is not unique and bears much resemblance to those of many of the SMOs that nurtured it into existence. There is no rigid hierarchy or formal leadership structure. The general coordinator is limited in his or her power. National chapters have their own structures that vary from country to country. "Lines of action," providing a general orientation rather than concrete goals, are established consensually at the continental meetings, leaving national chapters broad discretion about which of the issues will be emphasized and exactly how the policies will be carried out.

SERPAJ is an autonomous organization, not directly tied to the church, political parties, or any other organization, even though it draws heavily on its links to the Roman Catholic Church in many countries. In this regard it is a relatively new organizational form in Latin America. Its autonomy has been important in allowing SERPAJ to maintain the integrity of its tactical message. Also, because SERPAJ is not bound to any special interests, it is better able to function as a mediating and coordinating organization (Pérez Esquivel, Personal Communication, 1985).

Attempting to be a catalyst of nonviolent change, SERPAJ functions much as a vanguard elite (Pérez Esquivel, Personal Communication, 1985). The national secretariats of SERPAJ typically are composed of a few paid staff, along with church-affiliated social activists such as priests, and volunteers. The typical national secretariat had ten to 15 members. Several chapters, such as those in Brazil, Uruguay, and Chile, have priests in important leadership positions, although SERPAJ-Argentina, perhaps because of the unique situation of the church in that country, does not have any priests in prominent positions. Thus the actual number of people working for SERPAJ is small. However, SERPAJ was not intended to be a mass membership organization but, rather, a cadre service organization of *animadores*, or facilitators. Much like its predecessor, Servicio para Liberadora, SERPAJ helps nonviolent groups communicate with each other and publicizes and documents their actions; it organizes solidarity and support actions for these groups, organizes nonviolent training sessions, and provides literature on nonviolence; it helps mobilize groups for nonviolent action; and it helps organize new groups (see Schravesande, 1981: 3–8).

Mainwaring and Viola provide an excellent summary of the role of the *animador* as opposed to that of the *dirigente*, or director:

> They attempt to develop leadership as *animador* (facilitator) and supersede leadership as *dirigente* (director). The animador stimulates autonomous popular action and mobilization. The logic of the social movement is not pre-established according to the animador's orientation. The animador respects and values the logic of the movement and attempts to establish a relation of mutuality and respect with the members of the movement. By contrast, the dirigente attempts to control the nature of popular mobilization and to orient this mobilization towards his/her objectives. The dirigente believes in expertise and technocracy. (Mainwaring and Viola, 1984: 37)

The *animador* tries to stimulate the full participation of group members and, rather than providing the answers, asks the right questions (McManus, 1991b). This approach is supposed to empower people, to help them build the organization and acquire the skills they need to be able to act on their own. The *animador* does not recruit members into SERPAJ per se, although the groups are invited to continue to work with SERPAJ.

The transnational dimension of SERPAJ

As has been made clear, SERPAJ has had very close ties with European and US groups since its beginning, principally with FOR groups (AFOR and IFOR). SERPAJ-Europe was organized by Jean and Hildegard Goss-Mayr with the help of the IFOR. According to its 1984 yearly report, SERPAJ-Europe consisted of a variety of groups in 14 countries, "most of them linked in one way or another to the Fellowship of Reconciliation...the War Resisters International, or/and Pax Christi – in so far as they are interested in...SERPAJ" (SERPAJ-Europe, 1984: 1). The organization provides the bulk of SERPAJ-AL's financial budget and informs Europeans about the Latin American movement through speakers, literature, and its newsletter *INFO*, established in 1980. SERPAJ-Europe also organizes solidarity and support actions for SERPAJ-AL.

SERPAJ-AL relations with US groups have been of a different form – there is no SERPAJ-US for example. However, close ties are maintained with the AFOR – throughout the 1980s, Tyson was the official AFOR liaison with SERPAJ-AL – as well as through AFOR members such as Richard Chartier, and the AFOR Task Force on Latin America and the Caribbean, founded in 1983. Likewise SERPAJ-AL has close ties with the Resource Center on Nonviolence (which has several AFOR members on its staff), as well as the Committee in Solidarity with Latin American Non-violent Movements (CISLANM), founded by two AFOR members in 1982 after a meeting with Pérez Esquivel. These US groups provide information and educational materials to North Americans about Latin American non-violent movements in general, as well as SERPAJ-AL in particular, organize support actions, and have helped arrange meetings for SERPAJ-AL, members in the United States; however, US groups have not provided SERPAJ with substantial financial resources.

The modern world system is characterized by sovereign, territorial nation-states; the degree of governance provided by international institutions, most notably the United Nations, is minimal. INGOs, while providing "unofficial" linkages among citizens in these nation-states, are limited in their abilities to directly influence national policies. Yet, indirectly, they can influence political leaders in nation-states by appealing their local cases to international bodies, thereby seeking legitimacy for their claims by going over the heads of those who control their own states (see Nagel and Olzak, 1982; Smith, 1991). An exclusively state-centric model is inadequate for analyzing SERPAJ; while national chapters engaged in various activities in their respective territorial nation-states, SERPAJ actors regularly interacted with actors outside their state. These transnational ties were crucial for the very survival of SERPAJ. As Mainwaring and Viola (1984:30) write of human rights groups, including SERPAJ, in Argentina: "Without international support for the human rights organizations, the Argentine state could have – and probably would have – destroyed the human rights organizations. Thus the limits to state terror were set in part by the international community to which the regime itself aspired to become a more central part." They go on to note that "a movement with relatively few participants had a significant international impact and became the major challenge to a regime with an immense capacity to control civil society" (Mainwaring and Viola, 1984: 31).

SERPAJ as movement midwife

Aldon Morris (1984) coined the phrase "movement halfway house" to characterize the role of AFOR and SMOs like it in the 1960s civil rights movement. SMOs of this type, he argued, specialize in aiding other groups that are fighting for their own rights:

> A movement halfway house is an established group or organization that is only partially integrated into the larger society because its participants are actively involved in efforts to bring about a desired change in society... [They] develop a battery of social change resources, such as skilled activists, tactical knowledge, media contacts, workshops, knowledge of past movements and a vision of a future society. What they lack is broad support and a visible platform. (Morris, 1984: 139–40)

We prefer instead the imagery of the term "movement midwife" since it more clearly conveys the nature of the aid that such groups provide – skill and knowledge to facilitate creations that are ultimately out of their hands. SERPAJ has functioned as a movement midwife, as we have seen above and will illustrate in more detail below. It has created a distinctive form of midwifery adapted to its cultural and political context. The development and legitimation of the role of animador beyond the efforts of SERPAJ no doubt facilitated its work much in the same way that Marxism paved the way for a central role for intellectuals in the struggles of the working classes. Yet the activists of SERPAJ, as we have seen, do not envision a long-term leadership role for themselves in the movements they encourage and support.

SERPAJ and the Latin American Church and State

For most of its 500-year history, the Roman Catholic Church in Latin America has identified with dominant elites, although there have been some exceptions to this pattern (see Salinas, 1990; Smith, 1991). Social, economic, and political changes in the nineteenth and twentieth centuries somewhat diminished the political power of the church, which for centuries had been a key actor in the power elite in Latin America. Commenting on religion and politics in contemporary Latin America, Thomas G. Sanders observed that "the principal political actors are political parties, the military, and economic groups. Religion plays a role, but a secondary one" (Sanders, 1987: 115). The church's important, if not central, role in Latin American society and politics was amplified during the 1960s, 1970s, and 1980s as a wave of repressive military regimes hit many Latin American countries. Religious activists, and in some cases church leaders, became vocal critics of regime repression as political parties, labor unions, and other possible sources of organized opposition were silenced. Broader changes in the church contributed to the emergence of this new religious activism on behalf of human rights.

Vatican Council II (1962–5) marked an important turning point in church–society relations, calling for greater efforts to achieve political, social, and economic justice on the part of the church. The Latin American bishops responded to this call in a widely known conference in Medellín, Colombia, in 1968 (see Smith, 1991). The bishops produced a document condemning the violence of social structures that doom many to misery, criticizing the economic dependency of the developing world on the developed world, and supporting the newly emerging ecclesiastical base communities (CEBs), including many small lay-led groups of poor people who support each other and pray and read the Bible together, as well as several other typical forms (Smith, 1991). The document put the church in solidarity with the poor and oppressed, and it opened up the church to greater opportunities for lay leadership. These changes created "religious opportunity" akin to the political opportunity that scholars of movements in rich nations view as increasingly important to understanding their emergence and vitality (Smith, 1991). In a variety of ways organized religious structures may facilitate social movements.

It was in this new context that SERPAJ was formed. The importance of the Medellín CELAM conference for the reorientation of the Latin American church toward social justice advocacy was summed up best by Pérez Esquivel when he said, "we are all the children of Medellín" (quoted in Antoine, 1983: 4). However, not all of the national episcopates stood with the oppressed and their middle-class supporters, and some doubt the depth of commitment to liberal, individual human rights of those that did (Garrett, 1988).

The twentieth century has seen a cycle of military dictatorships interspersed by periods of less oppressive governance in most of the countries of Latin America (Skidmore and Smith, 1989). The first eight national chapters of SERPAJ, established between 1974 and 1982, were formed in countries with military dictatorships. Our case study, SERPAJ-Argentina, was established in 1974; its predecessor was formed in 1973 during a brief turbulent period of civilian rule between the military regimes of 1966–73 and 1976–83. In general, the military dictatorships eliminated or severely repressed the civil associations that might have opposed them, though the degree of repression varied by country. Under such circumstances the church hierarchy in some countries came to actively oppose the dictatorships, whereas in others, such as Argentina, it did not.

SERPAJ-Argentina

The development of SERPAJ in Argentina has a special place in the history of SERPAJ-AL, as its key organizer, Adolfo Pérez Esquivel, recognized for his work, was elected general coordinator of SERPAJ-AL at its formal establishment in 1974. In the 1960s Pérez Esquivel joined one of del Vasto's "Friends of the Ark" groups in Buenos Aires and met and befriended del Vasto. There were many such groups in Argentina, and del Vasto visited

Argentina regularly (Chartier, 1980; McManus, 1991b; Pérez Esquivel, Personal Communication, 1985). Committed to Gandhian nonviolence, the groups were small, predominantly Catholic, and very spiritual, and they fostered prayer and study rather than engaging in nonviolent direct action (Chartier, 1980; McManus, 1991a). Pérez Esquivel also met and befriended Jean and Hildegard Goss-Mayr in the 1960s and became a part of the network that they were building (Maciel, 1986).

In 1972, Pérez Esquivel, Chartier, and others participated in a public fast to protest the increasing violence of the left and right in Argentina. Perceiving a need for a publication to inform Argentines and other Latin Americans about nonviolence and the various nonviolent efforts throughout the world, in April of 1973 Pérez Esquivel, with a team of five assistants including Adolfo Obieta, a Catholic Friends of the Ark member, began publishing the monthly newsletter *Paz y Justicia: Acción No-Violenta Latinoamericana* – hereafter called *Paz* (Pérez Esquivel, Personal Communication, 1985; see also *Paz*, April 1973). Pérez Esquivel's group in Argentina at this time was called "Acción No-Violenta Latinoamérica." This group cooperated with the Friends of the Ark in Buenos Aires as well as the local FOR chapter. The Friends of the Ark have a place of prominence in the 1973–4 issues of *Paz* and clearly played an important role in the developing nonviolent community in Buenos Aires and in the emergence of SERPAJ-Argentina.

Among the broad range of issues addressed in the 1973–4 issues of *Paz* were the right to conscientious objection in Argentina; the ecology; human rights; economic development; French nuclear testing in the Pacific; and Argentina and nuclear weapons. The newsletter also carried stories about peace groups and nonviolent campaigns in numerous countries, listing the names and addresses of groups throughout the world. It also had essays on nonviolence by Europeans, North Americans, and Latin Americans. In 1974 when SERPAJ was formally established, *Paz* became its official publication, merging with the *Boletin* edited by Earl Smith in Montevideo, Uruguay.

Besides publishing *Paz*, Acción was involved in other activities. In one of the first major campaigns noted in the newsletter, Acción, the Friends, and the local FOR issued a statement protesting France's planned nuclear test in the Pacific (see *Paz*, August 1973). On August 3, 1973, Acción and the Friends, but not the FOR, sponsored a march in front of the French embassy to protest the nuclear test. Nine of the protestors, including Pérez Esquivel, were arrested by the Argentine federal police.

As can be seen, the precursor to SERPAJ-Argentina was not exclusively a human rights organization but, rather, a group of religious activists committed to nonviolence and pacifism. They addressed many peace and justice issues within the framework of religious, usually Christian, faith. These issues continued to be of interest to all of SERPAJ-AL, although work for human rights, the source of SERPAJ's and Pérez Esquivel's fame, became a more central concern. However, Pérez Esquivel traveled to Europe and

North America to talk about disarmament and conditions in Latin America and was known to peace activists before the 1976 coup. These contacts, already evident in the 1973 issues of *Paz*, were to prove invaluable.

As noted, the Argentine church hierarchy was quite conservative politically and theologically (Lehmann, 1990; Mignone, 1988). The church did not support SERPAJ and may have welcomed its suppression. One significant example of the hierarchy's conservatism occurred in 1975 as the political horizon was growing ever darker. At that time there was a lack of work in human rights in Argentina (Acuna, Personal Communication, 1985; Pérez Esquivel, Personal Communication, 1985), the only human rights organization was the Communist-dominated Argentine League for Human Rights, founded in 1937. In 1973 civilian rule was returned when Juan Perón was elected president; however, he gave his approval to crackdowns on leftist rallies and publications. After he died in 1974 the vice president, his wife, Isabel, succeeded him, but she was unable to stop the chaos in Argentina. Many believed that a military coup was inevitable; the future of human rights looked bleak. In March 1976 the military took power in "Argentina's best predicted coup" (Skidmore and Smith, 1989: 102). According to Carlos Acuna, a SERPAJ-Argentina staff member, Pérez Esquivel and SERPAJ-Argentina had proposed in 1975 that the Argentine church strengthen its Justice and Peace Commission and work on human rights. The bishops refused. Consequently, in February 1976 Pérez Esquivel helped start the Ecumenical Human Rights Movement, a group of religious and lay workers from several denominations. At the end of 1975, Pérez Esquivel and SERPAJ helped start the Permanent Assembly for Human Rights, a group of trade unionists, politicians, and intellectuals. The strategy of Pérez Esquivel and SERPAJ was to organize two human rights organizations with different constituencies and to coordinate their activities with those of SERPAJ (Acuna, 1985; Jelín, 1987).

In the March–May 1976 issue of *Paz*, SERPAJ announced, in the face of the military junta that seized power on March 24, a two-year campaign to get the United Nations General Assembly to hold a special convocation on human rights and to strengthen the enforcement of human rights throughout the world. Included in the issue was the entire Universal Declaration of Human Rights and a petition for people to sign and send to the Secretary General of the United Nations. On March 29, 1976, Pérez Esquivel began an international tour to drum up support for the campaign.

In spring 1977, Pérez Esquivel helped form the Mothers of the Plaza de Mayo, which appeared as a distinct group on April 30, 1977 (Acuna, 1985; Navarro, 1989). The Mothers were women who had children who "disappeared" and had good reason to believe the government was responsible. They gathered regularly in the plaza and marched in front of government offices demanding an account of their children. The Mothers became one of the most celebrated human rights groups in Latin America, and they continued to march regularly throughout the tenure of the military regime.

Also in spring 1977, SERPAJ arranged to hold the International Seminar for Training in Nonviolent Action during July in Cuernevaca, Mexico. As Pérez Esquivel prepared to travel throughout Latin America to recruit participants for the seminar, on April 4 he went to central police headquarters to get a passport. He was detained. Police told inquiring friends that they did not know where he was. He became one of the "disappeared."

An international campaign for the release of Pérez Esquivel, largely organized by the IFOR, was begun immediately. The response was quick and widespread; many groups in Europe and North America promptly joined the campaign. Amnesty International adopted him as a prisoner of conscience, and when Patricia Derian, the US State Department's human rights coordinator, visited Buenos Aires in August, she formally inquired into Pérez Esquivel's case, signaling the Carter administration's concern. Pérez Esquivel was imprisoned for 14 months, during which time he was tortured. He was released from prison in June 1978 as the World Cup soccer championship in Argentina drew the international spotlight there. He remained under house arrest for another 14 months. After his release, he resumed his activities in Buenos Aires as general coordinator of SERPAJ.

It was during Pérez Esquivel's imprisonment that Jim Forest of the international headquarters of IFOR informed Maeread Corrigan and Betty Williams, the 1976 Nobel Peace Prize winners, of Pérez Esquivel's plight. Corrigan and Williams subsequently nominated Pérez Esquivel for the Nobel Peace Prize, which he received in 1980 (Ready, Tyson, and Pagnucco, 1985). Using its international network, SERPAJ arranged for Corrigan to visit Buenos Aires for a one-week speaking tour late in August 1979. At that time she publicly praised Pérez Esquivel for his work and stated that she wanted to see him get the Nobel Peace Prize (see *Paz*, October–November 1979). SERPAJ strategically used its international network to criticize the military regime right before its eyes.

The news of Pérez Esquivel's receipt of the prize was greeted critically by the military regime and ignored or downplayed by the Argentine media. The Argentine Catholic Information Agency simply stated that SERPAJ was not associated with the church's Peace and Justice Commission (Ready, Tyson, and Pagnucco, 1985). In spite of such responses, Pérez Esquivel believed that his receipt of the prize strengthened the social movement for democracy in Argentina and gave him an international forum to talk about human rights abuses in Argentina and Latin America as a whole (Pérez Esquivel, 1985). According to the Argentine sociologist Elizabeth Jelín, the September 1979 visit of a delegation of the Organization of American States' Inter-American Commission on Human Rights, which resulted in criticism of the Argentine regime, along with Pérez Esquivel's receipt of the prize in 1980, helped create in Argentina an opening for public debate of human rights (Jelín, 1987). Part of a trend of awarding the prize to leaders of movements for domestic reform, the Nobel Committee expressed the hope that the award would assist Pérez Esquivel in his work (Ready, Tyson, and Pagnucco, 1985). Pérez Esquivel (1985) and Acuna (1985) both believe that the prize made life safer for SERPAJ-Argentina workers, as well as for other human rights activists. It would appear that the Nobel Committee's hopes were fulfilled.

Conclusion

IFOR and AFOR, social movement midwives themselves, were instrumental in nurturing the birth of SERPAJ, the TSMO that became the Latin American midwife to countless new collective efforts to bring about social change across the nations of central and south America. The Protestant and Roman Catholic churches, with their transnational organizational structures and networks, also played an important role in the emergence and growth of SERPAJ. Earlier, less successful efforts by IFOR and AFOR to midwife Latin American social change efforts were superseded by more successful SERPAJ efforts that grafted indigenous ideas, such as that of the *animador*, to the more abstract commitment to a more aggressive nonviolence in pursuit of justice for oppressed peoples.

The early organizing efforts of the FOR helped provide a transnational base for the eventual emergence of SERPAJ, but it was the work of Jean and Hildegard Goss-Mayr that proved especially valuable. Working in the changing political and religious opportunity structures of the 1960s, the Goss-Mayrs played a very important role in developing the Latin American network of Catholic bishops, priests, nuns, and lay people advocating the philosophy and technique of nonviolent direct action. It was largely this network, combined with the Protestant network cultivated by the FOR, that became the core of SERPAJ.

While SERPAJ mobilized a number of Latin American Catholics to work for political goals, it differed from earlier twentieth-century Catholic political action organizations. One such organization was the Christian Democratic Party, a political party embodying Catholic social principles, with Catholic lay people as political candidates. Established in Latin America during the 1930s, by 1949 the Christian Democratic Party had spread to several countries on the continent, contending for political office when and where it could.

SERPAJ took a different approach, however. Like many of its contemporary Latin American SMOs, SERPAJ strove to maintain its autonomy from political parties, trying to operate outside the realm of partisan politics as it worked for peace, social justice, and the empowerment of the popular classes. Also like its contemporaries, SERPAJ advocated "new ways of engaging in politics" as well as "new forms of social relations and social organization" (Jelín, 1990: 3; see also Lehmann, 1990; Munck, 1989). On the one hand, such an orientation is not surprising, given the limited structure of political opportunity in which SERPAJ was born. On the other hand, SERPAJ's ideology led it to advocate social and political transformation and to reject the centralized structure and dirigente approach of political parties in favor of a decentralized structure and animador approach. Likewise, SERPAJ wanted to preserve the integrity of its message by avoiding its identification with partisan politics. Indeed, given the continuing legacy of manipulation and corruption in Latin American politics, it is not surprising that SERPAJ chose autonomy. A key question for autonomous SMOs such as SERPAJ after the democratic transition was whether or not they could have any political impact without working with a political party in some way (Bidegain, 1985; Jelín, 1987). Under the dictatorships, the channels of political participation were closed; such conditions, combined with SERPAJ's ideology, provided a context for SERPAJ to advocate nonviolent direct action. Now that the political channels have opened somewhat, will SERPAJ adopt more conventional means of political action?

As we have seen, the transnational character of SERPAJ is important in understanding its success in several respects. First, it is based on transnational networks of faith-based communities. Religious communities are naturally transnational. As a result, there is an element of transnational solidarity among them that can be translated into pressure by a faith community, such as AFOR, upon the leaders of one state, such as the United States, to pressure the leaders of another state, such as Argentina, to take action in support of comrades in faith, such as SERPAJ. The advantages of this strategic approach may be summarized as (1) the creation of solidarity across national boundaries, (2) the communication of new ways of doing things, (3) the development of mechanisms of mutual support, (4) the creation of international legitimacy for local claims and action, and (5) international mobilization in support of local activists. The leaders of core states where religious freedom is a norm tend to be diffusely supportive of such freedom for members of such communities in non-core states. Second, the many other advantages of transnational SMO structures that we noted above allowed a cadre organization with few resources made up of a very small number of activists to exert telling pressure on parochial and repressive regimes.

The history of SERPAJ has been brief, tumultuous, and inspiring. It has now entered a new phase in which the tactical advice and principled commitment to nonviolence of its several national groups may become less central to the affairs of their political and social landscapes. The SERPAJ we have described existed mostly under military regimes. The transition to democracy in the mid- to late eighties has caused changes in the structure and role of SERPAJ, as well as of other social movement organizations (Cardoso, 1989; Jelín, 1986; (Pérez Esquivel, Personal Communication, 1985). If the experiences of North American "movement midwives" are any guide, however, SERPAJ has many new opportunities ahead to be of service to progressive causes, as both political and religious opportunity are likely to remain fleeting.

Notes

We are deeply indebted to the following: Dr. Brady Tyson, longtime AFOR liaison to SERPAJ and other Latin American nonviolent groups; Adolfo Pérez Esquivel; Creuza Maciel, executive secretary of SERPAJ from 1982 to 1986 and general coordinator from 1986 to 1990; Richard Chartier of AFOR, who worked with nonviolent groups and activists (including Adolfo Pérez Esquivel) in Latin America, particularly Argentina, from 1959 to 1973; Fr. José Alamiro Andrade da Silva, president of SERPAJ-Brazil (1982–84); and Timothy Ready. All of these were available for interviews and provided materials on various aspects of SERPAJ's history and structure and function. Scott Mainwaring, Michael Foley, Susan Eckstein, Jackie Smith, and Bob Edwards provided helpful advice on earlier versions of this manuscript. An earlier version of this manuscript appeared in the July and December 1986 issues of *Solidarity Solidaridad*, the newsletter of the Committee in Solidarity with Latin American Nonviolent Movements (CISLANM) and the Task Force on Latin America of the Fellowship of Reconciliation.

Our description of FOR's work in Latin America and the emergence and development of SERPAJ through 1985 draws heavily on key FOR organizing reports and SERPAJ documents, interviews with several principal FOR and SERPAJ activists, and a variety of secondary accounts of the activities of SERPAJ.

1 In SERPAJ's terminology, it advocates "active nonviolence," which is a new way of engaging in politics that seeks not only political but social transformation. McManus and Schlabach define active nonviolence as:

> A means of struggle for social change based on an unswerving commitment to speak the truth and a willingness to put oneself at risk in the process while refusing to harm others. Major components of nonviolent action include reflection, dialogue, education, challenging existing power relations, and building alternative structures to create a just and compassionate world. (McManus and Schlabach 1990: 300)

In this essay we focus on how a central component of active nonviolence, the philosophy and methods of nonviolent direct action, became part of SERPAJ's repertoire of contention. For a succinct summary of SERPAJ's approach to nonviolent direct action, see Goss 1974.

2 JAPLA shows the interest that civil rights veterans had in spreading the methods of nonviolent direct action in Latin America. Described as "a group of Methodist inspiration which gives instruction in non-violent action techniques" (Richardson Nute 1974: 22), JAPLA was founded in the late 1960s by Glenn Smiley, who achieved fame for his work with Martin Luther King, Jr., at Montgomery in 1956. As early as 1968, JAPLA held a seminar on the strategy of nonviolent action at Medellín, Colombia. In the early 1970s, JAPLA sponsored seminars in Mexico. By the early 1970s, several former colleagues of Martin Luther King, Jr.—Andrew Young and AFOR members James Lawson, Brady Tyson, and Bernard Lafayette—had joined JAPLA, with Lafayette replacing Smiley as executive director. Lafayette was a member of the Nashville, Tennessee, Sit-In Steering Committee in 1960–1, the precursor to the Student

Nonviolent Coordinating Committee (SNCC), and was a co-founder of the Raleigh, North Carolina, SNCC chapter. He later became a national staff member of the AFOR and the Southern Christian Leadership Conference (SCLC). In 1968, he was the national coordinator of the Poor People's Campaign. In 1971, Lafayette joined Smiley at the Alajuela, Costa Rica, meeting in which the Servicio para Liberadora was created.

References

Antoine, Charles, 1983, "Introduction," in Adolfo Pérez Esquivel, ed., *Christ in a Poncho*. Maryknoll, NY: Orbis, pp. 4–12.

Barton, Betty, L., 1974. *The Fellowship of Reconciliation: Pacifism, Labor and Social Welfare, 1915–1960*. PhD dissertation. Florida State University.

Bidegain, Ana Maria, 1985. "From Catholic action to liberation theology: The historical process of the laity in Latin America in the twentieth century," Working Paper no. 48. Notre Dame, IN: Kellogg Institute.

Boulding, Elise, 1988. *Building a Global Civic Culture*. Syracuse, NY: Syracuse University Press.

Cardoso, Ruth Correa Leite, 1989. "Popular movements in the context of the consolidation of democracy," Working Paper no. 120. Notre Dame, IN: Kellogg Institute.

Chartier, Richard, 1980. "Adolfo Pérez Esquivel: Behind the man and the prize," *Fellowship* 7–9 (December): 23.

Chatfield, Charles, 1971. *For Peace and Justice: Pacifism in America, 1914–1941*. Boston: Beacon Press.

Cornell, Tom, 1977. "Adolfo Pérez Esquivel," *Fellowship* (September): 6–9.

Deats, Richard, ed., 1991. *Ambassador of Reconciliation: A Muriel Lester Reader*. Philadelphia: New Society.

Deming, Marty, 1978. "What is SERVICIO?" *IFOR Report* (December): 7–8.

Eckstein, Susan, 1989. *Power and Popular Protest: Latin American Social Movements*. Berkeley: University of California Press.

Epstein, Barbara, 1991. *Political Protest and Cultural Revolution: Nonviolent Direct Action in the 1970s and 1980s*. Berkeley: University of California Press.

Freeman, Jo, 1979. "Resource mobilization and strategy: A model for analyzing social movement organization actions," in Mayer Zald and John McCarthy, eds., *The Dynamics of Social Movements*, pp. 167–89. Winthrop, MA: Winthrop.

Garrett, William R., 1988. "Liberation theology and the concept of human rights," in Anson Shupe and Jeffrey K. Hadden, eds., *The Politics of Religion and Social Change*. New York: Paragon House, pp. 128–43.

Goss-Mayr, Jean and Hildegard Goss-Mayr, 1984. "Antecedentes del 'Servicio Paz y Justicia' en America Latina." Rio de Janeiro: SERPAJ-AL.

——, 1971. "Report December 1st to February 15, 1971." Rio de Janeiro: SERPAJ-AL.

——, 1966. "Report on work in Latin America from May to August 1966," November 1966. Rio de Janeiro: SERPAJ-AL.

——, 1962a. "Confidential report on work in Latin America," June 11, 1962. Rio de Janeiro: SERPAJ-AL.

——, 1962b. "News from South America from Jean and Hildegard Goss," April 16, 1962. Rio de Janeiro: SERPAJ: AL.

Holsworth, Robert D. 1989. *Let Your Life Speak: A Study of Politics, Religion, and Antinuclear Weapons Activism.* Madison: University of Wisconsin Press.

Jelin, Elizabeth, 1990. "Introduction," in Elizabeth Jelin, ed., *Women and Social Change in Latin America.* Atlantic Highlands, NJ: Zed Books, pp. 1–12.

——, 1987. "The movement: Eclipsed by democracy?" *NACLA Report on the Americas* 21(4): 28–36, 39.

——, 1986. "Otros silencios, otras voces: El tiempo de la democratización en la Argentina," in Calderon G. Fernando, ed., *Los movimientos sociales antes de la crisis.* New York: United Nations University, pp. 17–44.

Jenkins, J. Craig, 1983. "Resource mobilization theory and the study of social movements," *Annual Review of Sociology* 9: 527–53.

Lehmann, David, 1990. *Democracy and Development in Latin America: Economics, Politics, and Religion in the Post-War Period.* Philadelphia: Temple University Press.

Maciel, Creuza, 1986. "SERPAJ facing the liberation process. Special: A summary of SERPAJ-AL's history," *Informative Letter* 3 no. 1.

Mainwaring, Scott and E. Viola, 1984. "New social movements, political culture and democracy: Brazil and Argentina in the 1980s," *Telos* (Fall) 61: 17–54.

McAdam, Doug, 1983. "Tactical innovation and the pace of insurgency," *American Sociological Review* 48(6): 735–54.

McManus, Philip, 1991a. "Introduction: In search of the Shalom society," in Philip McManus and Gerald Schlabach, eds., *Relentless Persistence: Non-violent Action in Latin America*, pp. 1–13. Santa Cruz, CA: New Society Publisher.

——, 1991b. "To discover our humanity: Adolfo Pérez Esquivel [an interview]," in Philip McManus and Gerald Schlabach, eds., *Relentless Persistence: Nonviolent Action in Latin America*, pp. 238–51. Santa Cruz, CA: New Society Publishers.

Mignone, Emilio, 1988. *Witness to the Truth: The Complicity of Church and Dictatorship in Argentina, 1976–1983*, Phillip Berryman, translator. Maryknoll, NY: Orbis.

Morris, Aldon, 1984. *The Origins of the Civil Rights Movement: Black Communities Organizing for Change.* New York: Free Press.

Munck, Ronaldo, 1989. *Latin America: The Transition to Democracy.* Atlantic Highlands, NJ: Zed Books.

Munoz, Carlos, Creuza Maciel, and Carmen de Souza, 1986. *Resena historica del SERPAJ-AL. Primer volumen: Una alternativa revolucionaria?* Rio de Janeiro: SERPAJ-AL.

Nagel, Joane and Susan Olzak, 1982. "Ethnic mobilization in new and old states," *Social Problems* 30(2): 127–43.

Navarro, Marysa, 1989. "The personal is political: Las madres de Plaza de Mayo," in Susan Eckstein, ed., *Power and Popular Protest: Latin American Social Movements*, pp. 241–58. Berkeley: University of California Press.

Parkman, Patricia, 1990. *Insurrectionary Civic Strikes in Latin America: 1931–1961.* Cambridge, MA: Albert Einstein Institution.

Ready, Timothy, Brady Tyson, and Ron Pagnucco, 1985. "The impact of the Nobel Peace Prize on the work of Adolfo Pérez Esquivel." Paper presented at the International Studies Association Annual Conference, March, Washington, D.C.

Salinas, Maximilliano, 1990. "The voices of those who spoke up for the victims," in Leonardo Boff and Virgil Elizondo, eds., *1491–1991: The Voice of the Victims*, pp. 101–110. Concilium Special. London: SCM Press.

Sanders, Thomas G., 1987. "Religion in Latin America," in Jack W. Hopkins, ed., *Latin America: Perspectives on a Region*. New York: Holmes and Meier, pp. 102–132.

Sayre, John Nevin, 1961. "The FOR and Latin America: Outline of work carried on 1919–1960." Nyack, NY: Fellowship of Reconciliation.

Schravesande, Joke, 1981. "Servicio Paz y Justicia en América Latina," *Info 3* (February): 2–9.

SERPAJ-AL, 1987. *Principles, Objectives, and Foundations of SERPAJ-LA*. Rio de Janeiro: SERPAJ-AL.

SERPAJ-Europe, 1984. *SERPAJ-Europe Year Report, 1984*. Leusden, Holland: SERPAJ-Europe.

Sharp, Gene, 1979. *Gandhi as a Political Strategist*. Boston: Porter Sargent.

Skidmore, Thomas and Peter H. Smith, 1989. *Modern Latin America*, 2nd edn. New York: Oxford University Press.

Slater, David, ed., 1985. *New Social Movements and the State in Latin America*. Amsterdam: Centre for Latin American Research and Documentation.

Smith, Christian, 1991. *The Emergence of Liberation Theology: Radical Religion and Social Movement Theory*. Chicago: University of Chicago Press.

Staggenborg, Suzanne, 1991. *The Pro-Choice Movement: Organization and Activism in the Abortion Conflict*. New York: Oxford University Press.

Tarrow, Sidney, 1988. "National politics and collective action: Recent theory and research in Western Europe and the United States," *Annual Review of Sociology* 14: 421–40.

Tilly, Charles, 1979. "Repertoires of contention in America and Britain, 1750–1830," in Mayer Zald and John D. McCarthy, eds., *The Dynamics of Social Movements*. Cambridge, MA: Winthrop, pp. 126–55.

Tyson, Brady, 1970. "Encounter in Recife," *Christian Century*, June 10: 720–22.

Willetts, Peter, 1982. "The impact of promotional pressure groups on global politics," in Peter Willets, ed., *Pressure Groups in the Global System*. New York: St. Martin's, pp. 179–200.

Zald, Mayer and John McCarthy, eds., 1987. *Social Movements in an Organizational Society: Collected Essays*. New Brunswick, NJ: Transaction Books.

13

The Brazilian Church–State Crisis of 1980: Effective Nonviolent Action in a Military Dictatorship

Daniel Zirker

Effective nonviolent resistance to military dictatorship in developing countries has become increasingly frequent during the past two decades, suggesting that nonviolent resistance can play a critical role in the democratization process. The following study[1] examines a nonviolent and effective political effort to weaken the 16-year-old Brazilian military dictatorship in 1980. It is an attempt to identify those political and socioeconomic conditions that contributed to its significant impact in the subsequent decline of military dictatorship in Brazil. Couched within this study, then, is a larger and more general question: under what conditions does nonviolence succeed in challenging the directly coercive power of military dictatorship?

Despite over a decade of overt authoritarianism in many Latin American countries by the early 1980s, military dictatorships in the region demonstrated a continuing willingness to hold on to power. Although most of the dictatorships turned to some form of political "liberalization" at this juncture, such policies tended to be accompanied by the random, if not pervasive, use of force, and an increasing emphasis upon nationalism. The use of scapegoats and appeals to xenophobia were particularly common.

Although some observers have argued that, in cases such as Brazil and Uruguay, deteriorating economic conditions reinforced the willingness of military officers and technocrats eventually to allow civilian politicians to take over "hopeless" domestic situations, in fact none of the military dictatorships of the period willingly relinquished power. Decisive moments arose late in each of them in which the authorities attempted to reinforce regime legitimacy through reliance upon a public appeal for popular support, confronted organized nonviolent resistance, and lost. In several of these cases, including that of Brazil, Liberation Theology was *central to* the organization and ultimate impact of nonviolent resistance. Also important

– particularly after dynamic nonviolent resistance spurred the necessary compromises from the military authorities – were electoral politics.

In Uruguay in 1980, the organization of nonviolent popular resistance to an authoritarian constitution led to a national referendum which resulted in an electoral defeat for the military dictatorship. A similar nonviolent (and, ultimately, electoral) campaign initiated the democratization process in Chile in 1988. Both countries had experienced a significant institutional resistance, growing out of campaigns of nonviolent resistance, to authoritarianism prior to those electoral defeats.

The military government in Brazil unsuccessfully attempted in 1980 to crush protracted and increasingly effective nonviolent resistance within the Catholic Church by strengthening its already considerable coercive powers. After more than 15 years in power, and in the midst of deteriorating economic circumstances, such a move would be politically costly at best, and hence appeared to require increasingly strident appeals for popular, nationalistic support. The central proponents of nonviolent resistance to the human rights violations of the dictatorship were Catholic clergy. The promulgation of a xenophobic new law in 1980, the Foreigners' Law, appears to have been directly aimed at challenging the pastoral activities of foreign priests, an important but by no means exclusive source of nonviolent resistance within the clergy, but one that was particularly vulnerable to nationalistic attacks. The military's ultimate target appears to have been to break a growing coalition of nonviolent resistance, one that threatened to thrust the country's two strongest institutions, the military and the Church, into open political conflict.

On November 1, 1980, the Brazilian government deported an Italian priest, Padre Vito Miracapillo, who had refused a request by the mayor in his Northeast Brazilian parish to celebrate an Independence Day mass. This form of nonviolent resistance to military dictatorship, while still rather dangerous in 1980, had become increasingly common. Padre Vito had stated that his noncompliance stemmed from the "non-effective independence of the people, [who have been] reduced to the condition of begging and abandonment of their rights" (*Veja*, October 29, 1981: 21). Padre Vito's subsequent arrest and expulsion, which represented an immediate response to a grassroots national movement in support of Liberation Theology, ultimately triggered a crisis in Brazilian church–state relations, and contributed, arguably significantly, to the subsequent weakening (and ultimate collapse) of the military dictatorship.

The determinant aspect of the crisis involved the association of Padre Vito, and a significant segment of the Brazilian clergy, with nonviolent resistance to military dictatorship, something that had become central to expressions of Liberation Theology by Brazilian theologians like Leonardo Boff. Liberation Theology had become a central political concern in Latin America by 1980. It is a philosophical and theological worldview[2] that calls for the active role of Catholicism in the temporal sphere on behalf of the rights and needs of the poor. While usually nonviolent in form, it involved violent struggles in opposition to oligarchy in some Latin American countries. Although a good deal has been written regarding the philosophical and theological implications of Liberation Theology, its definition broadens noticeably in specific political contexts,[3] often encompassing a whole range of actions that might, except for their immediate context in Church policy and national socioeconomic conditions, appear to have little direct theological relevance.[4] The mobilization of national public opinion in the presence of a nonviolent mass movement – over 100,000 ecclesiastical base communities and numerous parishes throughout the country – that provided the context of the Brazilian Church–state crisis of 1980, offers interesting insights into the conditions in which nonviolence might be said to represent an optimal tactic in resisting the apotheosis of institutionalized violence, military dictatorship.

Background to a Case of Effective Nonviolent Resistance: Regional Underdevelopment, Church Activism, and Historical Legacies

Brazil evinced an arguably unique set of circumstances in 1980, including national, regional, and local development disparities, and the rapid increase, for a variety of reasons, in the political activism of certain sectors of the Brazilian Catholic Church. The former requires little elaboration for the purposes of this study. Its most dramatic exemplification in the early 1980s was in the northeast, the region where the Italian priest, Padre Vito, worked, and where the worst drought of the century had transformed into refugees some 10 to 20 million peasants (*Veja*, August 17, 1983: 56), pushing them as *flagelados* ("beaten ones") into the swelling slums of Brazilian cities as far south as São Paulo.

Ironically, there was a significant reliance by the military dictatorship of General João Baptista Figueiredo upon the political support of elected and appointed legislators from the traditional oligarchic interests of the Northeast, as well as other underdeveloped regions, by 1980 (Sarles, 1982: 65–7). This constituted at least one of the major reasons for the regime's particular vulnerability to open displays of defiance in the Northeast. The nonviolent resistance of pastoral clergy in the North, Center-West and Northeast regions, of which the case of Padre Vito was a prominent example, immediately threatened to undercut the regime's political base of support in these key areas at a critical political juncture.

Of related and equally crucial significance was the breakdown nationally of societal support for Figueiredo's regime. This was also influenced by the growing hostility between Church and state during its last years,[5] although many economic and political factors had coalesced by 1980, with Brazilian public opinion balanced, awaiting a decisive event or condition upon which to judge the Figueiredo administration and, by extension, the legitimacy of the dictatorship itself.

Simmering Church–state hostility, it should be added, had been primed for just such an event; for one thing, the conflict between these two powerful institutions was both traditional and deeply felt, a legacy of the nineteenth century. The near absolute institutional domination of the Brazilian Church by the Imperial government, both in formal, organizational structure and in political control of the clergy (Bruneau, 1974: 23),[6] led to repeated outbursts of ultramontanism, one of which, in 1874, is thought to have contributed to the eventual collapse of the Brazilian Empire in 1889 (ibid.: 25; 26–30), and to unification of Church support for the republican government that emerged thereafter (Bruneau ibid.: 30). The Republic brought with it the values of European liberalism, including the separation of Church and state, initially seen as desirable by an institution that had been dominated by the state. Within several years, however, competition between the Church and state had again surfaced, and influential clergy had called for an end to separation of Church and state (ibid.: 123).

When the military effectively replaced the Brazilian Emperor in the role of *poder moderador*, or "moderating power," after 1889, further Church–state competition was encouraged. By the 1980s, significant segments of the Church had shifted their traditional, pastoral goals, and institutions such as the National Conference of Brazilian Bishops (CNBB)[7] sought to influence the political direction of the Brazilian Church while qualifying the strength of its ties with Rome (ibid.: 123), a tendency of national bishops' conferences in other countries as well.[8] Nonviolent resistance to the human rights violations and the abridgements of freedom of the dictatorship became a constant theme in this regard.

State power, on the other hand, appeared increasingly impotent. By the late 1980s, groups supportive of (and supported by) the *ancien régime* tended to find themselves isolated and increasingly dependent upon state power for their own survival. Hence, the calls by Northeastern landowners for the state to take legal sanctions against the activist Church came to constitute a key feature of the Padre Vito case.

Another legacy from the nineteenth century that affected the case is the overall size of the Brazilian Church. Emperor Dom Pedro II had strictly limited the number of clergy in Brazil, allowing only three new dioceses during his nearly 50 years on the throne (ibid.: 23). In 1889, with a population of 14 million, Brazil had only 700 priests, 12 dioceses, 13 bishops and nine seminaries, a situation regarded by analysts such as Luiz Gonzaga de Souza Lima as "extremely unfavorable [for the Church], even in comparison with other nations on the American continent" (Souza Lima, 1979: 15). During the "Old Republic" (1889–1930), the Church grew steadily in size, and although it continued to push for establishment (ibid.: 16), it fostered ties with Rome that were much closer than previously experienced in Brazil (ibid.: 19). The regional disparities in the numbers of clergy are an especially relevant aspect of the overall size of the Church in Brazil. Underdeveloped regions, such as the Northeast, tend to have far fewer clergy, and tend to depend disproportionately upon the ministering of foreign clergy (Bruneau, 1974: 48).[9]

A third and crucial legacy stems from the *getuliato*, the 15-year dictatorship (1930–45) of Getulio Vargas. Although this protracted rule did not alter the formal terms of Church–state relations in Brazil, Vargas did display a willingness to use Catholicism to his political advantage, putting an emphasis on the importance of his backing by the Church equal to that of the military (ibid.: 39–40). Increased competition between the two institutions was inevitable under the circumstances, although the nonviolence of the Church stood in stark contrast to the explicit violence of the military establishment.

A significant pattern, associated with the rapid growth and modernization of the country during this period, in effect transformed the demographic basis of the Church: foreign clergy became a crucial support. By 1946, fully 70 percent of the clerics and religious workers in Brazil were foreigners, and although the figure had stabilized by the 1970s at about 40 percent, the absolute number of foreign clergy and lay workers had actually increased (Souza Lima, 1979: 19; Bruneau, 1974: 63–4). The critical importance to the national Church of foreign clergy remains, and is heightened by the protracted shortage of clergy (Bruneau, 1974: 63–4); foreign clergy tended relatively easily to establish themselves and to achieve recognition in Brazil.

Liberation Theology, Nonviolent Opposition, and Church–State Crises after 1964

These legacies of nineteenth- and twentieth-century Church–State politics deeply influenced the relations between the Church and government after 1964, the year that the military seized power in Brazil. Three potentially explosive issues in the relationship pointed to the eventual Church–state crisis: the expulsion of foreign clergy, which threatened the institutional mission of the Church; the questioning by clergy of Brazil's political and economic independence, a specific form of nonviolent political resistance to military legitimacy which often precipitated stormy responses from the military dictatorship; and land tenure disputes between peasants and landowners in impoverished regions of the country, which elicited ambiguous responses from both institutions, particularly when related to the work of activist priests in some way.

The expulsion of foreign clergy during the post-1964 military dictatorships was perceived as a direct assault upon the institutional integrity and viability of the Church. Many of the foreign clergy came to Brazil as missionaries for the express purpose of ministering to the poor. The profound poverty and striking economic disparities of Brazil, particularly in such regions as the Northeast, shocked and radicalized many of these foreign clergy, and they in turn often encouraged the development within the Church hierarchy of a worldview that, if not always unified, tended increasingly to define the Church's mission in the context of the country's poverty.[10] This became a common theme in the Brazilian news media.[11]

Beginning with the influence of the CNBB and such papal encyclicals as *Populorum Progressio*, significant sectors of the Brazilian Church embarked upon a nonviolent leftward ideological transformation in the early 1960s that sporadically (but increasingly) collided with the policies of the right-leaning military dictatorship after 1964. Hence it should be emphasized that while the socioeconomic conditions of such regions as the Northeast clearly had a shocking and radicalizing effect upon foreign and native-born clergy in the 1960s and 1970s, a pervasive and sophisticated commitment to nonviolent political resistance as well as the relevant principles of Liberation Theology was already evident in a significant part of the national Church. By 1973, for example, there were some 40,000 Base Ecclesiastical Communities registered in Brazil, and this number mushroomed to over 100,000 by 1980. While the growth of Base Communities, moreover, was often attributed to the chronic shortage of priests (*Veja*, December 17, 1980: 21), they increasingly came to be seen as a burgeoning mass movement by Brazil's dictatorship.

Foreign clergy had often become the focal points of Church–state conflict after 1964, but not necessarily because of their extraordinary radicalization. Rather, as Bruneau suggests, this was due primarily to "the case with which the government [could] direct public opinion against them and deport them" (Bruneau, 1974: 218). Hence, while many Brazilian clergy consistently struggled on behalf of the rights and needs of the poor, the foreign clergy were frequently selected by the government to serve as "examples." After the imprisonment and deportation in 1968 of Padre Pedro Wauthier, a French worker-priest who had been ordained in Brazil, and who refused to comply with the request of the management of the São Paulo factory where he worked that he say a mass during a strike (ibid.: 199–200), the government began routinely punishing activist foreign clergy with imprisonment and deportation: during the worst years of political repression, cases of murder were also reported (ibid.: 218).[12]

The government responses to nonviolent resistance were usually tactical. An example of this involved an influential Belgian theologian, Padre Jose Comblin, who had served as an advisor to Dom Helder Camara, and who was denied reentry to Brazil in 1972 (ibid.: 198–9), effectively striking blows both at the commitment of the Church to the poor, which Comblin eloquently espoused, and at Camara, who was too prominent to punish directly.

Although the post-1964 military governments frequently resorted to the expulsion of foreign priests, apparently convinced of the comparative advantages of playing to nationalistic xenophobia, such actions were always potentially explosive. When a French priest, Padre Francisco Jentel, was imprisoned in 1974 and deported in 1975 after his implication in a land dispute between impoverished squatters and large landowners (*Veja*, December 29, 1976: 37), the Brazilian Church hierarchy, noted for its traditional conservatism in such matters, acted with unexpected stridency, attacking the regime directly for its human rights violations. The government responded by noting the "unpatriotic" activities of clergy such as bishops Camara and Pedro Casaldaliga (*Veja*, December 29, 1976: 37). Bruneau observes that a short period of Church-state harmony came to an end around 1976.[13]

By 1978, a momentum had developed which consolidated all of the progressive elements of the previous two decades. Briefly, this influence model is one in which the church has chosen to work primarily with the lower classes in assisting them to seek liberation in an environment characterized by repression and injustice. The other classes are not ignored but are regarded as being less in need of the few resources the church has available (Bruneau, 1982: 72). Padre Vito's expulsion represented yet another unexpected escalation of Church–state conflict based upon the expulsion of foreign clergy, and, even more significantly, the presence of this perceived new mass movement, guided as it was by clergy who espoused an uncompromising – if nonviolent – resistance to dictatorship in Brazil through the denial of its legitimacy.

A fundamental dimension of the case involved the passage, in August of 1980, of a strict new "foreigners' law," which prohibited virtually any "political" activities by foreigners in Brazil. The law was introduced to the Congress under a provision that ensured its becoming a law if no congressional objection were passed within 40 days – the Congress was not in session for 30 of the days in question (*New York Times*, October 17, 1980: 5); it was seen as a direct challenge to both democratization (the process of "opening", or abertura, as the Figueiredo dictatorship referred to it), and to the Church, and was bitterly criticized by the CNBB (*Jornal do Brasil*, November 5, 1980: 4; *O Globo*, November 6, 1980: 8), and even by the Pope (*O Estado de São Paulo*, December 13, 1980: 9). Padre Vito's case represented the first use of this law, which had undeniable implications for the 56 foreign bishops and more than 5,000 foreign priests working in Brazil, out of a total of less than 13,000 (*Veja*, October 20, 1980: 23).

A second basic catalyst in Brazilian Church–state competition after 1964 involved an oft-repeated tactic of nonviolent resistance to military dictatorship: the public questioning of Brazilian economic and political independence. Given the prominence of multinational corporate interests in Latin America, and the implications of the "internationalized" economic system in Brazil, such questioning, however innocently couched, became intensely provocative. The overt sympathy of the dictatorial juntas with foreign investors, and their consequent vulnerability (especially within the ranks of the officer corps) to questions of nationalism and national development, contributed to the sensitivity of the issue. General Golbery do Couto e Silva, one of the chief architects of the dictatorship, has been characterized by as a major exponent of the "internationalist" tendency (i.e., supporting the multinational corporate investment pattern in Brazil), and was serving as the chief of the president's civilian cabinet when Padre Vito's refusal to say an Independence Day mass became known. *Veja* notes his call for an immediate government response (October 29, 1980: 21). Examples of violent military responses to the nonviolent questioning of the character of Brazilian independence had by this time become common; the asymmetric response of the government to such apparently mild challenges, in fact, reinforced their utility as vehicles of nonviolent resistance. In 1967, for example, a Church-controlled radio station in the Brazilian Northeast presented an Independence Day program that was based on the question, "Is the independence we celebrate real?" The government's response was sharp: the radio station was closed down for over a week, and strict censorship of all subsequent programs in the series was imposed (Bruneau, 1974: 187). The conflict clearly had an explosive quality to it, developing, in Bruneau's words, "through public statements from all sides" (1974: 187). In May 1968, during a mass in the Northeast in honor of the Brazilian Expeditionary Force (which fought with the Allies in Italy during the Second World War II), Dom Edmilson da Cruz questioned the existence of liberty in Brazil, again to a stormy military response: military personnel walked out in the middle of the service, one of whom returned and physically "accosted" Dom Edmilson; a subsequent battle of "statements and counter-statements" was resolved by a de facto truce after one week, but Bruneau concludes that relations remained tense between the army and the Archdiocese of Sao Luis" (1974: 197–8).

The nonviolent opponents of military dictatorship had apparently found its Achilles tendon. The open questioning of Brazilian economic and political independence invariably came to be seen by the military establishment as an immediate threat to the regime's legitimacy. Revelations in the late 1970s of direct US involvement in the coup of 1964[14] sensitized this potentially explosive tool of nonviolent resistance, further explaining the strident response that Padre Vito's action would later provoke.[15]

A third basic catalyst in the ongoing Church–state crisis in Brazil in the post-1964 period involved a legal issue, the question of land tenure, particularly in the most impoverished regions of Brazil.[16] The archaic and repressive land-tenure pattern in the Northeast, for example, which occasionally led to vague promises by the dictatorship to enact land reform in the region (Sanders, 1981: 210), facilitated the mounting mass opposition to the dictatorship, most apparent initially within the base communities and Church-related organizations such as the CNBB. By late 1980, the intensity of this nonviolent opposition was demonstrated by a declaration by the bishops of Northeast Region III of the CNBB, which stated that

> the usury of the land tenure, exacerbated by an archaic land [ownership] structure and by the Brazilian economic model – exclusive, concentrated and

dependent – generates hunger and disease, forced migrations, lack of production and productivity, precariousness in housing, arbitrary imprisonment, injustices and other forms of oppression against the human person. (*Jornal do Brazil*, November 8, 1980: 4)

Dom Avelar Brandao, the Archbishop of Salvador and Primate of Brazil, argued in 1980 that the injustices and socioeconomic conflict resulting from the land-tenure system could not be left to "the government and its technicians," and that when such conditions "take the peace of the spirit, the Church can no longer remain indifferent to the phenomenon" (*Jornal do Brasil*, November 10, 1980: 2). The Church's Pastoral Land Commission (CPT), established in 1975, subsequently and significantly expanded its efforts on behalf of the landless peasantry (Paiva, 1985). It had increasingly been drawn into nonviolent opposition to military dictatorship because of its role – and the related radicalization of foreign and Brazilian clergy – in sponsoring the nonviolent struggles of its base communities and of the landless peasants of Brazil.

The Expulsion and its Aftermath: Institutional Responses

A nonviolent adaptation of Liberation Theology, debated within the national Church hierarchy, became the norm in Brazil during the 1960s and 1970s. The writings of such Brazilian theologians as Leonardo Boff, Paulo Freire and Dom Helder Camara were internationally known at the time of Padre Vito's expulsion. The CNBB, which had grown directly out of Catholic Action under the influence and direction of Camara, had concerned itself – and the national Church – with the problems of poverty and national development (Bruneau, 1974: 107–10).[17] In practice, this meant that the CNBB continually questioned the government over the brutality of the "Brazilian model," and thereby stimulated a broader Church response on a variety of issues relating to human rights and the rights and needs of the poor. Bruneau noted that "The CNBB statements from 1975 on and the formation of organizations concerned with human rights, land tenure, and Indians, and intrinsically linked to the church, are indications of substantial change in the Brazilian church's overall orientation. The new approach clearly favors the lower classes and other oppressed sectors and seeks to assist them by means of a variety of instruments and processes" (1982: 92).

Hence, Brazil can be characterized as a case in which a significant part of the national Church was ultimately influenced by a nonviolent adaptation of Liberation Theology originally espoused by a considerably smaller number of foreign and Brazilian clergy who worked with Brazil's poor. The bloc of support for nonviolent Liberation Theology soon came to be represented in virtually all levels of the Church hierarchy, with particular support emanating from foreign and Brazilian clergy that worked directly with the very poor, and from the CNBB. Conservative critics of Liberation Theology within the Church were very vocal in the late 1970s, however, and this appears to have encouraged the dictatorship, and may even have contributed to its continuing violations of human rights. Dom Luciano José Cabral Duarte, Archbishop of Aracaju and vice-president of the Latin American Episcopal Council (CELAM) publicly declared in an open letter released on November 13, 1979, that the CNBB was more interested in reconciling Marxism with Christianity than in accurately interpreting such Church policies as the final document of the Puebla Conference of 1979 (*Veja*, December 19, 1979: 67). Direct association with the option for the poor, and their burgeoning nonviolent resistance to the conditions fostered by protracted military dictatorship, seems originally to have had a determinant influence upon those clergy who opposed Dom Luciano's conservatism. Padre Vito Miracapillo's case – and its implications for a national Roman Catholic Church overwhelmingly dependent upon foreign clergy – could only further their position.

Padre Vito Miracapillo worked with impoverished sugar cane laborers in 1980 in an area of the state of Pernambuco, Ribeirão, that manifested the most brutal aspects of the latifundium: a dependent work force that tended to be paid in "credits" redeemable only at what have charitably been called "extortionist" rates at company stores (*Jornal do Brasil*, October 24, 1980: 10). The level of social repression necessary to maintain this system was high, and because of his questioning of the system, Padre Vito was regarded by the landowning elite in Ribeirão as a direct challenge to the status quo. The consequent tension was immediate: only a few days following his refusal to say an Independence Day mass, a group of landowners occupied the church in Ribeirão, impeding a mass of solidarity being held by 52 priests, and finally bringing it to a halt with physical threats and acts of vandalism (*Veja*, October 29, 1980: 24).

The case was closely linked to the brutal system of land-tenure. Padre Vito's "open letter," which he left in Ribeirão when he flew to Brasilia for his deportation, was released to the media on the eve of his Supreme Court hearing for habeas corpus, and directly questioned the land-tenure system, denying the nationalist integrity of the dictatorship, and underscoring his own nonviolent political commitment to eradicate the suffering and poverty brought on by the Brazilian economic "model" in his parish and region.

> The sugar factory owners, the mill owners, the suppliers of cane (dominating the workers and peasants), as well as the regional and federal authorities responsible for national security, demonstrate that they want to ignore absolutely the situation of semi-slavery in which the workers of Ribeirão live. They speak of patriotism. Is systematic violence against Brazilians in the country-side, in the factories, in the prisons, patriotic? Is it patriotic to maintain or import illiteracy to assure the supply of labor, to give alms in place of salaries, to eulogize "good men" who do everything to massacre the defenseless and

take from them bread, peace, dignity and life. (*Jornal do Brasil*, October 25, 1980: 4)

The uncompromising tenor of the questions posed by Padre Vito clearly situates the letter within the nonviolent campaign to deny the legitimacy of the military dictatorship.

October 1980 represented a period in which the Church–state crisis continually intensified. Padre Vito had left Ribeirão, and was cloistered in the CNBB headquarters in Brasilia (*Veja*, October 29, 1980: 21), awaiting the outcome of the Supreme Court's review of habeas corpus, and his imminent deportation. During this period, three important patterns emerged regarding the crisis which can be associated with strident reaction to nonviolent questioning of military legitimacy in general, and to Padre Vito's nonviolent resistance in particular; they appear to have weakened the political base of the military dictatorship significantly, especially in its subsequent competition with the Church. First, the Figeiredo government allowed senior officials to accuse the Church of protecting the practice of Marxism by many of its senior clergy. They named specific "Marxist" bishops and accused the Church of bringing in funds from outside the country for use by the Brazilian "communist movement." General José Luiz Coelho Neto, commander of the Fourth Army, was among those who made both of these accusations, charging that the Bishop of Teofilo Otoni, Dom Quirino Adolfo Schmitz, was "the major example in Minas [Gerais] of Marxist clergy" (*Veja*, October 29, 1980: 24). Justice Minister Ibrahim Abi-Ackel, in a widely publicized statement, rather unexpectedly denied that the government possessed any documents that substantiated these allegations (*Jornal do Brasil*, October 24, 1980: 1); this was not unexpected by most Brazilians, who by now had become familiar with the awkward responses of the dictatorship to nonviolent denial of its legitimacy.

A second pattern, one that emerged during October of 1980, and which also subsequently strengthened the Church's competitive position, was the establishment within the Church hierarchy of a unified stand against the deportation of Padre Vito. In its unanimous declarations, the Brazilian Catholic Church has always filled a strong tutelary role in national political culture. Although the government's harsh political repression in the late 1960s had exercised a unifying effect on the Brazilian Church (Kadt, 1970: 219), a good deal of disagreement vis-à-vis the dictatorship had nevertheless persisted within the hierarchy of the Church; the attack upon Padre Vito (and, by extension, upon thousands of other foreign clergy) was particularly significant in its unification of opinion among the Church hierarchy. Early expressions of ambivalence about the deportation from such conservative bishops as Cardinal Vicente Scherer of Porto Alegre, were hastily denied in favor of strong statements of support for Padre Vito (ibid., October 23, 1980: 1), and Cardinal Paulo Evaristo Arns, of São Paulo, declared to the media that "the Church reacts always as a body; if one member is touched, the reaction is from the whole body" (ibid., (October 23, 1980: 4). A former minister in the previous Geisel dictatorship, Severo Gomes, declared to the press that "Padre Vito Miracapillo has received the solidarity of all of the Bishops and sectors of the Church, including that of the Cardinal of Rio de Janeiro, Dom Eugênio Salles, considered a conservative" (ibid., October 27, 1990: 1). The national movement of nonviolent rejection of the legitimacy of the dictatorship had moved from the base communities and radicalized clergy to the Church hierarchy.

Acts of Church solidarity proliferated. Five Brazilian bishops attending the Vatican synod in late October of 1980, including conservative Salles and radical Claudio Hummes, boycotted a luncheon in their honor at the Brazilian Embassy (*Veja*, October 29, 1980: 22). The bishops of Ceará voted on November 5 to reaffirm their commitment to working with the poor and to the principles of Puebla, and explicitly lent their support to the CNBB in its resistance to the deportation of Padre Vito (*O Globo*, November 6, 1980: 8). Cardinal Avelar Brandão, archbishop of Salvador and primate of Brazil, announced that he also opposed the deportation, and that his "position [in favor] of dialogue [with the government] should not be confused with acceptance" (*convivencia*) *Jornal do Brasil*, November 8, 1980: 4). In an interview granted on November 8, Brandão emphasized the Church's growing fear that Padre Vito's deportation threatened many other foreign clergy (Jornal do Brasil, November 9, 1980: 3), a point that was raised again the next day when the Southern Regional Conference of the CNBB publicly thanked and expressed support for the foreign clergy in their pastoral work with the poor in Brazil, denouncing the government policies of harassment and deportation (ibid., November 10, 1980: 2). In mid-December, moderate cardinal, Aloísio Lorscheider, who had functioned as a mediator between conservative and radical wings of the Church hierarchy and hence had become an important spokesperson for the Church, contributed significantly to the breakdown in Church–state cooperation when he declared on Northeast regional television that "the regime is sinful." (*Veja*, 17, December 1980: 20).

The Church's fears of widespread government harassment of clergy were well-founded. There were strong indications by October, 1980, that a number of bishops and priests – both foreign and Brazilian – were vulnerable to similar action. Some of the more prominent foreign bishops, in fact, appeared to be the ultimate targets, depending upon the outcome of public reaction to Padre Vito's deportation. One of these, the Spanish bishop, Dom Pedro Casaldáliga, bishop of São Felíz do Araguaia (Mato Grosso), had already been indirectly attacked with the imprisonment and expulsion of one of his priests, Padre Jentel, in 1976 (*Veja*, December 29, 1976: 36–7). The federal deputy who first denounced Padre Vito, Severino Cavalcante, of the pro-government Democratic Social Party (PDS) in Pernambuco, accused Casaldáliga in October of engaging in similar activities (*Veja*,

October 29, 1980: 21); and Darcilio Aires, the PDS leader of the State of Rio de Janeiro in the Federal Chamber of Deputies, followed suit, complaining – in somewhat exaggerated terms – of the unacceptability of "the line adopted by this foreign clergyman, which exhorts the people to make a new revolution, capable of guaranteeing the expropriation of all of the properties of the country," and suggesting that the government review Casaldáliga's status in Brazil (*Jornal do Brasil*, October 29, 1980: 4).

In fact, the Figueiredo government was already investigating Dom Pedro, having requisitioned a tape of a speech that he had made (ibid., October 25, 1980: 4). The federal Minister of Justice, Abi-Ackel, denied that there was any link between the deportation of Padre Vito and the investigation of Casaldáliga, and insisted that "the Padre Vito case is a mere episode." Meanwhile, the minister of social communication, Said Farhat, suggested that a statement by Casaldaliga, describing the Supreme Court as subservient to the government, represented a proscribed political action (ibid., November 4, 1980: 4).

Government actions during this period were not limited to threats, moreover. In November, the Papal Nuncio expressed fears that new expulsions were being planned, including those of an Italian missionary and a French priest (ibid., November 7, 1980: 7), and three Italian nuns were briefly jailed during the demolition of a slum neighborhood in Goiania (ibid., November 8, 1980: 4). Two other Italian priests, Afonso Tebaldine and Giovanni Batista Zenotto, were charged with political crimes in November and December, respectively (ibid., November 8, 1980: 4; November 10, 1980: 2; *O Estado de São Paulo*, December 13, 1980: 9). The government seemed to be stepping up its campaign against "Marxist clergy," although the results of a Gallup Poll, which had been taken between October 25 and 29, which indicated that about 52 percent of all of the respondents – and over 70 percent of those who held an opinion in the case – opposed the expulsion of Padre Vito (*Jornal do Brasil*, November 4, 1980: 4), pointed to a profound government defeat in its struggle to capture Brazilian public opinion. The publication of the Gallup Poll indicated the extent to which the case of Padre Vito had weakened the legitimacy of the military dictatorship of General Figueiredo. Having gambled that the deportation of another foreign priest would once again inflame the potential xenophobia of lower income Brazilians, while the closely related land-tenure question (and latent xenophobia) would draw the support of the upper and middle classes, Figueiredo's government had, in actuality, submitted itself to a referendum with its expulsion of Padre Vito. As with the Uruguayan constitutional referendum that would follow Padre Vito's deportation by only a month, Brazilian public opinion overwhelmingly rejected the legitimacy of the dictatorship in this key case. Of those people polled who had an opinion regarding the deportation, the vast majority opposed it. Of all groups polled, and including the respondents with no opinion in the case, majorities, or near majorities, opposed the government's action, and very small minorities supported it.[18]

Of particular interest was the position of those with high incomes, given the salience of the land-tenure question in the case. Only 13 percent of this category supported the expulsion. The general unpopularity of the action, given the atmosphere of national crisis with which the dictatorship had surrounded it, significantly weakened the argument for continued military dictatorship in Brazil. The government had effectively limited its subsequent policy alternatives to two basic categories – escalation of overt authoritarianism, which it chose to pursue (to its own detriment) in the short-run, or a progressive and uncontrolled retreat from the political sphere, which it ultimately adopted, and which appears to have led directly to its own demise.

As early as September of 1980, the Figueiredo government had accelerated a campaign of harassment of Brazilian and foreign clergy, prompting the interim president of the CNBB, Dom Celso Queiroz, to compare the national political situation with that of 1964 and 1968, the years of the coup and the "white coup" (the authoritarian crackdown) in Brazil (*Jornal do Brasil*, October 23, 1980: 4). Cardinal Eugênio Sales announced that his phone had been tapped by the government (*Veja*, October 29, 1980: 23–4), and a Brazilian priest, Padre Reginaldo Veloso, was interrogated and charged under another law, the National Security Act, for composing and singing a song in support of Padre Vito, entitled "Vito, Vito, Vitoria" (*Jornal do Brasil*, November 7, 1980: 2), which directly attacked the dictatorship and the Supreme Court, and led to his trial by military court (*Diario de Pernambuco*, January 16, 1981: A4). In November, the Archbishop of Paraiba, Dom Jose Maria Pires (known popularly as "Dom Pelé" because he was black), was prevented by state police from holding a mass for peasants at a latifundium where social tensions were high (*Jornal do Brasil*, November 10, 1980: 2). Although the state government quickly backed down, evidently having received cautionary warnings from the federal government (ibid., November 11, 1980: 3), the national visibility of the Archbishop increased substantially, and he used it effectively in criticizing the violence practiced by landowners against the peasants and agricultural laborers of Paraiba (*O Estado de São Paulo*, December 13, 1980: 9). The military dictatorship had once again been given a graphic lesson in the unanticipated consequences of oppression – nonviolent resistance was clearly the more efficacious tactic.

The third salutary effect of the crisis upon the relative political position of the Church involved that institution's own process of internal adjustment to the crisis. The Church moved rapidly after September of 1980 to moderate its most radical elements – even while defending them – and hence arguably emerged from the crisis as a much more viable and popularly acceptable political competitor, particularly from the standpoint of the Brazilian middle class. This intentional moderation of Church radicalism, while not substantially transforming pastoral commitments to the rights and needs of the poor, was a direct response to the charges of Marxism that had been leveled at it by the military dictatorship. As Dom Ivo Lorscheiter commented, upon being told that Padre Vito had finally been deported, "the Church does not seek friction, but the Church will not renounce its way of understanding and realizing the Pastoral." He added that "although we condemn class conflict as we condemn savage capitalism [*capitalismo selvagem*], it would be a great lie to preach the Golden Rule if we, the priests, closed our eyes to the material necessities of the most impoverished" (*Jornal do Brasil*, October 26, 1980: 1).

Later, the Brazilian primate, Cardinal Avelar Brandão, addressed the question of the social structure of Brazil, noting that "savage capitalism does not interest [the Church], and Marxist collectivism will not resolve [the problems]" (ibid., November 9, 1980: 3). It was clear that the Church, and even the CNBB, while closing ranks in its response to the deportation, attempted at the same time to moderate its positions. CNBB bishops, believed by the conservatives to be a foco of radical resistance to the military dictatorship, were among those who dissuaded the Italian Ambassador to Brazil, Giuseppi Jacoangeli, from holding a solidarity dinner for Padre Vito just prior to his deportation (*LeLa*, October 29, 1980: 25).

The radicalization was ultimately the result of its option for the poor, and its consequent association with the nonviolent resistance to the "Brazilian system" – that poor Brazilians increasingly manifested through such institutions as the base communities. The Figueiredo government made charges in December of 1980 – which the Church did not wholly deny – that the ecclesiastical base communities had been infiltrated by leftists. Dom Ivo insisted that the Church was "anti-Communist," but lamented publicly that some leftists might be using the communities for their own political ends, while Cardinal Arns stressed that base communities were trained by clergy to resist (politically and ideologically) their takeover and manipulation by political groups (*O Estado de São Paulo*, December 10, 1980: 5). Clodovis Boff, a theologian and brother of Leonardo Boff, suggested that the infiltration of base communities had taken place to some extent, and that this might threaten their links with the Church. The bishop of Passo Fundo, Dom Jacó Hilgert, responded that the charges that the 100,000 base communities in Brazil, and their 2 million members, represented a threat to the country because of leftist infiltration were "ridiculous" (*O Estado de São Paulo*, December 12, 1980: 5; data from: *Veja*, December 17, 1980: 21).

While the strong anti-Communist statements made at this juncture by such conservative clergy as Cardinal Vicente Scherer, of Porto Alegre (*O Estado de Sao Paulo*, December 16, 1980: 2), and the qualified defense of the communities by such activist clergy as Dom Jose Maria Pires (ibid., December 24, 1980: 2), were expected, other responses revealed the profundity of the crisis. Dom Helder Câmara responded publicly in February of 1981 to an open letter by Franciso Julião calling for a union of Marxists and Christians. Câmara stridently insisted that there was a basic incompatibility between the two (*Diario de Pernambuco* (Recife), February 14, 1981: 1).

In effect, political pressures from both sides of the political spectrum were curbed, ultimately reinforcing the broader, moderate political appeal of the Church.

Conclusion

Nonviolent resistance to military dictatorship at this key juncture in Brazilian history appears to have met with significant success insofar as it was able to unify and consolidate the organized opposition within a powerful rival institution, the national Catholic Church. The principal nonviolent technique that came to be employed, public declarations that questioned the independence of Brazil and the basic rights of its citizens under dictatorship, often voiced by foreign and Brazilian clergy to their desperately poor congregations, led to at least four results: first, the level of violence normally evinced by government responses to challenges to its legitimacy was decidedly limited because of the nonviolent and public character of the actions; second, the Brazilian Catholic Church was, at least temporarily, unified in its response to human rights violations by the military; third, in the course of the subsequent nonviolent challenge, competitive appeals by both the Church and the military dictatorship to the people of Brazil for their support resulted in decisive support for the Roman Catholic Church, at the expense of the government; and finally, a pattern of mass-based nonviolent resistance to the antidemocratic policies of the dictatorship was initiated, and later became crucial in such events as the *diretas já* movement in 1984 and even the successful impeachment of President Fernando Collor de Mello in 1992.

The deportation of Padre Vito Miracapillo from Brazil in 1980, an all too apparent attempt by the dictatorship to win popular support through a xenophobic appeal to nationalism, precipitated a largely unanticipated Church–state crisis. Even Tancredo Neves, then the president of the Partido Popular, expressed his surprise at the severity of the crisis (*Jornal do Brasil*, November 4, 1980: 4). The specific conditions of this case were vital to the political outcome: the nonviolent tactics of Liberation Theology as practiced in Brazil, based in large measure on the writings of such Brazilian theologians as Leonardo Boff and apparent in the practice of millions of members of Brazil's basic communities; the socially explosive conditions of poverty in Padre Vito's parish and in the Northeast in general; the growing vulnerability of the dictatorship and its principal ideological supporters, the large landowners, to the nonviolent strategy of publicly questioning the legitimacy of the dictatorship; the increasingly isolated and mutually dependent relationship of the Northeast landed elite and the dictatorship; the Brazilian Church's overwhelming dependence upon foreign clergy; the propensity of foreign clergy to embrace the tenets of Brazilian nonviolent Liberation Theology; and the Church's previous two decades of commitment to the rights and needs of the poor. Moreover, the political adaptation of the Church to a crisis precipitated by an increasingly illegitimate dictatorship increased its own corporate solidarity and moderated its own most radical elements while, temporarily at least, opening it to the more general aspects of the nonviolent Brazilian variant of Liberation Theology, and even imparting upon it a sense of mission in this regard. As the bishop of Volta Redonda, Dom Waldyr Calheiros, was able to comment at the height of the crisis,

> the [Church–state] friction will only disappear when the state positions itself from the same side and angle as the Church positions itself: on the side of the unjustly treated, the poor, the squatters, those without land, the Indians, and the workers. (*Jornal do Brasil*, October 29, 1980: 1)

Ivan Vallier argued in 1970 that the absence of a Christian Democratic party in Brazil had, in effect, politicized the Church, funneling Catholic political activists into Church activities and ultimately provoking a backlash from the Church hierarchy, which had finally opted for more conservative policies. As Vallier put it, "a cycle of political involvement on the left breeds a new cycle of political involvement on the right" (Vallier, 1970: 94). The pendulum had apparently moved again, however – with inadvertent help from the military dictatorship.

Figueiredo's regime had isolated and undermined its most salient ideological focus: anti-communism. Military dictatorship came to be associated in Brazil – and particularly in the Northeast – with the protection of unqualified rights of large-scale landownership; the nonviolent threat to such unqualified property rights posed by leftist (and, particularly, foreign) clergy ultimately facilitated their ability to question the dictatorship publicly. By deporting Padre Vito, the military government only called attention to this, and hence intensified its receding legitimacy. In effect, it had underscored the hollowness of anti-communism as a justification for the violent suppression of the rights of the poor. Nonviolent resistance to military dictatorship at a key juncture forced it to appeal for support to the people of Brazil. The Brazilian public did indeed mull over the dictatorship's arguments and, as indicated by the Gallup Poll of late October, 1980, found them wanting: over 70 percent of those with an opinion (which encompassed about 74 percent of the Brazilian public) objected to the deportation.

The legitimacy of military dictatorship in Brazil had been effectively undermined in the public's eye and successive waves of organized political resistance, most notably that of the *diretas já* movement for direct presidential elections, soon persuaded the military, to retreat from national politics. In 1984 it scheduled presidential elections, and handed over power to civilians in the following year. The dictatorship's Achilles tendon, its fragile sense of legitimacy, had been stretched beyond the breaking point by modest acts of nonviolent resistance.

Notes

1 This study is broadly based upon field research, conducted in Brazil in 1980, 1981, 1987, 1991, and 1992, which included confidential interviews with Catholic clergy and laity, government officials, academics, and landowners. The author would especially like to thank Dom Helder Camâra for his helpful comments made during his visit to Idaho in 1988, and the Killam Foundation at the University of Alberta, the University of Idaho Research Council, and the Martin Institute for Peace Studies and Conflict Resolution for grants which facilitated travel and research in Brazil.

2 Gustavo Gutierrez observed in his classic work, *A Theology of Liberation*, that "the question regarding the theological meaning of liberation is, in truth, a question about the very meaning of Christianity and *about the mission of the Church*" (Gutierrez, 1973: xl). (*Emphasis in the original*).

3 Works that emphasize its wider socioeconomic implications include: Cardenal, 1977; Lernoux, 1982; Gutierrez and Schaull, 1977, to name a very few.

4 As Gutierrez (1973: 34) notes, *Populorum progressio* "speaks clearly of 'building a world where every man, no matter what his race, religion or nationality, can live a fully human life, freed of servitude imposed on him by other men or by natural forces over which he has not sufficient control.'"

5 As Bruneau wrote in 1982, "obviously the church is not going to bring on 'the revolution' singlehandedly, but neither is any other single group or institution. Rather, the church is promoting a general structural change in a great many ways, and thereby assisting a more general process" (154).

6 Roberto Romano notes in this regard that "perhaps only in revolutionary Mexico, in all of Latin America, did something more drastic occur than the acts of the Empire, imprisoning and sentencing bishops to forced labor" (1979: 94).

7 The formation of the CNBB in 1952, under the leadership of Dom Helder Câmara, played a major role in pushing the national Church into an activist, pastoral stance such that, by the early 1960s, it arguably "was socially more advanced than any other Latin American Church (except perhaps that of Chile)" (Bruneau, 1974: 107).

8 Edward J. Williams noted in 1973 that "in addition to extending their relative strength within the nation-state, the national conferences have become more independent of the international hierarchy. In part as a result of the pope's own initiative, Vatican II weakened the operational significance of the papacy with reference to the national churches. The national conferences deal with much more substantial problems than formerly, when they were almost entirely concerned with the implementation of detailed directives from Rome. Now Rome's communications are frequently in the form of general policy statements which leave considerable latitude for national initiative and innovation. Moreover, national conferences frequently by-pass the papal nuncio and communicate directly with the pope" (1973: 267).

9 Bruneau's 1968 data, given by states, yields the following averages: For seven South and Center-South states, there was an average of 5,993 Catholics per priest; for nine Northeastern states, the figure was 12,319. The national average in 1968 was 7,272.

10   Many authors have emphasized this point. Williams, for example, notes that "foreign ideas, priests and money have literally consumed the Latin American Church" (1973: 265).

11   E.g., an editorial in the prestigious Brazilian newspaper, *Jornal do Brasil*: "When he was Governor of [the state of] Bahia, [Luiz Viana Filho] had problems with foreign priests which acted in a way to provoke disturbances in the most backward and poor areas of the state...he concludes that the source of the [current Church–state] crisis is the inadaptation to the parishes entrusted to the foreign priests. Europeans coming from highly evolved countries with a solid social structure, such as Holland, Switzerland, Italy and Germany, suffer a traumatic shock in entering in intimate contact with the populations of the Northeast, where the social contrasts were produced in more than four hundred years of defective formation" (*Jornal do Brasil*, October 25, 1980: 10).

12   E.g., 11 foreign priests had been deported by late 1969. Bruneau mentions the murder of a priest by government agents in 1969. The murder of a priest by state police in 1976 in Matto Grosso is recounted by Peter Flynn (1979: 504–5).

13   Bruneau does not mention the Jentel incident, which appears to have been deeply influential.

14   Under the codename of "Operation Brother Sam", the US military had stationed strategic supplies for rapid delivery should the conspirators need support.

15   In the aftermath of his arrest, Padre Vito tried to minimize this aspect of the case, explaining that he "had not refused to conduct the mass – he refused merely to celebrate it on the day and hour marked by the mayor of Ribeirao" (*Veja*, October 29, 1980: 21).

16   *Veja* noted in a report in 1976 that "more, perhaps, than any other, the question of land, with its inextricable juridical and social puzzle[s], is at the center of the differences that involve the Church and the state today" (December 29, 1976: 36).

17   This was underscored by Gustavo Gutierrez's service as a personal advisor to Dom Helder Camara (Lernoux, 1982: 423).

18   For example, the following results were derived from a Gallup Poll conducted in Brazil between October 25 and 29, 1980, and published in the *Jornal do Brasil*, November 4, 1980: 4.

References

Bruneau, Thomas. 1982. *The Church in Brazil; The Politics of Religion*. Austin: University of Texas Press.

——. 1974. The *Political Transformation of the Brazilian Catholic Church*. London: Cambridge University Press.

Cardenal, Ernesto 1977. *The Gospel in Solentiname*, trans. Donald D. Walsh. Maryknoll, NY: Orbis Books.

Flynn, Peter. 1979. *Brazil: A Political Analysis*. Boulder: Westview Press.

Gutierrez, Gustavo. 1973. A *Theology of Liberation*, trans. and ed. Sister Caridad Inda and John Eagleson. Maryknoll, NY: Orbis Books.

Gutierrez, Gustavo and Richard Schaull. 1977. *Liberation and Change*, ed. Ronald H. Stone. Atlanta: John Knox Press.

Kadt, Emanuel de. 1970. "JUC and AP: The Rise of Catholic Radicalism in Brazil." In ed., *The Church and Social Change in Latin America*, by Notre Dame, Ind.: University of Notre Dame Press.

Lernoux, Penny. 1982. *Cry of the People*. New York: Doubleday.

Paiva, Vanilda, ed. 1985. *Igreja e Questao Agraria*. São Paulo: Edicaes Loyola.

Romano, Roberto. 1979. *Brasil: Igreja contra Estado*. São Paulo: Kairos.

Sanders, Thomas G. 1981. "Brazil in 1980: The Emerging Political Model." In Thomas Bruneau and Philippe Faucher, eds., *Authoritarian Capitalism*. Boulder: Westview Press.

Sarles, Margaret J. 1982. "Maintaining Political Control through Parties: The Brazilian Strategy," *Comparative Politics*, vol. 15, no. 1 (October), pp. 65–7.

Souza Lima, Luiz Gonzaga de. 1979. *Evolucão Política dos Católicos e da Igreja no Brasil*. Petropólis, Brazil: Vôzes.

Vallier, Ivan. 1970. *Catholicism, Social Control, and Modernization in Latin America*. Engelwood Cliffs, NJ: Prentice-Hall.

Williams, Edward J. 1973. "The Emergence of the Secular Nation-State and Latin American Catholicism," *Comparative Politics*, vol. 5, no. 2 (January).

PART VII
North America

Introduction

It is estimated that over half of the North American population of European ancestry are direct descendants of those who immigrated from Europe to avoid military conscription. The United States and Canada are, in effect, nations of draft resisters. Indeed, the "rugged individualism" that hallmarks American culture is based on the premise of defiance and noncooperation with government authority. The American political system is based on the principle, enshrined in the 1776 Declaration of Independence that people are endowed with such "unalienable Rights" as "Life, Liberty and the Pursuit of Happiness," and that "whenever any Form of Government becomes destructive of these Ends, it is the Right of the people to alter or to abolish it." It is not surprising, then, that there is a strong tradition of nonviolent resistance. Despite a tradition of order and a relatively responsive government, Canada has a long history of nonviolent resistance on such causes as trade unionism, native sovereignty, the environment, and the rights of the French-speaking minority. Greenpeace, founded in Canada in the early 1970s, soon expanded into a global movement against militarism and environmental desecration. In the United States, while the distrust of governmental authority and its laws has sometimes led to the emergence of right-wing and reactionary movements and the celebration of such outlaw heroes as Oliver North, it has also led to the emergence of pacifist heroes such as Martin Luther King. Interestingly, while his birthday is now officially recognized as a national holiday, it is only King's civil rights activism that is universally acknowledged, not his radical pacifism which also challenged the militarism and corporate capitalism which dominate American politics.

In the more than 200 years of American independence, the classical liberal notions of individual freedom have expanded to include the enfranchisement of larger segments of the population and the introduction of greater individual rights. This progress, largely taken for granted today, was largely the result of nonviolent movements by historically disenfranchised people: women, people of color, and the working class.

Furthermore, it is now known through recently released government documents that nonviolent resistance and the threat of greater nonviolent resistance in recent decades played a decisive role in deterring dramatic escalation in US military intervention in Indochina, Central America, and elsewhere in the Third World, as well as the increased nuclear arms race, the spread of nuclear power, and other elite-driven policies which conflicted with the wishes of the majority of Americans. While many decry decreased voter turnout and popular interest in political matters, a closer look reveals that, from Earth First! activists protecting ancient forests to strawberry workers striking for decent working conditions to protests against further US military assaults against Iraq, the tradition of nonviolent action is still alive and well today.

In this section, historian Charles Chatfield surveys this often hidden history of nonviolence in the United States.

14
Nonviolent Social Movements in the United States: A Historical Overview

Charles Chatfield

Organized nonviolence, in United States history, characterized sporadic and essentially religious or moral opposition to war and injustice in the nineteenth century. It was employed self-consciously as an organizing principle during the First World War. Following the war, it was studied intensively in relation to the campaigns of Mohandas Gandhi, and over the next 30 years, small groups emulated him by applying nonviolent tactics against racism and other violations of civil rights. In the second half of the twentieth century, nonviolent direct action was applied in campaigns against racism, nuclear weapons, war, and ecological degradation to such an extent that it became institutionalized in US political culture.

Nonviolence – the word, its variations, and related terms have had mixed connotations in a US context. In the most general sense, most social movements for change and justice have avoided violence and have mobilized essentially political, economic, and social resources. Indeed, the US political system was designed, as James Madison observed, to channel the claims of both self-interest and social justice through the same institutions in order to clip the claws of protest and subordinate conflict to political order. "Nonviolent," in this sense, is a very generalized adjective.

Historically, however, nonviolence has come to imply a characteristic of some social movements that is both sharper and more limited than being merely not violent. It connotes a particular form of conflict: *direct action undertaken at risk but without recourse to destructive force.* Here is the difference between *nonresistance* and *nonviolent resistance* – between the principled avoiding of violence, even at the price of complying with unjust authority on one hand, and actively resisting unjust authority without using violence at any cost. It is like the distinction between accepting conscientious objector status and courting arrest by engaging in civil disobedience. To the extent that it derives from religious or ethical precepts, nonviolence may be said to be *principled* (Woito 1997), even though it may also be valued as

prudent and practical. Accordingly, "nonviolent movements" may be understood to employ a wide range of direct actions, some of which put their
members at risk but none of which direct violence against others.

Roots of Nonviolent Activism

An ethic of principled nonviolence is threaded through US culture and
literature (True 1995), and it has roots in religious pacifism as well as the
antislavery, women's suffrage, and labor movements.

The main carriers of nonviolent principle – religious pacifism – were for a
long time the nonresistant free churches – the Mennonites, Brethren, and
especially the Society of Friends, or Quakers (Brock 1968, 1990).They are
often called the "peace churches." In colonial North America, Friends
consciously applied such principles as the equal worth of all persons
(male and female; Anglo-American, African American and native Indian),
the caring of persons for one another, the individual revelation of truth, the
merit of mutual trust, and the rejection of war and killing. As the governance of the Pennsylvania colony came to involve militias, military force,
and eventually armed rebellion, Friends withdrew from the seats of power.
Their ideals became particularly visible in their relationships with native
Indians along the frontier, in the antiwar testimony of Quaker Anthony
Benezet, and in the witness of Quakers who participated in the antebellum
antislavery movement of the 1830s and 1840s (Brock 1968).

By that time some pacifists, in the sense of people who totally rejected the
use of punitive force or violence, had become associated with small groups
that evangelized against war on mainly religious grounds. Beginning in New
York and Massachusetts (1815), these peace societies became national with
the founding of the American Peace Movement in 1829. Peace groups
focused primarily on international understanding and arbitration, and they
divided on the issue of whether to repudiate war and force altogether or to
make exceptions for just causes – the so-called Just War position that was still
the ethical norm for Western civilization. The absolutist position was carried
beyond the Peace Society and into the white antislavery movement, notably
by William Lloyd Garrison and his followers (Ziegler 1992, 48–149; Brock
1968). Various abolitionists spirited slaves to freedom along the Underground Railroad, and also used the boycott and tax resistance (as in the
case of Henry David Thoreau, who refused to pay his poll tax in protest
against the Mexican–American war, which he believed was for slavery).

Among generations of slaves, of course, a virtual culture of nonviolent
resistance had evolved, embedded in language, song, and forms of humor
that would embellish the more explicit African American nonviolence of
the twentieth century. In the antebellum era, moreover, nonviolent resistance was urged upon blacks and whites alike by leaders such as Frederick
Douglass and Sojourner Truth (Genovese 1974; Gutman 1974).

In the mid-nineteenth century, the civil war enlisted all but the most redoubtable advocates of nonviolence, Elihu Burritt, for example. Afterward, the peace movement revived. The absolute repudiation of war was reasserted then, notably by Alfred Love and the Universal Peace Union; but for the most part the movement attracted proponents of understanding among peoples, international law, and arbitration. By the outbreak of the First World War in Europe, the US peace movement was well organized and generously funded by an economic and professional elite, but it was not rigorously pacifist (Chatfield 1992, DeBenedetti 1980). On the other hand, by then a small core of humanitarian reformers had been inspired by the Russian Leo Tolstoy's advocacy and practice of religious pacifism in the most humanitarian and absolute sense.

A movement for woman's rights paralleled the women's antislavery campaigns from 1848; focusing on suffrage, it grew into a major political force by the end of the century. Like the peace movement, the women's movement was transnational and, moreover, it increasingly located the roots of warfare in social injustice, in this case the injustice of male repression. Suffrage activists in the United States employed assertive but not violent tactics such as rallies, marches, petitioning, strikes, vote-ins, picketing, fasting, and lobbying (Alonso 1993; Bacon 1994; Flexner 1975). Early in the twentieth century they were in contact with British women who employed civil disobedience in the cause. By the time of the First World War, women's suffrage was highly organized, frequently successful on the state level, and very articulate.

Nonviolent but active protest also characterized much of the labor movement in years prior to the First World War. For the most part, this was a practical matter: violence played into the hands of corporations which, linked as they were to government, had available overwhelming force. The workers' struggle was characterized by a great deal of violence in nineteenth–century United States, and laborers sometimes did adopt violent tactics. Indeed, the western mining states experienced periods of virtual civil war around the turn of the century. But major worker's organizations, the Knights of Labor among others, explicitly rejected violence. Even the most militant of unions, and rhetorically the most revolutionary of them – the Industrial Workers of the World – adopted disciplined nonviolent action in major strikes, notably in Lawrence, Massachusetts (1912). Moreover, the American Socialist Party, founded in 1901, shared with its European counterparts an explicit rejection of international wars (which was understood to be labor-exploiting), through nonviolent general strikes if necessary.

The First World War as a Defining Event

The defining event for the emergence of modern nonviolence was the First World War because it elicited a new constituency of progressive activists in the US peace movement (Chatfield 1971: 13–87). Among the earliest to respond to the war in Europe were leaders in the suffrage movement such as Jane Addams, director of Hull House, around whom formed the Woman's Peace Party (1915). She and Emily Green Balch, another settlement house director, represented US women at The Hague (1915), where over 1,000 women from over 12 nations appealed for a standing bloc of neutral nations to negotiate peace. Lillian Wald, a social worker like Addams and Balch, headed the activist American Union Against Militarism (1915), through which men and women progressives challenged President Wilson's budget for military preparedness in 1915 and 1916. Meanwhile, pacifist religious leaders, most of them politically progressive, emulated British pacifists in forming a Fellowship of Reconciliation (FOR, 1915).

In the spring of 1917 the Union Against Militarism and FOR were joined by socialists in a desperate, futile effort to stem US intervention. Once declared, on Good Friday (April 6), the war split the party and the peace movement. The older, well established peace societies swung in line behind the crusade, as did many younger progressives who had resisted intervention. Carrie Chapman Catt epitomized the overwhelming majority of the women in shifting to support the war effort, which she successfully merged with the cause of suffrage. The First World War thus drew a sharp line of principle between those progressives who would or would not sanction violence for the best of intentions.

Absolute pacifists – those who would not sanction even the so-called Great War – were an isolated few. They, like Addams and Balch, socialist leader Norman Thomas and his conscientious objector brother Evan, ministers John Nevin Sayre and A. J. Muste, journalist Devere Allen and YMCA leader Kirby Page, found solace and companionship in the FOR. Some of them got legal help from the National Civil Liberties Bureau (subsequently American Civil Liberties Union), founded to defend conscientious objectors (COs) to the war. Quakers organized the American Friends Service Committee (AFSC) in support of their COs.

Those groups became the principle carriers of principled nonviolence in active campaigns for justice and against war – the FOR and AFSC, a strong network of pacifist women (Alonso 1993: 56–84), the antiwar wing of the Socialist Party, and, after 1921, the War Resisters League. The wartime, reform-oriented pacifists and those who joined them later became convinced that even as war is a form of injustice, so the causes of peace and justice are one: what is wrong with war, they felt, is the injustice it does to all. They effectively articulated opposition to warfare *as a social process*, and urgently sought a process through which social justice might be pursued without violence – nonviolence. Without this core of persons who had combined progressive activism with pacifist principle, Gandhi would not have been studied and emulated in the United States as he was, and nonviolence would not have been articulated as it was when the time became ripe for its application.

Gandhi as a Defining Advocate of Nonviolence

Mohandas Karamchand Gandhi became the reference point for US advocates of modern nonviolence through people who popularized him, studied his movement, analyzed it in Western terms, and imbued it with revolutionary significance. For most Americans, Gandhi was a symbol of anti-imperialism, but for US pacifists he was a symbol and success story of nonviolent political activism (Chatfield 1976: 23–69). Unitarian minister and pacifist John Haynes Holmes was Gandhi's first prominent US advocate. Holmes valued Gandhi's example of principled nonviolent resistance in action. He widely compared the Mahatma to Jesus, and serialized the Indian leader's autobiography in his *Unity* magazine, beginning in 1926.

Beyond the image, however, was the man, beyond the slogan a movement. The dynamics of man and movement was the subject of two important studies by Clarence Marsh Case and Richard B. Gregg. Case (1874–1946) was both a Quaker minister and a distinguished professor of sociology. He began his study of the sociology of nonviolence as a graduate student (he earned his PhD at the University of Wisconsin in 1915), but completed it after the war, when new material became available on conscientious objectors and on the *satyagraha* movement in India. The result, *Non-Violent Coercion: A Study in Methods of Social Pressure* (1923), rejected the then-current image of Gandhi as an exotic oriental and distinguished his approach from passive resistance. Rather, Case identified nonviolence squarely as a form of coercion available to westerners and easterners alike, should persuasion alone fail.

Gregg, trained in law, but working in the labor movement, had been in India briefly in 1913. Back in the United States and in the midst of a major strike, he happened upon a piece about Gandhi. He read more, learned something of agriculture, and returned to India in 1925. There he worked and studied in the Gandhian movement, and he maintained a serious correspondence with Gandhi. The result was a series of books, produced in India and mainly for Indians, on Gandhian economics and on the psychology and strategy of Gandhi's nonviolent form of resistance. For Americans he synthesized Gandhian *satyagraha* (literally, "truth force") as an action strategy of practical power in his classic *The Power of Nonviolence* (1934).

Precisely because they were activists who rejected violence even in extremity, Kirby Page, John Nevin Sayre, Devere Allen, and A. J. Muste seized upon the political realism implied in Gregg's analysis of Gandhi. Page was the most important publicist for politically relevant religious pacifism in the decade, and he stressed the social power of Gandhi's movement. Sayre was the stabilizing force in the Fellowship of Reconciliation between the world wars, and he steered the organization through an intense dispute in the mid-thirties, from which it emerged committed to the cause of justice with all forms of direct action short of violence. Allen was a journalist and editor especially close to the Norman Thomas wing of the Socialist Party, which itself was torn in the thirties by a debate over whether or not violence was an acceptable strategy against authoritarian repression. Far from being an esoteric notion, then, nonviolence was a center of contention at that time.

By the time that the Second World War broke out in Europe, A. J. Muste had returned to leadership in the Fellowship of Reconciliation after working in the labor struggle (where he engaged in the novel sit-in tactic) and the Trotskyist movement, and he appreciated Gandhi's approach, synthesizing it with his own Christian vision of revolutionary nonviolence in the service of justice. Accordingly, Muste encouraged a young Indian, then a graduate student at Columbia University but formerly a Gandhian activist, to publish his interpretation of *satyagraha* in western terms. Krishnalal Shridharani's *War Without Violence* (1939) interpreted nonviolence as a form of force, even coercion, which can preserve political space for openness and mutuality. This book completed a basic analysis of Gandhian nonviolence. The way was open for its application.

Experiments During the Second World War

For the most part ignored by the public, two sets of wartime experiments with nonviolence established important precedents and leaders in nonviolent action.

One group consisted of conscientious objectors to war and conscription who had been placed in Civilian Public Service (CPS) camps that were operated by the peace churches and the FOR. CPS had been envisioned as a way of removing COs from military jurisdiction while conforming to Selective Service law. But while CPS operation and cost was relegated to pacifists, jurisdiction was retained by a government that acknowledged as legitimate only absolute, religious objection to all war. A difficulty was that some COs objected on political or philosophical grounds and objected not only to war but to conscription. A core of these COs ended up in federal prison. There they had time to study nonviolence, with which they melded a utopian and revolutionary vision for society. They also found occasion to apply nonviolent actions like fasts and noncooperation to racial injustice and violations of civil rights within their prison environment.

Out of this experience came a small core of radical pacifists that "set the tone and strategy for future campaigns of non-violent action" (Wittner 1984: 96).Out of it, too, nonviolence was coupled with their kind of philosophical individualism, now envisioned as a social revolution. In the immediate postwar years a few CPS radicals structured their vision as the Committee for Non-Violent Revolution (1946), and then they took over the War Resisters League, formed in 1923 as a home for nonreligious COs. Contrary to their expectation, and given an emerging Cold War and *Real-*

politik mind-set, the public was unreceptive. That reinforced, for the time being, a personal and inward orientation in the nonviolence of CPS radicals (Tracy 1996: 51–3).

Meanwhile, another group of pacifists (some of whom also went to CPS camps) experimented with nonviolent action to assault the walls of racial segregation. A. Philip Randolph, head of the Brotherhood of Sleeping Car Porters, had threatened Franklin Roosevelt with a massive March on Washington, which resulted in the president's appointment of a Fair Employment Commission in 1941. Randolph called, two years later, for "non-violent civil disobedience and non-cooperation... refusal of Negroes to obey any law which violates their basic citizenship rights..." (quoted in Chatfield 1971: 218).

Randolph did not carry out his 1941 threat, but by that time a small interracial group of young pacifists in Chicago was experimenting with various forms of nonviolent direct action to challenge segregation in housing, recreation, and eating places. They included James Farmer, George Houser, and Bayard Rustin, all of them familiar with the literature on Gandhian *satyagraha* (especially Shridharani). With the help of A. J. Muste and the FOR, their Committee of Racial Equality expanded into the Congress of Racial Equality(CORE), which developed a Gandhian sequence of nonviolent tactics: an objective assessment of any injustice, subsequent negotiations with those responsible for it, publicity to enlist popular support, self-sacrifice such as fasting, and if necessary civil disobedience or other direct action. CORE's early staff was on the FOR payroll, and until 1957 its office was at FOR headquarters. It continued to grow as branches grew up around the country, replicating one another's experiments in direct action. In 1947 CORE sponsored an interracial trip by interstate bus into the upper south – its "Journey of Reconciliation" (Tracy 1996: 20–35, 53–9; Meier and Rudwick 1973).

By mid-century, then, CORE and its experiments with nonviolent action against racism, together with the CPS radicals' notion of nonviolent social revolution, was connected to the close study and popularization of Gandhian *satyagraha* in the 1930s, to an intense debate then about the ethics of violence in the cause of justice, and to the First World War era when progressive activism was coupled with the principled rejection of violence.

Civil Rights: The Culminating Movement

It was only *after* the mid-century civil rights movement employed nonviolence dramatically and effectively that scholars recovered the history of African American nonviolent direct action earlier in the twentieth century. Then, August Meier and Elliot Rudwick (1976) documented early cases: the use of boycotts against segregation in transportation in the South and in the North against theaters; the 1915–16 actions against D. W. Griffith's film *Birth of a Nation* in Philadelphia and Boston, which included picketing, a mass march, and editor William Monroe Trotter's stand-in at a theater box office. African Americans in New York and other cities occasionally marched by the thousands in dignified response to mob violence and on behalf of antilynching legislation. In the twenties and thirties, they used boycotts to fight Jim Crow schools, usually in conjunction with legal action. The Great Depression led to widespread boycotts, pickets, and other creative direct actions in relation to job campaigns, and there were also rent strikes and actions against discrimination in public accommodation. There were, therefore, indigenous antecedents for CORE's Gandhian experiments in the 1940s and for the wholesale use of nonviolence in the next decade, although Meier and Rudwick caution that "its roots lay not in any past tradition of nonviolent direct action, but in the changing context of race relations which had emerged by the middle of the twentieth century" (1976: 301).

Although there was a successful black boycott of New Orleans busing in 1953, it was the Montgomery bus boycott three years later that dramatically captured the attention of African Americans in the deep South and of a national public. Montgomery elevated Martin Luther King, Jr. to leadership. It galvanized CORE, which expanded in the South and, with the FOR, provided training in nonviolence to the widespread sit-in movement of 1960. The following year CORE sponsored its famous Freedom Ride to challenge racial segregation in the deep South. Televised accounts of freedom riders (including James Farmer) enduring beatings and a fire bombing, put CORE alongside the Student Nonviolent Coordinating Committee (SNCC) and King's Southern Christian Leadership Conference (SCLC) as major institutions of organized, disciplined nonviolent action for African American civil rights.

The SNCC grew out of the sit-ins. At first a coalition of local groups, it soon attracted full-time organizers and activists, and expanded its agenda to include economic and political concerns. Initially reflecting the Christian idealism of leaders such as James Lawson, who was expelled from Vanderbilt Divinity School for his activism, SNCC's orientation became increasingly secularized, although it valued Gandhian civil disobedience and democratic decision-making. After 1965 its agenda changed to black nationalism and its political influence declined (Carson 1981; Stoper 1989).

Martin Luther King, meanwhile, enveloped Gandhian tactics in a Christian ethos and in African American culture. King had heard A. J. Muste and read Gandhi while in the seminary. In Montgomery he had the counsel of two men experienced in direct action: Glen Smiley of the FOR and Bayard Rustin of CORE. The SCLC grew out of Montgomery to become the strongest, most representative, and most influential civil rights institution. It became a community-based mass movement that employed boycotts, picketing, sit-ins, mass marches, and mass arrests. It paralyzed Birmingham and won its demands in 1963, the year it mobilized 200,000 people to March on

Washington. With direct action the movement challenged racists and their values directly; with civil disobedience it challenged, not law itself but racist laws and institutions. Thus, direct action that climaxed in the mass march from Selma to Montgomery was crucial to securing the 1965 Voting Rights Act. Nonviolence was the hammer by which the SCLC mobilized a mass African American constituency for change while it dared white Americans to adjust their institutions to be consistent with their stated values.

The SCLC broadened its agenda to include equal economic opportunity, north as well as south, and planned to use mass nonviolence in that cause. King's assassination in the spring of 1968 left his "Poor People's March on Washington" that summer a largely symbolic tribute to his vision rather than the opening event of a campaign for which he had hoped (Fairclough 1987; Garrow 1986; Morris 1984).

All three civil rights groups – CORE, SNCC, and SCLC – expanded their efforts through the mid-1960s, confronting racism in social, political, and economic forms. The frustration that accompanied those broad efforts led to divisive questions about philosophy as well as tactics, yielding a change of emphasis and leadership as new CORE and SNCC leaders advocated exclusively black empowerment. SCLC wrestled with similar challenges toward the end of the decade, as national attention shifted from civil rights and economic needs to the Vietnam War.

Nuclear Weapons: Another Field for Direct Action

At the same time that the Montgomery bus boycott occupied national attention, a campaign was being organized against the atmospheric testing of nuclear weapons, another field for nonviolent direct action. The issue was joined when nuclear scientists opened a debate with the government over the hazards of nuclear radiation. Opposition was heralded in 1955 when a few radical pacifists, including Dorothy Day and other Catholic Workers, challenged a compulsory air raid drill with civil disobedience.

In 1957 a pair of organizations was formed to "ban the bomb," at least from the atmosphere. One of them was created by established peace groups like the FOR, AFSC, and the Women's International League for Peace and Freedom. It was the Committee for a Sane Nuclear Policy (SANE), which campaigned through traditional means of education, speeches, advertisements, and lobbying (M. Katz 1986). The second group was created by radical pacifists and eventually called the Committee for Nonviolent Action (CNVA). It used the tactics of direct action to challenge not only atmospheric testing but nuclear weapons themselves (N. Katz 1974; Tracy 1996: 99–122; Wittner 1984: 245–53, 261–6). Although CNVA was identified with leading pacifists like A. J. Muste of the FOR, Larry Scott and Brad Lyttle of the AFSC, actually it was a loosely organized "collection of individuals who coalesced around certain projects" (N. Katz 1997: 107).

Each project was designed to publicize the threat of nuclear weapons and to be a symbol of personal resistance to militarism. All of them were the visible demand for alternatives to nuclear militarism and Cold War.

CNVA actions started on the 1957 anniversary of the atomic bombing of Hiroshima, when several of activists were arrested for intentionally trespassing at a Nevada test site. Subsequently pacifists attempted to sail into the Pacific Ocean test zone, and some did so (Bigelow 1959). Other projects were focused on the nuclear submarine construction works at New London, Connecticut, and missile bases in Cheyenne, Wyoming, and Omaha, Nebraska. In 1960–1, CNVA sponsored a"Walk," against nuclear weapons from San Francisco to Moscow (Lyttle 1966). CNVA followed that in 1963–4 with an integrated walk from Quebec to Cuba, which culminated in a civil rights confrontation in Albany, Georgia. The convergence of nuclear weapons issues and black civil rights was not coincidental: ban-the-bomb pacifists were inspired by the concurrent civil rights movement. Moreover, some young whites who volunteered for civil rights campaigns in the South were spurred upon their northward return to engage in other causes, including opposition to nuclear weapons and then to the war in Vietnam.

The Vietnam War and Nonviolence

Opposition to US policy in Vietnam preceded the spring offensive of 1965, but it coalesced then, when President Lyndon Johnson launched a campaign of sustained, escalating bombing of North Vietnam and committed troops to an open-ended ground war in the South. The antiwar movement of the Vietnam era was a loose, shifting but relentlessly growing movement with several centers of leadership (DeBenedetti 1990).

It was a fragile coalition, tenuously anchored in established peace organizations like the FOR, the AFSC, the Women's International League for Peace and Freedom, SANE, and Women Strike for Peace. Organized war opposition was formed also within part of the liberal wing of the Democratic party and among religious leaders (Clergy and Laymen Concerned about Vietnam – CALC), women (Another Mother for Peace), business and labor leaders, social workers, writers, scientists, and entertainers. An African American antiwar constituency included not only SNCC and eventually the SCLC but also soldiers (Cortright 1990). As the war wore on, civilian opponents of the war were joined by veterans (Cortright 1975). Collectively, this broad coalition employed tactics such as teach-ins and public education, advertising, petitions, lobbying and electoral politics, picketing, vigils, public meetings, the display of buttons and bumper stickers, demonstrations, street theater, tax resistance, conscientious objection to military service, and boycotts. Several Americans protested the war through self-immolation.

Another, less stable but more visible bloc of war opposition included the old left Socialist Workers Party and minuscule Communist Party, the new left Students for a Democratic Society, and radical pacifists associated mainly with the WRL or AFSC. Some radical pacifists linked war-resistance to other social causes in order to build the largest possible base for it; some, like Dellinger, hoped to find in the New Left wing a potential agent of nonviolent social revolution. Both hopes were dissipated in the chaos of 1968, and thereafter pacifists increasingly tended to value nonviolence as a limited antiwar tactic.

The tactics of the radical wing shifted during the war, but they included, in addition to actions noted above, attempting to block troop trains, burning draft cards, politicizing the military, engaging in guerrilla theater, harassing officials, and committing civil disobedience. Guerrilla theater included association with cultural radicals like hippies, as well as Abbie Hoffman and Jerry Rubin's so-called "Yippies," a street theater of the absurd. Civil disobedience sometimes elicited violence on the part of authorities and, for an extreme few (notably the Weatherman), violence on the part of antiwar elements themselves.

Draft resistance sprang from many sources and included publicly destroying draft cards, picketing or blockading draft boards or destroying their records, conscientious objection, and principled draft evasion – by flight to Canada if necessary. It was difficult to distinguish principled resistance to conscription from selfish evasion, of course, but both received increasing public support until the lottery system was introduced in 1970 and subsequently when the draft was ended (Useem 1973).

Antiwar actions thus had an extremely broad range. They were for the most part handled responsibly and nonviolently. Indeed, both activists and authorities learned ways to avoid violence, as for example to negotiate transportation and march routes, to coordinate arrangements, and to train marshals for mass walks and rallies.

Still, the media highlighted the exceptional and dramatic. This tendency, reinforced by some antiwar protest and also by the efforts of presidential administrations to put opposition on the politically margin, contributed to a public image of antiwar activism as culturally and politically radical, if not violence-prone. Ironically, a core group of pacifists mainly associated with the FOR and AFSC undertook to discipline civil disobedience tactics after 1968. In addition, war opposition became strong within the Democratic Party and increasingly within Congress. The more that direct action was conducted without violence and that antiwar effort flowed into the political mainstream, the less sensational and visible was the antiwar movement. It did not go away, though.

In the spring of 1971 activists put in motion a large repertoire of discrete actions that dramatized the breadth of nonviolence (DeBenedetti 1990: 303–6): through Easter weekend, religious leaders popularized proposals to "Set the Date Now" (for military withdrawal), a proposal echoed in Congress; early in April a People's Coalition sponsored rallies in which the war was addressed along with poverty and civil rights issues; about the same time dissenters in the advertising industry donated a million dollars worth of ads to "unsell" the war. In mid-April hundreds of antiwar veterans held a memorial service in Washington, staged a mock military operation there, lobbied, and demonstrated at the Capitol. Then perhaps a half-million people participated in an orderly, impressive demonstration, following which many of them lobbied with Congress for a People's Peace Treaty that had been drawn up by US students who had met with Vietnamese counterparts. Finally, a large-scale use of civil disobedience to shut down Washington traffic, organized by so-called May Day radicals, resulted in some 7,000 arrests and reinforced President Nixon's paranoia, but probably did not affect public policy.

A particular strand of direct action emerged within the Catholic Church during the war, and it reflected the personalist radical pacifism of Dorothy Day and the Catholic Worker movement (Klejment and Roberts 1996). It was personified by Daniel and Philip Berrigan, two socially conscious priests who, with seven others, publicly burned files taken from a draft board in Catonsville, Maryland in May 1968. Popularized in Daniel Berrigan's play, *The Trial of the Catonsville Nine* (1970), that action established a precedent for similar ones by Catholic antiwar protesters, and for the Plowshares campaigns against nuclear missiles in the 1980s.

Neither nonviolent direct action nor the antiwar movement itself directly brought about US withdrawal from war in Vietnam, though it is likely that both were major contributing factors. All too often it was uncoordinated and sometimes insufficiently disciplined, as activists concluded late in the war; it had not been effectively enough related to political issues and organizing. Nonetheless, nonviolence was applied in a great variety of ways, often very much to the point and as an integral part of the overall antiwar efforts.

Indeed, in the Civil Rights Movement and antiwar movement of 1956–75, nonviolent direct action had been attempted on a large scale to face urgent and profound national issues. A great many people had been trained in the philosophy and tactics of nonviolence. Television had dramatized (and sometimes distorted) it for the nation. A burgeoning literature on the nonviolence included: scholarly works like Joan Bondurant's interpretation of *satyagraha* in an Indian context, and Gene Sharp's systematic political assessment of it; thoughtful reflection by activists like Barbara Deming; anthologies that showed how pervasive was nonviolence in history (Lynd 1966; Sibley 1963; Weinberg and Weinberg 1963); an engaging, nearly commemorative popular treatment, *The Power of the People* (Cooney and Michalowski 1977); and various training manuals.

After Vietnam: The Dissemination of Nonviolence

Already in the 1960s, nonviolence was explicitly used in California by Cesar Chavez and the United Farm Workers. Actions beginning with strikes against grape growers expanded to include picketing, even against court orders, and then to nationwide boycotts. In 1968 Chavez undertook a 25–day fast, largely to discipline the movement, which enlisted further public support and new forms of direct action. The UFW negotiated contracts with grape growers in 1970, and in the following decade it expanded to producers of other kinds of produce. Conflict was renewed, not only with growers but also with Teamsters with whom owners had contracted as an alternative to UFW organization, until the state intervened to guarantee collective bargaining (Jenkins 1985).

In the wake of the Vietnam War, activists mounted effective campaigns against selected weapons systems, such as the B-1 Bomber and the MX missile, mobilizing public opinion in traditional ways. Moreover, the nuclear arms issue was given an additional boost by growing concern about environmental issues related to nuclear power.

The Union of Concerned Scientists epitomized that reorientation, which also characterized environmental organizations such as the Sierra Club and Friends of the Earth. The campaign against atomic power was generally decentralized, however, comprised of perhaps 1,000 local groups. Many of them were galvanized, when in 1975 German farmers and students halted the construction of a nuclear power plant in Wyhl by occupying its site. A political alliance of "Greens" became a major actor in German politics and helped generate a European-wide environmental and peace movement.

Inspired by Wyhl, Americans employed direct action, notably when the Clamshell Alliance committed civil disobedience in a 1977 action at the Seabrook, New Hampshire nuclear facility; there were 1,414 arrests. The Diablo Canyon complex in California was similarly challenged by the Abalone Alliance with more than 2,000 arrests. Dozens of actions involved thousands of arrests took place at nuclear power plant sites around the country. In 1979 the AFSC and FOR mobilized 15,000 people for demonstrations against the nuclear processing plant at Rocky Flats, Colorado, making the link between nuclear power and nuclear weaponry. Participants in these direct actions were disciplined by training in nonviolence. The Mobilization for Survival, concerned over both atomic power and nuclear arms, was formed through a coalition of some 280 local, regional, and national groups. It both foreshadowed and contributed to the Nuclear Freeze Campaign.

The 1980s saw a renewal of competition in nuclear arms. It started in the Carter administration but became aggressive under President Ronald Reagan, who was openly critical or arms control efforts and whom many feared believed a nuclear war against the Soviet Union was winnable. The administration was publicly challenged by arms control experts, which helped fuel an antinuclear movement that was international in scope.

In Western Europe and the United States there were massive rallies, supplemented by direct action focused on missiles, and even military suppliers. At a General Electric missile plant in Pennsylvania, the Daniel and

Philip Berrigan and their "Plowshares" group courted arrest by damaging missile-related equipment. Over a score of Plowshares actions followed. Other activists held vigils and walked picket lines, or attempted to block missile-bearing trains. The Women's Pentagon Action held several demonstrations at the Pentagon, symbolically blocking it and provoking arrests.

As in the 1950s, nonviolent direct action was but one element in a large campaign – in the 1980s was the "Nuclear Freeze." More of a grassroots-driven movement than previous peace campaigns (Kleidman 1993),the Freeze mobilized support for an expressly political agenda. More than 800,000 rallied in New York City in support of the Freeze in 1982 and hundreds of grassroots freeze groups sprung up across the country. It did not achieve its avowed goal of freezing the arms race, but it did result in restoring US arms control policy, and it played a key role in the process that led to the administration's reversal of the Cold War arms race (Meyer 1990). Important, but hardly noticed at the time, nonviolence was employed by groups besides radical pacifists and was largely accepted by the movement as a part of its overall repertoire.

Besides the Freeze, there was organized opposition to Reagan policy in Central America, most notably in Nicaragua. There, the administration sponsored a military force of Contras against the revolutionary Sandinistas, who had overthrown the dictatorial Somoza regime. At the same time, civil conflict erupted in El Salvador and Guatemala, where the US supported repressive regimes. Opponents of Reagan's policy mobilized US solidarity effectively, both in the capital and in country at large. Nonviolence was part of the campaign. in a number of respects. As with the case of Vietnam, there were large-scale demonstrations and civil disobedience against US policy. In addition, the civil wars generated thousands of refugees, many of whom applied for asylum in the United States but were refused. US activists smuggled Salvadoran and Guatemalan refugees along a modern underground railroad through a network of hundreds of churches and synagogues which offered them sanctuary, classic acts of civil disobedience. The government took legal action, but sanctuary continued until late in the decade when conditions improved in Central America and the refugee flow was reversed (Nepstad 1997; Crittenden 1988; Golden and McConnell 1986).

Some took their nonviolent resistance beyond US borders. Beginning in 1983, teams of trained North Americans were stationed in towns along the Nicaragua border that were threatened with Contra invasion. Highly publicized in the area, their presence was designed to deter attacks, but they also engaged in development work on site. They engaged in media work and lobbying upon their return home. Grounded in principled nonviolence, Witness for Peace expanded this work to other parts of Latin America following the end of US support for the Contras (1988).

Not only in Central America but in South Africa, self-government and human rights enlisted solidarity in the United States. National church denominations and other issue-oriented citizen groups opposed apartheid by pressing the government to issue economic sanctions and urging large corporations to either divest their investments in South Africa or abide by strict conditions for doing business there. On both fronts there was limited success. Resistance to sanctions led some activists to direct action, resulting in thousands of arrests on college campuses and before South African diplomatic offices.

Illustrative of this process were campaigns on college campuses to force their institutions to divest their stockholdings in corporations doing business in South Africa. Rallies, sit-ins, and the construction of shanty towns modeled on the squalid experience of black South Africans led to scores of universities divesting. As such campaigns increased, Congress finally voted in 1986 to impose limited sanctions on the apartheid regime.

Nonviolence also became part of the repertoire of the environmental movement from the 1970s on. Conservation and preservation societies date from the nineteenth century, but ecological activism grew sharply in the decade of Rachel Carson's *Silent Spring* (1962), Paul Ehrlich's *The Population Bomb* (1968), and Garrett Hardin's "The Tragedy of the Commons" (1968). On April 22, 1970 the new Friends of the Earth sponsored the first annual Earth Day. By then the issues of nuclear waste had been added to pollution and species preservation in the movement's agenda, and direct action had been added to its tactics of scientific study and monitoring, public education, and lobbying.

Principled nonviolence was, for many environmental activists, a corollary to respect for life. Direct action, effectively publicized, served to mobilize public opinion, and thus to strengthen educational and political efforts. Actions included chaining oneself to a threatened tree, sit-ins or sail- ins (to nuclear test zones), boycotts, blocking (clearing equipment from clearing forests, whaling ships in the open seas, etc.), and at the extreme end, industrial sabotage. Action-oriented groups included Sea Shepherds (1977) and Earth First! (1981), groups employing sabotage to property, and Greenpeace (1969). By far the most prominent and effective was Greenpeace.

With strong international connections, Greenpeace sent its own ship, the *Rainbow Warrior*, to confront activities from killing dolphin to dumping nuclear waste. The effectiveness of the ship in dramatizing issues was suggested in July 1985 when agents of the French government planted bombs that sunk the *Warrior* in the Auckland, New Zealand harbor. The incident was widely publicized the ship was replaced four years later to continue nonviolent direct action (Robie 1986; Brown and May 1989).

The environmental movement reflects two broad trends in current social movement organization. One is that it is part of a *transnational* social movement: it is integrally related to nongovernmental associations that span the globe, bringing pressure on both governments and international organizations (Smith, Chatfield, and Pagnucco 1997). A second characteristic of modern social movements is their decentralization and egalitarianism. Perhaps at least partly because of the influence of feminism and women's participation as Jane Meyerding argues (1997), recent groups employing principled nonviolence place a greater stress on group process and equal participation than earlier ones. On the other hand, the very diversity of nonviolent actions still causes rifts among the constituent groups in a social movement such as environmentalism, divisions which may be resolved through eclecticism or group specialization in specific tactics. Nonviolence is varied and it attracts differing commitments, but it is now generally understood as one tool among many in quests for peace and justice.

Nonviolent action in opposition to abortion was the cause that enlisted the largest numbers of arrests in recent decades, as abortion opponents blocked access to clinics. While most of the leadership of such campaigns were quite conservative politically and some anti-abortion activism has been violent, there have also been widespread participation by left-wing Catholics and others who had also been active in the peace and antinuclear movements. Accordingly, an explicitly nonviolent core emerged in the prolife movement. Sit-ins in front of medical facilities have led to judicial restraints and to legislation such as the Freedom of Access to Clinic Entrances Act, which severely curtailed the movement, and which even many supporters of legalized abortion fear may be setting a dangerous precedent against nonviolent action elsewhere. An outgrowth of such campaigns has been the Seamless Garment Network (1987), a coalition of some 140 peace, human rights, and prolife groups united in the belief that "war, abortion, poverty, racism, the arms race, the death penalty and euthanasia...are linked under a consistent ethic of life."

Conclusion

Initially viewed by the North American public as a kind of religious extremism or, in Gandhi's case, as alien and exotic, nonviolence has become part of the repertoire of social movements engaged in protest of any kind. Nonviolent direct action in this sense has become part of the language of public discourse in the United States. In a century of experimentation and application, nonviolence has been extended from the reflection of a few to an option widely understood in mainstream US social thought and institutions.

References

Alonso, Harriet Hyman. 1993. *Peace as a Women's Issue: A History of the U.S. Movement for World Peace and Women's Rights.* Syracuse, NY: Syracuse University Press.

Bacon, Margaret Hope. 1994. "By Moral Force Alone: The Antislavery Women and Non-resistance." In Jean Fagin Yellin and John C. Van Horne, eds., *The Abolitionist Sisterhood: Women's Political Culture in Antebellum America*, Ithaca, NY: Cornell University Press.

Berrigan, Daniel. 1970. *The Trial of the Catonsville Nine*. Boston: Beacon Press.

Bigelow, Albert. 1959. *The Voyage of the Golden Rule: An Experiment With Truth*. Garden City, NY: Doubleday.

Bondurant, Joan. 1958. *Conquest of Violence: The Gandhian Philosophy of Conflict*. Princeton: Princeton University Press.

Brock, Peter. 1968. *Pacifism in the United States from the Colonial Era to the First World War*. Princeton: Princeton University Press.

———. 1970. *Twentieth-Century Pacifism*. New York: Van Nostrand Reinhold.

———. 1990. *The Quaker Peace Testimony 1660 to 1914*. York, England: Sessions Book Trust.

Brown, Michael, and John May. 1989. *The Greenpeace Story*. New York: Dorling Kindersley.

Carson, Clayborne. 1981. *In Struggle: SNCC and the Black Awakening of the 1960s*. Cambridge, Mass.: Harvard University Press.

Case, Clarence Marsh. [1923] 1972. *Non-Violent Coercion: A Study in Methods of Social Pressure*. New York: Garland.

Chatfield, Charles. 1971. *For Peace and Justice: Pacifism in America: 1914–1941*. Knoxville, Tenn.: University of Tennessee Press.

———. 1976. *The Americanization of Gandhi: Images of the Mahatma*. New York: Garland.

———. 1992. *The American Peace Movement: Ideals and Activism*. New York: Twayne.

Cooney, Robert, and Helen Michalowski, eds. 1977. *The Power of the People: Active Nonviolence in the United States*. Cooperatively published.

Cortright, David. 1975. *Soldiers in Revolt: The American Military Today*. Garden City, NY: Doubleday, Anchor.

———. 1990. "Black GI Resistance During the Vietnam War". *Vietnam Generation* no. 2: 51–64.

Crittenden, Ann. 1988. *Sanctuary: A Story of American Conscience and the Law in Collision*. New York: Weidenfeld and Nicholson.

DeBenedetti, Charles. 1980. *The Peace Reform in American History*. Bloomington: Indiana University Press.

DeBenedetti, Charles, with Charles Chatfield. 1990. *An American Ordeal: The Antiwar Movement of the Vietnam Era*. Syracuse, NY: Syracuse University Press.

Deming, Barbara. 1971. *Revolution and Equilibrium*. New York: Grossman.

Dubofsky, Melvyn. 1969. *We Shall Be All: A History of the Wobblies*. Westport, Conn.: Greenwood.

Fairclough, Adam. 1987. *To Redeem the Soul of America: The Southern Christian Leadership Conference and Martin Luther King, Jr*. Athens: University of Georgia Press.

Flexner, Eleanor. 1975. *Century of Struggle: The Woman's Rights Movement in the United States*. Rev. ed. Cambridge, Mass.: Belknap.

Foner, Philip. 1965. *History of the Labor Movement in the United States*, 4 vols. New York: International.

Garrow, David J. 1986. *Bearing the Cross: Martin Luther King, Jr., and the Southern Christian Leadership Conference.* New York: William Morrow.

Genovese, Eugene D. 1974. *Roll, Jordan, Roll: The World the Slaves Made.* New York: Vintage Books.

Golden, Renny, and Michael McConnell. 1986. *Sanctuary: The New Underground Railroad.* Maryknoll, NY: Orbis.

Gregg, Richard B. 1934. *The Power of Non-Violence.* Philadelphia: J. B. Lippincott.

Gutman, Herbert G. 1974. *The Black Family in Slavery and Freedom, 1750–1925.* New York: Pantheon Books.

Jenkins, J. Craig. 1985. *The Politics of Insurgency: The Farm Worker Movement in the 1960s.* New York: Columbia University Press.

Katz, Milton S. 1986. *Ban the Bomb: A History of SANE, the Committee for a Sane Nuclear Policy, 1957–1985.* Westport, Conn.: Greenwood.

Katz, Neil H. 1974. "Radical Pacifism and the Contemporary American Peace Movement: The Committee for Nonviolent Action, 1957–1967." Unpublished PhD dissertation, University of Maryland.

——. 1997. "Committee for Nonviolent Action." In Roger S. Powers and William B. Vogele, eds., *Protest, Power, and Change: An Encyclopedia of Nonviolent Action from ACT-UP to Women's Suffrage* New York: Garland, 107–9.

Kleidman, Robert. 1993. *Organizing for Peace: Neutrality, the Test Ban, and the Freeze.* Syracuse: Syracuse University Press.

Klejment, Anne, and Nancy L. Roberts. 1996. "The Catholic Worker and the Vietnam War." In Klejment and Roberts, eds., *American Catholic Pacifism: The Influence of Dorothy Day and the Catholic Worker Movement.* Westport, Conn.: Praeger.

Lynd, Staughton, ed. 1966. *Nonviolence in America: A Documentary History.* Indianapolis, Ind.: Bobbs-Merrill.

Lyttle, Bradford. 1966. *You Come with Naked Hands – A Story of the San Francisco to Moscow Walk for Peace.* New Hampshire: Greenleaf Books.

Meier, August, and Elliot Rudwick. 1973. *CORE: A Study in the Civil Rights Movement.* New York: Oxford University Press.

——. 1976. "The Origins of Nonviolent Direct Action in Afro- American Protest: A Note on Historical Discontinuities." In *Along the Color Line: Explorations in the Black Experience,* Urbana: University of Illinois Press, 307–404.

Meyer, David S. 1990. *A Winter of Discontent: The Nuclear Freeze and American Politics.* New York: Praeger.

Meyerding, Jane. 1997. "Women and Nonviolent Action", In Roger S. Powers and William B. Vogele, eds., *Protest, Power, and Change: An Encyclopedia of Nonviolent Action from ACT-UP to Women's Suffrage* New York: Garland, 569–73.

Morris, Aldon D. 1984. *The Origins of the Civil Rights Movement: Black Communities Organizing for Change.* New York: Free Press.

Nepstad, Sharon Erickson. 1997. "Sanctuary Movement." In Roger S. Powers and William B. Vogele, eds., *Protest, Power, and Change: An Encyclopedia of Nonviolent Action from ACT-UP to Women's Suffrage.* New York: Garland, 456–8.

Robie, David. 1986. *Eyes of Fire: The Last Voyage of the Rainbow Warrior.* Philadelphia: New Society.

Shridharani, Krishnalal. 1939. *War Without Violence: The Sociology of Gandhi's Satyagraha.* New York: Harcourt, Brace.

Sibley, Mulford Q., ed. 1963. *The Quiet Battle: Writings on the Theory and Practice of Non-violent Resistance.* New York: Doubleday Anchor.

Smith, Jackie, Charles Chatfield, and Ron Pagnucco. 1997. *Transnational Social Movements and Global Politics: Solidarity Beyond the State*. Syracuse, NY: Syracuse University Press.

Stoper, Emily. 1989. *The Student Nonviolent Coordinating Committee: The Growth of Radicalism in a Civil Rights Organization*. Brooklyn, NY: Carlson.

Tracy, James. 1996. *Direct Action: Radical Pacifism from the Union Eight to the Chicago Seven*. Chicago: University of Chicago Press.

True, Michael. 1995. *An Energy Field More Intense Than War: The Nonviolent Tradition and American Literature*. Syracuse, NY: Syracuse University Press.

Useem, Michael. 1973. *Conscription, Protest, and Social Conflict: The Life and Death of a Draft Resistance Movement*. New York: John Wiley & Sons.

Weinberg, Arthur and Lila Weinberg. 1963. *Instead of Violence: Writings by the Great Advocates of Peace and Nonviolence throughout History*. New York: Grossman.

Wilcox, Fred A. 1991. *Uncommon Martyrs: The Berrigans, the Catholic Left, and the Plowshares Movement*. Reading, Mass.: Addison-Wesley.

Wittner, Lawrence S. 1984. *Rebels Against War: The American Peace Movement, 1933–1983*. Philadelphia: Temple University Press.

Woito, Robert. 1997. "Nonviolence, Principled." In Roger S. Powers and William B. Vogele, eds., *Protest, Power, and Change: An Encyclopedia of Nonviolent Action from ACT-UP to Women's Suffrage*, New York: Garland, 357–63.

Ziegler, Valarie H. 1992. *The Advocates of Peace in Antebellum America*. Bloomington: Indiana University Press.

Conclusion

Stephen Zunes and Lester R. Kurtz

The irony of what Gandhi called "Brute Force" is that it has reached both its apex and its nadir in the last century. On the one hand, the owners of the means of destruction now have the power to destroy not only their enemies but virtually all life on the planet. On the other hand, they are often impotent in the face of massive resistance. When the Commander of the Red Army, the Chairman of the Communist Party, and the head of the KGB ordered the special troops to storm the "White House" in Moscow in 1991, by shooting their way through unarmed demonstrators protecting its inhabitants, the troops simply refused to follow orders. Even the military brass at the Pentagon – with by far the superior military power in human history – increasingly raise questions about the value of using military force in many situations, apparently because they do not think they will succeed.

Modern attitudes toward violence are, in fact, genuinely ambivalent (see Turpin and Kurtz 1997). It is simultaneously condemned and condoned, denounced and employed, from the individual household to international conflict, resulting in considerable contradictory behavior among elites and masses alike. We have grown weary of war and violence and know their destructive possibilities. The dilemma for those who recoil from violence is whether there is an alternative to flight. Is it possible to engage in serious struggle without harming others, or even wreaking widespread destruction? C. Wright Mills (1958) contended, in the wake of the atomic bomb and the development of long-range delivery systems, that "We all now live in a war neighborhood." Moreover, the solution to the danger that humanity faces, he claimed, is not in the further development of the technologies of destruction, but in their banishment: "The utopians are now the realists," he insisted.

Indian physicist D. S. Kothari claims that there were two monumental events in the twentieth century: the development of the atomic bomb and Gandhi's "Salt March." In a sense he is right to place these two events – as symbols of two different kinds of force and struggle – at the center of that century's history.

Still, the pacifist option for those who abhor violence is simply too unsettling for most of us in a world filled with so much violence. One of the great questions of our time is whether or not nonviolent struggle provides an alternative to both militarism and pacifism, as Gandhi claimed it did. For those who would not give up the fight for fear that only evil forces would prevail, nonviolent struggle promised the possibility of resistance without violence. Indeed, the moral burden of proof may have shifted from those who refrain from violence to those who do; the jury is still out, however, on its efficacy. Whether we can develop, in William James's terms, a "moral equivalent of war" is too important a question to be left to chance. It is too significant an issue to be left to the generals, or the politicians, or even to the armed insurgents who struggle against injustice in their homelands. While we spend many billions of dollars annually preparing for violent conflict, developing the weapons, infrastructure, training, research and evaluation, of brute force, we have scarcely begun to explore the implications of nonviolent direct action. The handful of scholars and the few thousands of activists around the world who have given it serious thought are statistically insignificant compared to the military's research labs, academies, bases, and arsenals. And yet, without conventional resources, "People Power" movements have shaken the foundations of the modern order.

Nonviolent Social Movements

Nonviolence is a complex and multifaceted phenomenon that runs the gamut from a nonviolent lifestyle to a primarily utilitarian approach to struggle. Our focus in this volume has been on the latter, on nonviolent direct action as a deliberate means to bring about social change, rather than the various aspects of a nonviolent lifestyle. An identifiable network of "new social movements" of the twentieth century – despite disparate contexts and goals – is linked together not only by the social organization of the emerging global village and its communications technologies, but also by some shared history, self-conscious cross-fertilization, and even an embryonic institutional infrastructure.

Some of the key practioners of nonviolent action in the twentieth century have taken it up out of deep religious convictions about the morality and efficacy of nonviolence. Others have chosen nonviolence for more pragmatic reasons, as the most effective tool for social change in a particular context, given the resources and the nature of the opposition. Still others argue that these two approaches are, in fact, inseparable. In any case, the vast majority of leaders and participants in these nonviolent insurrections have not been pacifists. Similarly, many of the struggles examined in this volume have not been exclusively nonviolent; indeed, some have included rioting, sabotage, and murders of collaborators. However, such acts of violence were not the primary or most politically significant elements of the struggle and were sometimes committed by persons marginal to the movement's leadership or perhaps even by *agents provocateurs* bent on sabotaging its discipline.

Even the most exclusively nonviolent of these movements do not necessary subscribe to the Gandhian ethic, which implies the goal of converting an opponent through moral appeal; nonviolence can also assume a coercive component. In many cases the core of the movement is a handful of people acting on moral or religious principles who initiate the struggle or sustain it between mass mobilizations that necessarily involve people who are using nonviolence for its efficacy more than its ethics.

Finally, the use of unarmed methods in insurrections, even if successful in the overthrow of the regime, does not necessarily mean that a democratic or antimilitarist government will take its place. Indeed, one of the most problematic aspects of nonviolent practice is that it seldom lives up to its theory. In case after case transformations have occurred only to create new problems and sometimes new dictators.

It is not just nonviolent movements, of course, that have mixed chances for success; we do not we fully understand what facilitates the emergence, development, and success or failure of any social movements, despite the plethora of individual case studies of social movements.

Doug McAdam, John McCarthy, and Mayer Zald (1998) identify three factors seen by movement scholars as central to the understanding of social movements, why they emerge or do not, why they work or fail. These are: political opportunities, mobilizing structures, and framing processes. The first, the structure of political opportunities and constraints confronting the movement, is a contextual issue that involves the kinds of contingencies that are faced by anyone wishing to mobilize a nonviolent movement for social change. The dominant approach to analyzing this factor is the "political process" model that emphasizes the impact of shifting institutional structures and ideological dispositions of those in power on the timing and fate of any movement (see ibid.; McAdam 1988; Tarrow 1983; Tilly 1978).

A second key element that McAdam et al. (1998) identify in the emergence and performance of movements lies in the kind of mobilizing structures that insurgents employ in their efforts to bring about social change. These structures include both the social movement organizations emphasized by the *resource mobilization* perspective (Zald and McCarthy 1987, 1977) as well as the established institutions important to, but not created by the insurgents, such as religious, educational, and occupational institutions along with informal associational networks (McAdam 1982; Tilly 1978).

Political opportunities and mobilizing structures may be necessary but not sufficient conditions for bringing about social change, however. Indeed, most scholars of nonviolence focus on the actors themselves and the cognitive frames and definitions that insurgents, elites, and the broader publics bring to a situation. This aspect of social movement analysis is emphasized by proponents of the "frame analysis" perspective such as David Snow and

Robert Benford (see Snow et al. 1986; Snow and Benford 1988; Hunt, Benford and Snow 1994) as well as many new social movement scholars (McAdam et al. 1998; Brand 1985, 1982; Inglehart 1979, 1977; Melucci 1988, 1985, 1980; Touraine 1981).

As McAdam et al., (1998) contend, most of the research on social movements has focused on one of these three factors, especially the first two, leaving us with a fragmented picture of the rise and fall of movements for social change. A similar fate has befallen the nonviolence literature, with its origins in Gandhian studies and from those who have followed Gene Sharp's pragmatic lead in attempting to develop a systematic, historical, and pragmatic approach to analyzing nonviolent strategies with an eye toward making them more effective. Because nonviolent studies are often closely tied to the applied aspect of social movements and are thus written with the activist in mind, they often focus on the agency of the insurgents rather than the contingencies of institutions and broad-scale social and cultural structures within which activists operate. As Ron Pagnucco (1993) notes, one of the key issues in our understanding of social change is the ongoing debate between agency and structure, that is, the extent to which actors (such as movement activists) can act as agents of genuine change, on the one hand, and the degree to which social reality is determined by social structures that are not amenable to manipulation by individuals wishing to transform them. Structural approaches to social change contend such changes as democratization are essentially a consequence of changes in macro-sociological organization such as the growth of the middle class, etc. (see, e.g., Moore 1966; Skocpol 1979). From this "political opportunities" perspective, the main determinants of the US civil rights movement were such factors as demographic shifts, urbanization, the growth of African American institutions (especially religious and educational), and so forth, rather than the efforts of activists or the use of Gandhian nonviolent action.

Scholars who focus on the "political opportunities" aspect of movements – including most current theories of revolution – argue "that revolutions owe less to the effort of insurgents than to the work of systematic crises which render the existing regime weak and vulnerable to challenge from virtually any quarter" (McAdam et al. 1998: 4; see Arjomand 1988; Goldstone 1991; Skocpol 1979). This approach is valuable but only tells one side of movement stories.

Much of the literature on nonviolence, by contrast, posits a voluntarist approach, in which "they overemphasize the role of agency, claiming that the deliberate choice and use of nonviolent tactics by opposition actors often has brought about social change," according to Pagnucco (1993: 98). "The only real prerequisite for change," from this perspective, "is the right nonviolent action." This, too, is a fruitful but partial view of nonviolent social change, one that often misses the significance of structural conditions that shape the possibility for activist agency.

Terry Lynn Karl and Philippe Schmitter (1991) suggest that the relationship between agency and structure can be viewed as a "structured contingency," in which some historically created structures may constitute "confining conditions" that set boundaries on what can be accomplished by actors within this contexts. From this perspective, it is important to understand that the "conditions under which nonviolent movements are likely to be mobilized and bring about social change" are not all conditions that "can be created by activists" (Pagnucco 1993: 102). In order to rescue nonviolence studies from a sort of naive optimism, Pagnucco advocates the use of comparative methods that explore nonviolent movements within a variety of contexts in an effort to identify the impact of structural conditions.

Hundreds of studies about specific nonviolent movements, leaders, or theories are available, from studies of Mohandas Gandhi and the Indian Freedom Movement (see, e.g., Parekh 1989; Sharp 1973; Brown; etc.) to Martin Luther King, Jr. and the US civil rights movement (see McAdam 1988). The social movements literature explores the broader process of social change processes and social movement organization, but this literature has yet to be applied in a systematic way to the explosion of nonviolent movements around the world in recent decades. Few systematic efforts explore patterns and underlying themes of nonviolent movements across time and space, identifying the diffusion of these movements, evaluating the conditions under which they succeed and when they fail, and attempting to situate them as a major social phenomenon of the twentieth century.

Although we do not pretend to have provided the sort of comprehensive set of cases in this volume that would enable us to make a definitive comparative analysis, we do hope this volume has moved us in that direction and has encouraged the reader to ponder these issues further.

Social Change, Violence, and Nonviolence

No one can predict with any reliability how any given individual or historically situated social group will respond to injustice, oppression, violence, and poverty. Clearly the response of choice for most people is simply to acquiesce to their oppression, to find ways of surviving within the boundaries established by the social order imposed on them. Others may flee from intolerable circumstances, such as the millions of refugees that have flooded various parts of the modern world. Still others choose to fight.

Once the decision to fight is made, or when people suddenly find themselves engaged in struggle, then they must choose their method of struggle. That choice is determined by a combination of factors from personal preferences to contextual factors, including the cultural repertoire available to those who wish to struggle. The central story in this collection is that of the development in the twentieth century of new images of mass nonviolent struggle that stand in stark contrast to the militarized struggle that characterizes much large-scale conflict, with weapons of mass destruction, armed insurgencies, and a variety of wars from the streets to the planet.

Although nonviolent conflict shares much with its violent counterpart, differences between the two have an important impact on both the means and consequences of a conflict. The theoretical assumptions of nonviolent struggle are significant and provide a challenge to a great deal of conventional thinking in the social sciences. The relative success of so many nonviolent social movements implies that political power is ultimately "fragile because it depends on many groups for reinforcement of its power sources" (Sharp 1973, I: 8). In addition, "nonviolent action cuts off sources of [regimes] power rather than simply combating the final power products of these sources" thus it is more direct (ibid., III: 454). Furthermore, it implies a pluralistic model of power in which a ruler's power is determined by the degree of compliance by subjects, thereby even the most oppressive regime is based at least some level on consent (punishing someone for disobeying is not the same as accomplishing the original goals); this trend indicates that revolutions/revolts "grow out of the disintegration of concert", not simply from the act of armed struggle by rebels. (Sharp 1973)

However, some scholars familiar with civil resistance in Third World settings argue that Sharp's theory of power relies too heavily on individual and voluntaristic behavior. (Martin 1989; Koch 1984; Burrowes 1996) For example, Souad Dajani (1994: 99–100), in her pioneering study of the Palestinian intifada, argues that,

> social power is deeply rooted in social relationships and patterns of social behavior that are institutionalized over time and are pervasive throughout society. Power is located in the social structures in which these patterns exist and are reproduced. In any given society, social class arrangements are the more likely manifestations of this distribution of power. Social classes intersect in turn with different ethnic, religious, and other sociocultural elements of a given society. People's "obedience" to rulers, therefore, is not so much an element of free personal choice that can be reversed at will, but a characteristic of the way society is organized.

This does not mean that Dajani does not recognize that nonviolent action is a powerful and effective means of overcoming oppression, she just recognizes that there are processes of marginalization, dependency, and integration which need to be taken into account. She argues that once the power sources are recognized within established social patterns and structures and unmasked as such, then it becomes possible to identify avenues for countering this power effectively. At some point, when these patterns of domination are exposed and its sources are unmasked and discredited, then there can be mobilization of opposition forces to overcome it.

In short, Dajani argues that Sharp's theory of "withdrawal of consent" is unsatisfactory because it fails to analyze the structural roots of power in society. However, she argues that if one is able to account for such factors as the roots of social movements, the power and resources available to the opponent and the resistance, and the means available for changing power relationships; and, if the structural and/or ideological sources of the opponents' power is identified, as well as the political, social, economic, and ideological sources of power and methods that are available to the resistance to target these sources of power, then nonviolent action can indeed be the powerful force which Sharp claims. Since there is so often an asymmetry of power between the nonviolent movement and their opponents, it may be strategically necessary to target the defeat of the political will of the opponent rather than to destroy directly its structures of control; by understanding the location and operation of power, those advocating nonviolence can contribute to a more convincing assessment of the viability of the method of nonviolent civilian resistance.

A nonviolent opposition refuses to engage the state on their terms, i.e., with military confrontation in which the state has all the advantages. By doing so insurgents can choose their own "weapons system," nonviolent struggle that utilizes the opposition's advantage by means of popular support and the ability to mobilize large numbers of people to a greater degree than in guerrilla warfare. It is easier to mobilize people to demonstrate nonviolently than to ask them to pick up a gun or a hand grenade. This mobilizing capacity results in a "disequilibrium within the dynamics of the conflict" that works to the advantage of the unarmed group.

Nonviolent Insurgencies in the Third World and Beyond

Economist Kenneth Boulding once quipped that "That which exists is possible," a formula that some nonviolent activists have dubbed "Boulding's Law." Because colonial powers have been driven out of power and dictators toppled by nonviolent insurgency, it can be done. Nonviolent struggle will not always succeed, in a conventional sense, just as the use of violence never insures success. One of the most interesting spheres for nonviolent struggle has been the effort to bring about social change in Third World countries, many of which have suffered from a lack of democratic institutions, economies dominated by multinational corporations and other financial institutions beyond their borders, as well as the related legacies of colonialism.

Nonviolent resistance to colonialism dates back to the original conquests. In this century, nonviolent action was utilized in anticolonial struggles such as India and Zambia, in overthrowing military regimes such as those in El Salvador and Guatemala in 1944, and in specific campaigns for social justice, such as South Africa's Defiance Campaign against apartheid in the 1950s, and the resistance by the Druze of the Golan Heights against Israeli occupation authorities in the 1970s.

The dramatic upsurge in recent years does indicate a trend worthy of systematic exploration, of which this book offers only a brief overview. The targets of these insurrections have ranged from monarchies, to military juntas, to Communist dictatorships, and across cultural, religious, and geographic boundaries. In most of these nonviolent overthrows, the incumbent government had previously been thought to be relatively strong if not invincible, the opposition thought to be unorganized and weak, the monopoly of power thought to be firmly on the side of the status quo, and nothing short of a massive armed uprising or foreign intervention was thought to be sufficient to successfully challenge the regime in power. A bishop in the Philippines told nonviolence trainer Richard Deats that he admired nonviolent reform strategies but that they would never work against Ferdinand Marcos, who was the "Hitler of Asia." A few months later, Marcos fled into exile after being challenged by the nonviolent "People Power" revolution.

Not all Third World nonviolent movements have been successful, of course; a number of them were suppressed, such as those in El Salvador (1979–81), Burma (1987–88), China (1989), and Kenya (1989). What is surprising is not that some of them failed – as have *violent* insurgencies around the world – but that so many of them succeeded. The world is no less conflictual than it has been in years past. Indeed, the debt crisis, hunger, ethnic strife, environmental problems are worsening, and in many of the world's urban areas these factors all converge to provide what may be the most significant security threat of the twenty-first century. Despite the end of formal colonialism and the Cold War, imperialism still denies Third World nations true independence, and despite the decline of traditional dictatorships, real political power in most countries still remains in the hands of a tiny elite that are willing and able to suppress any real challenge to their privilege. The decline in armed struggle is less a matter of a more tolerable status quo than the shifting of the struggle to other means, such as nonviolent action.

This trend can be explained by three major factors: (1) the dramatically increased costs from counterinsurgency warfare; (2) an increased recognition that unarmed methods are more effective; and (3) a growing concern over the impact of militarism on postrevolutionary society which harms efforts at unity, democracy, independence, and development.

The costs of counterinsurgency warfare

As a mirror to Western national security managers who insisted that guerrilla warfare could easily be defeated (even in such cases as Algeria and Vietnam), many on the left and in the Third World created a counter-myth of the invincibility of such a movement. However, technology has given the status quo power an increasing advantage in recent years.

Even when an armed insurgency is victorious, the results are devastating. The Vietnamese victory against the Americans was at a cost of over 1 million lives, with millions more displaced, thousands of villages destroyed, several cities and much of the nation's infrastructure severely damaged, a wrecked economy, and environmental devastation. A generation later, as demonstrated in the recent Gulf War, the weapons now possessed by the United States and its allies are far more destructive than even those faced by the Vietnamese. The Afghans rebels defeated the Soviet Union, yet the legacy of their struggle is ongoing war, a theocratic totalitarianism, a heavily bombed countryside, and millions of refugees. Even when a superpower is not involved directly, the human costs of even a successful guerrilla war can be disastrous, as exemplified by the Ethiopian government's battle against armed rebel forces which resulted not only in tens of thousands of deaths outright, but hundreds of thousands of fatalities through starvation and disease brought on by the economic dislocation from warfare (Zwi, Macrae, and Ugalde 1992). (Interestingly, as with many "successful" armed rebellions, the victory of the EPLF and other insurgent forces in Ethiopia was at least as much a result of the collapse of any legitimacy by the ruling Dergue, which had held power primarily through violence and intimidation, than by victories on the battlefield (Zunes 1991).)

More insidious is the phenomenon of low-intensity warfare, where the United States, other major powers, and their client dictatorships have been highly effective in ruthlessly suppressing armed opposition groups and their allies through assassination, forced relocation of potentially sympathetic populations, conscription of peasants into progovernment militias, and selective but highly effective bombing and other military incursions which fall short of full-scale intervention but still have a devastating impact on society. The use of death squads – paramilitary units with ties to government security services – have taken the threat from armed insurgencies as an excuse to murder thousands of government opponents. Thus, as in the case of Argentina, not only did the armed insurgency fail to stimulate the radical social change, but led to a brutal "dirty war" which resulted in the deaths of as many as 10,000 Argentines, with the apparent acquiescence of much of Argentine society.

The net result is an increasing realization that the benefits of waging an armed insurrection may not be worth the costs.

Unarmed methods are more effective

The growing awareness of the power of nonviolent action grows out of several phenomena. First, more insurgents are convinced that armed resistance tends to push undecided elements of the population towards the government. When facing a violent insurgency, a government can easily justify its repression, but when used against unarmed resistance movements it usually creates greater sympathy for the regime's opponents. Second, unarmed movements allow for far larger numbers of participants, taking advantage of a popular movements' majority support. Finally, unarmed resistance allows for the creation of alternative institutions which further undermine the status quo and form the basis of a new independent and democratic order. It is worthwhile to consider each of these in turn.

Armed resistance often backfires by legitimating the use of repressive tactics, whereas the use of violence by the state against unarmed dictators often constitutes a turning point in nonviolent struggles, producing what Smithey and Kurtz (in this volume) call the "paradox of repression." From the massacre of peaceful demonstrators by the British at Amritsar in 1919 to the bombings and murder of civil rights activists in the southern US in the 1960s, and the indiscriminate shooting of civilians by Soviet soldiers at Tbilisi in 1991, incidents of violence against nonviolent protests have played a key role in cultivating sympathy for the movement. Attacks against unarmed demonstrators have often been the spark that turned periodic protests into full-scale insurrections. Examples include Iran's "Black Friday" – September 8, 1978 – when the Shah's forces opened fire on hundreds of thousands of unarmed demonstrators in Teheran, killing more than 3,000 people. Similarly, in the Philippines, the assassination of Benigno Aquino helped spark an organized resistance, and the massacre of dozens of peacefully protesting farmers in Escalante in September 1985 was a major episode in delegitimizing the Marcos regime in the Philippines.

The paradox of repression helps explain why violence from the opposition is often welcomed by authoritarian governments (hence the use of *agents provocateurs*): it justifies state repression. Violent repression of a movement often transforms popular and elite perceptions of legitimacy, which is why state officials usually use less repression against the more nonviolent movements. Unarmed resistance movements also tend to increase the chances of divisions within pro-government circles (see Sharp 1973, III: 676) for a number of reasons. First, disagreements surface internally regarding how to effectively deal with the resistance, since few regimes are as prepared to deal with unarmed revolts than armed ones. Second, some pro-government elements become less concerned about the consequences of a compromise with insurgents if they are nonviolent. Unarmed movements, especially if they are completely nonviolent, increase the likelihood of defections and noncooperation from police and military whereas armed revolts strengthen the role of the government's coercive apparatus. (Lakey 1970)

The efficacy of nonviolent resistance in dividing supporters of the status quo is not just apparent in rendering government troops less effective, but in challenging the attitudes of an entire nation and even foreign actors, as in the South African struggle against apartheid. Pictures of peaceful protesters – including whites, members of the clergy, and other "upstanding citizens"

– broadcast on television worldwide lent legitimacy to anti-apartheid forces and undermined the regime in a way that the armed struggle was unable to do. As nonviolent resistance within the country escalated, momentum grew for external pressure in the form of economic sanctions and other tactics by the international community that raised the costs of maintaining the apartheid system.

This dynamic was also appreciated by Palestinian activists. While there have certainly been Israelis who support the occupation for purely ideological or religious reasons, the majority (including most American supporters of Israeli policies) did so out of concerns for Israeli security. The use of armed forms of resistance perpetuated this rationale. By contrast, nonviolent action does nothing to threaten Israeli security. As Mubarak Awad, the exiled founder of the Palestine Center for the Study of Nonviolence, describes it, a commitment to nonviolence would remove "the irrational fear of 'Arab violence' which presently cements Israeli society together" (Awad 1983: 26). An Israeli soldier, even one who may personally oppose the occupation, is far more willing to serve in the occupied territories if he believes that it is necessary to protect him and his family from violence. Prior to the *intifada*, hundreds of Israelis had already risked jail by refusing to serve in the occupied territories. During the *intifada*, with their targets now either peaceful protesters or protesters using nonlethal weapons, the Yesh G'vul movement of selective draft resistance multiplied into the thousands. This created unprecedented divisions in Israeli society, and eventually weakened the ability of the Israeli Defense Forces to maintain an effective presence as a foreign occupation force. Palestinian attorney Jonathan Kuttab, in his account of one nonviolent campaign, observed, "The [Israeli] soldiers were really being torn apart, because they couldn't handle that type of nonviolence" (in Kennedy 1984: 18).

Because of increased global interdependence, the non-local audience for a conflict may be just as important as the immediate community. Just as Gandhi played to British citizens in Manchester and London, organizers of civil rights movements were communicating to the entire nation and especially to the Kennedy administration. Insurgency against the Soviet bloc was disseminated by television broadcasts that spread the news from country to country, legitimating local protests that no longer seemed like local events organized by unstable dissidents (see Brinton and Rinzler 1990). The prominent role of the global media during the anti-Marcos "People Power" movement in 1986 was instrumental in forcing the US government to pull back from its support of the Philippine dictator.

Israeli repression of nonviolent protests had a similar effect on Americans whose perception is significant because of the role of both private citizens and the US government in sustaining Israel's military, economic infrastructure, and so forth. As Rashid Khalidi (1988: 507) observes, the Palestinians had "succeeded at last in conveying the reality of their victimization to world public opinion."

This dynamic is crucial, as George Lakey notes, in the ability of the opposition to reframe the perceptions of key parties: the public, political elites, and the military, most of whom will have no difficulty supporting the use of violence against violent insurrections.

> The status quo must become too costly for the oppressor to find it in his interest to continue, *compared with the alternative* . . . , a variable which is often overlooked. Not only can [the revolutionaries] make the status quo *more* costly, but [they] can make the alternative appear *less* costly than he may first have believed, even though still detrimental to his interests. [They] must build a strategy, then, which encourages the oppressor to think rather than to fight irrationally, on the likelihood that some of this early protests about "holding out until the bitter end" will turn out to be only words. (Lakey 1970: 13–14)

Moreover, when authorities respond to nonviolent protests with violence, the instruments of oppression are directly challenged. Even soldiers, police, and people in power may begin to question the legitimacy of their actions and the system they support, resulting in divisions within the ruling elite. As Lakey (1971: 5–6) puts it, "Hard as it may be to believe, exploiters have an almost infinite capacity for self-delusion, the ability to believe that they are superior in every important way. Their own actions open their own eyes – they are taught by their life- experience that they are quite capable of atrocious behavior."

This importance of dividing the opponent is also true for external allies of the regime in question. Much of the West's traditional support to the Israelis, prior to the Palestinian *intifada* and the moderation of Arab attitudes towards the Jewish state, came from the terrorism and belligerent militarism of some of its Arab opponents. Similarly, armed revolutionaries during the liberation struggle in Zimbabwe were routinely depicted as "terrorists" in the Western press, which resulted in widespread sympathy for the white minority. Rhodesian raids against refugee camps and other civilian targets were rationalized in the Western media as attacks on "terrorist bases." By contrast, the nonviolent independence struggle in neighboring Zambia in the early 1960s had much greater support from many of these same countries.

Not only may nonviolence raise self-doubts among the elites, it may facilitate broader participation in the movement. Indeed, the breadth of participation is one of the hallmarks of nonviolent insurgency which, in contrast to violent rebellions that usually rely upon very small devoted cadres, can mobilize large numbers of people. In nonviolent action, there are no weapons to procure for distribution, only minimal training involved, and hardly any physical requirements. Even in uprisings that mix nonviolent and violent forms and resistance, far greater participation results from the nonviolent forms of resistance, even if the violent component is not usually lethal. For example, in the *intifada*, while the stone-throwing and related incidents have received the most publicity, the most widespread and effective components of the *intifada* have tended to be those of an exclusively nonviolent nature. A study of 17 leaflets released during the second year of the uprising by the Unified Leadership of the Uprising revealed that of 27 recommended actions of defiance to be taken by the population, 26 were nonviolent. Community response to the eight calls for the use of stones or molotov cocktails, (which represented only 4.9 percent of the total recommendations), was "slight in comparison to the great response to calls for civil disobedience and nonviolent activities" (Benn 1989).

The arrest or killing of even a dozen members of a guerrilla cell can devastate an armed campaign; the sheer numbers that have become involved in massive nonviolent campaigns of recent years where even the deaths of hundreds or even thousands has failed to weakened the movement. In addition, though the repression by authorities has often been severe, there is little question that the repression would be far greater were they facing an armed insurgency and often repression ironically strengthens the movement.

In addition, unlike most nonviolent methods of resistance, armed struggle does not allow for as broad a level of popular participation. According to South African Ben Turok,

> While sabotage provided the government with every excuse for unleashing a brutal wave of terror it failed to mobilize the mass of the people who seemed to be left outside the arena from the time of the first blasts. Sabotage remained the weapon of an elite corps in the liberation movement. As a consequence, sabotage had the effect of isolating the organization from the masses who felt unable to join in this new phase or even to defend the actionists when they were seized. (Callinicos and Rogers 1978, 78)

In addition to widespread participation, nonviolence facilitates the simultaneous resistance of the old structures and construction of their desired replacements. Parallel institutions are an integral part of nonviolent insurgency, so that elements of a reformed society and governance structure are already in place when the insurgents win their battles. Gandhi not only advocated a boycott of British cloth, for example, going to the heart of colonial economics in that instance, but also the construction of a grassroots economic structure for the production of homespun cloth that could mobilize people for resistance but also begin creating an economic base for the poorest people in the villages.

The creation of alternative structures provides both a moral and a practical underpinning for efforts aimed at bringing about fundamental social change.[1] Parallel structures in civil society may render state control increasingly impotent, as they did throughout Eastern Europe leading up to the events of 1989. As jailed Czech writer-cum-President Václav Havel (1990: 108) puts it:

These parallel structures, it may be said, represent the most articulated expressions so far of 'living within the truth'. One of the most important tasks the 'dissident movements' have set themselves is to support and develop them. What else are those initial attempts at self-organization than the efforts of a certain part of society to live – as a society – within the truth, to rid itself of the self-sustaining aspects of totalitarianism and, thus, to extricate itself radically from its involvement in the post-totalitarian system? What else is it but a non-violent attempt by people to negate the system within themselves and to establish their lives on a new basis, that of their own proper identity?

Growing out of this "second culture" were a series of independent institutions and networks throughout Eastern Europe, such as the *samizdat* (self-published) editions of various books, private concerts, and seminars. At one point, the underground press in Poland rivaled the official one in terms of its annual output. Often such structures were constructed out of previously existing, but unofficial or quasi-official organizations, frequently religious ones. In Leipzig, heart of the East German rebellion, people met in churches every Monday night for a worship service followed by demonstrations (Anderson 1990: 179).

In the Philippines, Marcos lost power not through the defeat of his troops in a long series of battles culminating with the storming the Malacanang Palace, but from the withdrawal of sufficient support of the regime so that Malacanang became the only part of the country that Marcos could effectively control. On the same day Marcos was sworn in for another term as president in an official ceremony, Corazon Aquino was sworn in simultaneously. Given that most Filipinos saw Marcos's election as fraudulent, the vast majority gave their allegiance to President Aquino instead of President Marcos. The transfer of allegiance from one source of authority and legitimacy to another is a key element of a successful nonviolent insurrection.

In the course of a successful nonviolent revolution, and with adequate popular participation, political authority may be wrested from the state and invested in institutions of civil society as these parallel institutions grow in effectiveness and legitimacy. The state may become increasingly impotent and irrelevant as parallel nongovernmental institutions take over an increasing proportion of the business of governing a society, providing services to the populace, and creating functional equivalents to the institutions of the state. The presence of these parallel structures, and the independent spaces created by them, may affect the outcome of a specific action, as evidenced by the apparent failure in China at Tiananman Square. It has been argued that one of the major reasons the Chinese demonstrations were not as effective as those taking place in other countries is that parallel structures were not adequately developed prior to the actual rebellion in Tiananman Square. Even apparent failures often result in eventual success for nonviolent movements, however; the government's action at Tiananman Square may have destroyed its last shred of legitimacy among large sectors of the population. Yet even prior to a dramatic culmination of nonviolent struggle, a situation of such dual power can be created.

The Impact on Postrevolutionary Society

A final consideration that causes many insurgents to weigh in on the side of nonviolence is the potential negative impact of armed insurgency on their postrevolutionary society, and its potential for unity, democracy, independence, and development. Jawaharlal Nehru was concerned, for example, about the kind of leadership that might be thrown up by a successful terrorist movement against the British colonial system. The most successful warriors or military strategists might not be the most capable leaders for the task of constructing the democratic institutions of a new order. Those who are now resisting authoritarian governments have been able to see the results of armed movements against previous dictatorships which, once in power, have failed to establish pluralistic, democratic, and independent political systems capable of supporting social and economic development. Many of these problems resulted in part from counterrevolution, natural disasters, foreign intervention, trade embargoes, and other circumstances beyond the movements' control. However, the choice of armed struggle as a means of securing power has tended to exacerbate these problems and create troubles of its own. For one, armed struggle often leads to an ethos of a secret elite vanguard which tends to create little democracy and less tolerance for pluralism. Often disagreements that could be resolved peaceably in non-militarized institutions, lead to bloody factional fighting. Some countries, such as Algeria and Guinea-Bissau, experienced military coups not long after armed revolutionary movements ousted colonialists. Others, such as Angola and Cambodia, experienced bloody civil wars.

Another problem is that keeping a strong military has required greater dependence on outside benefactors for arms supplies, which led several revolutionary governments to become reliant on the Soviet Union, which – like any major power – traditionally tied strings to its aid. Even the relatively low level of assistance during the course of the armed struggle starts a dependent relationship that is hard to break. This, in turn, may allow elements of the old dictatorship to ally with rival major powers seeking to overthrow the new government.

Having overthrown the Somoza dictatorship through armed force, the popular but heavily militarized Sandinista Front – despite largely avoiding the pitfalls of the Cuban revolution of sliding into a Communist dictatorship – was still faced with US-organized attacks by armed mercenaries. The Contras, as they were called, were justified by American policy makers on the (largely fabricated) grounds that the Sandinista military had aggressive designs on neighboring countries. The national security threat from the United States reinforced the military wing of the Sandinistas, taking precious funds away from desperately needed domestic programs, and led to military conscription and counterinsurgency efforts that alienated some important segments of the population. The result of the Contra War was widespread destruction, a collapse of the economy, and the Sandinistas' eventual electoral defeat.

The degree of problems affecting the Third World is so extensive that it is clear that a successful armed movement against an authoritarian regime – even if it has a strong organization, proven mobilization skills, and a coherent ideology – is not sufficient to address the pressing concerns facing a country in transition after a devastating civil war. As a result, there is growing interest in the utilization of tactics that will minimize the degree of dislocation in the country and maximize the segments of the population that can become contributing members of a postauthoritarian political order to help build a new society.

Obstacles to Nonviolent Insurrections

Some limitations regarding the viability of unarmed insurrections against authoritarian regimes are very real despite the remarkable record of success in recent decades. This does not mean that armed insurrections in these cases are necessarily more likely to be successful, but these problems are illustrative of some of the real obstacles remaining for nonviolent democratic movements. Authoritarian governments make it very difficult – though by no means impossible – to engage in the effective mobilization of popular forces for mass action through legal restrictions, terror, and a media monopoly. Years of repression lead to a sense of despair and a lack of empowerment of the population, a key element to the critique of Sharp's pluralistic concepts of power. More problematic are the cases of suppressed ethnic minorities which would have particular difficulty winning the support of majority sectors against government repression due to widespread popular prejudice. Another problem is in impoverished dependent societies, in which many basic necessities are in short supply and are controlled by local elites and foreigners. The threshold for survival is marginal, and unarmed movements simply may not be able to hold out indefinitely in a protracted struggle. In addition, governments with outside economic support can survive the near total collapse of domestic economic activity, as demonstrated with the Salvadoran junta which withstood a series of general strikes in the early 1980s, as a result of a commitment from the United States to finance 80 percent of the government's budget.

A particularly problematic example of the latter phenomenon is demonstrated in the way that a number of governments – particularly those which rely on substantial foreign support – have developed a means by which they apparently have been able to effectively suppress nonviolent movements by using violence without fatally undermining their legitimacy. This method we refer to as the "privatization of the repressive apparatus." This takes place when elements of a regime, ranging from middle-ranked military officers to top political officials, allow or encourage private vigilantes, often with the direct support of elements of the police and the military, to violently suppress leaders and participants in nonviolent movements as a means of terrorizing the population into submission. Despite being sanctioned by key sectors of the governing apparatus, these "death squads" are distinct enough from the official chain of command so that the regime can plausibly deny responsibility. While most of the nonviolent actionists still blame the government, important neutral sectors of the population as well as foreign backers of the regime, critical players in the political jiu-jitsu equation, may accept the portrayal of the regime as a moderate force doing its best to curb violence and extremism on all sides.

The adaptation of this privatization of the repressive apparatus grows out of "low-intensity conflict", a counter- insurgency strategy advocated by US military advisers over the past decade. LIC has several components, including economic development programs, propaganda, and anti-guerrilla military campaigns. Acknowledging that overt repression by the government against popular civilian movements is counterproductive, the doctrine advocates other forms of neutralizing opposition forces. This concept evolved into its current phase in the late 1970s and early 1980s in El Salvador and has been utilized in other counterinsurgency situations as well, such as Guatemala, Colombia, and the Philippines. Shooting into crowds, it was realized, doesn't work; it merely strengthens the opposition. Overkill can win battles, but lose the war. The government, it was argued, needed to combine repression with nominal civilian control of administration to help convert the population to its cause. Training and cleaning up the local armed forces is an integral part of restoring respectability to the government. At the same time, the government had to go through several levels to neutralize the opposition: wipe out trade union, academic and religious leaders; identify and annihilate grassroots supporters of opposition; and, limit and repress independent human rights groups. This is where the use of death squads have played an important role.

For example, there have been some substantiated reports regarding the emphasis by American military trainers on responsible crowd control methods while encouraging other forms of violence (see McClintock 1985).The now-famous secret CIA report to its Nicaraguan contras units advocates "the selective use of violence" by paramilitary units as preferable to "indiscriminate" repression as a means of "decapitating" the leadership of the opposition. Meanwhile, in Sri Lanka, with a nominally democratic government challenging two simultaneous insurrections, efforts by human rights activists and others to salvage some semblance of the rule of law being met by widespread death squad activity.

The result of the privatization of the repressive apparatus has had a chilling effect on the prospects of successful nonviolent insurrections. One counter-measure has been "nonviolent intervention" by teams of international volunteers organized by Peace Brigades International and similar groups. Growing out of the Gandhian tradition, PBI and its sister organizations have sent teams to Guatemala, El Salvador, Sri Lanka, and the West Bank to accompany prominent nonviolent activists as essentially unarmed bodyguards. The potential diplomatic fallout from international observers, particularly North Americans or Europeans, being casualties of – or even just witnessing – death squad attacks, have allowed these teams, despite their small numbers, to become remarkably successful deterrents. (Mahoney and Eguren, 1997) If civilian-based defense and nonviolent insurrections constitute two forms of organized nonviolent action, this nonviolent intervention could be considered a third type, albeit in an embryonic stage. These efforts have been extremely limited, however, and while there is certainly some potential for further development, they have yet to evolve to a scope that would constitute an effective means of addressing this phenomenon.

The Future of Nonviolence

This volume is a comparison of nonviolent struggles within particular nation-states. In most cases, a particular national government is the target of the nonviolent campaigns. However, the future of nonviolent action may rest less with challenging state authority as with certain transnational institutions. Organized labor, which – in many countries – has engaged in some of the most important nonviolent struggles, is increasingly recognized the need that their activism go beyond their national borders. Many unions have seen effective nonviolent action result in management giving in to their demands only to have the factory shut down operations and move to a poorer country where wages and working conditions are grossly inferior. Similarly, environmental movements have been able to obtain stricter environmental laws or close down a dangerous site only to have the polluter move overseas to where there are lax environmental laws.

This phenomenon has worked in the other direction as well. There have been movements in Third World countries which have shaken the foundations of authoritarian rule only to have the regime bailed out by large infusions of aid and assistance from the United States and other Western governments. It is unlikely the Salvarodean junta could have survived the nonviolent uprising in the early 1980s were it not for US support; the failure of the nonviolent movement led to a bloody civil war which cost the lives of tens of thousands of people, mostly civilians. In many respects, it was not the failure of nonviolence by the Salvadoreans but the failure of nonviolent action by those in the United States to change US policy of support for the Salvadorean junta. Similarly, it is unlikely that Israel could have afforded the enormous financial and diplomatic costs of its suppression of the Palestinian *intifada* were it not for the more than $4 billion of annual subsidies the US sends to prop up the Israeli occupation. There was virtually no nonviolent action in the United States to challenge US policies of large-scale support to Israel's right-wing government, resulting in the current US-led "peace process" which still denies the Palestinians national self-determination and encourages violence and instability.

Perhaps the most telling example of the promise and obstacles to nonviolent action in Latin America today came in the spring of 1997, when tens of thousands of Nicaraguans engaged in a general strike to protest the austerity programs of President Alemain's government. Former Sandinista soldiers and former Contras left their guns at home to work together to set up roadblocks and engage in street protests where they adhered strictly to a disciplined nonviolence. The government, in the face of massive nonviolent resistance, relented and the austerity measures were withdrawn. However, the United States, through the International Monetary Fund, forced the government to implement the austerity plan anyway. As Alejandro Badana, a leading Sandinista intellectual told an American audience a few months later, "Will the United States allow the people of Latin America to succeed with nonviolence?" (Bandana 1997).

Thus, just as militarism and corporate capitalism has become global, so must nonviolent movements. For nonviolence to continue being an effective force, it must be within the context of transnational movements which struggle not just at where the worse manifestations of institutional violence occur, but at their source - which is often in the advanced industrialized countries, particularly the United States.

This study has probably raised more questions than answers, since the study of nonviolence is at such an early stage. Yet we have been able to present a broad sweep of geographical regions and economic and political circumstances in which these nonviolent movements take, as well as a variety of ways they can be analyzed. There seems to be evidence that there is declining faith in both the efficacy and morality of armed struggle as well as a decline in faith in electoral politics. As a result, the time may be right to both explore and expound on the power of nonviolent action. Governments around the world spend billions of dollars not just in developing their own military preparedness but exporting their hardware and know-how to other countries, many of which can least afford it. Perhaps those of us with an appreciation for nonviolence should, despite our more limited resources, be more aggressive in developing and disseminating what we know about nonviolence and be willing to use it ourselves.

Notes

1 Havel (1990) attributes the idea of parallel structures in Czechoslovakia to Van Giros, who developed the concept of a "second culture," at first chiefly in the sphere of nonconformist rock music, but it very rapidly diffused to "the whole area of independent and repressed culture, that is, not only for art and its various currents but also for the humanities, the social sciences, and philosophical thought" (1990: 107).

References

Anderson, Edith. 1990. "Town Mice and Country Mice: The East German Revolution." In W. M. Brinton and A. Rinzler eds, *Without Force or Lies*. San Francisco: Mercury House.

Arjomand, Said, ed. 1988. *Authority and Political Culture in Shi'ism*. Albany: State University of New York Press.

Awad, Mubarak. 1983. "Nonviolent Resistance: A Strategy for the Occupied Territories." In David Albert (ed.), *Nonviolent Struggle in the Middle East*, Philadelphia: New Society Publishers.

Bandana, Alejandro. 1997. Speech before the joint conference of the Peace Studies Association and the Consortium on Peace Research, Education and Development, Georgetown University, Washington, DC, June 5.

Benn, Ruth. Quoting a study by the Palestinian Center for the Study of Nonviolence in Ruth Benn, "West Bank/Gaza Report: The Occupation Must End", *Nonviolent Activist*, March 1989.

Brinton, William M., and Alan Rinzler, eds. 1990. *Without Force or Lies: Voices from the Revolution of Central Europe in 1989–90: Essays, Speeches, and Eyewitness Accounts*. San Francisco: Mercury House.

Burrowes, Robert J. 1996. *The Strategy of Nonviolent Defense: A Gandhian Approach*. Albany: State University of New York Press.

Callinicos, Alex, and John Rogers. 1978. *Southern Africa after Soweto*. London: Pluto Press.

Dajani, Souad. 1994. *Eyes without Country: Searching for a Palestinian Strategy of Liberation*. Philadelphia: Temple University Press.

Goldstone, Jack A., Ted Robert Gurr and Farrokh Moshiri, eds. 1991. *Revolutions of the Late Twentieth Century*. Boulder: Westview Press.

Havel, Václav. 1990. "The Power of the Powerless." In W. Brinton and A. Rinzler eds, *Without Force or Lies*, San Francisco: Mercury House.

Homer-Dixon, Thomas F. 1993. "Environmental change and violent conflict: growing scarcities of renewable resources can contribute to social instability and civil strife." *Scientific American* 268 (Feb): 38–46.

Karl, Terry Lynn, and Philippe C. Schmitter. 1991. "Modes of transition in Latin America, Southern and Eastern Europe." *International Social Science Journal* 43 (May): 269–85.

Kennedy, Scott. 1984. "The Golani Druze: A Case of Nonviolent Resistance." *Journal of Palestine Studies* vol. XIII no. 2 (Winter 1984), pp. 48–64.

Khalidi, Rashid. 1988. "The Uprising and the Palestine Question." *World Policy Journal*, vol. V, no. 3 (Summer 1988), pp. 497–517.

Koch, Koen. 1984. "Civilian Defence: An Alternative to Military Defence?" The *Netherlands Journal of Sociology* 20(0).

Lakey, George. 1970. "Revolution: Violent or Nonviolent." Store Restrup Holjskele, Danmark: 070-orenes utfordringer til nordist fredsbelgelse.

Mahony, Liam, and Lluis Enrique Eguren. 1997. *Unarmed Bodyguards: International Accompaniment for the Protection of Human Rights*. West Hartford, CT: Kumarian Press.

Martin, Brian. 1989. "Gene Sharp's Theory of Power." *Journal of Peace Research* 26 (2): 213–23.

McAdam, Doug. 1988. *Freedom Summer*. New York: Oxford University Press.

McAdam, Doug, John D. McCarthy, and Mayer N. Zald, eds. 1998. *Comparative Perspectives on Social Movements: Political Opportunities, Mobilizing Structures, and Cultural Framings*. Cambridge: Cambridge University Press.

McClintock, Michael. 1985. *The American Connection: State Terror and Popular Resistance in El Salvador*. London: Zed Books.

Mills, C. Wright. 1958. *The Causes of World War III*. New York: Simon and Schuster.

Pagnucco, Ron. 1993. "Teaching about Agency and Structure in Nonviolent Social Change." *Journal for Peace and Justice Studies* 5 (2): 97–107.

Parekh, Bikkhu. 1989. *Colonialism, Tradition and Reform: An Analysis of Gandhi's Political Discourse*. New Delhi: Sage.

Sharp, Gene. 1973. *The Politics of Nonviolent Action*. 3 vols. Boston: Porter Sargent.

Skocpol, Theda. 1979. *States and Social Revolutions: A Comparative analysis of France, Russia, and China*. Cambridge: Cambridge University Press.

Smith, Jackie, Charles Chatfield, and Ron Pagnucco, eds. 1997. *Transnational Social Movements and Global Politics: Solidarity Beyond the State*. Syracuse, NY: Syracuse University Press.

Tarrow, Sidney G. 1994. *Power in Movement: Social Movements, Collective Action and Politics*. Cambridge: Cambridge University Press.

Tilly, Charles. 1978. *From Mobilization to Revolution*. Reading, Mass.: Addison-Wesley.

Turpin, Jennifer, and Lester R. Kurtz, eds. 1997. *The Web of Violence*. Urbana: University of Illinois Press.

Zald, Mayer N., and John D. McCarthy, eds. 1987. *Social Movements in an Organizational Society: Collected Essays*. New Brunswick: Transaction Books.

Zald, Mayer N., and John D. McCarthy, eds. 1977. *The Dynamics of Social Movements: Resource Mobilization, Social Control, and Tactics*. Cambridge: Winthrop Publishers.

Zwi, Anthony, Joanne Macrae, and Antonio Ugalde. 1992. "Children and War." *Kangaroo* (December): 46–50.

Index